FORTY YEARS WITH THE FAIRIES

The Collected Fairy Manuscripts of Daphne Charters

Volume I

Author:
Daphne Charters

Compiled by Michael Pilarski
Cover by Ethan Radcliffe

R.J. Stewart
Books
P.O. Box 802
Arcata, CA 95518
www.rjstewart.net

Forty Years With The Fairies
By Daphne Charters, edited by Michael Pilarski

Published by:
R. J. Stewart Books

First Edition

Printed in the United States of America

A Catalogue record for this book is available from the Library of Congress.

ISBN: 978-0-9791402-9-7

R. J. Stewart Books
P.O. Box 802
Arcata, CA 95518
www.rjstewart.net

TABLE OF CONTENTS

* * *

These manuscripts span a 40-year time period from December 25, 1950 to December 11, 1990.

There are 154 stories of varying lengths. Some of the stories are Daphne's personal accounts but most of them are told to Daphne by 33 fairies, 14 humans from the astral realm & 1 deva. Volume 1 contains 60 of the stories.

A MESSAGE FROM THE FAIRY, NORMUS, TO HUMANS:

"We hope that this book will show you that we are individuals and not flickers of only semi-conscious light. We are sometimes seen as flashes because the watcher is unable to maintain our high speed of vibration for more than a second or two at a time. We are quite solid to ourselves and to each other when we want to be, and when we are without our bodies, we experience much greater freedom than you can possibly know".

— *Normus.*

ACKNOWLEDGEMENTS

Many people contributed to bringing this portion of the *Collected Manuscripts* into print.

* First and foremost is Daphne Charters herself.
* Thanks to her devoted friends in England who typed up Daphne's handwritten notes and sent them on the United States: Philip Groom, David Nall-Cain and her niece Gay Burdett.
* The people who assisted with typesetting include: Howard Berg, Rosemary Warden, Anahata Pomeroy, Fatima, Kiela, Anya and others.
* Scanning: Roni Freund and Stephanie Rafnson.
* The many artists include:
  - Cover for this volume was painted by Ethan Radcliffe, © 2007.
  - Shirley Musgrove, June Landerholm, Barbara Ligren, Valerie, Gita, Miguel Guizar. Sara Shaffer, Louisa McCuskey, Nancy Leshinsky, and Tom Giffen.
  - Daphne Charter's friend, Susan Anderson, painted the cover for the 2nd printing of the 2nd edition of *A True Fairy Tale* and for many of the chapter heading illustrations *in Volume I.*
  - Daphne Charters is the artist of Luna Magic, the cover of the original edition of *A True Fairy Tale,* which is reproduced on the back cover of *Volume I.*
* Thanks to Aera Spreckley for being my chief assistant in preparing *Volume I.*
* Thanks to Camilla Bishop for proofreading and advice.
* Thanks to Willow-Duir Foxwood for overseeing book layout and production.
* Thanks to the many other friends who helped and encouraged me over the years including Marianne Aylmer and Anahata Pomeroy.
* A big thanks to the present-day members of the Fairy Congress Council for their assistance in organizing the Fairy & Human Relations Congress.

* My special appreciation to my good friend R. J. Stewart for making this book one of the first ventures of his new publishing house.
* And finally a multi-colored thank you to all the fairies, devas and humans who assisted this multi-evolutionary project from behind the scenes.

– *Michael Pilarski*

BRITISH SPELLING VS. AMERICAN SPELLING

Some words have a different spelling in British than in American. We have kept the British spelling.

Some words include 'ou' instead of 'o,' such as clamour, colour, endeavour, glamour, honour, labour, moulded, neighbour, saviour, savour, and splendour.

Some words use re instead of er, such as centre.

Some words use double letters where in the US we would only use one, such as marvelled, travelling, and modeling. Conversely some words use single letters where in the US we would use two, such as fulfilment.

Some words use s instead of z, such as exercise, harmonise, neutralise, organise and recognise.

For a complete rundown on the differences between British and American spelling visit www2.gsu.edu/~wwwesl/egw/jones/differences.htm.

FOREWORD
by R. J. Stewart

The faery tradition encompasses a wide range of themes, sources, and interpretations. The core tradition is many centuries old, and new presentations appear with each generation, in tradition, in story and song, and nowadays in popular entertainment. There has been a disturbing tendency in recent years to reduce faery material down to the most simplistic trite entertainment possible…a contrived simulation of faery lore rather than a true connection to this most ancient spiritual tradition.

No matter what form it takes, the main premise of faery magic is that there are spirit beings that occupy the land and sea, that are of the mysterious world behind, within, and beneath, manifest nature. This premise is thousands of years old, and found in traditions worldwide: every country, race, and culture, has its version of the faery tradition. Next come practices, which are ways of building and sustaining relationships between humans and the many faery races. These practices vary widely, but all have a core of connection with one another, no matter where they are found. It might seem, to the thoughtful reader that while religion so often brings strife, the faery tradition implies and offers unity and amity, worldwide.

The work of Daphne Charters is a classic example of a particular way of relating to faeries, something which is uniquely British, and specifically English. It carries the stamp of English culture of the early 20th century, rather than (say) that of the Ireland or Britanny, Scotland or Scandinavia, each having related but very different faery traditions. The seership and writings that Daphne produced are in a direct line from the upsurge of interest in faeries that swept through Britain, England especially, during and after the First World War of 1914-1918. Her understanding and presentation of the faery allies is closer to that of Sir Arthur Conan Doyle, creator of Sherlock Holmes, who strongly believed in faeries, than it is to that of W B Yeats, or of Fiona Macleod who is perhaps the most profound esoteric writer on faery mysticism and magic, who wrote in the late 19th century, before the First World War swept away the old Europe forever.

The upsurge of interest in faeries that manifested in Britain in the early 20th century was part of the intense cathartic changes brought about by the First World War, and went hand in hand with an upsurge of Spiritualism, which in those days was often linked not so much to the ancient folkloric faery tradition, but to psychic explorations regarding faeries. This approach continued well into the 1950's, and is, indeed, the overall ambience of Daphne's visions, vocabulary, and writing. Nowadays this uniquely English vision and interpretation has been absorbed into the world of the fantasy novel or cartoon or fairy postcard. Yet to

Daphne this was not whimsy or fantasy, but the real experiences of her direct communion with spirit beings who were close to her, and who, she asserted, are always close to us all.

While her language and approach to the faeries is strongly cultural, strongly 20th century middle-class English, much that Daphne reveals is timeless, and could equally well have been found in ancient Greece or Celtic Europe thousands of years ago. The cultural viewpoint is different, but the core insights remain more or less unchanged. An interesting example of this is found in her descriptions of her guide or ally Normus, revealing the depths of the Earth to her. She seems to be uncomfortable with this vision, but does not (as Christians tend to do) describe it as evil or to be shunned. These episodes might remind us of the testimony of the 17th century Scottish witch Isobel Gowdie who said at her trial that she was taken to the center of the earth, where she dined with the faery king and queen in a place full of light.

We can trace this UnderWorld theme in faery tradition back to the most ancient sources. It is found in the metaphysics of the Greek/Sicilian philosopher Empedocles (circa 490-430 BC), who saw the volcanic core of the Earth as a source of cosmic birth and creation: the star power within our planet. Nowadays marine biologists have discovered that where the volcanic fires rise deep in the oceans, new life forms abound, hitherto unknown to modern science. This reiterates the deepest teachings of the esoteric faery tradition, namely that life originates in the heart of the planet and rises to the surface. Curiously, materialist evolutionary theory based on the work of Darwin, says something similar.

There are many connections in Daphne's work to ancient philosophy, magic, and metaphysics. Nevertheless, her visions and her writing are uniquely her own, and certainly not based on source books or study. This gives them a powerful naïve quality, an undeniable genuineness, so different from those fairy-fashion pot-boilers that merely quote and regurgitate lore and information from other books. Indeed, in her day, such copyist commercial faery books hardly existed.

As someone who has experienced lived and taught the esoteric faery and UnderWorld tradition for over 30 years as a source of transformative and power spiritual magic, I recommend to you the collected writings of Daphne Charters.

R J Stewart, California, 2008

INTRODUCTION TO VOLUME I

by Michael Pilarski

The Collected Fairy Manuscripts of Daphne Charters are one of the great, fairy literary treasures of the twentieth century. These manuscripts will provide you with hours of captivating, entertaining and uplifting reading. The first part of *Volume I* gives the background for the manuscripts. The stories themselves will take you to places you never, ever imagined. Enjoy the journey.

Daphne Charters worked with three groups of fairies. Her initial contact was with a group of eleven nature fairies. The area of plants which they tended was about a half-mile square according to Daphne. Daphne also came to work with nine house fairies at her housing flat. Years later a second group of twelve nature fairies was added to her circle. A female fairy named Rhelia joined the first group of nature fairies sometime during this intervening period. This is a total of 33 fairies whom Daphne knew by name and worked with.

There are many branches of fairies as outlined by the Deva Marusis in this book. Here are some of the characteristics and level of evolution attained by Daphne's fairy friends.

Attributes of the fairies with whom Daphne worked:

* Their size in their human-like astral bodies, when Daphne first met them, were eight to twelve inches tall. Fairies have to "earn" their size, unlike humans. In Daphne's later writings she says that the fairies were growing taller as a result of their accelerated spiritual growth. Normus in particular, grew from one foot to over three feet tall during his forty years of working with Daphne. Many of the other fairies grew to between one and two feet tall.

* Although small in stature they are generally equivalent to, or even higher than the average human in intellect and spiritual development, particularly in regards to the latter.

* The fairies Daphne worked with commonly spend 100 years on the earth plane in each incarnation with longer, intervening periods in fairy "heaven."

* Their adolescence includes trials, tribulations and lots of learning as they learn to function on the etheric earth plane. Years of experience bring more wisdom and capabilities.

* The fairies have their "jobs". They all serve to the best of their ability, generally. Sometimes they change jobs, change careers so to speak. They don't work all the time, but also have time for play, recreation and socializing.
* They have relationships. There are male and female fairies. They couple up. Some couples form lifelong partnerships. Others break up and take new partners. Not all fairies have a partner.
* They experience emotions, joys, elatedness, pains, and sadness. For example, the clearcutting of their forest or the wanton tearing up of flowers causes them sorrow.
* Spiritual advancement is a lifelong goal. They meditate and take trainings and schooling.

There are a number of ways to explain the origin of Daphne Charters' manuscripts.

One explanation is that she simply made up these stories from her imagination and wrote them down; and if so, they should be regarded as fiction stories such as would be found in the fantasy sections of bookstores. This would be the only acceptable explanation to people who do not believe in fairies or communication with people in the afterlife.

For those people who believe in communication with unseen realms, there are a number of other possible explanations. For instance, that Daphne channeled the material or used automatic writing. In which case, what being(s) did she channel?

The explanation that Daphne herself gave for these stories is that Daphne could see the fairies with her inner eye and carry on long conversations with them. She had ongoing friendships with fairies for decades. The fairies told Daphne about their lives, their exploits, their work and their spiritual development. Daphne wrote it all down. In this explanation, these manuscripts are narrations which Daphne transcribed. As such, they are stories about the lives of the fairies told by the fairies themselves.

Whether one approaches Daphne's stories as purely fiction, or whether one sees them as true communications from the fairy realm, they are fascinating and entertaining reading and are filled with spiritual insights.

I have been a serious student of the fairy realm for thirty years. I have read hundreds of books and articles and am always on the lookout for more. Over the years I have talked with many people who see and/or communicate with fairies and I have done my own personal, experiential explorations, both privately and in group sessions with experienced leaders. Of the many authors I have read and people I have met, only a few come anywhere close to describing a depth of relationship that Daphne had with her fairies. Daphne is in a class all by herself.

Despite the vast amount of fairy and metaphysical writings available, there are a number of unique things about Daphne Charters' manuscripts.

* One is the sheer volume of her writings. It is one of the largest compilations of information on fairies.
* Another is the length of the 40-year period of time over which the writings were done.
* This is the only source I know of whereby fairies tell the stories.
* Daphne not only had long-term, close, personal friendships with 33 individual fairies, she also worked with them.
* Daphne's manuscripts include over 50 characters from many different evolutions and planes of being. Most are fairies, but there are also humans who are not alive on the physical plane and who live on the astral plane. Some of the humans are spiritually evolved, while others would seem quite normal to us.
* Daphne introduced her fairy friends to the astral humans she was working with on the astral plane. Each fairy, or fairy couple, formed a special friendship with one of the astral humans. Daphne referred to them as "observers". They did far more than just observe though. They described the fairies, their homes and their character. They became friends. Fairies live and work on the etheric plane which is one plane higher (in vibration) than the astral plane. Fairies are generally invisible to the humans on the astral plane. Daphne's human friends had a hard time seeing the fairies at first and it was only with practice that the humans were able to see the fairies and their homes.
* The fairies and astral humans would meditate together. When meditating they could journey to higher planes of beings. Some of the most fascinating stories from the *Collected Manuscripts* are about journeys that the fairies and humans take together to other planes of beings, both above and below their usual plane of residence.
* Daphne's astral human friends formed a group to travel to lower earth planes, which they called "the underworld", to rescue lost human souls which they called the "earthbound". After a period of time some of the fairies also joined these expeditions. In exchange, some of the humans joined fairy teams to rescue fairies who had sunk to lower planes. These stories are in Manuscript Set #10 in *Volume II*.
* Another unusual aspect to these stories is that some of Daphne's fairy friends begin visiting the realms of other evolutions/sectors (in addition to fairy and human realms). For instance, the realms of the evolutions concerned with color, with sound, with scent, with movement, and with mind. There they forge friendships with individual beings from these other

evolutions. Eventually the fairies, humans and members of other evolutions are able to merge their consciousnesses and journey together. These are new developments in inter-evolutionary communication and cooperation.

* Due to the success of linking up humans and fairies to encourage friendships and greater understanding between the two evolutions, a Fairy & Human Relations Depot was set up on the astral plane. This became very successful with tens of thousands of fairies and humans being involved as detailed by Betty in her 1990 report. It was eventually re-named the Fairy & Human Relations Centre.

* Over the course of the decades that Daphne worked with the fairies, additional fairies were assigned to work with her. Some of the fairies she works with early on are given promotions as they grow rapidly because of their contact with humans and other evolutions.

* Daphne's language is simple and there are few, long, unfamiliar words. This is not the work of a literary scholar, but it can certainly expand your mind and is fun to read at the same time.

* Other famous fairy writers such as Dora Van Gelder, Geoffrey Hodson, Dorothy Maclean, Rudolph Steiner and R. J. Stewart offer insights into the fairy/devic realm but none of them have the long-term, intimate relationships that Daphne shared with her fairy friends.

* One of the most far-reaching outcomes of the friendship between Daphne and the fairies was the establishment of their annual Fairy & Human Relations Congress. The story of the Congress is found in Manuscript Set # 8 in *Volume I*.

* This Congress held in the fairy realm has inspired the creation of a Fairy & Human Relations Congress on the physical Earth plane. The first was held in 2001.

Adults, interested teens and even some pre-teens would enjoy reading the whole of *Volume I*. Daphne's manuscripts were not intended to be a story book for reading to young children before they go to bed. However, it turns out that the vivid images in the stories make many of the stories enjoyable by children. If read to children, I would advise the reader to select a story ahead of time which is appropriate to the age group and understanding of the audience.

Some of Daphne's language may seem antiquated and trite to modern readers. Please realize that Daphne was raised in the culture and language of England in the early 1900s (born 1910), so her language is different than in the US today. We are less likely to use the male pronouns (his, him) or the term negro. Please don't take offense at some of her language. Daphne was limited to the words in her vocabulary and the cultural context and grammar of the time. We have not changed the British spelling to American spelling for words such as colour and centre, nor have we have edited Daphne's writings to make them more palatable or familiar to modern readers. It is part of the uniqueness of her manuscripts. Some of Daphne's writings can be seen as symbolic, allegorical or as metaphors.

There is a great deal more interest in fairies today than a short thirty years ago. This fairy renaissance is part of a general upsurge of people seeking a reconnection to the Divine.

With this spiritual renaissance, many new doors into the "unseen realms" open to our sight – including the world of the fairies, devas and angels. The natural world is teeming with conscious, loving life; far beyond what humanity perceives at present.

The fairies are God's servants in the nature realms. Without their ministrations, plant life as we know it would not be able to exist. The fairies have always wished to work with humanity and, at one time, did so; but as humanity lost touch with God, we also lost touch with many of the unseen kingdoms. And, as we abused the Earth, it became harder for the nature spirits to maintain links with humanity except for the purer hearts of children and cultures who live close to nature.

Daphne Charters is no longer with us on the physical earth plane, but the effects of her work continue to ripple out as more people read her *Collected Manuscripts*. Daphne Charters is playing a part in improving fairy-human relationships. We can all participate, bringing us closer to that day when humans and fairies work hand-in-hand in loving cooperation for the benefit of all life.

Enjoy the journey.

Michael Francis Pilarski
April, 2007

THE STORY OF HOW MICHAEL PILARSKI MET DAPHNE CHARTERS & SUBSEQUENT HISTORY

by Michael Pilarski

Not so long ago as a young man, I was living in the Okanogan Highlands of north-central Washington. I especially loved ponderosa pine, the waving bunchgrasses, bigbush sagebrush, and bitterroot. I loved all the plants and even the hills, mountains, rivers and the land. My love for the natural world led me to begin a period of spiritual searching. I read prodigiously in the metaphysical and the occult sciences.

One day a beautiful woman named Barbara who lived at Snake Ranch in the Aeneas Valley gave me a book which was to change my life forever. She said "I think you'll like this book." The year was 1976.

The book had a plain brown cover and the title was *A True Fairy Tale* by Daphne Charters. A very plain book, not a single illustration, and a simple layout. Plain exterior notwithstanding, I dove into the book and found it to be wonderful indeed. I could hardly put it down and read it within several days.

My spiritual readings had made me a little familiar with nature spirits and the devic realm, but here, within the plain brown cover was the most elaborate description of the fairy realms I have ever seen before or since. All made possible because Daphne learned to communicate with the nature fairies where she lived. Daphne became friends with them and the fairies formed a partnership with her to rescue lost souls in lower realms. Since Daphne was so good at hearing the fairies she did interviews with them wherein they described their fairy lives, their work, their loves and their challenges. She wrote down many of their stories.

I loved the book so much and my heart was so opened up that when I finished the last page, I jumped up and said "I want to share this book with all my friends!"

So I looked in the book to see where I could get more. But there was no address, no publisher, no ISBN number, nothing. Just the name of the author, a foreword by Lord Air Marshal Dowding, and the text. From the stories it was obvious that the author lived in London. Looking more closely I found a printer's mark at the end of the book with an address. I hopefully sent an airmail letter to the London address. Several weeks later the envelope was returned by the London post. There was no such printer at that address. So I sent another letter to the address and it too came back. Dead end. What to do? The book's foreword by Lord Air Marshal Dowding was dated by him as April, 1956. So in 1976, 20 years later, I didn't know if Daphne was even alive.

But I didn't give up and would mention the book to new friends and groups of people and ask if any of them knew about the book. No one ever had. In the spring of 1977, I helped organize the 3rd Annual Spring Healing Gathering near the tiny town of Curlew in northeast Washington. On Friday night I was helping a van load of nice people from British Columbia set up their camp and at one point I started telling them about this great fairy book *A True Fairy Tale*. Through the darkness a woman's voice called out "Oh, you mean the book by Daphne Charters?" "Yes, yes!", I cried. "You are the first person I've met who knows about it." Her name was Joyce and she was from Castlegar, British Columbia. Joyce says it is a lovely book and her mother is a friend of Daphne's and she will ask her mother for Daphne's address and send it to me later.

About two months later, she did just that and I finally obtained Daphne's address after over a year of looking. So I drafted Daphne a letter and told her how much I loved her book and I wanted to share it with all my friends and would she consider letting me reprint it in the US. Those days it took about a week for airmail to go one-way between US and England. So, two weeks later I am elated to receive a letter from Daphne giving me permission to reprint *A True Fairy Tale*.

She wrote "How fortuitous that you should come along just now, since I am in the process of cleaning up the grammar to make the book more readable and I was wondering how to get it published". Daphne had been approaching publishers in England, but no one was interested. So it was a "match made in heaven," or perhaps in fairyland.

At that time I didn't have any money, but I didn't let that stop me. I found a couple of young artist friends to create some illustrations. I found a sympathetic typesetter who typed the whole text for only several hundred dollars. I found someone to loan me $3,000 to pay the printer, and in 1979 3,000 copies were printed. The price didn't include collating or binding, so a few friends and I collated them by hand and used a big, saddle stapler to bind them.

Well, once the books were finished and in my hands I wasted no time in sharing them with all my friends. They sold like hotcakes plus I gave many away. I sold them for $3 each. By 1982 I was down to the end of the printing and I still didn't have any money. How was I going to get more printed?

One of my best customers for the book was the Association of Sananda and Sunat Kumara, based in Mt. Shasta at the time. ASSK was founded by Sister Thedra who channeled a lot of material from ascended master Sananda. ASSK sold Sister Thedra's channelings plus other metaphysical books. When I told them I was sold out of Daphne's book they said it was a good seller for them and would I give ASSK permission to do a reprinting. Daphne agreed to this and so in 1982 ASSK had several thousand copies printed in New Zealand. The front cover of my 1979 edition featured a watercolor painting of fairies by Daphne. The ASSK printing had Daphne's watercolor on the back cover and the front cover was a fairy illustration done by Daphne's friend Susan Anderson. They sold the books for many years.

In the early 1990s, ASSK moved to Arizona. After Sister Thedra passed on, their book sales gradually wound down. Sometime in the mid-1990s ASSK sold me the remainder of their printing, which was about 300 copies. Those 300 copies lasted a couple years and since then I have been xeroxing copies in small batches.

Daphne and I kept up a correspondence from 1977 till her death in 1991 at 82 years old. She had been working closely with the fairies for over 40 years during which time she had written down over 150 stories.

Although Daphne had friends, there was no one in England to carry on her work. So she asked me if I would be willing to take on the mission of publishing her many stories which had piled up over the years. I said I would be honored to do so. After Daphne's passing a few of her steadfast friends compiled all Daphne's stories and typed them up, notably Gay Burdett, Philip Groom and David Nall-Cain. Installments arrived in my mailbox over several years as they gradually typed them up. Every time an installment arrived, I would gleefully unwrap it and dive into the new batch of stories. So many wonderful stories! And I still want to share them with all my friends.

Progress has been much slower on this mission than I had hoped. Many other missions kept intervening. Finally I had the idea to create a Fairy and Human Relations Congress to attract people to assist getting Daphne's books published. The first Fairy & Human Relations Congress on the physical plane was held in 2001 and it was an instant success. Our first three congresses were held at the Skalitude Retreat Center in a remote valley in the North Cascades. Congresses IV and V were held at the Riversong Forest Sanctuary on the Hood River, Oregon. The 2006 and 2007 congresses are back at Skalitude. And the strategy finally worked! R. J. Stewart, one of our main presenters, started a publishing house and is publishing Daphne's works in three volumes.

This is a brief account of my 32-year history with Daphne Charters and her Collected Fairy Manuscripts.

– Michael Pilarski

SEQUENCE OF EVENTS

1910. Daphne is born in Berkshire, England.

1940s. Daphne marries Jack Charters, a captain in the army during WWII.

1948. Jack dies tragically as a result of being caught in a blizzard in Canada (where they were living after the war).

* Daphne is able to communicate with Jack after his death, where he was living on one of the astral planes.

* Jack introduces Daphne to some of his new friends on the astral plane and she is able to communicate with them.

* Together they begin the work of descending to lower planes to rescue lost souls and bring them up to higher planes.

* After a period of time, Daphne is able to see the fairies who work in her garden and to communicate with them.

1950. Daphne meets Lord Dowding at a lecture he is giving on fairies.

1951. Daphne publishes her first pamphlet on the fairies. *The Origin, Life and Evolution of the Fairies* with a foreword by Lord Dowding. This corresponds to Manuscript Set #2 in *Volume I.*

1951. A French language edition of Daphne's pamphlet is published in Paris. *Les Origines, La Vie, El L'Evolution des Fees.*

1954 ca. The first Fairy & Human Relations Congress is held in the fairy realm. It is hosted by Daphne's fairy friends. The Congress was held annually until at least 1985.

1956. *A True Fairy Tale* is self-published by Daphne with a foreword by Lord Dowding.

1969. A Spanish language edition of *A True Fairy Tale* is published in Buenas Aires, Argentina.

1969. Daphne writes a report on her first 20 years of work with the fairies.

1976. A copy of *A True Fairy Tale* is given to Michael Pilarski by a friend.

1979. Michael Pilarski publishes the 2nd edition of *A True Fairy Tale* in the USA with a new addendum by Daphne.

1981. The first printing sells out and the Association of Sananda and Sunat Kumara does a 2nd printing in New Zealand. Susan Anderson, a friend of Daphne's, draws a new cover.

1985. Daphne transcribes a report from the fairies on the 1985 Fairy & Human Relations Congress held in the fairy realm.

1990. Betty describes the development of the Fairy & Human Relations Center. Betty is the human coordinator from her residence on the astral plane.

1990. Daphne writes several addendums to some of the stories she is transcribing.

1991. Daphne Charters passes on from the Earth plane after asking Michael Pilarski to publish her *Collected Manuscripts*.

1992. Daphne's friends type up her manuscripts and send them to Michael.

2001. The first annual Fairy & Human Relations Congress is held on the physical Earth plane. Organized by Michael and friends and held in the North Cascades of Washington State, USA.

2002-2006. Five more annual Fairy & Human Relations Congress are held in Oregon and Washington.

2007. *Forty Years With the Fairies, The Collected Fairy Manuscripts of Daphne Charters, Volume I* goes to press.

2007. June 22-24. The 7th annual Fairy & Human Relations Congress is held in the North Cascades of Washington.

2008. Volumes II and III are to be published.

TYPES OF STORIES

17 stories by Daphne.

10 stories by Father John, Daphne's spirit-guide.

81 stories by fairies:
  - about their lives.
  - about travels to higher fairy realms, usually in company with a human.
  - about travels to the realms of other evolutions.

32 stories by astral humans.
  - Describing the fairies and their homes.
  - Describing visits to higher fairy realms, usually in company with one or more fairies.
  - Describing life on the astral plane where they live.

Blending & Becoming.
A series of stories about collaboration between fairy, human and other evolutions.

Stories about "The Underworld."
  - Rescuing humans and fairies from lower realms.
  - by Daphne
  - by Humans
  - by Father John
  - by Fairies

Perima: The Adventures of a House Fairy.
Perima is the longest story by far with 435 pages. It is an epic adventure. The fairies Perima and Tepi along with Augustine (a human being) undertake arduous and adventurous journeys to the Underworld where Perima and Augustine assist Tepi to recover parts of his lost soul.

LIST OF CHARACTERS

The following list includes the characters from *Volume II* and *Volume III* as well as *Volume I*. Numbers in parentheses ( ) refer to how many of the stories are by that individual.

Daphne Charters (17) The only human in physical embodiment in the stories. The person who wrote it all down. Daphne transcribes the stories of all the other characters.

Father John (10) Daphne's spirit-guide. A spiritually-advanced human living on one of the higher planes of being. As you will see, he is a full participant in the action as well as a wise helper to Daphne, the fairies and the astral humans. [Father John is my counselor and beloved companion of many incarnations. This time, alas, he is not with me in the flesh but neither are we lost to one another. It was through him that I originally met the fairies, and it was his power in the early months of our contact which acted as a bridge between the two Evolutions. He is the loving friend of many including the fairies. – Daphne Charters]

Deva Marusis (1) A high-level deva of the fairy/deva evolution.

Nature Fairies (1st group – featured in *A True Fairy Tale*)
Normus (12). The leader and most advanced of the fairies. When he first met Daphne he was one foot in height but after 40 years of working with Daphne he had evolved to three feet tall, had been promoted up the ladder and was now overseeing 18 local groups.
Movus (4) He became leader of the local group when Normus was promoted.
Nixus (3)
Gorjus (2)
Myrris (2)
Merella (2)
Mirilla (2)
Lyssis (2)
Namsos (2)
Sirilla (2)
Nuvic (2)
Rhelia (2)

House Fairies
Maire (12)
Herus (4)
Perima (3) The main character in *Volume III*.
Mairus (2)
Pino (2)
Sheena (2)
Sulic (1)
Tepi (1) A main character in *Volume III*.

Nature Fairies (2nd group)
Fina (1)
Sulan (1)
Finto (1)
Pirilla (1)
Horrus (1)
Reena (1)
Silvyl (1)
Nella (1)
Julus (1)
Lunine (1)
Festus (1)
Pellus (1)

Gnomes
Tanchon
Parsion

Other Fairies
Damon, Normus' overleader, boss, mentor, counselor.
Serrus
Fello
Miniva, in Sheena's story
Friamista, a fairy musician
Lerralina, a fairy musician
Master of Music,
The Arienes. Singers mentioned by Rudolph in the Spider-Musicians.

Fares, better known on earth as fairies

Farices, fairies who work with healing

Farallis, singular. Spiritually-advanced fairies. At this point they are at the point of reaching deva status. Their work could be with nature, with humans, or many other tasks.

Faralles, plural.

Maratumel/Marata, Also called the Nameless One by the fairies.
Maratumel is the male aspect.
Marata is the feminine aspect and is the Goddess of Nature.

Humans (living on the astral plane)
Jack (5) Daphne's husband, who died in 1948.
Peter (4)
Ludwig (4)
John (4)
Rudolph (3)
Ronald (3)
Betty (2)
George (2)
Simon (2)
Andrew (1)
Bill (1)
Cecil (1)
Cecile
Joe
Marie Louise
Lerra
Estian
Augustine, A main character in *Volume III*.

Beings from other Evolutions.

Ceres (Beings from the evolution concerned with mind)
Rimago, (6) a young Ceris.
Lorise, Rimago's guide
Marki, a more evolved Ceris, Rimago's teacher.

Thormes (Beings from the sound evolution/sector)

Kojan

Harneles (Beings from the color evolution)
Farre

Gravines (Beings from the scent evolution)
Rerety

Drones (Beings from the movement evolution)

Vibration Evolution (No fairy term given)
Lofer

Other Beings:
Ra-Arus, a fire-being. A main character in *Volume III.*
Marano
Harodino
Ponterinus
Soperon
Sai Baba's higher self

Beings from lower planes.
Hatreds
Monserros

MANUSCRIPTS
SET #1

INTRODUCING
DAPHNE CHARTERS

Preface

𝕴n this section we have gathered together Daphne's manuscripts that were specifically about herself and her work with the fairies. Daphne is much more than just the "channeler" or secretary doing note-taking and transcription. Daphne is one of the key ringleaders in the manuscripts. Daphne developed the capacity to descend into very dark realms to rescue people and fairies and bring them up to lighter realms. Daphne was also able to ascend into higher realms. I am sure that Daphne would be far too humble to categorize herself as a master, but few physical-embodied humans can slip so easily into both higher and lower dimensions and function there. Through the Fairy & Human Relations Centre, Daphne has been responsible for linking up thousands of humans and fairies. She has helped further human/fairy communication more then we can ever know.

– *Michael Pilarski*

A BIOGRAPHY OF DAPHNE CHARTERS
by Gay Burdett

*[Gay Burdett was Daphne's niece and one of her closest friends in England. –
M.P.]*

Born February 24, 1910 in Berkshire, England.
The youngest of 3. Father: retired army officer.

She had 'the brains of the family' and could
successfully, either have continued her
studies after leaving school, or have had a career.
But in those days, neither option was open to a
young girl whose parents were of independent
means. Unmarried daughters simply stayed at
home with their parents and participated in social
life locally.

However, hobbies were accepted. Daphne was
intere98sted in painting; and during the pre-war
years, attended classes at Cedric Morris' art school
in Dedham, Essex. At that time, her parents lived
not far from there, near Colchester.

During the war she successfully ran the food office in Colchester. (Food of-
fices were responsible for ration books which were issued to everyone when food
supplies were restricted.)

Also during the war, she married Jack Charters who was serving as a captain
in the army. After the war, they went to Canada where Jack died tragically as
a result of being caught in a snowstorm. No doubt it was Jack's death which
prompted Daphne's interest in spiritualism.

In the late 1940's, shortly after Jack's death, Daphne returned to England and
lived in Colchester with her widowed mother. It was during this period that she
wrote her *book A True Fairy Tale*. She also became a vegetarian, which led to
her joining 'Beauty Without Cruelty' – at that time a pioneer organisation in the
field of cosmetics free of animal substances, and therefore manufactured without
causing the suffering of any animals.

After her mother's death in 1962, Daphne moved to London. This gave her
the opportunity to participate actively in 'Beauty Without Cruelty.' She became
manageress of their shop in central London, and on their behalf, promoted good
quality simulation fur coats, by organizing dress shows not only in England, but
also abroad.

For the greater part of her life, Daphne was not a physically robust person, and during her latter years she did not have much respite from problems caused by poor health. However, in spite of this, she continued to record, in writing, her experiences inspired by fairies. Unfortunately the last nine months of her life had to be spent in a nursing home where she died on July 7, 1991.

She was wonderfully brave, was always good company and interested in other people, right up until the end.

She once said: "There is only one thing I regret in my life, and that is not to have had a career, because I know I would have made a success of it." And she would.

Daphne was more than a charity worker: She helped many people personally, but always discreetly, 'by stealth.'

– Gay Burdett

SOME BIOGRAPHICAL NOTES ON DAPHNE CHARTERS
by Michael Pilarski

Although I never met Daphne Charters in person, here are a few things I would like to add to the Biography written by her niece and good friend, Gay Burdett. I talked to Daphne several times on the phone, but mostly we just had voluminous correspondence – Daphne in her horrible handwriting and me typing replies on an old clunky, manual typewriter. Alas, almost all of our correspondence was destroyed in several tragic fires. Tragic for the papers that is, no person was injured.

Although we lived thousands of miles apart and never met we became fast friends. Daphne was always so thrilled that I was helping get her writings out to people. She was one of those people who seemed to not have a mean bone in her body. I was always thrilled that she would allow me to serve her and the fairies.

Daphne was a sweet and charming person. She was good with people as well as with fairies. Much of her later life was devoted to her work with the *Beauty Without Cruelty* movement which was headquartered in London. *Beauty Without Cruelty* sold body products that did not involve experimentation on animals. They also promoted alternatives to fur clothing. I never knew the full extent of Daphne's work with them, but she ran their shop in London for many years. She would go to fur shows and talk to people about switching to other forms of clothing. She was an activist in her day.

Daphne and her husband Jack must have had an extra-ordinarily close relationship. Not only did they vow "til death do us part" in their marriage vows, they also vowed to stay in touch even if one died before the other. Jack's life did end tragically when he was still young. Jack and Daphne had emigrated to

Canada after World War II and were living on the Great Plains. Jack got caught in a blizzard and froze to death. Daphne was able to continue her communication with Jack at his new plane of residence (on some other Earth plane) where he lived with other "dead" humans. Daphne uses the term "astral plane" to describe this place. It was not a life totally unlike the world he had just left. Over time, Jack introduced Daphne to some of his new friends and Daphne was able to communicate with them and become their friend as well. Sometime after this, Daphne discovered she has developed the capacity to see and communicate with the local fairies. After some time she had the idea to link up some of her astral human friends with some of her fairy friends. Sort of like a cross-evolutionary pen-pal relationship. This is all explained in more detail in Manuscript Set #3 and in other places throughout the manuscripts.

Lord Chief Air Marshall Dowding was a well-known high-ranking, military officer and the Chief Air Marshall for Britain during WWII. Lord Dowding believed in fairies and at a talk he gave on fairies in 1950 met Daphne Charters and was impressed with her advanced abilities to communicate with fairies. He encouraged her to publish her writings and wrote the foreword for her small, first publication in 1951 titled *The Origin, Life and Evolution of the Fairies* (Manuscript Set #2 in *Volume I*). Later on he amended this foreword to use in Daphne's self-published, 1956 book *A True Fairy Tale*.

Daphne lived for many years in London at a series of flats called the Delaware Mansions. There was a garden and lawn out back where Daphne met and had tea with friends and her band of nature fairies. Daphne loved trees and would visit her favorite trees in and around London for the enjoyment and strength they gave her.

As Daphne became older she was beset by various illnesses and conditions. Daphne was not above complaining about her aches and pains. At least she confided some of her health problems to me. She would get better and then something else would happen. The world is full of examples of spiritually-evolved people who are plagued with ill health or other kinds of trials and tribulations. With Daphne it was mainly her health as she had good friends and a stable life. She kept her keen mind up till the end when she passed from the physical realm at 82 years old. I am sure they had a huge welcoming party in fairyland when Daphne passed from this realm.

Daphne never received the fame and recognition she deserved while she was alive. but her work is still alive and continuing. Through these publications her writings can thrill and inspire thousands of people and generations to come.

It took a lot of time and dedication for Daphne to write down all these manuscripts over the years. She was steadfast. Not long before she died, when she requested me to see to it that all her unpublished manuscripts would eventually get published, she said to me. "Now Michael, I don't think they would have had me go to all this work for nothing."

My apologies, Daphne, for taking so long. Suffice it to say that I have been busy working for the plants, the planet and the people.

Here, dear reader, is Volume I, a tribute to all of Daphne Charters' hard work and dedication.

– Michael Pilarski

INTRODUCTION TO THE 1ST EDITION
OF *A TRUE FAIRY TALE* (1956)
by Air Chief Marshall Lord Dowding

[Air Chief Marshall Lord Dowding was he commander-in-chief of the British forces during the Battle of Britain (WWII). Here was a popular, public figure from the military, openly lecturing about fairies. – M.P.]

The first chapter of this book was published in 1951 as a booklet entitled *The Origin, Life and Evolution of the Fairies.*

To that booklet I wrote a Foreword which, in an amended form, will serve as an introduction to this volume.

In 1950, with the valour of ignorance, I took upon myself to give a public lecture on Angels and Fairies. I knew little enough about my subject but I supposed that my audience would know even less. I was wrong.

At the end of my lecture a lady came up to me and told me that she was on the most intimate terms with all the fairies in her house and garden; she knew them all by name and she knew what they looked like (although she could not see them directly) and what sort of work they each did.

That lady was Mrs. Charters, the recorder of the script of which the booklet was composed.

She tells me that the transmitter is one of the healing Devas (a Deva may be thought of as an Angel of the Fairy line of evolution); and intelligible communications between Devas and humanity are extremely rare for a variety of reasons, of which the principal is the very great technical difficulty of the process.

When I have spoken to Spiritualist and Theosophical friends about Mrs. Charters and her work, they have said, "Is she a hysterical person?" or "Does she live much alone?" I am writing this foreword mainly to testify that Mrs. Charters is a very normal, matter-of-fact person, largely occupied (like the majority of contemporary Englishwomen) with housekeeping and domestic duties. I do not propose to enter into a lengthy discussion about the probable accuracy

This black and white graphic is adapted from the watercolor painted
by Daphne Charters for the dust cover of the 1956 first edition.

or otherwise of the script; I merely wish to state that, in my opinion, little or none of it emanates from Mrs. Charter's subconscious mind. I rather say to the reader:

"Here is a very remarkable document. It is the first serious attempt that I have ever seen to trace the Fairy line of evolution through all its stages from a tiny speck of light right through to its ultimate stage as a Deva, ultimate, that is to say, except for the final process of Union with the Absolute. Geoffrey Hodson has given us his fascinating books on Fairy life, and Conan Doyle and others have given us photographs of the Fairy folk, but nobody (in my limited experience) has given us a comprehensive picture of Fairy life and its objectives, and also of the process of Rebirth into the Etheric by which one stage of development merges into the next.

"Don't think of me as saying that this is the Revelation of a great truth which should be unhesitatingly accepted. What I do say is that here is a remarkable, perhaps a unique, document - read it for yourself and see what you make of it."

The thing that has puzzled me more than any other is the obvious Latin origin of the names given for the different types of Fairy and for most of their personal names. Most of the roots are Latin, as also are the singular and plural forms, ending in -is and -es respectively.

In my original foreword I raised the query as to whether Chinese Fairies (for instance) had similar Latin-type names or names of Chinese form. I have just had an answer to this query. Mrs. Charters had recently made the acquaintance of two Chinese Fairies and their names are Perima and Sulic. Perima has a distinct Latin tang about it. Perhaps the fact may be, not that Fairies have Latin names, but that the Romans had Fairy names!

The other thing that comes as a surprise to me is the idea that we all have House Fairies working regularly in-doors. I have believed in Fairies for many years, but chiefly as an adjunct necessary for all vegetable growth. Of course, the Romans had their Lares and Penates, their household gods; but I thought that was all part of their not very elevated religion. There is not smoke without fire, and maybe it was the House Fairies who were adopted as household gods.

I fear that this book is years ahead of its time. People are so hard-headed! Fairies are seen today in thousands of cases, but mainly by very simple people, as for instance, Celtic peasants and children of all nationalities. Now and then they are seen by psychic adults. And yet, to say of a person, "He believes in Fairies." almost amounts to saying, "He isn't right in the head." Personally I believe that we shall all eventually come not only to accept the existence of fairies as a fact, but also to recognise the essential work which they do for humanity, and to accept the obligation therein implicit to afford them our loving cooperation, and so help them along their path of evolution. For their evolution is no less important than ours in the sight of God, and both lead to a common goal.

– Dowding, April, 1956

Foreword to the 1ST edition
of *A True Fairy Tale* (1956)

By Daphne Charters

From the beginning I want to make it clear that this book is not a fantasy. On the contrary, to the best of my knowledge, every word in it is true. There is, however, always a margin of error in extra-sensory communication and, for this reason, I think that no one should ever blindly accept any statement, however impeccable the source. If the medium has a fixed idea, it is very difficult for the communicator instantaneously to eradicate it but, given time, he is able gradually to mould the mistaken mind to a more accurate point of view. On the other hand, I often ask a question and receive another answer to the one I had anticipated – but there is a vast difference between expectation and a supposed certainty.

Because of this possibility of inadvertent mistakes I am in the habit of leaving any communication for approximately three months before examining it again and, during the interval, those who are helping me are able to readjust my ideas. When I again read what I have previously written in good faith, sometimes I pause before a statement and "something" inside me says, "No." Then I think again and I find that I know the correct answer or, if it is not completely accurate it will, at any rate, be nearer the truth. Of course you may say, "Well, in that case if she reads this in a year's time 'something' inside her may say, 'No' to the entire book." I do not think that anything quite so drastic as that will happen and, if it does, I hope that I shall have the courage to admit it.

Work

It is necessary for me to tell you a little about myself and the work in which I am engaged, otherwise you may be misled. I am not clairvoyant in the usual sense. I can, however, see a little, as it might be described, with my mind. If I say to you, "Last week I watched the sun setting between two ranges of snow-capped mountains and the lake lying between looked as though it were on fire," unless you are very unimaginative, I feel sure that some kind of picture will take form in your mind. In other words, you will be seeing with your "mind's eye" as opposed to your physical or psychic eye. This is how I "see."

Vibrations

This ability to see is not due entirely to the mind's eye but to vibrations. These are known to all who are interested in the next world and also by those who have an elementary knowledge of physics in this.

I am sure that, at any rate, some of you must have entered an apparently empty room and yet have known that you were not alone. This is often called the sixth sense but actually you are receiving the invisible vibrations of the other person present. All things vibrate, some fast, some slow and every object, building, continent and person has his or her individual vibration, a kind of indestructible identity card. You may think that a chair is static but elementary physics gives us the number of times it vibrates to a second. We vibrate at a somewhat higher speed but, owing to the fact that we are both within the same vibratory range, we can both see and touch the chair. We are only unable to see the dead because they are vibrating faster than our much slower physical eye. (Fairies' vibrations are higher than the dead who live on the Astral Plane and that is why they are not visible to most clairvoyant mediums).

Mediumship

Now, I expect that most of you have a radio and you will know that the waves of sound are captured by your set so that you can hear music and talks coming from many miles away. These waves or vibrations are in your room all the time, but you cannot hear them unless you tune in to them. In other words, your radio is the medium through which your ears are enabled to receive the sounds which are already present.

Being a medium merely means that a person is able to receive sights and sounds not visible or audible to the normal eye and ear.

I have no doubt that many of you are convinced that fairies are imaginary beings which have been invented for the amusement of children and, in stating that I have conversations with them every day, I am in grave danger of being labeled an amiable lunatic.

However, it is not always wise to scoff at people who have access to experiences which, up to the present, you have not. I will take the question of hearing. Tests have been made by various groups of people and indeed you could carry out a similar experiment yourself, with the aid of several friends, if you are able to buy or borrow a super-sonic whistle. The pitch of this instrument varies from a tone which all with normal ears can hear, to so high a note that no human being can detect it. We will imagine that you are with eleven trusted friends and, to begin with, all can hear the whistle. Gradually the pitch of this instrument is raised until in ones and twos your friends drop out of the group, as the note becomes inaudible to them. You are the eighth to retire, leaving four who maintain that they can still hear the whistle. If you are a scoffer, you must now make up your mind whether:

(1) Your four friends are experiencing something beyond your own capacity.
(2) Their hearing is a figment of their imagination.
(3) They are just plain liars.

If you decide on (2) or (3), remember that the seven friends who dropped out before you are equally entitled to think these same thoughts of you.

In 1950 a big sheep-dog trial was won by a dog whose handler used a super-sonic whistle. Once again you have a choice before you:

(1) The dog could hear the whistle with which his handler was issuing directions, although all was silence to the human watchers.
(2) The winner was a miracle dog who knew instinctively what he should do.
(3) Although his handler had an object between his lips, he and the dog were really practicing telepathy.

I have stressed this point in order to dissuade you from laughing at children when they come and tell you of their fairy friends. Young people are often psychic up to the age of adolescence, so encourage them to share these playmates who, although unseen by you, are as real as you yourselves.

In this book I am using the words "see" and "hear" although I do not mean them in the ordinary sense.

How it all began

My husband Jack died unexpectedly and tragically in 1948. 1 had always had a vague interest in psychic matters but I had been too afraid to delve further. With Jack's death, however, came the realization that, the worst having happened, there was nothing of which to be afraid any more and I knew that I must find out where and what he was. About four, months later, when I was a trifle calmer, every-thing, as were, fell into my lap and I was able to speak to him through a medium.

On my return to England I continued with this method of communication about once a month and on the fourth visit I was told that Jack wished to try "au-tomatic writing" with me. With this form of communication the dead person takes the hand and guides the pen. Sometimes the medium is in full trance, sometimes partial or, as in my own case, fully conscious. After two failures we succeeded and then, once a week, we wrote one or two sentences together.

13

Interference

I was becoming quite confident when I came across my first snag. Unknown to me, some earth-bound entities came and took my hand, Jack not being powerful enough at the time to prevent them, and continued the conversation. I was completely taken in and it was only after I had made a fool of myself and had gone on a false journey that I realized I was being tricked and that it was not Jack who was the writer. Let this be a warning to seekers. Do not try to work alone. I have done it and I have experienced some of the many difficulties. It can be dangerous as well as unpleasant so, if you wish to develop, sit about once a week with a medium who is strong enough to keep unwanted intruders away.

You may wonder how these troublesome people can possible know when you are about to communicate. When you, as it were, open out to make contact, you show a light. Undeveloped and earth-bound spirits are those who, by their behaviour on Earth, such as habitual drunkenness or drug addiction, have prevented themselves from reaching the Other Side in the normal way, at death. They live in a dark and dreary world and a light naturally attracts them. Some of the more frivolous ones enjoy baiting mediums, particularly those new to communication, who are, of course, far more gullible than old hands at the game. When I look back at my notes, I am amazed that I could have been taken in by such rubbish but, at the time, I was often more than upset. On the first occasion I was horrified at the thought of some ghoul-like creature clutching my hand. I felt unclean and not a little frightened. There was one thing that I knew, though, and that was that I must get rid of the intruder. But how? Then the word "exorcise" came into my mind. I had heard that clergymen were sometimes called in to exorcise evil spirits from haunted houses. I did not know how they did it, any more than you probably do, but I succeeded and when, trembling in every limb, I again took up my pen, Jack came through.

The next night he told me that there was a sequel to this event which, at the time, caused me considerable distress, for I was to try and persuade these same earth-bounds to go with him to the Astral Plane. So, once again, shaking like jelly, I knew that strangers were guiding my hand. No dramatic exhortation was necessary on my part because they were easily persuaded and I had my first psychic proof of "Out of evil cometh good." That was by no means the end of my work with these temporarily lost souls; in fact, it was the beginning and I found that most of them were far from ghoulish, cheeky or unkind. In fact, many were terrified and I needed all my powers of tact and persuasion to make them understand that they, and only they, were punishing themselves, that would-be friends were eager to help them, and that life on the Astral Plane is quite different from the atonement and everlasting Hymn singing which most of them imagined it to be.

The Book

When I first contacted the fairies, I knew nothing about them at all. I found them charming and often amusing companions and the idea came to me that one day I might write a little book for children. However, I soon realized that the fairies' activities merited something far more serious than this slight tribute.

I obtained a wonderful book entitled "Fairies at Work and Play" by Geoffrey Hodson and I was fascinated to read his vivid descriptions of many types of fairies, from the tiny entities who spend their lives tending plants to the wonderful Devas who, with the Shining Ones of the other evolutions, preside over and govern the Universe. I was, however, somewhat surprised to learn that fairies do not speak and, although they sometimes perform imitative gestures, such as opening and shutting their mouths, they are incapable of communication.

Very soon after I had read this book I attended a lecture entitled "Angels and Fairies" by Lord Dowding. Again, to my amazement, he stated that, as far as he knew, it was not possible to converse with the little people. I spoke to him after the lecture and I verified that I had not misunderstood him on this point. I then told him that I talked with fairies every day, and he advised me to keep notes, which actually I had just commenced doing. It was then that I decided to write a book that might shed a light on this fascinating subject.

The Other Side

I imagine that some of you will not have previously given much thought to where you go and what happens to you when you die. As the evolution to which the fairies belong grows side by side with Man, not only on Earth, I must tell you a little about the life after death in order that you may understand how the fairies work.

The place to which we normally go when we die is generally known as the Astral Plane and it is situated in what we know as space. Here, in reality, are fields, rivers, mountains, valleys, villages and towns very similar to those on Earth, but we are unable to see them because they are vibrating, like their occupants, faster than our physical eyes can record.

Dying is just like casting off an overcoat when Spring arrives. Our physical body is the overcoat and underneath it we have another one; in other words, we have a second, invisible body living inside the one we know, and it is this body which we use when we die. To take a not very attractive simile, we are rather like an onion with the coarse, brown, outside skin as the physical body. As we progress and move to a higher sphere, we require a finer body, because the atmosphere is clearer. With the onion, when one skin is peeled off, another takes its place so, as we cast one body, there is another ready for our use.

Between the physical and this Astral body is the Etheric body, which may be regarded as the liaison between the two. Quite a number of people, while still on Earth, consciously use this Etheric body, which they extricate from the physical, and travel at will. I have this ability although, unfortunately, I have not the added talent which many enjoy, of a clear vision of the places I visit and the people I meet.

At death the Etheric body is used for a short while and is then discarded for that of the Astral. The "Earth-bound" are still using their Etheric bodies because they are living in a "No Man's Land" between Earth and Astral. This is also the body used in dreams, the Etheric being the plane of the subconscious mind, through which all extra-sensory communications must pass before reaching the factual brain consciousness.

Fairies' Bodies

Fairies, too, naturally differ in their consciousness and are present on every plane. They live and work either with or without a body and their usual form can temporarily be changed by an act of will. When they are without their bodies they appear as small lights, their color and strength depending on their work and individual state of progress.

Power

The main work of the fairies consists of absorbing Power in order to coarsen it sufficiently for use on the Earth Plane and exhaling it into the etheric bodies of their charges. Power is in and around every one and everything in the Universe and as you advance on your upward path you become capable of absorbing and passing through your body more of it for the many purposes for which it is used. I do not think that I can do better than quote Father John on the subject: "To us it is that which sustains Life itself; it is in every mineral, plant and person; it draws, it breaks, it raises up and it casts down; it Is food and drink; it heals, it comforts and it lifts us literally to the stars." [Father John is my most frequent communicator, being my guide, friend and counselor.]

When people wish to give power to another, whether to heal, comfort or to make love, they, as it were, open out and the power flows through them.

Young fairies and smaller entities of their evolution must first absorb and then expel it; in other words, there is a double action, as in breathing. As they evolve they, too, become able to act as generators for the ever-flowing stream.

Love on the Astral

I understand that there is no marriage after Earth life; in other words, there is no ceremony, either religious or legal, which forces two people to live together when love has died. Love, and love only, is the tie for Man, Fairy and all the other evolutions as well.

When two people cease to love on the Astral, they part. Do not, however, think that they are encouraged to be promiscuous. In the next chapter the Deva explains a few of the precautions taken to ensure happiness. After anyone has been over on the Other Side for a short while, he understands that life goes on for eternity. Why, therefore, this headlong rush to find your true love? Everyone has an affinity. Some say that they begin and end as one, others that they are separate parts of a whole. I understand from Father John that the general opinion is that affinities are formed from identical atoms but others maintain that the soul splits, forming two separate parts of a whole, and that each part goes its way through mineral, vegetable and animal kingdoms until finally they meet again. It is this searching for one's twin, or affinity, which causes us to make unions which are not always a success. Time has not been wasted, however, because it is necessary for us to have all kinds of experience, both good and bad, before we are sufficiently tempered to make much progress.

With the fairies, the twin souls - or affinities, whichever you prefer - are called duo and dua. These exchange power with each other alone and also with their leader if of the opposite sex. It is a reward and a spiritual experience to receive power from a leader for he or she is invariably more advanced than the receiver. Fairies who have a special love for one another and therefore live together, are called pares, but there is no ill-feeling or jealousy if either or both exchange power with other fairies as well.

Fairies and Man

Although the evolution to which the fairies belong grows side by side with man, its members are usually unseen by him until both are living on the Higher Astral Plane.

When I first began talking to my discarnate friends I found, to my surprise, that they were unable to see or hear them. However, with a little concentration on the part of both men and fairies, they were soon able to communicate. Like me, they do not hear them with their ears but with their minds; indeed, this is essential for fairies do not speak with their voices. They project a picture of their thoughts onto the atmosphere or, for greater privacy, onto the mind of the person with whom they wish to converse. Rather an interesting fact concerning the unconscious translation from pictures into words was disclosed quite early in my acquaintance with the fairies and may supply the answer to the biblical term, "gift of tongues," for when people die I find that they are not able to speak French, Greek or Sanskrit at will, any more than they could on Earth. However, the people who are able to use this method of projecting their thoughts have no difficulty in understanding others, no matter what the nationality of the speaker.

Among those contributing to this book is a German called Ludwig. He writes good English but naturally German is the language in which he normally speaks and thinks. One day I said to him, "You're often with me when I'm talking to the fairies and you must be receiving the same projections that I am. To me they're talking in English, what about you?" After considering the matter, he replied that he had not until that moment given it a thought but that he definitely heard them in German.

To make these men see the fairies was a much more difficult task. Days or weeks of study on their part and a certain amount of power had to be used on three or four occasions before success was achieved. However, once they had found the correct vibration, the men had but to tune in to it to see the little people quite normally with their eyes.

There are so many tiny entities of various evolutions in every corner of the Universe that life would become like a drunkard's nightmare if everyone was tuned in to all of them at once. We would realise that we sucked minute people in and blew them out again each time we draw breath; we would see them in our soup and in our favourite chair, popping out of the television and into the flour bin. Therefore everyone keeps tuned in to his own vibratory range and, when he has learned how to do so, to any of the others for long or short periods at will. Thus nobody gets in anyone else's way.

Owing to their actual sight, my friends have been able to describe to me the fairies' exquisite beauty, often transcending anything on Earth. The little people are entirely unconceited and their sole desire is that others may derive pleasure from it too. They make charmingly naive remarks about themselves such as when I said to one of them, "You know, until George gave me that description of you,

I had no idea what a handsome fellow you are." He said, "Oh, Daphne, I do wish that you could see me because I really am very beautiful."

I laughingly chided him on his conceit but he did not appear to grasp my meaning so I explained to him that on Earth, when people applaud their own beauty, for which they are in no way responsible, we say that they are conceited. "But I don't understand," he insisted. "We delight in our looks and love others to enjoy them. In any case, our beauty is earned," he added proudly. 'We can't make ourselves better looking than we deserve."

Help with the Book

I am not the sole author of this book as my psychic faculties are limited and unfortunately I cannot give as much time to talking to the fairies as I could wish.

I have already mentioned my guide, Father John. Of the rest who have helped me, six were once earthbounds whom I was instrumental in sending over to the Other Side. All these six have given up what might be termed by some, the pleasanter occupations of astral life, to return to the Earth plane and below to help others who are now suffering for their past misdeeds, even as did they themselves.

As this book is not about the earthbound, except incidentally, I will not give you the stories of these men now, interesting though they are. I will just mention, with their names, their occupations when they were on Earth. (1) George was a tea planter. (2) Ludwig, a German princeling. (3) Ronald, a stockbroker. (4) Peter was, more than anything else, a playboy. (5) Andrew, a factory foreman. (6) John, an estate agent. Also mentioned are Betty, who was not earthbound but went over in the usual way (although before her proper time, owing to the fact that she was killed in World War II while driving an ambulance in Germany), and my husband Jack. These two being "Guardians" of the House-fairies, whose stories are not told in this book, make but a fleeting appearance.

These eight visit me periodically and one day, soon after I had become aware of the fairies, I suggested to them that each should adopt, or be adopted by, one or a pair of the little people. Both sides were delighted with the idea although, at the time, the men and Betty could only hear but not see them. This love between Man and Fairy has led to many enchanting revelations which would be quite beyond my ability to describe owing to my lack of vision. In each case I have named the human observer or the fairy who has given me the information which follows.

All the people concerned in our evolution are discarnate or what we know as dead.

None of these friends has been over long, and some of their communications may come as a shock to those who have never studied life after death.

Evolution of the physical body has been proved to be very slow; it is therefore logical to conclude that there will be no large gaps when, although the same individuals, we happen to be vibrating somewhat faster than we are at present, i.e. when we're dead.

All evolution, whether of the body, mind or spirit, is slow and immediately after death we look to those also dead, identical in appearance to when we were "alive." We very definitely have bodies which are perfectly solid to us and until we have learned the efficacy of thought, they require attention, clothing and feeding.

Many people live for years in almost exactly the same conditions as those they knew on Earth, either because they are satisfied with them or because they are afraid to try anything else. Naturally some people become acclimatized quicker than others, depending on their state of progress and whether they are young or comparatively old and experienced souls.

Added to their short span on the Astral, most of the friends who have helped me with the book are working with people who are either earthbound or living on planes below that of Earth, the deeper spheres of which we know as Hell. To exist in the prevailing conditions there, it is necessary for them to slow down the vibrations of their bodies considerably. In order to make this change less arduous, they are residing in a fairly low sphere of the Astral plane, therefore do not be surprised, dismayed or filled with righteous indignation when they talk about shaving brushes, dinner parties or wearing their second-best suits because they are but speaking the truth.

I admit that I cannot prove any of these facts to you, nor will I be able to do so until you, too, are dead and, even then, you may be sufficiently advanced to pass through the Astral plane quickly without indulging in its more material aspects. Or, again, you may be one of the elect who will shoot like a meteor through the Astral, Third and Fourth planes to take your shimmering self to conditions indescribable to us on Earth, to twang your harp, I hope tunefully, into Infinity.

It is more than possible that you may think that the fairies and my astral friends all relate their parts of the story in the same way. Remember, though, that it is my brain which is translating into words the ideas which they give me and even when the automatic writing comes into use I am fully conscious at the time and the communication is still, to a large extent, mental. Bear in mind, too, that none of my friends nor I are professional writers. We have no literary style which is the hallmark of the good author; we only have some facts which we wish to lay before you and our main endeavour is to keep them as clear and as simple as possible.

If you find a similarity in the reading, I can assure you that there has been a vast difference in the writing, according to whether I am struggling with the composition myself or the ideas are being given to me. In the former case, I re-write whole sentences time and time again; I delete phrases, add paragraphs or move them from one place to another and my wastepaper basket fills and refills. In the latter, the sequence of events is orderly, if not literary, and, apart from the fact that in the translation I may have repeated the same word twice, too closely for comfortable reading, and a synonym has to be found, I merely copy down what has been dictated to me with comparatively little alteration.

"The Deva Marusis Speaks," has already been published as a separate booklet by the Greater World Association under the title, *The Origin, Life and Evolution of the Fairies*. I have made one or two amendments and alterations due to increased knowledge. This communication was the most difficult and tiring in which I have ever taken part.

My average output was about twenty lines an hour and often I was obliged to leave gaps for words which I could not, at the time, translate. Once I wrote five lines in three quarters of an hour and always I felt extremely tired when I stopped.

With the fairies, approximate meaning of a word or phrase satisfied them but, with the Deva, the exact one must be found and sometimes I made ten or twelve suggestions with equivalent meanings before He appeared satisfied.

When you have read the chapter you may say, "Well, it wasn't worth all the trouble. After all, apart from a few names and numbers, it's really only what I could have worked out for myself if I'd thought about it," – and there lies the key. *If* you had thought about it. All truth is available for those who think and if I can succeed in making a few people seek for the Truth which has been since the Beginning, then this book will have achieved its purpose.

– Daphne Charters

FAIRIES

by Daphne Charters

[This piece is not dated but would have been written around 1970. – M.P.]

Fairies have been so much part of my life for over twenty years that it is sometimes quite difficult for me to realize that most people know nothing of their existence. If they think of them at all, they probably regard them as attractive figments of the imagination, conjured up by some obliging person for the amusement of young children. But, if we have studied, even a little, we find that the main esoteric systems, whether of East of West, wherein the knowledge has been handed down from Master to pupil, often verbally, all recognize the various orders of Angels and the existence of nature spirits.

I am sure that most of you here must at some time, have wondered what makes plants grow and come to flower and fruit at different times of the year instead of all together which might be expected considering the conditions in a district of sun, moon, rain and soil are identical.

I believe that all effects are brought about by different Cosmic Forces playing upon, penetrating and permeating the substance not only of our Earth but of the Universe. These Forces are habitually playing and any action which is habitual over eons of time eventually becomes conscious and finally, intelligent. In other woods these are not blind forces which are bringing about the wonders of Nature by chance, but highly evolved Intelligences, with which can be linked the well-known term 'Angel.' Very little has been told us about these Beings by orthodoxy except in a highly symbolic way, extremely difficult to understand by anyone who has not made a study of symbolic forms. We have been told however that they are messengers and is not a messengers a conveyor? So may they not be the conveyors of the Force and the Will which turns an idea into a reality? I know this sounds somewhat ambiguous so I will give a very elementary example. The idea of the future oak lies within the acorn, but it is the playing of these Intelligent Forces on it that takes it through its many stages which turn the idea in the acorn into the fact of the oak.

I have already suggested that any action which is habitual eventually becomes conscious, self-conscious and intelligent. This was the sequence followed by the Cosmic Forces with which we have linked the term Angel. Now these Intelligent Forces are habitually playing on matter, the degree of intensity being governed by certain cosmic cyclic changes some of which are reflected in our four seasons. These Forces cause certain stresses, actions and reactions to take place within the matter, varying according to whether it is of a solid, liquid or gaseous nature or of the physicist's ether. Again, constant repetition has it's effect and these stereotyped actions acquire an increasing degree of consciousness until they gain a separate existence no longer dependent on the activity which brought them into being. These existences are the elementals of Earth, water, air and fire of which we have all heard. Their activities continue and, like the molecules of physical matter they act and re-act among themselves, unite with or repel one another until they become more complex in nature. If there is an "official" term for these little existences, I'm afraid I don't know it but I think the word "complexity" serves to differentiate them from the elementals which are capable of only one type of function within a single idea. Elementals, then, come into being as the result of the Angelic Forces playing on matter in order to stimulate it into certain activities. To put it in very simple language, one might say that they are the "children" of Angels and matter, and from them evolve the complexities, nature spirits and fairies.

If we link the Fairies to the Cosmic Forces in this way, I think we will begin to realize that there are occult truths in fairy stories, for instance the gifts bestowed by the good and bad fairies at a child's christening. Are not these references to the astrological influences under which we are all born? Linking the fairies with the science of Astrology should lead to the idea that all manifestation is part of a Whole, so don't shut fairies up in a box as though they were something apart from our everyday lives because whether we know it or not, the evolution to which they belong contributes a great deal to our very existence, in fact it has been stated on good authority that if it weren't for the ministrations

Artist: Louisa McCuskey

of the Nature Spirits, there would be no agriculture.

There is, of course, a vast Nature Spirit World containing countless categories in type and consciousness which includes those of microscopic size which work in their teeming millions building up and breaking down the bodies of the plant and animal Kingdoms. Then there are the innumerable little creatures whose movement in play or other compulsive activities unconsciously contribute to evolution by distributing the forces in which they live. These might be compared to ants or bees in consciousness or, higher up the scale, to a bird in a flock or an animal in a herd. Consciousness in each varies but in no case is there individual awareness, the ant, bee, bird, animal or little nature-spirit being part of the whole. One might say that the ant hill, bee-hive, flock or herd is the incarnating personality within the group-soul of the species. However I think that in some instances when there has been contact with an understanding Man, although remaining a member of its group, some could achieve a greater awareness than is usual in a member of a herd or possibly of a flock of birds.

Gradually the numbers in a group diminish as consciousness grows, until there are two fairies working as a single unit or a leader, controlling a group of lesser nature spirits.

Wherever there is a natural division of land such as a valley, a forest or a range of mountains there develops an over-soul and these great Devas brood over and bring about the changes in their area through the intermediary of the innumerable lesser nature spirits who live there.

We have compared the consciousness of the little non-human part-entities to groups of animals. We know that animals through their association with Man, become domesticated. They become self-conscious because they are aware of someone outside themselves. Some learn to obey. Some learn to love. It is this last attainment which I believe is the key to individualization, for to learn to love is to find God, or an aspect of Him-It even if the finder knows nothing of the existence of what we call God. It is the nucleus and beginning of a new type of being, that of individual living.

Like animals, complexities or nature spirits too can be "domesticated." They are used by Adepts in their work and discarnate or incarnate man, even though not as Adept, if he understands these matters, can "adopt" one or some of these non-human existences and provide them with an object for observation. By loving them the man brings them into contact with a Force that is not their own and, as with the animals, Love causes Individualization. This is not sentimentality on my part for as you know Love is a great Force and one of the Factors which built the manifested Universe and continues to sustain it to this day.

Through this contact with the human being , there becomes available to the nature spirit a whole new magnetic field containing the concrete thinking mind or Man's logical way of thinking and becomes capable of making his own plans and carrying them out.

I am not saying that there are not other methods of individualization, indeed I am sure there are, but I think that this particular process is probably the occult truth being the so-called "marriage" of a man and a fairy in traditional Fairy Stories. This act is always regarded as a necessity before the fairy can acquire a soul and thus immortality. Occultly of course, marriage does not mean what we mean by the word but the conjunction of two Forces bringing them into equilibrium.

I believe that all fairies who have been seen by psychics are these individuals. I am not however including under the world "Psychic" such seers as Geoffrey Hodson and Rudolph Steiner whose vision goes far deeper, enabling them to observe the nature spirits in their own sphere rather than cloaked with etheric matter, giving them a degree of materialization. Yet it is interesting that these two advanced occultists vary considerably in some of their findings. For instance Geoffrey Hodson says that gnomes have very little consciousness and their atmosphere is inclined to be evil. Whereas Rudolph Steiner says they are filled with inherent wisdom and regard Man's complicated way of thinking with amused tolerance. One can only presume that there is a whole world of gnomes, who like human beings and fairies vary widely in type and degree of consciousness.

Among these individualized existences are those whom I like to call "my Fairies." They reached this status many years ago, are highly intelligent, some of course more so than others as one finds with the Human race. They are quite different in character, some being grave, some gay, some impetuous, others patient and plodding.

Twenty years ago the group around me consisted of ten outdoor fairies with their leader and six house fairies, but in ones and twos, sometimes in groups, others have joined us until there are now about thirty-five whom I have identified and whose names I know, although I am sure that there are many "observers" of whom I am quite ignorant.

I am now going to return to the question of individualization. A member of the outer group who visits me once a week is called Rhelia. On one of those occasions I became aware that she was not alone and on concentrating further, I realized that there were some what I must call "children" with her. I questioned her about them and I asked her if she would come and tell me how they come into being. As is usual, she was delighted to have this opportunity of telling a human being a little about an aspect of fairy life, but she had to have some help with what one might call the composition. She turned to one called Father John who is my counselor and beloved companion of many incarnations. This time, alas, he is not with me in the flesh but neither are we lost to one another. It was through him that I originally met the fairies, and it was his power in the early months of our contact, which acted as a bridge between the two evolutions. He is the loving friend of many including the fairies, and with his help Rhelia was able to express herself so that a human being could understand.

– *Daphne Charters*

[Rhelia's story is told at the end of the Nature Fairies section of Vol I. – M.P.]

ADDENDUM FROM THE 2ND EDITION
OF *A TRUE FAIRY TALE* (1979)

by Daphne Charters

Many years have passed since *A True Fairy Tale* was published. It was written in almost total ignorance of the subject but, paradoxically, this proved to be an advantage because I had no fixed ideas about fairies which could have interfered with the communications given to me by those who, in reality, "wrote" the book.

Having now re-read it for the first time since publication, I find that there is factually little that needs altering. I have, however, changed words or phrases in order to clarify a meaning, have qualified a few statements and have added one or two footnotes.

There was also a good deal of "sloppy" grammar and, doubtless, some remains but I think the corrections are at least an improvement on the original.

After my mother's death, when I moved from the flat and garden outside a country town to London, I received a number of letters from "fairy friends" worried that the group would no longer be with me, but severance of both work and love would be impossible.

These fairies are not Nature Spirits whose work lies solely with the Plant Kingdom and, although I did not know it at the time, they were already training for life in a big city for, although to me the future was unknown, my move to London was already part of the "blueprint" of my life.

I do not think it was by chance that I found a quiet flat that was both close to a large Nursery Garden and overlooking a spacious rectangle of grass and trees, so there was no sudden change to the suffocating pressure of massed brick and concrete.

However, it is not only the constraining face of solid matter that had to be experienced by the fairies and overcome before they were ready to live in its midst. There was also the onslaught of noise and pollution that had to be encountered – not only that of traffic but that of vice, for vice is not contained in a vicinity but spreads like an infectious disease through the atmosphere. Its etheric forms are both ferocious and voracious, for these man-made creatures have a life of their own which needs the sustenance of further vice to keep them alive and, like everything manifesting in form, they, too, want to live.

We humans are fortunate in that we cannot see these awesome creatures because our physical bodies and brains form a barrier; but fairies do not have this protection and they must build their own safeguards by keeping their auras filled with light, for the creatures of darkness are afraid of the light and will keep their distance in its presence.

During the years since the book was written, we have all grown in knowledge and, in the case of the fairies, in stature as well. As garden fairies moving among flowers and leaves, their small size was a necessity but now that their work no longer lies mainly with the Plant Kingdom, their height has increased with their expansion in consciousness. Normus is now an impressive three feet (bless him) and the others vary between one and a half feet and two and a half feet.

I think it was probably from the time of the first Fairy Congress that their lives changed radically, as their desire for service to Mankind as well as to Nature became a compulsive force. They now join with thousands of their own evolution from many countries and with the Great Ones from the Higher Planes to work on World Projects.

Normus is no longer the leader of our own band of fairies. Before I came to London, he entered a Hall of Learning to train as a super-leader with others who had also proved of outstanding merit. After the completion of their training, they began by acting as advisers to two or three other leaders. As confidence and ability grew, more came under their "command" until, at the present day, Normus is super-leader to eighteen groups.

During the beginning of his training, he remained as adviser to his friend Movus, who was promoted to the leadership. After about two years, Movus also left to become a super-leader and, from that time until the present day, the group has been guided jointly by Mirilla and Merella. Either would have been capable of taking over the leadership but both preferred to continue with their active work with the Plant World, Mirilla as adviser to those working with flowers and Merella in her experimental work, not only with plant seeds but with human embryos.

A True Fairy Tale is about a small band of fairies who were especially brought together to cooperate with Man on certain projects. Through daily contact with them I have come to know each as an individual but, at the time of writing, I knew very little about Fairy origins and their evolution.

After the book was finished I had more time to devote to study and I learned that the Esoteric Traditions of both East and West, wherein the Ancient Wisdom has been handed down – often verbally – from Initiate Master to pupil, mostly, if not all, acknowledge the Orders of Angels and accept the existence of Nature Spirits.

Like many people, I wondered what makes plants grow and come to flower and fruit at different times of the year instead of together, which might be expected, considering the conditions in a district of sun, moon, rain and soil are identical.

I now believe that these and all effects are brought about by different Cosmic Forces playing upon, penetrating and permeating the substance not only of our Earth but of the Universe. These Forces are habitually playing and any action which is habitual over eons of time eventually becomes conscious, then, after further countless ages have passed, it becomes self-conscious and finally, intelligent. In other words, these are not blind forces which are bringing about the wonders of Nature by chance, but highly evolved Intelligences with which can be linked the well-known term Angel.

Very little has been told us about these Beings by orthodoxy except in a symbolic way most difficult to understand by anyone who has not made a study of symbolic forms. We have been told, however, that they are Messengers, and are not messengers conveyors? and may they not be the conveyors of the Force and the Will which turn an idea into a reality?

I know this sounds somewhat ambiguous so I will give an example: The idea of the oak lies within the acorn and it is the playing of these Intelligent Forces on it that takes it through its many stages, transforming the idea within the acorn into the fact ... the oak.

I have already suggested that any action which is habitual becomes conscious, self-conscious and intelligent. This was the sequence followed by the Cosmic Forces with which we have linked the term Angel. These Intelligent Forces are habitually playing on matter, the degree of intensity being governed by certain cosmic cyclic changes which include our four seasons. These Forces cause certain stresses, actions and reactions to take place in the matter, varying according to whether it is of a solid, liquid or gaseous nature or of the physicist's ether.

Again, constant repetition has its effect and these stereotyped actions acquire an increasing degree of consciousness until they gain a separate existence no longer dependent on the activity which brought them into being. These existences are the elementals of Earth, Air, Fire and Water.

Their activities continue and, like the molecules of physical matter, they act and react among themselves, unite with or repel one another, until they become more complex in nature. If there is an "official" term for these little existences, I'm afraid I am unaware of it but I think the word "complexity" serves to differentiate them from the elementals which are capable of only one type of function within a single idea. Elementals, then, come into being as the result of the Angelic Forces playing on matter in order to stimulate it into certain activities.

To put it very simply, one might say that they are the "children" of Angels and matter and from them evolve the complexities, nature spirits and fairies.

When fairies are linked to the Cosmic Forces in this way, we begin to realize that there are occult truths in fairy stories; for instance, the gifts bestowed by the good and bad fairies at a child's christening are obviously a reference to the astrological influences under which each one of us is born.

Thus, linking fairies with the science of Astrology should lead to the idea that all manifestation is part of a Whole, so don't shut fairies up in a box as though they were something apart from our everyday lives, because whether we know it or not, the evolution to which fairies belong contributes a great deal to our very existence. In fact, it has been stated on good authority that if it weren't for the ministrations of the Nature Spirits, there would be no agriculture.

There is, of course, a vast Nature Spirit World containing countless categories in type and degrees of consciousness, including those of microscopic size which work in their teeming millions building up and breaking down the bodies of the Animal and Vegetable Kingdoms.

Then there are the innumerable little creatures whose movement in play and other forms of compulsive activity contribute to Evolution by distributing the cosmic powers in which they live. These might be compared to ants or bees in consciousness or, higher up the scale, to a bird in a flock or an animal in a herd. Consciousness in each varies but in no case is there individual awareness, the ant, bee, bird, animal or nature spirit being part of the whole.

One might say that the ant-hill, bee hive, flock or herd is the incarnating personality within the Group Soul of the species. An exception to this would occur should an animal or a bird come into contact with an understanding Man when, while remaining a member of its group, it would develop a far greater awareness than is usual in a member of a herd or a flock.

Gradually the numbers in a group diminish as consciousness grows, until there might be two elves working as a single unit or a leader controlling a group of lesser nature spirits.

Wherever there is a natural division of land, such as a valley, a forest or a range of mountain, there develops an oversoul and these great Devas brood over and bring about the changes in their area through the intermediary of the innumerable lesser nature spirits who live there.

The consciousness of the little non-human part-entities has already been compared with that of different insects and animals. Through their association with Man, the higher animals become domesticated. They gain self-consciousness because they are aware of someone outside themselves. Some learn to obey and/ or to love and it is this latter which I believe is the key to individualization, for to learn to love is to find God, or an aspect of Him, even if the finder knows nothing of That which we call God. It is the nucleus and beginning of a new type of being, that of individual existence.

Like animals, nature spirits, too, can be domesticated. Adepts use them in their work and any man, whether incarnate or discarnate, if he has knowledge of these matters, can "adopt" one or more nature spirits and provide them with an object for observation (himself). In loving them, he brings them into contact with a force which is not their own and, as with the animals, love causes individualization.

This is not sentimentality on my part because Love is a great Force and was one of the factors which built the manifested Universe and which continues to sustain it to this day. Through this contact with the human being, there becomes available to the nature spirit a whole new magnetic field containing the concrete thinking mind or Man's logical mode of mentation. Gradually the nature spirit acquires this way of thinking and becomes capable of making his own plans and carrying them out.

This is not the only method of individualization but this particular process probably explains the occult Truth in traditional fairy stories of the necessity for a fairy to marry a Man before it can acquire a soul and thus gain immortality. Of course, occultly, marriage does not mean what we mean by the word, but a conjunction of two forces, bringing them into equilibrium.

I believe that all fairies who have been seen by psychics are these individualized ones, however, I am not including under the word "psychic" such seers as Geoffrey Hodson and Rudolph Steiner, whose vision goes far deeper, enabling them to observe the nature spirit in its own sphere rather than cloaked in etheric matter giving it a degree of materialization.

Yet it is interesting that these two advanced occultists sometimes vary considerably in their findings. For instance, Geoffrey Hodson says that gnomes have very little consciousness and that their atmosphere is inclined to be unpleasant, whereas Rudolph Steiner found them to be filled with inherent wisdom and that they regard Man's complicated way of thinking with amused tolerance. These divergent opinions can only lead to the assumption that there is a whole world of gnomes, the inhabitants varying as widely in type and consciousness as do the members of the human race.

The line of evolution to which Angels and fairies belong might be described as running parallel to that of Man. Normally they do not meet for Man's ignorance of their existence forms a barrier through which they cannot pass. But the powers which they yield MUST pass and blend with that of Man if there is ever to be peace on our planet. Man needs these forces for his continued existence and the Angels need Man to speed their evolution.

They are intelligent but they have not the ability to ensure that their power is used only for good. Paradoxically, the power of Peace is also that of War, the one being the positive and the other the negative aspect of the same force. When they are in equilibrium, we get Perfection.

The Angelic powers, acting and reacting, one with the others according to immutable laws, built and sustain all that is in existence in Nature. They bring to perfection each flower and tree; they hold each planet on its course and every star in its place in this fantastic whirling universe. What then, we may well ask, has gone wrong? I would reply that the answer is undoubtedly Man.

Nature is ever true to Herself. Each plant follows the set pattern of the species, as does every bee in a hive and animal in a herd.

Man is the one creation that has free will, giving him a choice in the shaping of his Destiny, but this choice is still within the limitation of the Cosmic Laws and he breaks them at his peril. He, too, has a blueprint to which he must eventually conform. His choice is not whether he will do so, but when.

If he refuses to be guided by the Angelic Forces he may obtain his immediate desires but he will inevitably lose not only his "Way" but his True Self as well. However, the loss is only temporary as, after he has learned the error of his behaviour through the resultant suffering he has brought upon himself, he will have another chance and, if necessary, a further one, until that particular lesson has been learned, even though it takes him several incarnations.

Most men's downfall is caused by greed and the lust for power and this lust can, not only retard his own progress but, at worst, destroy whole Nations.

The successful, as judged by Earth standards, are rarely of the True Elite, so become a Watcher. You may find your neighbour is a Great One. Was not Jesus of Nazareth a carpenter?

We are all at different stages of evolution; we have all been as savage as the murderers, rapists and terrorists of today. This is the beginning of a New Age when many young souls come into incarnation and much Power is flowing. Remember the Power can be used for Good or Evil but, because of its Cosmic source, Good must eventually prevail.

We can all help to overcome the Powers of Darkness which are activating the villains in the world today, by consciously blending with and using for good these ever-flowing Angelic Forces, if only by performing a kindly act to someone near us, or by planting a flower. We cannot all save the World. It is presumptuous to think that we can, but at least we can make our own tiny corner of it a pleasant place to live in by becoming generators of the Light, which is individually within and without and universally Transcendent and Omnipresent; and in performing this service, we will not only help others, but ourselves as well, for That is the Law.

– Daphne C.

WHO AM I?

By Daphne Charters

When I say "I," I am not alluding to my "I." I am referring to the "I" of every single entity whether incarnate or discarnate.

I have been prompted to put into words the conclusion to which I have come after probing my higher consciousness and receiving the memory of two experiences on planes far above Earth. Conclusion is a misleading word to use for in our language a conclusion is conclusive. I know though that what lives must also evolve and, like everything else, my conclusion will grow.

This probing of my mind takes place while I am fully conscious. Although this enables me to bring down to the Earth plane events which have taken place on others, it also restricts me to Earth comprehension. As when one remembers an event in one's past life, one can visualize oneself smelling a rose but one cannot recall the perfume, one can bring back the visit to an orchestral concert but one cannot re-experience the sound, so when I remember my visits to the higher spheres, I am likewise restricted in knowledge by the very consciousness which I must retain to bring the memory down.

My husband, Jack, is dead, and in my sleep we meet to work with the "lost ones" who reside on planes below that of Earth, or to rise for brief periods of refreshment to the highest sphere that we can reach.

Hand in hand we drifted along a passage of light. I could see the light in my memory but I could not recall the perfume which must also have been guiding us because the path led us to the Marata, a Shining One of the Gravinis evolution.

The Gravine['s] outward manifestation is scent and their part in the Plan is to persuade us into more spiritual aspects of our present consciousness.

She is an old friend and we talked of love and how the power produced by love is used on every plane. "Come," she said, and casting off our form we blended and became one.

I had no body and I stood alone in space. There were no trees. I was conscious of no music, perfume, movement or will. I was aware of one fact only. "I" was there and nothing else – but GOD. I returned to Earth but soon I began to search my mind once more.

Again Jack and I were together hand in hand, this time moving up a ray of purple and I knew that soon we would be with the Marano, a master not of Man but Mind.

"You know," I said to Him, or was it Jack?

"Yes, I know," he replied smiling.

"It was extraordinary," I continued, stretching out my hand to Jack in apology to meet his seeking mine.

"Jack wasn't there," I said. "And I didn't mind because I was. There was only I and God." Then I paused. "Was I wrong? Was that presumptuous of me – that I should have been aware of I as well as God.

He drew me into him. "If there had been no 'I,' there would have been no knowledge of God."

I felt my form melting and I was alone. There was no Jack, no Marano – nothing but an even more intense awareness of myself and God.

Again I returned to Earth and I thought deeply. First there had been a Man, Jack – a Gravinis, the Marata and a woman, I. Yet each of us had known that 'I' was all but God. Then it had been a Man, Jack – a Ceris, the Marano and a Woman, and still for each there had only been I.

I knew then that had there been five thousand or five million of each evolution present, for each there would have been the knowledge that there was only 'I' and God. I knew then that the 'I' is God manifest each experiencing Him to the state of his evolution.

Then I pondered on the seven planes of consciousness and the 'I' which simultaneously dwells on each.

On Earth I am a minute particle of God, aware of my tiny corner of the Universe and of the other minute particles that come my way, but as a rule I have no realization of any direct connection with them outside the ties of family and friendship. I am restricted by time and space and the limitations of a physical body although I can, if I will, escape from them through seeking my higher consciousness.

On the next plane, the astral, I am less limited by time and space and I can, if I wish, be in more than one place at a time.

On the third plane 'I' am again less restricted. I can manifest in more forms or I can do without one.

On the fourth plane, 'I' have the ability of blending myself with other forms and minds which, like me, are traveling through births on Earth and other planets plunging into and rising out of matter to varying degrees, until each through suffering has paid the debts which he has accumulated in his different guises on the lower planes. When all is balanced, each ascends to his fourth plane consciousness and on entering his particular Group-soul, he realizes that in reality, he is not a part of it but the whole.

All this I already knew although I had never forced my mind to put these varying thoughts into words.

I had been content to regard the planes above the fourth as beyond my comprehension, but now I knew that I must follow the 'I' to the end of the journey which has no end.

On the fifth plane I am the eternal male or the eternal female of my evolution. I do not understand exactly what this means for I know that we are both, with one predominating until another birth may change us from one sex to another. On considering this matter again, I re-received the idea that Male is the eternal seeker and Female the revealer. Bringing this thought right down to this plane, I considered the physical act of love between the male and female and I understood the symbolism – the male knocking on the door, ever the seeker and the female answering, revealing.

And then I pondered on the sixth plane and I remembered the seven seraphims who stood before the throne of God. I knew then that they are not Man or the vague term "Angel" as usually interpreted by Man, but the seven evolutions each with his separate part in the Plan. So on the sixth plane 'I' am my evolution in my case, Man.

And on the seventh, where all the evolutions will blend into one, 'I' am the whole of God manifest. That brings us to the very brink of eternity itself. If 'I' outside the GODHEAD am GOD manifest, when I finally return whence I came, I must then be God.

– Daphne Charters

MANUSCRIPTS
SET #2

THE DEVA
MARUSIS SPEAKS

Preface

This set is actually one manuscript, but it stands on its own. It is the only manuscript channeled by a high deva and it outlines the fairy evolution from tiny specks of being to immense, powerful and loving beings who exist in a realm where time as we know it, ceases to exist.

Deva is the Sanskrit word for "Shining One" and refers to angelic beings of love and great power. Deva is most commonly used nowadays in The West to mean a highly-evolved nature spirit who works with the plants, the land, the seas, the air or other macro-scale aspects of our world.

Many spiritual and metaphysical traditions teach that fairies are younger, smaller aspects of a reincarnational stream and that after many reincarnations a fairy will eventually evolve into a deva and then into even higher forms of devas. In this book we use the term nature fairy/deva evolution.

The following manuscript dictated to Daphne by the Deva Marusis is one of the clearest descriptions of the nature fairy/deva evolution we have available in print today. At the same time it is concise. It is corroborated in many ways by other main texts on this topic.

Clearly, the Deva Marusis is a highly-evolved Light Being.

Reading this portion of the book will give the reader a better grasp of the evolutionary stage of the fairies that are the main characters in these manuscripts.

– Michael Pilarski

THE ORIGIN, LIFE AND EVOLUTION OF THE FAIRIES
by the Deva Marusis

I wish to tell you now about the lowest forms of fairy life. These are known as *Rudimes* and they are approximately 1/8 inch high. They have practically no intelligence as their consciousness is naturally minute. They have, however, that instinct, also found among insects, which prompts them to keep moving, the continuous motion stimulating the plant life among which they live. They do not absorb and give out power, as do most of the lower grades of fairy, as they are below even this form of activity.

Their Earth-span is approximately one month, after which period they return to the Astral plane for about ten years. *[Our time cycles of months and years should not be taken literally but used as a guideline to denote short, long or very long periods – D.C.]*

Their next visit to Earth is as a *Unitis* and, as such, they experience individual consciousness for the first time; before they have been existing as separate parts of a whole, now they are capable of very limited thought but they are now able to absorb and give power, although it requires many of them to produce sufficient to keep a small patch of grass alive. They are about 1/2 inch in height and their Earth-span is one year, after which they return to the Astral for a period of about one hundred years.

Their next advance is when they become *Minutes*. *[Pronounced min-you-tees. – D.C.]* They have now grown to between one and two inches and they still work in groups in order to produce enough power to stimulate plants. Their Earth-span is five years, and then they spend a further period of about five hundred years on the Astral plane. At this time they reach the stage in their evolution when they begin making decisions for themselves and, from now on, it is the individual entity who decides when he or she desires further Earth experiences. If they do not wish to return, they are permitted to continue working on the Astral plane until they do.

Their visit to Earth, which is for a period of twenty-five years, is as a *Nomenes* (gnomes). These little people work with the earth and with roots, especially those of trees, and they are now capable of separating their work from their play. Previously, the absorbing and giving of power was both to them, but gnomes enjoy their recreation and they play games such as children do. They are fond of copying the actions and objects which they observe around them, such as carrying shopping baskets filled with parcels or making themselves hats similar to those which they have seen women wear. You may imagine the amusement such simple pleasures give them; when they are alone, they will laugh hilariously, but if they know themselves to be watched they will carry out these actions with mock-solemnity as though they were busy with their normal tasks.

The next rung of the fairy ladder is reached when they become *Elfines* (elves and brownies). This is during their sojourn on the Astral of another five hundred years. Elves, as a rule, work away from mankind, in woodland glades, on moor and common, or in the mountains. It is at this stage that they learn to guide the minutes and unites; they perform this task by making barriers of power through which the smaller entities are unable to pass, and they are thus kept within a certain area to carry out their work. They gambol in the force emanating from the elves, absorbing it and enhancing it with vigor from their own particles of life before exhaling it again. As the elves move and work so the minutes and unites follow them in order to keep within their power range, thus the elves are able to guide them where they will.

Elves enjoy their recreation and people who are clairvoyant have often seen them performing simple dances and chasing and bowling each other over in high spirits. They are happy little people for they have not yet been called upon to suffer. They vary in size, as do the gnomes, for their bodies are of their own making and they can alter their proportions at will. They are not often more than a foot in height and sometimes they are but a few inches. After their Earth-span of fifty years, they return to the Astral and, once again, the choice of returning to Earth lies within themselves; but they rarely descend again before a thousand years have passed. During this period they gradually change into fairies, improving in appearance and growing mentally.

Elves on Earth are nearly always males, although the younger entities are of either sex. As in the human race, males are generally more adventurous than females and the latter are quite happy developing in the Astral. However, if they wish to come to Earth they are permitted to do so.

Fares, or fairies, are far more developed mentally than any of the lower ranks that I have already mentioned and during their span on Earth they experience suffering for the first time.

They are permitted, whilst on the Astral plane, to choose the category which they desire to study. Until this stage in their development, all fairies work with the vegetable or mineral kingdom, but now many new tasks become available to them. They can work with man, with Thought-forms, in healing the sick; they can learn to control the elements, fire, water or the air, with its various currents and the vibrations which pass through it. They can also study colour composition, which plays a very important part in life on Earth and, in increasing magnitude, on the higher planes.

On Earth each object has its own particular colour. Have you ever wondered whence it came? You have an example in the rainbow; the atmosphere is full of colour but you are able to see it only when the sun and raindrops combine to give you a glimpse of what is always there. Each colour is directed by specialists towards the flower of a leaf which needs it. A leaf, you understand, could not live if, say, red instead of green was guided to it, and likewise every flower is of the colour it needs. To be a certain colour is an experience, it is not chance. Every flower must live a span on Earth of each colour. It is therefore interfering with the course of evolution if you give a plant chemicals which cause it to change from, say, cream to blue. Even if it is a shade which fails to please your eye, there is a reason for it so do not seek to alter it for, if you do, the flower must continue to be born and reborn on Earth until someone permits it to live its few months or years with that particular colour. Whatever the degree of consciousness, colour is always an essential part of life, so do not regard it merely as a decoration.

The fairy, having decided upon the work which he wishes to study, attends a Hall of Learning. When he has become sufficiently skilled, he works on the Astral plane and, continuing his studies, he thus gains new knowledge and practical experience at the same time. It is often several thousands of years, however, before he wishes to test himself amidst the difficulties of the Earth plane. As with Man, there are always fairies waiting to come to Earth and sometime many years may pass before suitable conditions are found for a particular entity. He then descends for a period of one hundred years, after which he returns, enriched with the experience which enables him to take the next step up the ladder. He will often choose to be a Farris, or teacher, but if he does not desire to do so, he becomes that which you on Earth would call a specialist.

I have already told you that fairies may work with the elements of fire, water and air; to begin with they work with all of them, infusing them with power and guiding them, but now they choose which of the three they desire to study as the more advanced stages of each demand all their energy and intelligence.

- The inland water fairy is known as an Undinis (f) or a Wallinis (m) (nymphs, naiads). These are usually very beautiful as judged by Earth standards. There are more undines than wallines as, once again, the males are more adventurous and prefer the excitement of working with fire, air or the sea. They live on Earth for approximately two hundred years when, once again, they return to the Astral for a period of about five thousand years.
- The fire fairies are known as *Farisilles* (Salamanders). Girls do not often take up this work but those who do so are called *Shallores*. These do not have an Earth-span but they live in its vicinity.
- Those who work with the air are known as *Wallotes* and the girls as *Arienes*.
- The next rung of the ladder is mounted when they become *Faralles*, or leaders in their chosen line of duty. It is no longer possible to give definite

periods of work for, when they reach this stage, Time, as you know it, ceases to exist.

- Above the faralles are the *Aspirites*, who control the various sections, i.e color, water, healing, etc.
- Above these preside the *Hiarus* and, one rung higher, the *Ra-Arus*.
- Above is HE WHOM we all worship.

*** *** ***

We will now return to the foot of the ladder and I will give you in greater detail the work of the entities whom I have already brought before you.

The rudimes work in groups of many thousands. They have form such as you know it on a minute scale and they are clothed by the fairies who work with thought forms on the Astral plane. I cannot give you much information about them for their consciousness is too small for any marked intelligence, apart from the physical desire for continuous movement. They know love, but not as male and female, although they are of different sexes. They love all the other members of the group and the plant life which they stimulate but, as they are incapable of separate thought, so they cannot experience individual love.

The unites have the power of singling out several from their group to whom they give their especial love and with whom they exchange power. They are still incapable of sexual love and they give and receive power regardless of sex, the usual practice being for a group within the group to give and receive communal power. Now that they have individual intelligence, they are able to think and thus they clothe themselves but, apart from this, their lives consist of continually giving power to the plants and, more rarely, to each other, interspersed with periods of rest.

The minutes are similar in every respect, except that they are capable of sex distinction and they give and take power only from members of the opposite sex. They are also sufficiently intelligent consciously to follow the guidance of the fairies who are in authority over them.

The gnomes, with whose appearance you are all familiar through your fairy tales, have advanced considerably and they now have sufficient power to work in pairs. They are usually like little old men or women in appearance, and the males sometimes grow beards of varying lengths. To you they might appear ugly, comic or quaint but their looks are pleasing to themselves. They make their own bodies by thought and they adopt the appearance and manner of the other gnomes about them.

Only a very small part of the whole consciousness is being manifested; in fact, they are but young spirits so, if provoked, they are somewhat vindictive. If, for example, you cut down a tree among whose roots they dwell and work, it is a probability that you will have annoyed them. I am sure that you would not be happy if your house was destroyed and all your life's work brought to nothing in a brief hour. They may therefore endeavour to cause you discomfort or even harm. It is possible that your garden tools will snap when you are working with them, your lawn mower may run crooked or a wheel come off your barrow. You naturally will not connect these little setbacks with the felled tree, but that will have been the cause.

You may think it is strange, that whereas the minutes and gnomes are able to make love to the opposite sex, elves are usually obligated to forego this happiness as they are mostly males. This is to teach them control. The giving and the taking of power between the minutes and, to a certain extent, with the gnomes as well, is almost entirely without forethought; it is automatic, at the presence of a member of the opposite sex. You might think that this lack of a female to love would lead to that which you call perversion, but this is not so. The elves know that one of the Universal Laws is that a male may only give power to a female to obtain ecstasy and Universal Laws cannot, in Truth, be broken. Their desires are but faint and, as their work entails the frequent giving of power, they do not suffer any physical discomfort. For companionship they have each other and, as a rule, there is much love within the groups of elves who live together.

Their clothes as you know them, usually being brown or green. They are younger in appearance than the gnomes and, whereas the latter sometimes give themselves somewhat thickset bodies, elves are always slim. They are kindlier than the gnomes but full of mischief and it is possible that you may at times find yourself a victim of one of their pranks. Have you ever walked across a field and tripped without apparent reason? You will probably have been a little hurt and somewhat annoyed. The greater your anger, the more the elves laugh. As they grow older they mellow somewhat and sometimes you may find yourself the happy recipient of some little kindness. Perhaps you may be walking along a pleasant lane when suddenly you perceive a patch of green so vivid in color, you had not thought that such existed. The elves are shining their power upon it to give you this sudden flash of pleasure and they are rewarded by the halt in your journey and the smile which lights your face. You will realize from their simple pleasures and jokes that they are still as children and as such they should be treated.

Their work is uncomplicated but they are at the beginning of the road of individual endeavour. They now know the difference between right and wrong; they are responsible for their own actions and they are aware that the path is long, the hazards many but that ultimately they will reach the light.

We will now turn to the Fairies who are altogether more advanced and thus more complex. Their tasks are many and each effort brings them fresh experience and further progress.

To come to Earth and to know cold winds and drenching rain is new to them. Before, as gnomes and elves, they were more of a pleasure; they felt the wind as a gentle breeze and the rain as a refreshment for their charges – they scarcely affected them except as a faintly stimulating touch. Now they know the seasons as you do for they are at first unable to use the faculty which is theirs to combat their misery, the cold and the damp seemingly deaden their neutralising powers. They suffer intensely and through this they grow; their perceptions are awakened to a higher degree and eventually they experience far greater happiness.

First we will take the Nature fairies, who spend their lives in the open. They work from dawn till dark in the winter and from dawn until late evening in summer. Their tasks are many and varied but always the nucleus of their work is the giving of power to the plant life which surrounds them. At first they give it themselves but, as they learn to control the various entities in their charge, they are able to turn off their own power and leave the younger workers to finish their tasks, until once more they turn on their power and lead them to a fresh area for replenishment.

Some fairies fly and others do not, according to their work and their degree of progress. When beginning to fly they usually grow themselves wings, using bees, moths and butterflies as their models but, after many years, they are able to travel by thought and thus, if they wish, dispense with their wings.

Fairies spend much of their lives without tangible form as you know it. They are as lights varying in brightness according to their progress, their colour harmonising with their work. The boy fairies are usually green, red, blue or amber and the girls mauve, cream, blue, pink, and pale gold. This comparative formlessness restricts their experience, however. As a light they can be happy but they cannot laugh; they can be sad and yet they are unable to weep. Likewise, in their lovemaking they are not yet sufficiently advanced to appreciate the highest forms of spiritual ecstasy so they prefer to use their bodies in order to experience love to the fullest extent of their present progress. Normally they rest in their light forms and often they work thus as well, for the giving of power to plants, though a mental joy, is not a physical one.

They make their own bodies with thought according to their state of progress. They cannot give themselves a more beautiful body than they have earned but they can make it gentle or gay, bold or graceful, according to their individual character and desires. They can choose their own height within certain limits but, as a rule, they prefer to remain small until they have earned the privilege of size; for the higher grades of fairy are usually much larger than their counterpart in Man. Nature fairies, as a rule, vary between six inches and a foot in height.

Apart from the weather, they have other difficulties with which to contend. Insects, in their Earth bodies, are far more virulent and less easy to guide than they are in the Astral plane. Their physical jackets make them impervious to the power with which the fairies endeavour to control them, but they never cease to strive for in their efforts lie all future results, and one day the fairies will be masters of the insect instead of the reverse.

There are also elementals which they must overcome. These, too, are a new experience because if one encroaches on the fairies' domain on the Astral, it is several planes higher than its normal habitat and its evil is automatically diminished; thus the fairies find it easy to send it back whence it came by turning on their power. On Earth, however, it is different. The elemental, although on a higher

plane than usual, is nearer its own conditions. If the fairies are vigilant and are aware of its approach, they can greet it with the full strength of their power and are thus able to turn it back before it has set its own evil forces at work. Should they be caught unawares, however, it is a very different story and may have lost their consciousness for years, during which period other fairies give them power until the evil is finally overcome and returned to its own environment.

Among other difficulties is that of understanding why they now must overcome all their misfortunes apparently alone. This, of course, is not really so, for always there are those who watch, ready to aid them should their troubles prove too great. This may appear to be a contradiction but unless the fairies ask, however, much we desire so to do, we cannot, for instance, give them enough power to overcome an elemental should the fairy be caught unawares. But, even when they fail to ask, we are able to supply them with sufficient to comfort and to give them the strength to make the necessary effort to overcome the difficulty themselves. On the Astral plane, even a slight distress signal calls to their aid helpers, whom they can see, but on Earth our workers are invisible to them and although the fairies know that they are there, as indeed you should know that willing helpers are with you as soon as you seek aid, they, like you, find it more difficult to appreciate their presence when they are unable to see them.

I have so far dwelt mostly on the fairies' misfortunes and, of course, for many years these are uppermost in their minds, but once they have been overcome, they then taste truer happiness, for to have battled against difficulty and despair, and to have won, gives for greater joy than is known to those whose path is smooth with no pitfalls or encumbrances.

Each fairy comes to Earth, having learned a particular branch of Nature work. He decides whether he wishes to work with trees or flowers, with plants that grow close to the ground or with those which reach out to the sky. Once again it is usually the males who choose the more adventurous tasks among the trees, although the females often like to work with shrubs. They spend approximately thirty years with their especial charges on the Astral before they are considered efficient to work with them on Earth. At first they live far from Man in the uncultivated areas. After about twenty years they are moved to a country garden, still far from the noise of traffic and town, but here they experience the proximity of Man and they learn to counteract his vibrations should they prove unpleasant to them. The next step is usually a removal to a village where there are people and more noise. After another twenty years they will be sent to the quieter parts of town and finally, if it is considered wise, they will move to tend the small private gardens of the large public parks amidst the rumble and smoke of some great city.

At first each change leads to new fears and discomforts but once acclimatized to the new conditions, the knowledge that they have overcome yet more hazards rewards them with greater happiness and their power grows with each new experience; the more power they develop, the speedier is their progress in every way.

Power is the key which controls all life in growth, in colour and in form; the greater the power, the greater the progress of both giver and receiver. As it increases, so the capacity for giving grows and, with each advance, the giver evolves in sensitivity and is thus enabled to enjoy each ensuing experience with added understanding and pleasure. Power is that which enables all events to take place and without it Life would become extinct. You may think that a plant extracts all the nourishment that it requires from the soil and so, in a small measure, it does, for there is power of Life in the earth too and without this individual effort of plant or tree, it could not progress. We can come a little more than halfway, but each entity, or part of one, whether it be man, beast or plant, must make his contribution too. However much power we give, unless the recipient, by his own endeavour, opens himself to receive it, very little can penetrate his physical jacket, and if he relaxes his efforts altogether, he dies; to live again, it is true, but as it is not permitted for a Man to take his life, so it is not good for a plant to die because it has ceased to strive. Remember, I pray, when you are weary and wish to give in, if you relax and ask for help, we will respond immediately, for by your request you have built the bridge over which we must pass to aid you. We are waiting, not miles up in the sky, but right by your side, and that one simple effort to contact us will serve as the breeze which will revive the almost dormant spark of courage within you.

Power to the fairies is work, food, drink, recreation, and love-making combined; in fact, the giving and taking of it in its various forms constitutes their entire lives.

In love-making there are many ways of exchanging power. Fairies do not view their unions the same way that you do. Marriage for you is often a matter of convenience; in a man, it is for sexual satisfaction and the desire to have someone to look after his home and children. In a woman, it is security for which she often exchanges her freedom to love where love lies. None of these reasons for unions exists in the spheres above the Earth. All are free to choose the beloved with whom to exchange power and affection and whom they eagerly endeavour to serve and protect. There is nothing to bind two beings except love and when it dies, they go their separate ways until they love again.

Experience is the essence of all life but not indiscriminate experience. Great care is taken by both participants to ensure happiness for many years. Sometimes, in the case of young entities, this care is not taken – you would describe it as a violent physical attraction between a man and a woman – and the same thing occurs among the other evolutions as well, and the same indifference or even hatred follows, causing much misery to both. When the proper procedure is followed, there is first a blending of the auras, then that which is known as the love vibration is given. This is a minor power within each being. You yourself know that at the approach of the loved one, the heart beats more strongly. Although you probably are unaware of the fact, you are giving out the love vibration. The next step is the exchanging of power, still within each other's aura. It is usually at this stage that one may decide to go no further, for if the power is not approximately equal, the stronger will derive little pleasure from the weaker. If they decide to proceed, they, unlike those upon Earth, can at will blend their bodies and later power is given again. This giving of power, even from within the aura only, gives ecstasy beyond anything known upon Earth, for the fulfillment extends over the entire body and infinite happiness enfolds the pair. To us, love-making is intermingled with work, progress in one, improving the other.

The fairies which live in your houses are equal in development and sometimes they surpass the young Nature spirits who work in gardens and in the countryside.

Naturally their state of evolvement differs according to the desire and capacity of each entity and the work varies according to their ability.

When any fairy has decided that he wishes to work with Man instead of Nature, he resides for many years in houses on the Astral plane. At first he may be with people who know of his presence, but later he will live in the lower regions of the Astral with men and women who are unable to see him and who are probably unaware of his existence. He is therefore prepared to be ignored when he eventually comes to Earth even though he is actively employed assisting people in their daily tasks.

Always there is a fairy present when you light a fire, whether it is an open grate of crackling logs or the kitchen boiler; it is his duty to give power to the astral body of the fuel and thus stimulate it so that it will burn brighter for your benefit. Others, likewise, must give power to the water in your pipes, or else it would lose all its health-giving properties. The air, too, has constantly to be revitalized or that which you draw your lungs would choke rather than keep you alive. As with those who work with Nature, the indoor fairies guide minutes and unites to the work while they themselves are in a supervisory capacity. All the material objects in your home, whether of fabric, wood or metal, must receive power, otherwise they would fall to pieces, for power is a necessity to an astral body whether of Man, beast or inanimate object, as are food and drink to the physical body of the animal and even vegetable kingdom.

The more advanced fairies now begin a most valuable work, which becomes increasingly important as they progress and take their place in the higher spheres; it is that of working by thought. To begin with, they weave forms, which are material to them; they can see and touch them and thus they are able to understand them. As they progress, the forms become less tangible but always they are beautiful in colour and design and they naturally increase in effect as the power of the individual or group of fairies grows. There is a great art in their composition and always they are made of the thoughts of both Man and fairy. When they are on Earth, unless there is someone near to them who understands these matters, and, alas, these conditions are all too rare, the fairies must rely on prayers or, for less important work, the ordinary thoughts of those living in the house. As they advance, they are able to use the dimmer reflections caused by thoughts which have travelled from farther afield.

In order to make this statement clearer I will endeavour to record the process rather more explicitly. As a rule, fairies are unable to exchange thoughts with Man, and those given out by him must evolve before they become tangible enough for use. There is no set period between the birth of a thought and the moment when it becomes sufficiently mature for inclusion in a thought form, but on average, it takes about three days. During this time, the thoughts of those living in the house, have at birth, sped away from their creator to return, in a fraction of a second, augmented by the reflections of similar thoughts – happy attracting happy thoughts, and gloomy, other gloomy ones which, in their turn add to the happiness or the gloom of the person who gave them birth. Now, in this light, wherever the original thought touches; it leaves the equivalent of a photographic print of itself, containing not only its form but its qualities. These prints also mature before they fade and disappear, unlike the original thought which ever remains. The fairies must therefore find and utilize these thought-prints when they are at the height of their maturity for otherwise their power is negligible. To them and to the stronger true-thoughts already in the house, they add their own, and from this combination they are able to make forms capable of helping the sick or destitute and comforting the lonely and the bereaved. These forms can attain great powers as well as beauty so when you are in need, ask the fairies around you for aid. Although your thoughts cannot reach them as the pictures they become on maturity, your vibrations will tell them. Do not doubt their ability to aid you for their efficacy is proved many thousands of times each day.

It is a little known fact that members of the fairy evolution are always present when any act of healing takes place. We are in attendance in every doctor's surgery although our efforts are almost brought to naught by Man's lack of knowledge of our powers. Even healers who invariably invoke spirit aid, are usually quite unaware of the part we play, equal in every way and sometimes surpassing the service rendered by discarnate Man. Know therefore that there is our separate power upon which you can call at any time. Ask and we will be with you as soon as the thought, desiring to summon us, has formed in your mind. Do not doubt our presence, for this very doubt can and will nullify our work. In case you are not aware of the fact, we use rays for healing similar to, but more effective than, the ultra-violet and the infra-red rays which you already know. These are but two of our rays which your scientists, with our inspiration, have discovered, but there are many others which orthodox practitioners are unable to use because no machine has yet been invented through which these rays may be passed. That which is known as a medium, or healer, is necessary before they become effective because, in their natural state, they are too fine to pierce the coarse substance of the physical body.

Mediums have the power of refining their bodies and thus the higher rays can be passed through them and sufficiently coarsened to enable them to enter the body of the sufferer. On our side, these rays are passed through a succession of mediums, each one from a plane lower than the one above, thus they pass from their source, through a chain of gradually coarsening bodies, until they are in a condition to heal Earth diseases. Each ray has its individual quality which can be used separately or collectively. There is no disease, no bone displacement, no infirmity that we cannot cure absolutely. The power is there, we who know how to use it are there, but we lack mediums of the necessary sensitivity to heal more than a lamentably small proportion of those who need us. Everyone has this power within them. I appeal to any of you who have even one hour a day which you are able and willing to expend in the service of the suffering, to ask our aid or, preferably, to join a healing group where the little power that you produce at first may be blended with that of those who have developed a little and thus can be used at once instead of after several months or even years of individual effort. If it is necessary for you to develop alone, please do not think that we are not eager to help you; with patience you will, in time, be of great assistance to us.

I will tell you a little of the part which the fairies play in the healing process. The ray has passed through the medium's hands and is entering the body of the sufferer. Some of the ray is also exuding through the pores of the healer's skin, apart from the hands. The fairies take up their positions around the psychic centre of the patient's body, that is, the pituitary gland in the centre of the forehead, the throat, the heart, the solar plexus, which lies between the breast and the stomach, the pineal gland, which is at the back of the head, the spleen, which is to the left of and below the heart and the centre which lies at the base of the spine. Thus the ray is entering the sufferer's body not only through the centre upon which the medium has laid his hands, but through all the others as well. Thus healer and fairies together are pouring the ray into the patient from every direction, and the whole of the afflicted area is bathed in its healing properties.

More advanced than the fairies in development are the *Farrices*. It is they who act as the mediums on our side. They train for many years and it is by their thoughts and guidance that the rays are directed to the right parts of the body and the remainder is returned to the Source. This is especially so in the case of the green ray, which, in one of its aspects, is a destroyer, used in cases of cancer and other tumors. You will understand that if this ray were not rigidly controlled it could destroy not only the unwanted tissues but the healthy flesh through which it passes of both patient and healer. Do not fear however; the farrices have spent a hundred years in learning absolutely control and until they have attained perfection in this respect, they are not permitted to work with bodies on Earth. Until they have reached the necessary efficiency, they are employed in destroying the waste matter which so often comes away in certain diseases. The suppurations not only from cancer, but from wounds and minor abrasions, would cause infinite harm if not destroyed in their astral form as well as their physical.

*** *** ***

We will now turn to the element of water. The fairies who work with water endeavour to guide it along the route which Nature has prepared for it but when Man seeks to divert it for his own use, they do their best to help him. It is guided,

49

as is all else in Nature, by power. The fairies give power along the route and the minutes follow, attracting the water in the desired locations.

I do not know whether it is possible for you to visualize the countless millions of these small entities who are always at work. Their ceaseless activities continue from dawn until dusk, when others take their place until the following dawn, they cover every inch, not only of Earth but of the mediums through which the distribution of power is made possible.

There are times, of course, when the power of the great fairies is not sufficient to control the water. I am speaking of the conditions which you call floods. These, as you know, are caused by heavy rainfall swelling the rivers to abnormal proportions so that the prepared water course is unable to contain them. If Man took proper precautions these floods would not occur. To begin with, heavy rainfall is caused by Man's failure to understand the laws of nature and to harmonize with Her in all her works. This you will doubtless find difficult to believe but I can assure you that it is so. On the Astral plane, where the Law is better understood, there is no rain unless it is desired for personal satisfaction and yet the ground is ever moist.

In normal conditions the fairies are capable of preventing minor troubles which, were they permitted to occur, would cause much inconvenience.

The undines and the wallines are the leaders of all the inland water fairies. They love the water and they live to a greater extent in its depths. Each is in charge of an area up to fifty square miles but naturally where the waterways are numerous a smaller division is allotted. Undines and wallines preside over the water from its source until it reaches the sea, when it comes under the direction of the *Nerenes* and the *Ensinnes* (nereids). Their work is more strenuous than the inland water undines, thus there are more males than females. Great concentration is necessary, particularly when the sea is rough, as without their control it could do much harm to the land against which it hurls itself. When the sea is calm, their watch can be somewhat relaxed and it is during these quiet periods that they indulge in the more pleasurable occupation of joining the fairies and the lesser entities as they ride the waves, giving power, playing games and chasing each other through the foam. For their hours of rest they betake themselves to the quiet depths far out to sea. Here they relax whilst others take over the constant vigil. The nerenis finds his beloved among the ensinnes, but if he has no loved one, he seeks compensation in the gently heaving water in which he reposes. To him, to relax in the cool deep is as revitalizing as experiencing the beloved's caress.

These sea fairies perform the most arduous work of all the water fairies. Those who work inland lead a comparatively peaceful existence interspersed with periods of great activity. But the constant and unpredictable surges of the sea call for continuous vigilance, the ability to make immediate decisions and the speed to travel vast distances in the fraction of a second.

These fairies are ever anxious to be of assistance to Man and the ships which he steers through the waves. In storms, if sailors would but invoke their aid, their tasks would be lightened and sometimes even disaster averted. To the sea fairies, the sailors are all friends and fellow workers and their mutual love of the sea draws them together. Even though they are unaware of their presence, many are the little tasks which fairies perform to help them. By acknowledging their presence, the men would give happiness to them and, in their gratitude, they would work even harder to assist them in times of trouble.

We will now consider the air fairies. They are those who control the wind. To you, possibly a gale is a frightening act of Nature which comes without warning and ceases often as unexpectedly as it began. Actually there is no element of chance in a high wind; in fact, a great deal of preparation is necessary. The air is driven by the power given out by the wallotes and the arienes. As there are waterways which you can see, so are there air channels which, although invisible to you, are quite tangible to them. Sometimes, as with the water, the air becomes out of control and a tempest ensues, causing havoc to Man and Fairy alike. You must understand that as the Earth fairy has to learn to combat the elementals which seek to destroy his work, so the water and the air fairies must endeavour to overcome the evil work of other elementals. A constant vigilance is necessary and if one error is permitted, evil ones are ever present to turn the fairies' omission to their own advantage. As the fairies thrive on kindness, so the elementals can exist only in terror, misery and discord. They, too, desire to live so a constant struggle is in progress between them and the Nature fairies.

In size, air fairies are somewhat larger than a tall man, being between seven and eight feet in height. By Earth standards they would be regarded as incredibly beautiful, with a grace of movement unknown to Man. They seek and find their beloved among their own kind and they work side by side, in pairs. Their tasks lie close to Earth and many miles around it. Their recreation is to dive, swoop and climb in a somewhat similar manner to the aerobatics familiar to you in your planes, and they rest in zones where the air is still.

They are not in close contact with Man but if, when the wind is high, you would appeal to them with strength of purpose, you would give to them the additional power which they need to overcome those who seek victory over them. The wind is a force for good when it is controlled; is stimulates plant life; it drives the clouds so that rain may fall; it dries the land after periods of flood. If Man could but learn to control it and keep it constant, he could utilize it in many ways. You know the great power of a typhoon, when it uproots large trees and hurls houses through the air; imagine then if this force were tempered and guided along organized channels, the power it could lend to industry.

The fire fairies, the farisilles and shallors, are if possible, even more skilled than those working with the elements already discussed. You all know the comfort of your own fireside, the companionship bestowed by the gaily-leaping flames; you also know of the terrible ravages caused by fire when it becomes out of control. Fire is the most difficult element to direct; it is less easily restrained by power because its action tends to increase the fire's activities and to make it more ungovernable than before. The fairies, therefore, utilize the wind and, when Man is present, water to help them in their tasks. The air fairies endeavour to guide the wind so that it drives the fire back into itself but this is often beyond their powers. At the same time, the fire fairies are striving to release as much power as possible from the flames so that it is dispersed in the air and can then be used by the air fairies to quench the flames to which it originally gave strength.

Many more actions are performed by these fire fairies but I am unable to tell you about them owing to the average man's lack of knowledge of power and to the limitations of the writer. Lightning also comes under their influence and great is their activity during storms. Lightning can do much damage when it strikes and the farisilles strive to direct it so that is does the least possible harm. Sometimes, of course, it flashes past their defenses and then a building or a tree is destroyed.

You are sometimes horrified by the fact that a man or woman is struck by lightning. You may think that it is a tragic accident but this is not so. No one ever dies by accident; he dies by design and by his own wish, expressed before he comes to Earth. So know that when someone is struck, it is the day and hour for him to die.

There are fewer shallores than farisilles as it is unusual for females to desire such existing work, but for those who are of an adventurous nature fire control is an absorbing and rigorous task. As with the air and sea fairies, great speed and the ability to make instantaneous decisions are essential qualities, combined with calmness and control. Fire fairies must always be prepared for interference from the enemy, who is ever on the alert for an opportunity to infiltrate their defenses.

They spend their periods of rest in the essence of which fire is made. It is not hot but is charged with Life. This source of fire is soothing and strengthening and from it the farisilles obtain the necessary power to combat it in its sometimes dangerous physical forms. It is during these times of rest that they receive the reward of their labours for the essence in which they relax has the power to reveal to them the Truth as it is known in the regions above those in which they normally work. They thus experience fulfillment without the necessity of a loved one, although at times they seek the one they love and then even greater happiness is enjoyed.

If Man could succeed in coordinating his work with the Fairies during a fire-fighting operation, his task would become easier for they, with their immeasurable influence over fire, could enable it to be brought under immediate control.

At present, Man, in his ignorance, often gives greater power to flames rather than diminishing them, by omitting to counteract the force of the wind.

Fire and air fairies are always present wherever there is a conflagration, big or small, and they do everything they can to help those who are trying to extinguish the flames. If the wind suddenly changes, know that it is for a purpose; at first it may appear to set at naught all the work already performed but if you quickly use every breeze to advantage, you will soon be able to observe the plan and you should endeavour to follow it.

Their work calls for tremendous strength and versatility; in the fraction of a second they must be able to vary their power from the height of their capability to the faintest trace. Their knowledge of fire's habits is extensive as they have spent several thousand years studying which operations cause it to increase in volume and which Man is liable to take when he is endeavouring to regain control over this element, which can bring to him either great pleasure, or cause his house or business to fall in ruins about him.

These beings strive to give to fire the exact amount of power to enable it to be used by Man in his home, in his industries and for many forms of transport. They help to temper your steel, to clear your wasteland for cultivation, they bring warmth to the cold and comfort to old and young alike.

If their charge sometimes destroys, it more often builds. Fire has played its part in making the bricks, the steel, the iron, the tin and the many manufactured substances you now use in the construction of houses, factories, churches and bridges. They work day and night in the service of Man and Nature, therefore help them with constructive thought and you will find that your fires will burn brighter when you wish, and will lose their power more swiftly when they become out of control. If Man and

Fairy would work together as they should, the Earth would bring forth fruits such as Man has never known.

Each of the types of fairy which I have mentioned has its leaders. They teach and guide those in their charge and they take command when an important operation is to take place. One of the first lessons which every Fairy learns, no matter to which status he belongs, is implicit and instant obedience to his leader. After many years of experience as such, a Fairy may become a Farallis, or a teaching-leader, who trains other leaders for more responsible work. Those desiring to become faralles, once they have attained the necessary efficiency as leaders, are sent to Halls of Learning where they study the next category in which they desire to serve. They remain as teachers to the section which they have left and then, after about fifty years, they become members of the next division. Thus, you will understand, they spend many years in studying and teaching the theory of a subject before they are permitted to participate in the work.

Aspirites are the organizers in each section. They are the entities who carry out the plans which offset the damage when fire, air or water have temporarily become out of control. It is they who endeavour to combat disease as a whole, leaving individual cases to their healing farrices. If the work of the farisilles, wallotes and nerenes requires constant vigilance and the ability to make immediate decisions, you may imagine that the aspirites who are in authority over many storms, floods, and outbreaks of fire, not only on Earth but on other planets, must have all these qualities and great mental strength as well. Their periods of rest are spent in relaxing in the combined essences of the elements, together with the spiritual power with which the atmosphere where they live is charged. They require no other being to experience ecstasy for all that they need is within themselves. Their work and their leisure are all that is necessary to make a life of intense interest and great joy. They know a little of the fulfillment which will be theirs as soon as they are worthy and they constantly strive to attain the necessary degree of Goodness so that they may experience the beginning of At-Oneness. This incredible ecstasy is the aim of every member of our evolution from the gnome to the highest Deva for We who know a little ever seek to know more.

The Hiarus are those who are the governors. It is they who make the plans for the aspirites to follow. They are the creators of all great ideas, and it is the work of those below them to devise the methods by which their plans should carry out.

The Ra-Arus, in the Fairy evolution, are equal to the Archangels of Man and it is together with the leaders of the other evolutions that we rule the Universe for Each adds Power to the Others and without the inspiration of All, None could fulfill His Purpose.

– Deva Marusis

MANUSCRIPTS
SET #3

DAPHNE MEETS
THE FAIRIES

Preface

In this section Daphne describes how she meets the fairies, and the development of her relationships with them. It also shows one way that fairies help unknowing humans in the physical world. This is the only part of the manuscripts that discusses gnomes, one of the stages in fairy evolution. This section also first introduces the underworld.

– Michael Pilarski

I MEET THE FAIRIES

By Daphne Charters

I began my psychic work at our old house not far from Colchester but, although I am sure that many worked in the walled-in garden there, I did not think of trying to contact the fairies until we came to our present home.

My interest was growing all the time, however, and a short while after our arrival, in the valour of ignorance, I asked Father John if I could try to talk to them. He accompanied me into the tiny garden and as far as I can understand he acted as a kind of medium between the two evolutions. I do not mean that he translated our thoughts from one to the other but his power formed the bridge which enabled us to communicate. On this first occasion I did not attempt to listen to the fairies, but I talked to them and Father John assured me that they could hear me. On the second day, I tried to hear them and to my delight, I found that I could understand the little people in exactly the same way that I can any other discarnate being and they were able to tell me their names, their particular branch of Nature work and several other facts about themselves.

I should have been even more pleased had I realized that I was achieving anything unusual from a psychic point of view.

The Leader

Normus was the first to introduce himself and this is natural and also correct for he is the leader of this band of Nature Fairies whose territory covers all the gardens between the road in front of this house and a second one at the back, forming a quadrangle of about half a square mile.

I was highly delighted with his name and later I tried to explain to him its incongruity considering how small he is. "Normus-Enormous," I repeated to him, but obviously there is no "play" in the projections as there is in the words and he was unable to understand what caused my amusement.

On this first occasion he introduced me to the fairies in pairs, not apparently according to precedence but by chance as they happened to be standing at the time, and this is the order in which I have kept their stories in this book.

He informed me that there were five boys and five girls, all pares or husband and wife. "Have you no paris.?" I enquired.

"All the girls are my pares," he replied, to my amusement.

"In that case, you must be kept pretty busy," I said.

"I have a great deal of trouble with them," he informed me.

"And doubtless they have a lot of bother with you too," I countered.

"They're a lazy bunch," he said, "and unless I'm running around after them all day, they do no work at all." I took this statement with a large pinch of salt as I could feel that they were all enjoying the joke as much as Normus.

As the fairies were presented, they came and stood on my knee to give me their names.

The first one, I was enchanted to hear, rejoiced in the name of Gorjus and I learned that he works with the trees. Later I discovered that there is a play in the projection of "Gorjus," unlike that of "Normus." The fairies were gathered 'round me one day and they were all praising Normus' good looks. I remarked, "I do hope that Gorjus doesn't belie his name."

"Oh no," they chorused. "Gorjus is gorgeous."

I next met his paris who is called Myrris and I learned that bulbs and corms are her special charges.

The second pair to be presented were Movus and Mirilla. I discovered later that Movus is Normus' greatest friend and that Mirilla, with her golden hair and exquisite beauty, is his favourite paris. Movus works with the shrubs and Mirilla with the tall flowers.

At this stage of the proceedings there was a slight setback. I sensed that all was not as it should be and I enquired whether something had gone wrong.

"Namsos is very shy," Normus explained, and I had a mental picture of a little figure hanging his head and sucking a finger nervously. "Never mind," I said quickly. "Don't press him. Namsos, dear," I added in the direction of the ground, "would you like to tell me about your work?" There was no reply.

"It's with worms and insects," Normus told me.

"He likes even the worms?" I enquired.

"He really loves them," Normus assured me.

"Well, I think that's wonderful," I said. "I know, of course, that we should love all creatures but it isn't always easy.

His paris, Sirilla, on the contrary was far from retiring and she told me that her work was . . . but, alas, I could not understand. "I seem to see a tree," I said doubtfully, "but Gorjus works with those."

"Yes, yes," they said. "it is a tree, but a special part." I received a picture then of the trunk of a tree with a tiny figure working halfway up. "The bark," I said triumphantly. "Yes, yes, the bark," they echoed delightedly.

Next I met Nuvic, who is the rose specialist, and his paris, Merella, who works with seeds. On Earth Merella would be regarded as a shameless hussy for she gives and takes power from any fairy whenever the opportunity arises, but it is in her approach to the subject in which she differs so essentially from the promiscuous on Earth. She regards each experience in the light of a scientific experiment and always she emerges from her love-making wiser than before, with the result that she has become exceptionally evolved for a fairy of her class. I used to tease her for her flirtatious habits, which she loved, but always she looked forward to the time when she could make me understand how her experiments have helped her.

Finally we came to Nixus and Lyssis, who respectively tend the grass and the low flowers. We had made a great beginning and I was filled with excitement at this new interest which had entered my life.

The Gnomes

It was some time later that I met my gnomes. I had not done so previously, owing to the fact that I had misunderstood Normus when I had enquired whether there were any elves or gnomes in the garden. I had thought that he had given me a negative answer to both questions whereas, in reality, he was referring to elves only.

I have always had an idea that if I had gnomes, they would live under the big tree in the far corner of the garden and I was delighted when I discovered that this is exactly where they have their home. They told me that their names were Tanchon and Persion and that they both had beards and wore pointed caps.

I asked the two gnomes whether they had in any way been responsible for the quite extraordinary manner in which a young boy whom I had employed to help in the garden, had managed to smash nearly all my tools. Heads flew off, handles snapped and the lawn mower broke in two. I could see them talking to one another and fidgeting. "I won't be cross," I promised.

"We didn't actually break them," they said, "but we encouraged the boy to be rough with them."

I grinned. "If you do that again, I shall plait your beards and tie the ends up with ribbon and then all the fairies will laugh at you," I threatened.

"Oh, Daphne, you wouldn't do that, would you?" they chuckled, highly amused.

"And tell me another thing," I continued, "Do you copy my mother and me with our big shopping baskets?"

"Yes," they admitted, not quite sure of my reactions.

"And I'm sure you've made yourselves that blue straw hat of hers with the red flowers."

"Oh, yes," they said, gaining confidence, "and we often dress up in that brown one of yours with the bow in the front."

Now, I rather fancy myself in this hat but the mental picture of a bearded, wrinkled face beneath it was too much for my sense of dignity and we all burst out laughing together.

The Full Moon

Some gardeners and old country people always plant their seeds either forty-eight hours before the full moon if, like flowers, green peas or cabbages, they grow up, or forty-eight hours after if, as in the case of carrots and other root vegetables, they grow down. This idea is generally regarded as just an old wives' tale by the uninitiated but Rudolf Steiner, in his very interesting science known as anthroposophy, proves that there is a definite reason for planting in this manner, owing to the fact that the ground is in its most fertile and rhythmic state, helping the seeds to grow.

Mairus (one of the house fairies) gave me the following account the day after one full moon:

> We went to rest early and arose at half-past eleven, when the festivities were beginning. We walked down the steps leading into the garden to find a great gathering on the lawn, for last night this was the meeting place for all the fairies in the district. We moved about, talking to each other and exchanging the news of the past month, we from this house and garden being much in demand because our work with Daphne is of great interest to all.

> Shortly before midnight the music began. We have an orchestra of twenty which is constantly changing so that those who play an instrument can take their turn in the dance.

> At the beginning, Maire, Herus and I stood on the hill under the chestnut tree (referring to my tiny rockery - D.C.) and watched the proceedings. At first the movements of the dance in progress were comparatively slow and graceful, but gradually the speed increased, which was very exciting as a great deal of power was being exhaled. Soon we ran down the hill and joined the merrymakers, adding our power to the ever-growing concentration already formed.

> After awhile we rested for a short time in order to replenish ourselves, not, of course, from the main body which we had been so busy making, but from the surrounding atmosphere. Soon we were refreshed and ready to begin all over again. This time I played my flutella but I was able to keep my eye on Maire as she took part in the dance.

> *[I asked him if this was to ascertain whether she was flirting with the boys. "No," he answered quite seriously, "I just like to watch her, that's all." – D.C.]*

The absorbing and giving out of the power continued until midnight, when the real reason for the evening's activities began.

By that time we had a large mass of power, which is visible to us and can be handled and distributed at will. This was escorted by all the fairies, some carrying it, some hovering over it and others running along the ground underneath it, to the accompaniment of the entire orchestra.

The power is like a great white light shedding its beams in all directions. We carried it over the surface of the ground so that its rays entered the earth, enriching it and giving energy to the seeds and roots buried in it. The power passed through each plant and tree until every living thing in the vegetable kingdom had received of its life-giving force.

You will understand that we can cover many miles in the fraction of a second so by half-past twelve our work was finished, but the festivities continued far into the morning. We house fairies are not very happy when we are out of doors except for essential work, so we left the others to their merrymaking and retired to rest, content in the knowledge that we not only help Man but the Nature kingdom as well."

The Peace Ray

When our position during the war in Korea deteriorated considerably before Christmas, 1950, the idea came to me that I should try to send out a peace ray which, I hoped, would be more powerful than transmitting thoughts alone.

I asked the fairies to join me and at first I concentrated on the idea of peace and the traditional emblems of the dove and olive branch came into my mind. After a week or two had passed, an extraordinary feeling of peace came over me as I worked and eventually I knew that a force was indeed passing through me because I could feel it as plainly as I can whenever I am healing or helping the earthbound.

After a few days I became convinced that not only my Teacher and the fairies were with me, and when I made enquiries I was informed that indeed many were present.

Remember the countless dead of the numerous wars which have taken place all over the world during the last century alone. Even if we are inclined to forget them, they do not forget us. Behind them stand thousands of more evolved souls who work endlessly in the cause of peace. You may not think that they have been very successful but, on the other hand, we do not know how much worse conditions might be without their aid.

A concentrated thought from anyone in a physical body adds power to theirs. I do not understand why this is so but I know that all their work is greatly enhanced by our thoughts and our desire to help them. If there are any among you who would spend even one minute a day to further the cause of peace, do not imagine that your little inexperienced thought will be waging a lone battle against the power of the ruthless war mongers. Know that as soon as you sit quietly, for however short a time, men, fairies and members of the other evolutions will gather 'round you, making your single thought into a real force for good.

Please do not think that I am a Pacifist or that I am advocating meeting guns with sweet thoughts, for that is far from my intention. Too many people jeopardise the chances of peace by frequently pondering on the horrors of war. Fear is one of the greatest gifts to the forces of evil and if, during times of what these days passes for peace, you would think constructively, you can do much to help those whose most earnest desire is to lighten the burdens of all who are plunged in matter.

Fairy Visitors

One day Normus was telling me how happy all in his band of fairies are, so I said to him, "You do a great deal to help Nature and Man; couldn't you do something further by sharing that happiness with your own evolution? You've told me how desperately miserable you were for several years after you first came down to Earth. Why not help some recently arrived fairies who are unhappy now?"

I know that during the working week they all live in a community house but that each pair of fairies has the equivalent of a weekend cottage. I continued, "Now the big house must be practically empty on Saturday and Sunday why not invite some sad little fairies and give them a good time?"

As with all my simple suggestions, he was delighted. I have noticed many times that the fairies do not seem to have the ability of thinking out quite ordinary little schemes for themselves but, once I have given them the idea, they make plans and carry them out far better than I could myself. I imagine that fairy thoughts are somehow different from ours and that the human ideas I am giving them, being more stable than theirs, can be put to good use.

Anyhow, every weekend, four sad little people arrive at noon each Saturday. All my fairy friends have been on Earth for many years and they have thus developed a good deal of power. A little of this force emanates from them without effort when they are not working and this acts as a soothing balm. Consciously they are also able to eliminate the vibration of Man, motor cars and other noises which might be distressing to these little entities who have done but five of their 100-year Earth span.

Saturday afternoon is a period of great activity here, when many discarnate beings of various nationalities come and aid us in the work which I need not here describe. This tremendous display of power and the presence of the different races, with their gaily coloured clothes and skins of varying hue, is a never-ending source of excitement to my own fairies who are naturally always present on these occasions. To the little visitors, it is a great wonder which jerks them out of their unhappiness and prepares them for the gaiety of the Power party in the evening.

A Fairy Party

I asked Normus one day what fairies do to entertain their guests. I explained to him that the provision of food and drink is the chief means by which we show hospitality to our friends and, as fairies do neither, I was interested to hear what occurs when they have a party. Here are Normus' own words:

> To begin with, we all meet at some pre-arranged place and give out power until there's a concentration rather like a big ball in the middle. We make it as beautiful as we can, each adding his own colour and vibration so that it is all shades of the rainbow and full of life and movement.
>
> During the party we enter the ball, either alone, with several friends or with a member of the opposite sex. We absorb the power and come out feeling wonderful. We try not to go into it too often though, because if we inhale too much of it, we're unable to control our movements. Those fairies who can't fly may find themselves floating over the tops of the flowers or even shrubs, and we who can will perhaps regain consciousness in a cloud. I did this once and I can assure you that it wasn't nearly as attractive to be in as it looks from the ground. I became very wet and the power began to ooze out of me. I found that I couldn't think properly and I was very frightened when I realized how far above Earth I'd wandered. I began to drop much faster than I liked but I managed to pull myself together and as soon as I reached a few feet above the tops of the trees, I seemed to regain control and all was well. I swore that I'd never do it again but I have . . . not very often . . . but you just don't know how irresistible that ball of power is."

Hostile Elements

I can well recall the day that George saw his first fairy, that is, apart from Normus. All my Astral friends became aware of the leader before any of the others, I presume because he has the most power, but on this occasion George was endeavouring to see one or more of the others and he finally met Gorjus for the first time.

I had asked all the fairies to stand or sit on George's knee so that he would know where to look for them, then I realized that Normus was still on my lap. I asked him where he was going and he replied, "Oh, I'll just stay here and watch."

"But aren't you going to do anything to help?" I enquired.

"No, I'll just watch," he replied.

"Normus," I admonished him, "you're a lazy, good-for-nothing rogue. If you'd been a human being during the last war, you'd have been a spy and a drone and a black marketeer." I had no idea how these terms would be translated by him but I realized that I had called him something extremely unpleasant when he said earnestly, "Oh, Daphne, you don't really think that of me, do you? I'm truly not as bad as all that." I hastened to assure him that I was only teasing him for of course I really know what a good little worker he is and he appeared to be comforted.

However, this turned out to be far from the end of this incident and after awhile I began to wonder what it was in fairy language that I had called him to cause him such dismay. I asked him one day if he could give me a picture of a fairy spy and he flashed back at me a form which looked to me somewhat like a miniature black octopus.

"It's a terrible thing," he said solemnly. "It sucks the goodness out of the ground or anything that it is able to dominate."

"'Has it a name?" I enquired.

"Yes, it's a monserros," he replied.

"Can you see them?" I enquired.

"Not as a rule, unless we are specially tuned in to them, but we can detect their presence by the evil vibrations."

"Do you fight them?" I asked, my mind filling with illustrations of fairies armed with pins facing up to miniature dragons, as in children's books.

"We overcome them with thought and power," he said. "We form a protective circle 'round an area and we drive them out, warning the fairies in the next territory in case they escape."

"But where do you drive them, because you obviously can't send them into anyone else's district?"

"We drive them down to their own country," he said.

"And where is that?" I asked.

"The 'dark places'," he replied.

I was not entirely satisfied with this explanation so I approached my Teacher on the subject, explaining that Normus had shown me mentally a creature like an octopus and I was wondering whether the monserros were always like that. He told me that they take what form they wish so I enquired exactly what these creatures are.

"Evil desires to express itself, as well as Good," he replied, "and when it becomes sufficiently strong it will take form. "

I then asked whether the monserros sap the strength from plants and the earth, as I had understood from Normus.

"My daughter," was the reply, "you have had experience of their work yourself. Do you not remember those two plants . . . ?" and instantly I recalled the big, strong aster with several fine branches, that had withered in a night and how, a few days later, a sturdy verbena had commenced to flower and suddenly died. I had asked Normus why this had happened at the time.

"Oh, I expect insects have killed them," he had said. I could see no sign of half-eaten leaves, nor yet of blight, so I dug them up and examined the roots, but they were whole and apparently strong. "That was the work of a monserros," my Teacher continued. I was deeply distressed and I asked if there was a remedy.

"More vigilance," he replied.

That morning I called the fairies together and I told them that I had something to discuss with them. I reminded them of the two dead flowers and I told them the cause.

"That part of a soul which was manifesting in each of those plants has literally been devoured by evil and, until the time comes, possibly millions of years hence, when Good conquers that particular evil – as it always does – the whole soul will be retarded in its evolution, owing to the loss of that part. It's only a tiny part but nonetheless, it is a part." I could feel the tension – the distress.

"I think that sometimes we may get a little overconfident and perhaps a bit slack," I continued. "Now we all know that these plants had died for some reason, and yet we presumed that it was from a normal cause. That's where our fault lies. In presuming. We should have made further enquiries from your super-leader – he would surely have suspected the real cause.

However, it's not all our fault for I was told too that there must have been a fundamental weakness in these flower part-souls to have permitted the monserros to devour them. There are many smaller and apparently weaker plants in the garden and I've no doubt that the monserros was far from satiated and, yet, for some reason, it was just these two which were overcome."

"Now, dears," I concluded, "you mustn't distress yourselves unduly because you'll pass on your unhappiness to the rest of your charges and that won't be good for them. We must be thankful that only two have been lost and we must ensure that they will be the last. It's only through experience that we really learn, so let's profit by this one, that the other plants may benefit.

"Now, you know much more about this sort of thing than I do and I'm confident that you'll do everything in your power to combat this evil."

I could see them talking among themselves very seriously, then Normus thanked me and assured me that they would immediately make plans for keeping the monserros away.

"Anything I can do, you know I will," I said before I left them, "but remember what I've said – no moping."

The following day Normus told me how upset they had been at my news. However, they had thought out a plan of defense which they had already put into action, but they wished to discuss the matter with me further. Unfortunately, I was especially busy at the time and it was not until another five days had passed that we were able to have another meeting.

The first precaution which had been taken was that of asking for guardians for their land and plants whenever the fairies were occupied with my work. These were not to take over any of their tasks but were in the nature of a patrol. At the first sign of danger, they would give the alarm and reinforcements would arrive. Thus the fairies would not themselves be disturbed when occupied with healing or other work.

The second action taken was that of guarding their charges at night. Normally while the fairies rest, others take their place, but those who do this work at night do not stay on Earth, but return to the Astral each day. They do not have a particular territory under their charge, as they may be sent to any part of the country. I gather that this night work is in the nature of a preparation for their future 100-year span but they do not take on Earth conditions as the other fairies do, nor do they have the responsibility of looking after the welfare of certain plants. They therefore cannot have the same interest as the day fairies whose charges are their absolute responsibility. The little people, therefore, were taking it in turns to keep watch at night, not actually leaving their home but continuously alert for the warning vibrations. I asked Normus whether this lack of proper rest was affecting their work and he confessed that, unfortunately, it was proving a great strain.

"Go to your leader and tell him what you have done and the effect it is having on you," I advised. "All fairies have their tasks and I'm sure that none should be deprived of rest. There must be an instrument which will flash a light or cause a vibration which will awaken you at approaching danger. Make enquiries and if there isn't already one, I'm sure that one can soon be made."

He then told me how, during the day, each would stop for a fraction of a second every few minutes and relax so that, if any evil influence was about, they could detect it.

I congratulated him and then he asked me if I had any suggestions to make. I thought back over my own encounters with evil. "The cross," I thought, "the sign of the cross." But would a monserros understand its significance?

I took this problem to my Teacher, who replied, "the power of the cross is there whether it is understood or not."

"Normus," I said, "the cross is the only symbol I understand but you know about many others and their meaning. Use them. They'll want replenishing, of course, but I'm sure that Jack, Peter and the others will give power for the purpose and, of course, I will too."

The men proved only too anxious to help their little friends and so it was that Man and Fairy combined to keep a common foe at bay.

Still, that was not the end of the incident. After several months had passed, I asked if there was no way by which we could retrieve the lost part-souls which the monserros had taken, owing to our carelessness.

"I will lead you to him," my Teacher said, "and the fairies will overcome him."

The day for the venture at last arrived and we set out. Soon we were in an inky land of squelching mud. Nothing grew and yet I had an impression of one solitary tree lifting its two leafless branches to the unresponsive sky.

I'm giving you Normus' version of the events which followed as I could go but part of the way with them and I did not know until later exactly what had happened during their absence underground.

For some time we had been greatly distressed by the loss to a mon-serros of two of our charges. We had taken several precautions, we had increased our vigilance and we had done everything in our power to prevent further trouble.

Then, at last, one day Daphne told us that we were to go with her Teacher and her and force the monserros to give back what he had taken. We set out and immediately we found ourselves in pitch dark-ness. At first we could see nothing but we kept close to Daphne and she seemed to know the way.

[I myself was, of course, being led. – D.C.]

Eventually we came to a hole in the mud and she told us that the monserros was inside and that we were to go in and fetch him out. I led the others down into the earth; the deeper we went, the thicker the atmosphere became. We had taken the precaution of closing our power-pipes before we left Earth and so we were still quite comfort-able.

At last we found him, a slowly vibrating mass of black sponge. We stood 'round him and opened our outlet ducts and the power, stored inside us, began to flow. He shuddered and tried to back further down the hole but we had him surrounded, leaving only the passage leading to the exit.

For some time we could not make him move so I ordered the fairies to climb onto him so that we could give him the power direct. This was a horrible experience, as we seemed to sink into him and, if we had not used all our willpower, he would have absorbed us too.

At last he could stand the conditions no longer and slowly he slith-ered his way up the hole. We were becoming very exhausted and our power was nearly spent; in fact, as we reached the top only Merella, Movus and I had any left. As soon as we came out, Daphne turned on hers and we were able to replenish ourselves.

We formed a circle 'round him, keeping the hole well covered, and it was as well that we did because he did his best to escape down below again. At last he could stand no more; he looked as though he were on fire and the life which was in him was literally burned out. We gathered the flakes and, when we arrived home, we scattered them on the garden to be absorbed by the earth. Thus the part-souls which we had lost re-entered the life cycle again – lower down the scale, it is true, but far higher than if they had been left in that vale of darkness with their terrible guardian.

Christmas Day

A few days before Christmas I received a letter from a girl in Vancouver, containing the news that a mutual medium friend of ours was giving a party for Astral children. The writer was to assist in decorating the tree with balloons and small presents with which the children would somehow be able to play.

The idea appealed to me and I began considering giving a party myself, but then I decided that as I had such a pathetically small tree the children would probably have a much better time on the Astral.

Suddenly a thought struck me. "Fool," I said to myself, "put up an astral tree, a huge one, with astral presents."

(I must here explain that for some time I have been able to create my own conditions when I am working. For example, if I have wanted flowers or the song of a bird to pierce the gloom to cheer some earthbound whom I am endeavouring to help, the thought has scarcely been formed in my mind before the flowers or song come into being. I do not think that I make them myself, but my thought forms the nucleus for those who do this work, to create the things for which I have asked.)

However, for the party I decided that I would not rely on my own powers as I should probably give the children far too rich food and unsuitable presents. I spoke to Father John and he arranged for a woman to arrive at 3 o'clock on Christmas Day to make the necessary preparations.

I felt her presence at the exact time and she told me that her name was Hermine. Upon my questioning her, she also informed me that she had been over the Other Side for forty years and that her work consisted of bringing up Earth children who have died and have no parents already over there. She is in charge of a school and children's home, combined, and here young people live and grow among ideal surroundings.

I learned, too, that astral children are subjected to strict discipline and privileges such as pony riding and taking care of animals are earned by conscientious work; food, except on party occasions, is plain and hours regular. Always they are surrounded by love and understanding, these two factors ensuring the progress and happiness of these young people during their growing years. I understand that they learn much more quickly than those on Earth and that their interests are wider. For instance, on later visits, I have given them details of my work of healing and with the earthbound and I have held their rapt attention even to the extent of their forgetting to eat their tea. With Hermine's permission, I have also told them of my visits to the very dark places, usually thought of on Earth as Hell. Not very suitable subjects for children, you may think, yet how much more so than the story of Bluebeard and the other more gruesome so-called Fairy Tales.

On this first occasion I kept very much in the background because I knew that these children, two Irish, two Indians, two Arabs and two Negroes, had all experienced sad Earth lives and I feared that my vibrations would remind them of their past unhappiness. Since then, when they visit me about once a month, we have become firm friends and I understand from Hermine that sitting next to me is considered quite a privilege. However, although they now come to see me with such enthusiasm, I know really that the fairies and not I are the chief attraction.

– Daphne Charters

CHRISTMAS DAY – THE CHILDREN'S PARTY
by Normus

We had been looking forward to Christmas Day for many weeks but when the time came it was all even more wonderful than we had dared to hope.

Fairies always love children and when Daphne told us that she was having a party, we were very excited, and when we heard that our astral human friends were coming later, our anticipation ran high.

When we arrived we saw that Daphne had called down astral conditions because at first we did not recognize her room. Everything was covered with leaves and flowers, the furniture and walls were all hidden and in the window was, not as we had expected, the little tree which we had helped to decorate the previous evening, but a giant one which reached right up to the ceiling. Daphne told us that we were to be part of the decorations so we flew, climbed and helped each other up until we were all standing or sitting on a branch or on one of the shiny decorations, some of which were in the shape of birds and we were able to perch on their backs.

Then the children came in. To our astonishment, they seemed rather frightened, but they had all been badly treated on Earth and the necessary lowering of their vibrations had brought back to them their unhappy memories. Daphne is always so affectionate with us that we had imagined her going forward with arms outstretched, but she remained sitting in her chair, just smiling as she welcomed them.

71

'They came in the charge of a lovely lady called Hermine, and a young girl who gave them their tea. The big cake, covered with candles and a Father Christmas in the centre of the table, held them spellbound for awhile and then the good things to eat soon dispersed their remaining doubts.

All this time the tree had been hidden from their view but, of course, that did not prevent us from watching them. Then the great moment arrived. With a thought, the screen was removed and the children gasped.

"Look at the lights," one cried.

"Look at the presents," shouted another.

"Look at the balloons," screamed a third.

But nobody said, "Look at the fairies."

We realized then that they couldn't see us and our hearts sank because we had so looked forward to playing with them.

"Can't the children see the fairies?" Daphne asked Hermine.

"I'm afraid not," she replied."

"Then we must make them," said Daphne decisively, and we knew that she would.

She lit us up and suddenly the little Indian boy began dancing and pointing at me in wild excitement. He couldn't even speak, he was so overcome, but somehow his gesticulations seemed to give the others sight and finally each child could see at least one of us.

When they had opened their gifts, we came down and played with them and I'm not sure which, to them, was the greatest thrill.

Then Daphne said, "Has every fairy been seen by someone?"

I'm afraid we had been so excited by our own success that we hadn't noticed poor Herus standing disconsolately alone. Although Daphne cannot see, she always seems to know, and she went straight up to the little black girl who seemed quite happy playing with her toys.

"Look, dear," she said, "there's a lonely little fairy nearly as shy as you are. Try to see him, will you?"

The child looked up at her with big, frightened eyes but Daphne already had her power turned on and she did as she was told. Then she began to laugh and she laughed until tears rolled down her cheeks and we knew that Herus had made a friend for life.

– Normus

CHRISTMAS DAY, 1950

by Ludwig

It is always a great pleasure for us to visit Daphne on Earth and, naturally, when she invited us to her children's party on Christmas Day, we were delighted. Some of the others confessed that such entertainment was hardly in their line but they would not have hurt her feelings for anything. As it turned out, it would have been a great loss to any of us had we not attended.

The children had eaten their tea when we arrived and were busy playing with their toys and the fairies. We were not quite sure what part we were to play but, after welcoming us, Daphne told us to sit on the ground as the decorations were about to be lit up. Her room had been transformed into a bower of flowers and greenery and she herself was sitting among a mass of bluebells which filled the air with their perfume.

Gradually the normal light faded, except for that around where Daphne sat. She appeared as though in a mist of blue jewels but she was obviously quite unaware that anything out of the ordinary was in progress. A great white beam shone down from above, lighting the whole scene, and yet it had changed for the four decorated walls had gone and a woodland glade, flooded by moonlight, appeared.

The children shrieked with delight as they saw countless baby rabbits playing between the trees. A gentle breeze rustled the leaves, which seemed to be whispering a message of hope for the world.

Then the fairies made their entry and I have seldom seen a more enchanting sight. They floated slowly and gracefully between the trees, trailing behind them garlands of ethereal flowers and what appeared to be wisps of gossamer. After awhile there was a sigh, the leaves began to fall, the baby rabbits returned to their burrows and the fairies sank to the ground, as though to sleep, everything fading behind a curtain of descending foliage.

We began to clap our hands, thinking that the show was over, but the scene again changed. We were in an Eastern market, with dazzling colour everywhere, the sun turning the streets to pure gold. The activity of the many buyers and sellers was in complete contrast to the peaceful woodland scene. The air was filled with music which our unaccustomed western ears found strange, and exotic perfume assailed our nostrils.

A clash of cymbals introduced a series of poetic Indian dances in which each gesture has a spiritual meaning. None of us has ever studied this fascinating subject and yet all was clear to us. We understood the tragedy behind the recent strife in that unhappy country, where men have murdered their neighbours to the glory of

God. The incalculable became understandable, the secrets of the mystics became simple and we knew that we had taken yet another step in the direction of ultimate Truth. To the children, I think the dance was solely a thing of beauty and grace but, in later years, I have no doubt that they will realize the true significance.

The scene disappeared in a rising crescendo of Indian pipes, which gradually faded into the distance to be replaced by a note – a note that was then new to us but to which we have now become attuned. It is the note which always leads to a new experience – the mantric note of our evolution. That first time, when we heard it, we did not know – and yet we did. Our hearts stood still and a peace which none can describe descended upon us.

The note swelled into a mighty voluntary and three vast arches filled with light came into view – they were as of coloured glass such as you find in churches, yet the stories they told were alive, moving, constantly changing.

A great ray shone through them and down the beams floated the fairies, a look of rapture on their upturned faces. When they reached the ground, they turned and, in the distance, through the central arch, we beheld a light which dimmed all others.

We rose and knelt, the children too. It came nearer until one and all must bow his head. We remained thus until some of the power was withdrawn and we could once again raise our eyes to watch the ray slowly fading until nothing was left. Nothing visible, that is, but once you have been touched by the light and felt its radiance, you can never rest until you find it again.

– Ludwig

THE GNOMES, TANCHON AND PERSION
by Themselves

We'll tell you about our work. We give power to the roots and the earth 'round them. We love our tasks because we understand that from the roots, the whole tree grows. We like to look high above our heads and to know that our work, or rather that of gnomes living here hundreds of years ago, has made it possible for the tree to be as he is today.

We can go a long way into the ground for the roots of a big tree reach far below the surface. Sometimes when we get to the end of a root we go even deeper, partly to prepare the soil for its future growth, but partly too out of curiosity. You who must stay on the surface would be surprised at the life which goes on deep down.

Wherever the rain falls, the water causes growth. We don't mean in size and we don't mean things that you can see, either. You've heard of the minerals in the soil; they're material, but there are all kinds of people-in-embryo down there too;

74

they contribute to the growth of the minerals and the minerals help them. They are dependent on each other in the same way that the roots rely on us to help them but, whereas we are more advanced than the roots, the minerals and the attendant entities unconsciously help each other, absorbing and returning the power for their mental and physical needs."

The message had obviously come to an end so I thanked the gnomes and told them that I thought it very good.

Gnomes (chuckling): "So do we."

D.C.: "I feel sure that you were helped."

Gnomes: "Yes. Normus did. We couldn't have remembered all that at once. He made thought forms for us and gave them to us, one by one."

One of them, Tanchon I think, turned a somersault, obviously as a sign of relief that the ordeal was over. I asked him what else he could do and he tried to stand on his hands but he overbalanced. He made another attempt and was more successful. I then suggested that they should stand on their heads. They did so but fell over, roaring with laughter.

I asked them to show me something else, whereupon they linked arms and performed a little dance. One, two, three, hop, and back again. Then they joined hands and ambled 'round in a circle, to fall over again with guffaws of laughter.

D.C.: "That was very clever."

Gnomes: "Yes, wasn't it. We made it up as we went along, Can we go now?"

And without waiting for my reply, off they went.

I turned to Normus, who confessed that he was glad the interview was safely over. I told him that I had been a little worried at the beginning because I was unable to hear anything at all, to which he replied that he was not surprised as, instead of looking at the thought forms which he was showing them, the gnomes were both busy trying to dig into the carpet!

He told me that he had been rehearsing them every day and that he had been obliged to give me the thoughts with them at the beginning but that, later, they had succeeded in transmitting the message correctly themselves.

– Tanchon and Person

TANCHON AND PERSION

by Father John

[When I met the gnomes, I told them that they would be welcome to join the fairies in any of their activities concerning my work and I hoped that, at any rate, they would join the Saturday afternoon tea party which takes place on the lawn.

After several weeks, I asked Andrew how they were all getting on with the gnomes and he told me that they no longer came to see them. He said that they had been wise but that they had all found them somewhat difficult because, if the conversation deviated even to a small degree from roots and the soil, they began muttering in their beards and edging away.

However absorbing these two subjects may be to gnomes, I did not regard them as very promising material of which to make a chapter for this book. I therefore asked Father John if he would interview them for me, because I felt that if there was anything profound in these quaint l little men, he, with his far more advanced powers of perception, would find it, however deeply it might be embedded. – D.C.]

At Daphne's request, I visited the gnomes yesterday afternoon. They were very busy digging the earth around the roots of a tree in the garden. They had miniature spades and were emulating the actions of any gardener engaged in a similar task.

I watched them for awhile from a higher vibration, which means that I was invisible to them. They would dig energetically for about three minutes, then their minds would wander from their work and they would knock each other over amidst roars of mirth until they once again recollected the task in hand.

Gnomes, as a rule, are merry little souls who love to play jokes on each other and on Man when an opportunity arises. Their games are similar to children's and their fat, cumbersome bodies make them amusing to watch as they are very clumsy and frequently fall over their own or each other's feet. The consequent bump appears to cause them no discomfort and each tumble leads to more laughter and horseplay.

Their work is similar to the fairies' but simpler. Again, power is distributed through them to the roots of trees and to the soil, which they are able to enter, sometimes for many miles.

The two gnomes in question have been on Earth for twenty-one years, so they have but four years of their span to run. They are fairly advanced in that they understand the reason for their work, but they have expressed no desire to enter into Daphne's tasks, as some would undoubtedly have done.

Gnomes are sometimes used with not very developed members of the human evolution in producing elementary forms of physical phenomena at seances. As an entity develops, so it becomes increasingly difficult for him to make himself seen and heard by non-psychics. Gnomes often produce knocks and taps and are instrumental in the conveyance of "apports," or objects from places miles away from the locality of the seance room.

In healing they can be of assistance in the mending of bones or with any disease of the flesh, but nerves or mental disorders would be beyond their capacity.

When I first spoke to Tanchon and Persion, I was given a hearty welcome. I arranged for my appearance to coincide with one of their periods of work and as soon as they heard me speak, they began puffing and blowing and mopping their brows to prove to me how busy they had been. They both stuck their spades into the newly turned earth and sat down beside me.

"We've been expecting you," Tanchon said. "We've a good deal to tell you. Shall we begin right away?"

I nodded and he began. "We haven't far to go in this Earth span now and we aren't quite sure whether we want to leave."

"You love this garden very much then?" I enquired.

"Well, yes – but we want to stay as we are."

"You mean that you wish to remain as gnomes forever?" I asked gravely.

"No – " they said, "but the fairies work so hard. Couldn't we miss out being fairies and just be big editions of ourselves?"

" If you wish to stay as you are, no one can make you advance," I told them. "You might even grow as big as I am if you wanted to very much, but size, in your evolution, also indicates growth of mind. There would be little point in having large bodies if your interests were still as restricted as they are today."

"We have lots of interests," they protested.

"Tell me what they are," I said.

"We have such grand games," said Persion.

"Ssh!" said Tanchon quickly. "Our work is very important," he continued, stroking his beard like a venerable scholar.

"And your work consists of . . . ?" I prompted.

"Giving power to the soil that all that grows therein may flourish," he quoted fluently and correctly.

"And what else do you do?" I persisted.

"We give power to the roots of the largest members of the vegetable kingdom . . . " said Tanchon.

"That they may provide Man with shade from the sun . . . " said Persion.

"'Wood for his fires . . . " said Tanchon.

"And material for many of his needs," added Persion. All this was quoted quite accurately from the thought forms, which serve them as books.

"What else?" I enquired.

"We give power to the soil that all that grows therein . . . " began Persion.

"Yes, you've told me that," I reminded him gently.

"We have lovely games," he tried again.

"Well, tell me about them."

"Ho-ho!" They began rolling about with laughter before they had even begun to describe any of their uproarous amusements. I waited for them to stop, but they began pulling each other's beards and punching one another in the stomach, causing fresh paroxysms every other second.

When they were quiet for a moment, obviously thinking of fresh tricks to play, I said, "Show me some of your other games."

They began whispering to each other, then Persion rose to his feet and disappeared behind a tree. After about three minutes, he came out the other side dressed in Daphne's green winter coat, fur-lined boots and a small brown hat perched on top of his long grey hair.

I confess that I, myself, laughed at this strange spectacle, then Tanchon said, "It's my turn now."

He, too, disappeared behind a tree and later appeared as Daphne again, dressed up to go to a party. He had on a long evening dress, cut very low, so that the hairs on his chest were prominently displayed. He lifted his skirts to show me his high heeled shoes. I do not think that he had even seen Daphne in evening dress and I should not have known whom he represented had it not been for the incongruous presence of her red tartan umbrella.

That appeared to be the end of their repertoire, so I waited to see what else they would do to entertain me. They eventually began to play leap-frog, turn somersaults, and do headstands. I applauded every turn enthusiastically but I noticed that each exhibition was taking them farther away from me until, eventually, they hid behind a tree in the next garden.

I followed them and found them pulling each other's beards. I made as much noise as I could as I drew near, so that when I became visible to them they were very busy digging 'round a root.

"What about all the interesting things which you were to tell me," I reminded them.

They looked puzzled.

"But we've told you," they said.

I sat down again.

"Come," I said, patting the ground and, obediently, they sat down beside me.

"You have told me everything that you know?" I asked them.

" It's for Daphne's book. It's very important," they chanted in unison.

"Shall we analyze what you have told and shown me?" I suggested. They were longing, I knew, to pull each other's beards but somehow they restrained themselves. I received no direct answer so I continued.

"You give power to the soil."

"So that all therein . . . " began Tanchon.

"We will just keep to essentials," I said. "You give power to the soil and to the roots of trees."

"So that they may provide Man . . . " said Persion.

"Yes, we know that," I cut in. "You disguise yourselves very cleverly. You turn somersaults, play leap-frog and can stand on your heads." Person was already standing on his by the time I reached this point. "Do you really not wish to do anything else, ever?"

"We give power to the soil . . . " Tanchon was singing now.

"And power to the roots," joined in Person as they rose to their feet and marched off, arm in arm, to attend to their important duties.

I remained seated. Could it be true that Normus, Movus or Marus were at one time like this? It did not seem possible but, as I myself have many times been a babe in arms, so, too, were they once gnomes.

My thoughts next turned to Him Whom we love to call "Our Deva," Who manifests in the body of a beautiful youth and yet Who has Wisdom unimaginable. One day Tanchon and Person will be such as He, watching tenderly, even as He, over quaint little, pot-bellied gnomes, gamboling their seemingly foolish lives away. In time, they, too, will reach the Heights as surely as will you or I. Who knows, we may even cross the threshold of Infinity together.

– Father John

MANUSCRIPTS
SET #4

THE NATURE FAIRIES

Preface

This is the largest section in Volume I. Ten of the eleven members of the fairy band get to tell their own stories. (Their leader, Normus, has a whole section following this one), Each fairy couple is also described by one of Daphne's astral human friends; herein referred to as observers. Fairies operate at the etheric level when working with nature. This section includes some of the most intimate details about the lives of the fairies in The Collected Fairy Manuscripts. The fairies introduced in this set of manuscripts are the main characters and authors of many of the latter manuscripts.

– Michael Pilarski

GORJUS AND MYRRIS
OBSERVER: GEORGE

TREES
by Gorjus

To begin with, I would like to tell you about my work, which, as you already know, is with the trees. Each has a presiding soul and, as the tree grows, so more and more of the soul, or consciousness, is able to manifest. When the tree is young, I have to think for him (trees are either male or female) and impress on him the necessity for reaching out for power which he needs to produce leaves and to grow.

As the years pass, he himself gradually becomes aware of this reason for his existence but, naturally, the time required for this realization varies, according to the number of times that he has incarnated before, some taking many years and others understanding a little even in their first season.

I can't tell you how exciting it is when I receive the first intimation that the tree has grasped my oft-repeated message, for then I know that I've succeeded in helping a soul to be reborn. Eventually he's capable of taking charge of his activities himself and I merely direct the unites and minutes who supply him with the power necessary to carry out his work.

The first autumn is always a sad time for the newly awakened tree-souls, for they haven't yet sufficient consciousness to understand that their past labors aren't being lost with their falling leaves. They are perplexed and unhappy and, however hard I try, I'm unable to make them understand that God in His Wisdom is giving them a period of rest in which to recuperate from the toil of the past half year. But when realization at last dawns, they rejoice that they have been able to bring a successful conclusion to that which they had set out to do.

Like Man and the more advanced entities of each evolution, they have their joys and their sorrows which, once again, are limited by the degrees of consciousness which they have reached. As they grow, although they are able to experience a little pain, so also is their power for happiness increased and, until some tragedy enters their lives, their joy is far greater than their sorrow.

Pain and unhappiness descend on them only when their branches are lopped or, at worst, the whole tree is cut down; these actions bringing despair not only to the tree himself, but to all the surrounding plants.

When they are comparatively advanced in years, I can make them understand that Man needs their Earth bodies and that when they are felled, they have fulfilled their function and have earned the right to a period amidst the pleasanter conditions of the Astral.

If I know that a tree is to be cut down, and I have time to impress the fact on his consciousness beforehand, he sometimes even greets the ax man with joy but, if the felling is an unexpected development as far I am concerned, I can but endeavor to soothe him in the limited time which I have at my disposal.

Trees and other plants invariably respond to love; we, in whose charge they are placed, always love them but, when Man in their vicinity does too, then they truly flourish. Children touching their lower branches as they play is a great joy to them and young couples absorbed in love beneath their boughs bring them added happiness.

Trees are sensitive to any attention and when a necessity, such as pruning, is performed with knowledge and affection, they are encouraged to give of their best, whether it is a prolific crop of leaves, flowers or fruit that Man desires. Their pleasures are supplied by the weather, each change being a welcome diversion. I often see them lifting themselves hopefully towards the sun after a sudden burst of rain, while the wind helps them grow and to express themselves through movement.

A gale is a great source of excitement to them for their branches are often bent until they fear that they must snap, and of, course sometimes they do. Then remorse follows, for this proves that some weakness is present, that work which should have been performed to sustain growth has been neglected.

We all do our best to bring comfort to the maimed tree, telling him to cease wasting his energy on useless regrets and to set to work to ensure that a similar disaster doesn't occur again. Usually we can persuade him and an important lesson is learned, but, if the tree has been very neglectful, the break and the consequent outpouring of power only serves to weaken him further and we know, to our sorrow, that the next gale may bring his great body crashing to the ground.

Trees often form close attachments to each other and for the other plants and shrubs around them; this love helps them to grow, for they obtain great joy in showing their friends as much beauty as they are able.

The smaller plants respond and they also do their best to increase in statue in order to emulate the grandeur of their elder brothers. Thus all should grow in harmony and love, each contributing in his own way to the pleasure of the others.

– Gorjus

BULBS

by Myrris

When I was on the Astral plane, I used to work with the low flowers until one day I met a fairy whose tasks lay among the bulbs. We became great friends and my interest in her charges grew. I've never lost my love for the other flowers but to watch a bulb's growth from the time when it is a hard globe until it bursts forth in all its beauty, I find a most satisfying experience.

I tend them all the year 'round, whether they are planted snugly in the earth, bringing themselves to flower, or when they are dug up and left in a corner until it is time for them to be placed in the ground again.

There is not, as a rule, much actual growth before they are planted but they are, nonetheless, full of life and a certain amount of power and attention are necessary to keep them in good health. As soon as the bulb is placed in the earth, much more power is required, as it is immediately stimulated by the warmth and moisture and it commences to work.

I can't tell you how wonderful it is to watch its awakening, its consciousness becoming gradually more active in controlling the growth in each section of its form. After awhile I begin to influence each bulb to push out roots that it may draw from the soil the necessary water and minerals to feed its physical body. Day by day, I give it more and more power so that the astral body which I tend, responds and passes on my message of encouragement to the physical.

I watch each in turn and always I have a sense of achievement when the first green shoot, which has been busy unfurling itself inside the bulb, pushes its way through the top and begins its journey up to the light and air.

You will understand that it isn't I who supply all the power for this growth; I have many smaller entities who help me with my work and I have only to guide them to the bulbs which need their attention. If one isn't doing as well as it should, I take some of the entities from another which doesn't need as much help. As with more advanced people, some bulbs do more work for themselves than others, and those which require more unites to give them power rarely do as well as those who are filled with an eagerness to grow.

I think that my happiness reaches its peak when my charges attain their full beauty and come to flower. But sometimes I feel an even greater joy when I find that a tiny bulb has formed under the parent plant, and then I know that she has succeeded not only in bringing herself to her annual perfection, but that she has brought into being another life to enrich the world with her beauty.

– Myrris

GORJUS AND MYRRIS

by George

I shall never forget the day when Daphne told me about the fairies. I thought at first she was pulling my leg, but she appeared quite serious. She knew that I didn't believe her, although I had said nothing, and when she challenged me, I rather diffidently admitted that I was sure that she wouldn't lie to me without, at the same time, giving the fact away.

She told me that her garden fairies were with us and that she wanted me to try to hear them. She called Normus who, she explained, was their leader, and she told him to lower his vibrations while I was able to raise mine. After about a minute, she asked me if I had heard anything but, to my regret, I had to tell her that I hadn't.

"Now, Normus," she admonished him with mock severity, "you aren't trying. Get on George's shoulder and give him the projection as directly as you can. I shall be very cross with you if you don't succeed."

I had no doubt that this latter remark was far from the truth and I am also sure that Normus was equally aware of the fact.

After a good deal of concentration, I thought that I heard a voice saying, "Please hear me, George, because if you don't, Daphne will beat me." She laughed and, when I repeated his remark, she confirmed that I really had heard a fairy for the first time in my life. I was naturally pretty pleased with myself.

I was then solemnly introduced to two other fairies whose names I learned were Gorjus and Myrris. I could hear them too but I wanted to see them as well, because we're never content with what we've got and always we want to take the next step. This ambition I was able to achieve another time when I was with Daphne. She called all the fairies and she told us that we were to make a combined effort, during which she would give some power.

This was the first time that Daphne had done this to help me and, as the surroundings grew lighter, I looked intently, first at one leg and then at the other, because this was where she had told the fairies to take up their positions. For a bit, nothing happened, and then I began to see the outline of a tiny figure near my right knee. By degrees, the form became solid and I held out a finger.

"Bet it's a girl," said Daphne.

"No, it's a boy," the fairies and I enlightened her. It turned out to be Gorjus, to whom I had already been formally introduced and, before I returned to the Astral, we had a polite little chat.

Some time elapsed before another opportunity arose and, in the interval, Daphne told us of her plan for each of us to adopt one or two of the little people.

At that time, five of us from the Astral plane used to have tea in her garden each Saturday so, one day when we were gathered there, we decided that we'd try to see the fairies even though she wasn't there to help us. We took it in turns to search while the others gave power and, when my time came, a figure began to materialize. To my delight, it was Myrris, Gorjus' paris, so I now had my pair complete.

I first asked them to tell me how they had met. Gorjus apparently was working in a country garden and Myrris was living about eight miles away when a certain celebration took place. Gorjus was playing his flutella when his eyes fell on what he thought was the most beautiful fairy he had ever seen.

She was not in her materialized form, but a pink light. (I have no idea how one pink light can differ from another and, so far, in spite of detailed explanations, I have completely failed to understand.)

Gorjus attracted her attention by sending a vibration of his own green light towards her and she traveled along it until she was motionless before him. He almost lost consciousness as she approached and he knew that if she refused to share his life, his light would fade and perhaps even become extinguished.

I then asked Myrris how she had felt at the time of this meeting.

"I knew that something wonderful was about to happen as soon as his vibration touched me," she replied. "There were hundreds of other vibrations all 'round me but suddenly I felt as though I were opening like a flower to welcome the sun; I made no conscious effort, I just felt myself drawn along the beam.

"This sensation of coming to full bloom became stronger, until I knew I could unfold no more, then I felt a little stab and I knew that he and I were one and that, instead of being two lights, one pink and one green, we were a single, bi-coloured glow."

They explained to me that this sudden blending of their two selves is most unusual in- their evolution and that, normally, many months or years of entering each other's auras and of exchanging power, pass before the all-pervading merging of two souls. I imagine that this is a most passionate love affair, for they rarely take their eyes off one another. I have heard of similar sudden urges for physical union in the human race, but none so swift and yet so lasting, for they have been together for thirty years.

I'll now try to give you a description of these two little friends of mine. Gorjus, as his name indicates, is very good looking, a perfect Adonis in miniature, in fact. He's about six inches high and, as his light suggests, he usually wears green.

He doesn't always have the same clothes, however, for sometimes he has brown leggings and a green tunic and, at others, he changes the colours 'round. His jacket often has square "scallops," I think they're called (like little turrets upside down); his shoes, unlike some of the other fairies', which are pointed, are squaretoed, and his hat is like a peaked cap turned up at the sides, rather like the old-fashioned "deer stalker."

His work being with the trees, he has wings which are long and thin like a dragon fly's and, when he uses them, they sparkle in the sun – otherwise they're transparent and colourless. His skin is handsomely sunburned, his features are beautifully modelled and he has blue eyes and fair, curly hair.

Myrris, in contrast, is very dark, with an almost alabaster skin. She always wears flowing pink gowns which display her pretty legs through the material. Her hair is straight and reaches to her waist; her eyelashes are exceptionally sweeping, framing her soft, brown eyes.

All the girls are beautiful but, to me, at any rate, she is more exquisite than any of the others.

I'm sure that if fairies had babies, she would make a wonderful mother but, as they don't, she lavishes her maternal instinct on her bulbs. I've seen her fondle one of these as devotedly as any parent its child and she's never happier than when Daphne gives her new ones to tend.

As her work is on the ground, she has no wings and, except when Gorjus carries her, she's unable to fly. *[True at the time of writing. – D.C.]* She once confided to me that she is always a little frightened on these trips but she swore me to secrecy for fear of hurting Gorjus' feelings. She explained that he loves so much to show her his work high up in the boughs of the trees that she prefers to suffer her fears during these excursions, rather than risk upsetting him.

One day they tried to show me the part of the communal house where they live. Outwardly, it has the appearance of one of the large, solid, Victorian buildings which surround them; in fact, it is very similar to the one in which Daphne lives. It has windows but no glass, and by getting down on my hands and knees, I was able to place my eye against one of these apertures and peer in.

To them, this room is perfect but, to tell you the truth, I couldn't see anything at all. It had four walls and some sort of covering on the floor but, apart from a few tiny mounds which I imagine must have been a bed and some chairs, I could see nothing to account for their enthusiasm. However, I told them that I thought it beautiful and they appeared satisfied.

Another day they escorted me up the road to the spot where they have their weekend cottage. Normally they live in the big community house but each pares also has a sort of hideout where they can go when their work is finished.

Outwardly, its appearance was in every way similar to the big house, apart from its size, and I'm afraid that I could see as little of the inside as of the other. I'm hoping, however, that as I progress, my sight will improve, because it would give me the greatest pleasure to share their pride in their possessions. To them, this home is obviously the dream cottage which all lovers have in mind, but so rarely in fact.

On another visit, they asked me to show them something which they hadn't previously seen. I produced my watch but I'm afraid it meant almost as little to them as their possessions did to me. They could see a circular object and the hands, but when I opened the back and displayed the works, they didn't seem to see anything at all. I'm hoping that they, too, will advance sufficiently for the exciting little wheels and their movement to become visible to them, because I'm sure that Gorjus, at any rate, if initiated, must share the curiosity which most males exhibit towards "what make the wheels go 'round."

Their devotion is most touching and there's never any sign of the human failure of vying one against the other; in fact, each tries to add to the other's understanding as they learn.

A Year Later

Daphne and I have just realized that over a year has passed since we last wrote about fairies.

At that time I couldn't see their home but now I'll do my best to describe it to you.

It's situated in one of the unused building sites near here and I imagine that they made it there because the long grass gives them the impression of living in a wood.

The house itself is of a distinctly strange design and, when I asked them where they got the idea for it, they replied, "From us. We wanted something different."

Originally, I had seen only the outside, which appeared quite normal, but on looking inside, there didn't seem to be anything there. After a bit, I could see what appeared to be one big room taking up all the space. It was oval like an egg and I presumed that they had but this one all-purpose apartment.

On later visits, however, the egg filled in and rooms of queer shapes came into view; one, which was Gorjus' "den," being rather like a fir cone. Another had the appearance of an electric bulb, but I suppose it really represented one of Myrris' charges. This one turned out to be her special room where she plans out her work for the following weeks or possibly years.

Their bedroom is composed of a lot of circular festoons, each intertwining with others and holding the whole together. They're immensely proud of what is obviously a terrifically ingenious piece of engineering but, although I wouldn't tell them for anything in the world, it doesn't look exactly cozy.

I've got the idea that the inside of my watch is partly responsible because they told me a short while after they began to see it properly, that they were redecorating their rest-room. Anyway, it seems to have created quite a sensation in the fairy world and I must admit that I'm not surprised. Their home has become quite a showplace, to which the neighbouring fairies flock, and I understand that it has begun quite a new style in house designing.

I only hope that the bed, at any rate, is more comfortable than it looks. When I asked where it was, Myrris draped herself over a slender, circular piece of stalk so that her head was on a level with her toes, her body forming a loop.

"Are you comfortable?" I asked, doing my best not to look surprised.

"It's wonderful," she cooed delightedly. "It's much the comfiest way of sleeping that I've ever tried."

I then asked Gorjus where his bed was.

"It's over here," he said, as he proceeded to climb up inside of a circle until he was facing the ground with his body fitting neatly 'round the half-arc.

"You'll fall out when you're asleep," I warned him.

"I don't," he assured me. "It's lovely. I can watch Myrris from here without turning my head."

"But why don't you fall?" I asked him.

He looked puzzled. "Why should I?" he said.

'Well, if I draped myself like that from my ceiling, I'd fall," I replied.

"Because you think you would," he said. "You try after making up your mind that you won't, and you won't."

That evening as I climbed onto my bed, I looked up at the ceiling.

"Of course I'd fall," I thought. "No, that's no good," I admonished myself. "Think 'you won't' and you won't." "I wouldn't fall." I kept repeating. "Of course I wouldn't." But it was no good because I really didn't believe it. I will one day, though. It's ridiculous being beaten by a little chap like Gorjus, but perhaps it's because I've no incentive. You see, I've no Myrris on whom I could gaze without turning my head.

When I went to see the fairies the next time, they were very excited. On making enquiries, they told me that their house was to be one of the star attractions of the Congress. They had spent hours redecorating it and they now wanted to show me the result.

The bedroom was still the inside of my watch but it was now lit in graduated shades of pale pink. Myrris' hoop was looped with threads of pink flummery stuff, which she informed me were thought forms composed of messages of welcome, and I resisted the obvious temptation of telling her that on Earth, these would hardly be considered a suitable decoration for a beautiful girl's bedroom.

Gorjus' part of the room was hung with different materials which he explained showed the vibrationary colours of some of the countries from which the delegates were coming.

Next I was shown Myrris' "bulb room," which had now grown a magnificent daffodil. One couldn't see it from the outside, although it was much taller than the roof-fairy magic, I suppose. Although they could both move about this room quite easily, it appeared to be solid and showed the inside of a bulb in the process of flowering. At the same time, one was somehow able to see not only its present state of progress but its activities from the moment it came to life until its period of repose had descended again.

Gorjus' fir cone had been replace by the inside of a tree trunk. I asked him why he had banished the cone and he explained that it was represented in the story, even then being unfolded, of the growth of the whole tree. Again I looked, and this time I could see that it was as he said. I was shown the evolving life from the moment that it first began to stir in the cone until it had become a magnificent fir tree, many feet high.

"That ridiculous," I said to Gorjus. "That's an enormous tree. How can you get it inside your tiny house?"

"It was a bit difficult," he said airily. "In fact we had to do quite a lot of experimenting before we finally solved the problem. As the tree grows, the house does too."

I looked to make sure, but the house was its normal size, so I asked him to show me the proceedings again.

I saw the room with its cone as I lay in the grass with one eye glued to the window. Exciting things began to happen and the tree was once more fully grown before I remembered the problem of the expanding house. I took my eye from the window and looked up to where the tree should have been but there was nothing there and the house was its usual size.

"Where is it?" I asked.

"There," said Gorjus, as he pointed to the window. I looked again but we were back at the cone stage.

"I give up," I said. Gorjus smiled in rather a superior way, I thought. I still haven't solved the problem.

We had decided, on a previous visit, that we would meditate so, when the excitement of the Congress was over and I again visited my two little friends, I sat down by their cottage and waited for instructions, because I was anxious to meditate as though I were a fairy and not a man.

"Absorb as much power as you can," they told me, "then relax and see what happens. That's all."

I did as I was told and, as soon as I had unflexed my muscles, I could feel that I was on the move. This was rather interesting to me because I've always understood that one must raise one's thoughts and that it is their height which governs one's ultimate destination. I've also found that, as a rule, several minutes elapse after the initial relaxation before a movement is felt, but now, with this simpler method, I found that I was obtaining results much earlier in the proceedings.

We stopped quite soon, however, and I opened my eyes to a familiar scene. My room.

"What in Heaven's name are we doing here?" I asked.

"We so wanted to see it, George," they said apologetically, "and we aren't allowed to come except during meditation."

I felt very flattered that they should so ardently desire to see my very ordinary possessions that they had voluntarily given up the opportunity of some far more uplifting experience.

I wondered what would interest them the most, but I needn't have worried because everything they touched and peered into might have been from the Fourth plane, at least, judging by their excitement.

My shaving brush fascinated them beyond belief. In fact, I had to lather my face with it and complete operations with my razor before they would believe its normal purpose. They rocked with laughter at my appearance, buried in white foam, and each sweep of the razor had to be examined for hairs.

My pyjamas caused great amusement and I confess that I was obliged to undress and put them on before they were satisfied. They wanted me to get into bed but I put my foot down because I know that they frequently see Daphne in hers.

"But we want to see *you*," they insisted, so – yes, I meekly obeyed. There's no question about it, those two can twist me 'round their minute fingers in no mean tune.

I won't go through a list of everything that fascinated them. I can only tell you that I began to take a new interest in the familiar objects about me. They wanted to know what kept the bristles in my toothbrush. I'd never even thought about this and I was obliged to admit ignorance on the subject – however, I've found the answer for them now.

They asked me why I drink whiskey. I explained to them that it gives me a pleasant feeling of stimulation.

"But power does that," they argued.

"It wouldn't be much fun to invite people to a party and just absorb power though." I tried to explain but I knew that I'd never get it across.

"But we have lovely parties doing just that," they said.

"Yes, but you dance - there isn't room here," I said hopefully.

"You could do a little dance," they insisted.

I've often been tempted to try out their advice, just to watch the expression on my friends' faces, but I haven't. If I did, I don't somehow feel that anyone would come to a party of mine again.

The next time I visited them, we meditated again and, on this occasion, we reached quite a high plane of the Astral. They were as pleased as though we'd attained seventh heaven and they overwhelmed me with gratitude for helping them.

"We aren't awfully good at meditation," they confessed. "Sometimes we think that we're too happy together. Our lovely home means so much to us; in fact, we're really too contented with our ordinary, everyday I lives."

"Well, don't be sad about it," I said. "It's what we all want but most of us don't get. It's suffering that makes people turn to spiritual comfort. It's just the same on Earth; the happiest people are often those who have a satisfactory family life, a nice fat income and a comfortable home. Occasionally, of course, you do find people who are happy without a lot of material possessions and that's better still."

"We've reached great heights of spirituality occasionally, but it's always been when we're exchanging power and not during meditation."

"But isn't that the time you're supposed to get your best results?"

They seemed doubtful. "You see," Gorjus continued, "it just happens. It isn't when we're striving mentally so, in a way, we don't deserve it."

"But that's a ridiculous thing to say," I said. "Apart from material possessions, you know quite well that we can't have things that we haven't earned. People can make thought forms of china and furniture and things like that, but nobody can make thought forms of spiritual growth and understanding, and they're the only things worth having."

I paused to think about what I'd just said. I'd never put the facts into words before. To talk to my human friends like that would embarrass me. I should feel stuffy and as though I were preaching and being rather a prig, but fairies are different because their understanding is streets ahead of most human beings.

They've never been confused by the necessity of acquiring possessions in order to keep warm and to feed themselves. Granted, they have the equivalent in their houses, their jewels, their all-important promotions in status and the privileges which are attached. But all these are rewards for the work which they have accomplished and for the performance of acts of kindness, which so often go unrewarded on Earth.

I came out of my daydream and I could see that the words which had been spoken almost without preliminary thought had comforted them.

"Why don't you try and set up a standard for pares," I suggested. "Be an ideal couple to whom others whose union hasn't been so successful can come for advice."

They held hands and gazed at each other.

"Ideal couple," they repeated and, wreathed in smiles, they wandered away, leaving me to ponder on the fact that perhaps, in some strange way, I, a member of quite a different evolution, had supplied them with the key which may one day unlock the door guarding the mysteries of the universe.

– George

MOVUS AND MIRILLA
OBSERVER: LUDWIG

SHRUBS

by Movus

As you already know, I work with the shrubs. I tended them for many years on the Astral plane and, when I wished to come to earth, I requested that I might continue to work with them, as I love them more than all the other plants. At one time I worked with trees, and I loved them too, but I always felt that they were so large, and I so small, that they couldn't really need me. Shrubs, not being so big, seem more friendly; not that the trees had ever been anything but kind and grateful for my care.

There are so many species of shrubs that I feel my work includes that of all the other fairies. There are the beautiful flowering ones, both large and small; there are evergreens and those which bloom and fade in a few weeks. Each is as individual as another fairy to me, or as a man to you. Some are bold, other shy; some flaunt their beauty proudly while others seem amazed at what they achieve year by year.

There is always a bond of love between a fairy and his charges, and to fly in and out of the twigs of advanced shrubs which I have tended for many years is a very pleasant experience. It is as though I'm being bathed in a gently stimulating sunbeam and I'm filled with happiness at their spontaneous affection and their desire to please me.

95

I have many minutes under my control and these tiny entities are guided by my power to any shrub which needs replenishing. They are able to enter the stem and to penetrate any part of the plant towards whom they feel a warm comradeship, for the power which they are exhaling is a gentle form of love-making to them. When the shrub is filled with power, he too feels happy, so he, in his turn, gives pleasure to the minutes who serve him.

In the spring I am particularly busy as all the shrubs which have been recuperating during the winter from the previous year's toil, throw off their lethargy and are filled with the desire to grow and to bring forth flower and fruit. You cannot know the joy with which each one enlarges his first shoots, and when hope thus becomes a fact, I too share in their happiness, for I know that I have contributed to their success.

– Movus

TALL FLOWERS

by Mirilla

My work with the tall flowers remains one of the greatest wonders in life. Each unfoldment is a miracle and the mystery of Nature is my absorbing interest. All my thoughts, during my waking hours, are centred on the idea behind each stage of development, until finally the flower, in all her perfection, opens to bring satisfaction to herself and happiness to all who see her.

Some, naturally, are more beautiful than others, but those who are simple in colour and form are younger sisters, and we know that if they can successfully be brought to flower and seed, in due course they will come to Earth again, more beautiful than before. The young ones require, if possible, even more tender care than those who are more experienced, for their consciousness is minute and it is mostly my thoughts and those of the other attendant entities which convey to them the next stage in their growth. A more advanced flower, such as the larkspur, needs less encouragement from us to persuade her to make further progress.

To do this I give the thought showing the next stage of its activities to the plant and the minutes give it power and strengthen it with their own projections. After awhile I can leave the work to the minutes who continue to add power to my original thought until the work illustrated therein is completed.

I cannot give you any definite period during which a plant requires power as, naturally, they vary, but a healthy, normal one receives it approximately every three days.

It is always a great joy to me when a once sickly flower becomes strong and healthy. If she is very weak she is given power every day. We cannot always

96

make a sick plant well, because she too must make an effort to progress, and sometimes, in spite of all our endeavours, we fail. We are always a little sad when this happens, but we can but do our best and we know that she will soon have another chance. As a rule, plants respond to our love immediately and they thrive on the power which they are given, but sometimes, although every care is bestowed, a healthy one fades, and then we know that the powers of evil have infiltrated our defenses and have sapped the strength from our charge. This is a sad day for us, for we know that we have failed, not in the performance of our duty, but in our vigilance.

To us, our work is more important than anything but spiritual wisdom, although, of course, our studies add to our efficiency. We love attending our halls of learning but we experience greater satisfaction when we are able to prove in practice the knowledge which we have acquired here.

– Mirilla

MOVUS AND MIRILLA
by Ludwig

[At the time that Ludwig met the fairies, he had been learning how to help the earthbound, among whose ranks he himself had so recently been. – D.C.]

At last the great day arrived when, having passed my tests, I was to return to Earth in an endeavour to bring over to our side a temporarily lost soul. Naturally those whom we beginners are sent to aid are carefully picked so that we do not experience failure but, although I was armed with this knowledge, I confess that I was nervous. All went well, however, and I escorted my first "lost one" to the Astral plane.

I was to take tea with Daphne, whatever the result, and when the time came I found the liquid most welcome, but I was too excited to eat. She made me rest and, after a short while, I began to feel refreshed.

"I think you deserve a reward," she said. "I've been talking to Normus and we're going to try to make you see some of the other fairies."

I was still overwrought and I am sure that Daphne had thought out this diversion to help me to forget my weariness.

"We'll try a new experiment," she continued. "I'll turn on some power and we'll see if that will do the trick. In any case, Normus has prepared an address in your honour which he is most anxious to deliver."

I raised my vibrations as high as I was able and Daphne turned on her power. I could already see Normus, who had arrayed himself in magnificent trappings for the occasion. He had been wearing a plain green jacket and leggings when I had seen him before but today he shone in a suit of green brilliants; his belt was of gold and, in place of a feather in his cap, he had a facsimile which appeared also to be made of gold and was crisp to the touch.

One by one, the fairies took shape before my eyes and what a lovely sight they were, the girls in long, pale-coloured robes of lustrous sheen and the boys, like Normus, in suits of brilliants with belts and feathers of silver and bronze.

"I can see!" I said delightedly, and they laughed and jumped in the air, clapping their hands with glee.

"Now, attention," said Normus firmly and, obediently they formed two lines behind him, the girls in the front and the boys in the rear.

He produced a small scroll from apparently nowhere as he commenced to speak.

"Oh, Ludwig, this is a great day for all, for us fairies as well as for you. Unfortunately it is not often that we are seen by Man on Earth or on the Astral, and it is a great joy to us to be able to display our beauty before you. Today is the beginning of a new road and we feel honoured to be among the first to congratulate you. We wish you to know that from now onwards, whenever you set forth, our thoughts will go with you. We are but small, but our thoughts are strong and we know that they will help both you and the person whom you seek to aid. If, at any time, you need more power, please call on us, and one or all will answer, according to your need. We have composed a ceremonial dance in your honour and we hope that you will be able to follow the movements, for each has its meaning and will be seeking to convey our esteem."

Daphne asked me whether I thought that I should be able to see the dance, to which I replied that I would because I was determined that I should. At first, I confess that there appeared before me little more than a series of coloured flashes but, by concentrating deeply, the individual figures soon took shape. The movements, now that I was tuned in, seemed comparatively slow and I could see the fairies bowing, curtseying, doffing their hats and offering invisible gifts.

It was exquisite in every detail and my heart beat strongly with gratitude for this new beauty which my eyes were but now permitted to behold.

After awhile the movements became more rapid and the boys lifted the girls in their arms, floating with them around my head. This all but took my breath away and my one sorrow was that Daphne was unable to share this newfound joy with me.

It was over all too soon. When they had taken up their final poses, I thanked them from the bottom of my heart and I knew that they would now take an increasing part in my life.

When they had gone, Daphne told me of her plan that each of us should adopt a fairy and she asked me if there were any towards whom I had felt particularly attracted. I replied that they were all so exquisite that I should be happy with any and that they should do the choosing.

The next evening she informed me that Movus and Mirilla had expressed a wish to become my fairies and, although I could not remember which they were, I felt sure that, as they wanted to have me for their especial friend, I should love them.

The next occasion that I came to tea, Daphne called and two lovely little people arrived and talked to us.

Mirilla has fair, curly hair falling to her shoulders and normally she wears

white, which is tinged with the colour of the blossoms which she has been tending. She works with the tall flowers and she has wings like a butterfly's, snowy-white and opaque.

I asked her if I might touch them although I was almost afraid that I might injure them.

"Do not fear; they are not nearly as delicate as they look." she encouraged me.

Very carefully I stroked one with the tip of my finger and it felt like the sheerest satin.

Movus is a good-looking little fellow with black hair and sparkling, near-black eyes. He attends the shrubs, which necessitates his flying, his wings being more pointed than Mirilla's.

They are obviously very devoted to one another and on my next visit they related to me the story of their meeting twenty years ago. I will give it to you in their own words.

"I am usually rather a gay fairy," began Movus, for some reason, I had been feeling somewhat off-colour. As a rule, I am a clear, fresh green, like a leaf in spring but, at that time I had gone dull like a tree in August, after a hot summer. I did not know what was wrong with me so I asked my leader if he had any suggestions to make, as I knew that I was not doing my work properly.

" 'You should go out more,' he said. 'You have wings: why stay around here all the time? Fly away to another district - the change of scenery and the fairies around you will do you good. Go for a week. I will do your work.'

"I thanked him for his kindness but, to be truthful, I did not think that a change of scenery would help me. The shrubs are all my friends and I did not like the idea of leaving them, but as I knew that, owing to my faded condition, I was not able to help them as I should, I agreed to go.

"I duly set out and, as I did not mind in which direction I went, I just relaxed and let my wings take me where they would. The shrubs greeted me cheerfully as I flew past, their friendliness helping a little to banish my unhappiness, and I rested that night in the branches of a hawthorn. I do not usually remain with my charges when my work is done but I wished to live as differently as possible for this one week.

"The next day I felt a little refreshed and I noticed that my tone of green was a shade brighter. This, in itself, pleased me for I have always loved beauty and it distressed me to know that my own was dimmed.

"Day followed day, my wings taking me I knew not where. This was not, I knew, the chance meandering of my temporarily ailing consciousness, but the fulfillment of a carefully laid plan by advanced entities whose task in life is guiding those in trouble. I became aware of things on every side which I had not known existed and, at each surprise, I felt new strength enter me.

"On the sixth day I was flying over a field of corn, bright with poppies. I was hovering over a large clump, drinking in the splendour of the scarlet mingled with the gold, when all power seemed to leave me. In the centre of that brilliant array was the most beautiful creature I had ever seen."

He held out his hand to Mirilla and smiled. "I need not describe her to you and I am sure that you will endorse my enthusiasm."

I nodded appreciatively and the little man continued.

100

"My power returned, after a second, like a raging hurricane and I felt as a plant after a storm; it seemed to have swept right through me, taking with it, in its hurried flight, all that remained of my sickness and, in spite of my limpness, I could see that I was shining brighter than ever before."

Mirilla then took up the tale. "As a rule, when I am tending my flowers I do not notice any passerby but, on this occasion I suddenly felt compelled to raise my eyes and there I, too, saw the most beautiful fairy I had ever seen, either here or on the Astral. His body was poised in absolute peace and yet his wings were beating in a fast, steady rhythm. His eyes were closed and yet I knew that he was intensely aware of me.

"I watched him, fascinated, until his eyelids quivered and I beheld eyes as black as soot and yet as gentle as a butterfly's. He hovered for a few seconds more but now his body was straight and strong. He alighted on the flower on which I stood and we gazed at each other in silence. Then he gently took my hand in his. 'We were made for each other,' he whispered."

"She hung her head," broke in Movus, "and for what seemed an entire Earth span I trembled in terror lest she should turn away."

"I was overcome," explained Mirilla. "He has great power, you know. Then my knees gave way and I sank down among the poppy's big black stamens."

"I was horrified in case I had injured her and yet I knew that that could not be," said Movus. "I knelt beside her and I gave her the biggest love-vibration in the world. Soon she opened her eyes and smiled. 'I feel as though I have known you forever,' she said, and I knew that all was well.

"We went straight to her leader and I asked if I might take her with me immediately. He beamed on us both and said that, although she was an excellent worker and would be hard to replace, love must come first.

"That was the beginning of true happiness for me," he said. "Not only has it never left me since that day but at times it becomes almost more than I can bear."

"Then he gives some of it to a poor fairy who hasn't enough so that others, too, benefit from our love," said Mirilla.

"Do you ever feel that his love is too much for you?" I asked her.

She shook her head. "Even when I want more I, too, give some away, for that is what love is for; it should benefit others as well as the two people most concerned."

"It is a pity that more do not understand this fact," I said. "Love between a man and a woman is, as a rule, a selfish thing, to be kept for themselves alone."

"It is not meant to be so," they said firmly, "and we, ourselves, have experienced an added joy after we have given some of this, our most precious possession, to one less fortunate than ourselves."

On another occasion they invited me to their cottage. At their request, I went down on my hands and knees and peered through one of the tiny apertures but, alas, I could see nothing.

"Very pretty," I said politely.

"Oh, Ludwig dear, do not feel that you will distress us. Please tell us truly what you see."

"I feel that I am a bad actor," I said. "I confess that I cannot see anything."

"We did not expect that you would the first time," they said, "but you will. It has taken us years of thought to make all that we have. You are seeing that which we made first, which is just the house, but we are confident that, little by little, the treasures which we have earned will be revealed to you."

"I am happy that I need not pretend," I said. "It would have distressed me that there should be anything but the truth between us and indeed I am sure that I should have been unable to mislead you for long. I will now tell you exactly what I see and I know that you will be as delighted as I when, as you suppose, the things which you love are shown to me.

A Year Later

Since last I wrote I have learned to attune myself far more to the fairies' vibrations and, consequently, I am now better equipped to tell you about them than I was before. Their house has become visible to me in all its beauty and I will do my best to describe it to you.

At first sight, I thought that the house looked very similar to the full-sized ones in the district. However, on studying it with the greater powers of perception which I have now acquired, I noticed that, in reality, the roof was but a mirage and that their home was open to the sky. I asked them how they counteracted the unpleasantness of wind, rain and cold.

"There is a vibration there which prevents them from affecting us," Movus explained. "We feel that unless we can look up to heaven when we relax, we cannot reach as high as we otherwise might."

This is quite understandable as I, myself, have found that I experience far greater spiritual fulfillment when I am in the open air, with the stars to guide my thoughts.

In the hall there is a white staircase spiralling its seemingly endless way to the heights. It does not, of course, end at the first or second floors, nor yet at the roof, but it winds into the distance as far as my human eye can see.

"Have you ever reached the top?" I asked.

Movus smiled. "There is no top or, if there is, we have not found it. We have often tried but always it stretches as far into the sky as it appears to do from here."

'What happens when you reach your highest point," I enquired, "and why cannot you go further?"

"Always something happens," he said gravely, "and when we regain consciousness, we are at the foot again."

He began: 'There have been so many occasions that I scarcely know which one to choose.' I waited patiently while he pondered and I could see that even the dull reflection of his memories filled him and Mirilla, too, with indescribable bliss.

Always, to put these experiences into words is to remove most of the glory, for it is what one *feels* rather than what one sees or hears which is so uplifting and yet, at the same time, so unbearable.

I have spent many hours endeavouring to put my own reactions into a form which can be grasped and at least partially understood by those who have not been as fortunate as I. I fear, though, that I invariably fail, so I can scarcely hope successfully to bring before you the enthralling sensations of another evolution.

As Movus spoke he somehow enabled me to participate in their experiences too. I will give you his own words or, rather, the words which came to my mind as my little friend gave me his thoughts.

"I think that one of the most wonderful of our experiences occurred two nights ago. Mirilla and I had spent a quiet day, it being Sunday, and in the evening we decided to climb the stairs. We stood at the foot, hand in hand, gazing upwards for awhile, and then we began to mount.

"We always enjoy every moment of this journey for there are so many things to see. Quite soon we look down on the houses of the other fairies and if any of them notice us, we wave and they send thought forms to us, wishing us well. Later we have the birds as our companions and then we leave the Earth plane for the Astral.

"On this occasion, our hearts soon became lighter and our bodies too. We felt more buoyant than the air and our thoughts seemed to bubble out of our minds to make exciting patterns on the atmosphere above us. Later they became less personal and formed without any effort on our part; they seemed to embrace all humanity, the Earth, the sky and every living thing within them.

"It is difficult to explain this loss of self; we knew that we were still together and yet we did not seem to be anywhere. This may sound as though we were only half-conscious but that would be very far from the truth; we were wider awake than we had ever been before. We did not actually understand a great deal more than we usually do, as is sometimes the case, but we knew that we were seeking the Ultimate Purpose.

"If only we had an inkling of what that is. When we're down here it does not seem to matter so very much; there is all Time before us and we know that eventually we shall understand. But up there, it is entirely different; it is essential that we should know, otherwise there is no reason for our constant toil.

"We experienced a feeling of futility and yet we sensed that we were closer to 'knowing' than we had ever been before. I think that we half expected the sky to open and for GOD to come and reveal Himself." He paused. "We felt, not only that, but that He should reveal Himself. I think that we actually expected it as something inevitable, something which had to be.

"Of course, it did not happen. In reality, although we felt that He must, we also knew that He would not, so that there was no sense of frustration, only a glorious certainty that one day He would."

I, myself, know that feeling so well, so I can endorse Movus' words. On paper the experience probably sounds disappointing . . . unreal . . . perhaps even pointless, but I can assure you that nothing can be further from the truth. Each of these experiences is for a purpose; they are given to us at the exact moment that we are ready for them; they are essential to our development and without them no one can progress far.

On my next visit I was shown the communal room which Movus and Mirilla share for sleeping and for entertaining their friends. It is decorated in silver and blue, with a soft light coming from I know not where, unless it emanates from the little people themselves. There is a dais at one end upon which they rest. It is softly draped from ceiling to floor with a protecting veil behind which they can retire and remain unseen when others are present. This desire for privacy when possibly a conference is in progress has nothing to do with the love-act of exchanging power.

When many are gathered together, whether Man, Fairy or members of the other evolutions, there is always an outflow of power which may be used for many purposes. Movus and Mirilla are very spiritual entities and with the added power of their friends, they love to retire and seek for enlightenment on whatever subject they have been discussing.

It is as they did of old, when the priests consulted the Oracle. This was no imaginary act for the purpose of deluding the public, for the priests either were themselves mediums, or worked with them, and were indeed capable of receiving advice from those who had died. If the priests were sincere, the messages received were from worthy sources; it was only when they had fallen from grace through sin that the power was withdrawn and lesser entities took the place of the great ones, giving useless and sometimes harmful counsel.

Thus, when the fairies are in doubt about some action to be taken, they meet to discuss the matter and then give power and pray for assistance.

I asked what happened behind the veil on these occasions but Movus shook his head. "We do not know, ourselves," he replied. "Whoever retires goes into trance and, through them, those who wait receive the instructions which we seek."

I was a little puzzled as obviously there could be no voice as with human trance mediumship. "Do you receive thought forms?" I enquired.

104

"I do not think so," he replied. "At least, we never see them. We just KNOW, that is all."

"But is it necessary for any to go into trance? Would not the answer come if you just asked and waited?"

"No," he replied, "we have tried but nothing happens. One or two must retire and, through them, the answer comes."

On my next visit they showed me the room in which they work. It is filled with golden light, like the sun, and is, they explained, very helpful in evolving ideas. Perhaps a thought strikes them just before they are leaving home for essential work and they have no time to ponder upon it or to decide whether it can be put to use. They therefore leave it trapped in the confines of the room and, in the invigorating golden ray, the thought grows. When they return, possibly a week later, they will scrutinize it carefully to ascertain whether the original idea is worth studying or whether it should be released in the outside world to evolve in its own time.

I asked them how the thought differed after its bath of gold from the time they had conceived it. They assured me that during the week it would become sufficiently tangible for them to judge its quality. Without this ability to hold it in the ray, the thought would evolve so slowly that months might go by before they would notice it again, by which time its term of possible usefulness might have elapsed.

They seem to use this room as an incubator, or forcing house, for all their ideas. They showed me a thought form of a plan devised by Movus for connecting several shrubs n one area by power channels, somewhat as a house is wired for electricity, his idea being that power, instead of feeding one shrub only, would supply all in the circuit. I thought it an excellent plan but Movus shook his head. On enquiring as to the reason of its failure, he explained that it had not made the least difference because his own power was insufficient to travel beyond the first shrub.

I suggested that he must also discover how to harness the main stream, which is limitless, so that it would flow along the channels without first passing through his own body. But this suggestion was not practical because, of course, it is essential for the power to make its way through the fairies' bodies before it is coarse enough to be of use to the plants. They showed me many such thoughts, each one promising in theory, but it may be many months, years or even lives, before some of them can be proved in practice. They know, however, that the idea behind each is good, and that even if they are unable to enlarge upon it so that it may be brought to a successful conclusion, they were among those who helped to create it and that, in time, it will bear fruit. This is how we all should work for to take the long view is the only satisfactory way of making plans. When we are on Earth, many of us think that a lifetime is all that we have, but it is, in reality, such a very small I flash in the eternity of time.

To me, who made far from a success of my last life, this is a comforting thought, but to many it may be just the opposite, for the idea of returning again and again to expiate long forgotten sins may seem unfair.

However, a sin, whether recent or a million years old, is still a sin and is part of one's true self until it has been blotted out by suffering physically and mentally a similar hurt to the one which we, ourselves, inflicted on somebody else. We have all lived in crueler times than these, when to torture those who displeased us was quite a normal practice; we should, therefore, not be surprised if pain grips us in our limbs, head, or our abdomen, according to which part of the anatomy we inflicted the agony for which we are now making restitution.

How often does the self-righteous cry, "What have I done to deserve this?" cross the lips of those who suffer? Always this question should be asked and, if it is asked with a genuine desire for understanding, the truth will always be given.

The fairies understand this idea of the long view so much better than do most human beings at a similar stage of evolution. Naturally they prefer to obtain results themselves, but if they do not achieve success even after they have toiled for years, they have the philosophical outlook that nothing is wasted, for they know that the idea to which they have contributed so much time and thought will be brought to perfection by other minds more advanced than their own.

It is hard that we must cease to describe our experiences, which grow more wonderful as we all advance and as we become more attuned to the little people who now play such an enchanting part in our lives. I know that I do not speak for myself alone when I say that, with so much left unsaid, we all hope that several years from now another true fairy story will be told, by which time we may be able to take you with us mentally to spheres at present beyond our reach.

– Ludwig

NAMSOS AND SIRILLA
OBSERVER: RONALD

INSECTS
by Namsos

Sirilla and I have been waiting many months for this opportunity to tell you about our tasks and a little about ourselves.

Life has always been full of interest but it was restricted to our work with Nature. Now, so many exciting experiences have been ours that we have all come to the realization that, although Nature is wonderful, there are many other ways by which we can use our powers to help man as well as the plants and animals.

Healing is the work which, apart from the task which I mainly came to Earth to perform, appeals to me the most. To be able to see the rays at work and to watch the gradual improvement in the sufferer's body is both interesting and gratifying. Each session brings new knowledge and an increased desire to give more, in order that the healing may be hastened.

My main work lies among the smallest members of the animal kingdom. The worms are my favourites for they do only good to the soil and the plants draw the nourishment which they require for their physical bodies from it. I love all animals and insects, even the ones that do harm to the plants, because they, too, have a desire to live and it is beyond their understanding that it is wrong to destroy their younger brothers and sisters.

I always strive to persuade them to eat the grass, for that thrives when the blades are constantly removed, but I haven't had much success. Occasionally, if I give all my thoughts for a long time, I have urged a snail onto the lawn, but they don't enjoy the slim grass blades like they do a tender shoot.

I know, though, that I mustn't give in, for it is the ambition of every fairy who is in charge of the little animals to guide them so that they may live without doing harm. I know that when your plants are eaten by caterpillars and slugs it is very distressing for you, but please understand that they have the desire to live just as you have and, to live, they must eat and, like you, they prefer something that tastes good. I know that you must destroy them to save your plants, but please do it without hatred in your hearts and remember that you are depriving them of this particular Earth span. Therefore, kill them with thoughts of kindness, because they are really very lovable when you know them as I do.

Many of the insects do good in the garden as their movement stimulates the physical bodies of the plants. Unfortunately, I am unable to guide them as I used to do on the Astral plane, and so they usually stay in one small sector close to their homes instead of moving from place to place and helping the plants to grow as well as themselves. I have tried many ways to make them follow me but I never succeed. It is a pity, because so much valuable energy is expended in doing good to such a small area.

Dealing with these little animals has taught me many things and I am very grateful to them, for they have helped me to progress. They have shown me how even the tiniest creatures will respond to love and, even though they don't obey me, I know that they love me in return.

I've learned, too, to be patient; it is only after hours of concentration that I can sometimes make them move even one inch in the direction in which I desire them to go, but I realize that if I can do only that, then it must be possible to guide them completely if I could but concentrate more deeply for longer periods.

To me, my work is the most interesting of any, because animals, however small, are in a higher state of evolution than even trees, however big and old. It is true that a tree understands more, but that is because he is more limited physically and is unable to move from place to place, nor has he any desire to do so.

My little animals are experiencing the beginning of a new existence and, naturally, they aren't sensitive enough to answer my attempts at direction. The fault is partly mine, though; I am not sufficiently determined because, if I was, I could control them. I've watched fairies in a higher status than mine guide them from place to place at will, and one day I shall be able to do the same.

– *Namsos*

BARKS OF TREES
by Sirilla

When I came to Earth, I had the fixed intention of devoting my entire span to my work. I have already told Daphne that I am a comparative novice with the barks of trees because I had always worked with the tall flowers. But there was no vacancy on Earth with them for years to come, so I agreed to learn my present task.

As a rule, fairies spend many years with their particular charges on the Astral before coming to Earth to work with them, but I was with the trees for only seven before I received my appointment to come down. I decided, therefore that under no circumstances would I divide my interests by becoming involved with a boy fairy.

I carried out my intentions faithfully for fifteen years and then, one day as I was working halfway up a tree trunk, I heard a scratching coming from far below me. I took no notice because this is a very common method by which boys who can't fly try to attract my attention.

This time, though, the scratching continued and, as I found that the noise was interfering with my concentration, I stopped and said, "will you please go away? I'm busy."

The fairy looked so dejected at my rebuke that I was touched. I had been expecting a cheeky grin, but this one hung his head and turned away. I hesitated a moment and then I said, "Don't go. I shall be finished here soon and perhaps we could have a little talk."

The fairy smiled back shyly and sat down.

When I had completed my work, I flew down and he rose to his feet. He seemed very nervous so I gave him a little love-vibration. He was almost overcome and he told me, when he had recovered sufficiently, that he had never before received a vibration from anyone whom he truly loved.

It was not very long after this that he asked me to become his paris; I told him that I had made up my mind to devote my Earth span to my work but that I was quite willing to exchange power with him. This offer didn't appear to satisfy him; he told me that he wanted the right to look after me and to know that should danger threaten me, he would be aware of it even before I was.

It was ten years before I agreed to abandon my principle, and what a poor thing it was in comparison to what I have received in exchange, for Namsos is the kindest little fairy in the Universe and I am the most fortunate entity in existence. He gives so much and asks so little but, despite this, he declares that I give him far more than he had dared to hope.

My work with the trunks of trees is exceedingly interesting. You are probably aware of the activity which takes place there and, of course, many of Namsos' little animals run up and down the cracks, performing physically what the unites do astrally.

To you, a tree trunk may be a somewhat cumbersome thing but, although it is strong, it is very sensitive; it opens to receive the sun and the rain; it turns itself inward when the wind is cold; it quivers with delight at the touch of either Fairy or Man. You will realize that the trunk is the main home of the tree-soul; of course he lives in his branches as well as in each leaf and flower, but the work is directed there from the trunk.

A tree is a very evolved member of the plant kingdom and many of them have been on Earth, in their present form, for thousands of years. Being so big, they require more than one fairy to direct operations; Gorjus is my co-partner, but his work is somewhat different from mine, his task being to aid the tree to come to flower and fruit, while I help with his general growth.

When the tree is old, he is able to perform his duty without prompting from us and our work then entails only the directing of the unites and minutes to give power, but a young tree must be coaxed and petted and instructions given by his various attendant-entities daily. As he grows in body, so he also does in mind and, by degrees, we are able to leave more of the mental work to him.

Year by year as I watch the trunks grow, not only upward but in strength and thickness, I rejoice because I know that unless Man needs him for his own use, he will still be there, growing in knowledge and stature thousands of years after my own Earth span is over.

I know, too, that my striving on his behalf has helped him to become what he is today and that when I return to the Astral plane, my thoughts will still be embedded in his consciousness, not just lying dormant, their work done, but ever urging him on to greater glory.

The charges of the other fairies may sometimes be more exquisite in colour and form, but in comparison, their span is short. Long after they have returned to the Astral and have come back to Earth again and again, my charges will still be giving of their same beauty to a generation of Man as yet unborn. There may even be some who have loved a particular tree who will return to Earth perhaps thousands of years hence to enjoy him again.

Sometimes I feel that my work is almost too big for so small a person, and yet I know that if I were not capable, I would never have been entrusted with my wonderful task.

– Sirilla

NAMSOS AND SIRILLA

by Ronald

[When at last it became his turn to write, Ronald was obliged to look a long way back in his notebook in order to find the beginning of his friendship with the fairies. I had asked him to keep a record of events one afternoon soon after he had met Namsos and Sirilla, when they had told us their love story. – D.C.]

I will give you the tale as the two fairies told it to us. Namsos began:

I'm not a very good-looking fairy, I'm afraid, and that used to worry me. Eventually it became like a nightmare and I was unable to perform my tasks properly. Because my work was bad, my looks didn't improve and so it might have gone on indefinitely.

But one day, when I was wandering along rather aimlessly, I came to a tree and halfway up the trunk I saw the most beautiful fairy I had ever seen. As I watched her, I wondered how I could attract her attention.

I gave a little scratch on the bark but she didn't take any notice. I scratched again and, after a pause, she looked at me. I hung my head, overcome by my boldness, but I could feel that she wasn't really annoyed.

My courage returned to me sufficiently to look at her again and I saw that she was smiling. We became friends – indeed, I loved her from the moment I saw her. After a short time I begged her to become my paris, but she told me that she had dedicated her Earth span to her work. I refused to give up hope and, after ten years, she gave me her consent.

He beamed. "Isn't she beautiful?" he said proudly, putting his arm 'round her waist.

Sirilla regarded him fondly. "I used to think him plain," she said, "but now I know he's beautiful."

I smiled with them then, because what she said is quite true. He has a light of great sweetness and patience in his eyes. Doubtless Sirilla's love for him has given him the former, and his work, which is waging a seemingly losing battle with insects, the latter, or rather, has augmented it, because no one without the patience of the Sphinx would ever undertake such a maddening task in the first place.

I watched him the other day spend half an hour trying to persuade a slug to move away from a plant with no result at all. He didn't appear in the least put out by his apparent failure and he remarked that, after another two or three hours, he would possibly succeed.

"If I don't," he added, "I shall know that I wasn't concentrating enough." He shook his head. "If only I could really concentrate for even three minutes at a time, I know I could succeed, but I can't, and there the whole trouble lies."

Sirilla is indeed a lovely little person, with her fair, curly hair and intensely dark eyes. Her complexion is very pale and her lips the colour of pink rose petals. She often wears pink or pale yellow and has cream-coloured butterfly wings.

Namsos' hair is straight and brown and is usually hidden under a round cap. He wears brown, with red laces in his leggings, or red boots made of soft material, tapering to a point at the toe and with a jagged edge 'round the ankle. His face is brown, too, and he looks rather older than the others.

He is really very wise for so young an entity and he has a quiet philosophy of his own. He told me once that he has never worried about anything since the moment that Sirilla agreed to become his paris. He maintains that if he has done his best, he can do no more, and if he has failed in what he was endeavouring to accomplish, then there are others more powerful than he to take over the work. He is a great believer in the goodness of an experience even though, at the time, everything appears desperately bad.

"Once I used to fight unpleasantness," he said to me one day, "but now I just let it roar and rush past me and I find that, whatever the outward conditions, inside I remain the same. Fighting troubles only attracts elementals, you know," he continued gravely, "and they're much more difficult to overcome than the original misfortune. The more you fight, the more are they able to sap your will and strength, because you, yourself, are giving them the power to do so. Just relax," he ended. "Ask for help from those above and the trouble will die a natural death and leave you stronger than you were before."

I was most anxious to learn how they entertain their friends and, as always, they were only too keen to enlighten me. But first I had to give them minute descriptions of my mother's dinner parties: what I wore, the colour and shape of all the women's dresses, what flowers were on the table and the exact arrangement of each dish of food and the colour of the wines. The first time they questioned me, I fear that I was a great disappointment to them because I'm not very observant about these sorts of things. I remembered that my mother had been wearing blue and that she had given me a rose to put in my buttonhole, but that was about all.

However, now I'm as greedy for detail as any society gossip writer and, to my mother's amazement, and the cook's delight, I insist on viewing each dish before it leaves the kitchen. I've no doubt that the guests think it a little strange that I leave the table between each course, but I let them put their own construction upon my frequent absences.

In exchange for this small concession to good manners, I've received a wealth of most interesting information. At the beginning of a fairy party, each guest gives out some power. To me, each power flash looks the same but both my little friends were amazed when I informed them of this point.

"But, Ronald, you must see how Namsos' differs from mine," said Sirilla.

"Show me," I said, and she shot out a tiny dart of white light, which was followed almost immediately by an identical one from Namsos.

"They look the same to me," I said.

"Oh, Ronald, they can't," they said in unison. "Now, look again, carefully."

I tried hard but it was no good; I couldn't see any difference at all.

"But can't you see that there's much more patience in Namsos' power?" Sirilla insisted.

"But how can I see an abstract thing like patience in a tiny, momentary flash?"

They were really shocked this time. "Abstract?" they chorused. "Patience, abstract? How can you say such a thing? It's as definite as we are."

"Show me some then," I said.

"Go on, Namsos. You're better at it than I am," urged Sirilla.

I looked at Namsos and slowly he lit up with a pale blue light.

"He's going blue," I said triumphantly.

"Doesn't he look lovely?" sighed Sirilla ecstatically. I looked at him again and I saw that he really was beautiful. Before, I had been aware only of his kind little face, but now he revealed a mental maturity beyond his years.

He returned to normal. "Now, Sirilla, you show him determination."

I watched her and her whole tiny face as wrapt in concentration, as though each atom was working overtime.

"She hasn't changed colour," I remarked.

"No, but all the matter in her body is transformed. Can't you see it?"

"Yes, I think I can," I said, "but I was expecting her to change colour too."

"Oh, Ronald, dear, you've a lot to learn," they said. "Our power differs in colour, substance, transparency, movement and many other ways."

"I'll never be able to see all that in that flash," I said dejectedly.

"You will," they said. "You must, because otherwise you won't know the real us at all. Our bodies are only like a suit of clothes to you; it's what's inside that can tell you every little thing about us."

I tried awfully hard; they were very patient over my shortcomings and, after several efforts, I really did begin to see the difference; in fact, I can't think now how I could have been so blind. Each power is, indeed, quite distinct and when they blend it, a third person seems to be present, which, I suppose, in fact, there is; the person which they'll become when they have lost the desire for bodies, separate thoughts and individual actions and reactions. With Namsos' patience and Sirilla's determination, combined with their other qualities, I feel sure that one day they will be someone very great.

I seem to have lost track of the fairy party so we'll have to retrace our steps, or thoughts, a bit. Having given some power, each guest is escorted into the enclosure so that they can absorb some of it themselves, then, refreshed, they take part in the dancing, games or discussions.

If they prefer, they can relax and watch sequences of thought formations which have been devised especially for the occasion. These, I imagine, are in the nature of a cinema show to us, some making them laugh, others leaving them in a state of near-ecstasy, while yet others fill them with an increased desire to learn and serve.

Sometimes a leader, far above their own status, comes and talks to them, not necessarily about their work, but his presence adds interest to the party and his power enables them to understand, without being told, some of the hidden truths which each fairy desires to know.

Perhaps this all sounds rather dull but, after all, what do we do at parties on Earth? We eat, drink, dance, gossip and play cards. For the younger guests, fairies, too, have dancing and there is always the power enclosure, which I myself can assure you gives you a far greater feeling of elation than any whiskey.

On several occasions, they had both asked me to their home but, each time, although I accepted with pleasure, we talked so much that I always had to leave before the promised visit took place.

One day they greeted me by saying that they refused to speak one word until we were outside their cottage. They escorted me to a neighbouring garden and, there in the corner, by the vegetables, I saw a true fairy house. It was pale pink and looked exactly as though it was made of icing sugar. The shape was somewhat similar to the surrounding houses but they had definitely succeeded in giving it the fairy touch, I could easily believe, by waving a magic wand. The roof was green, rather like cut crystal, and it shone in the sun, emerald beams, turning the surrounding atmosphere into a sparkling, transparent mist.

No acting was required when I expressed my appreciation.

"Just wait until you've seen inside," they said confidently, but I was far from being sure of myself. I knew that all the others had failed to see anything at their first attempt and some could see little now.

"Don't you think that we had better wait a bit?" I suggested diffidently.

They smiled. "We'll make you see," they replied, so I went on my hands and knees and I placed my eye against one of the tiny windows. I could see a room but that was all. They knew from my expression that we had failed, so they hid their own disappointment and hastened to comfort me.

Two Months Later

Since writing the above, I have reached the stage when I can unravel a few of the simpler thought formations with which their house is decorated. It's fascinating pulling them to pieces, but how much more gratifying it must be to make them.

Here's an example: there was one floating about the fairies' home and I asked them whether it would drift away. They replied that it was quite safe as they had anchored it, but that it could move at will within a certain area. The form was about an inch square and mostly green in colour, with streaks of orange and small blue dots.

I watched it for some time to see whether my brain would translate its meaning without conscious effort on my part, as it does the fairies' projections.

Nothing happened, however, so I set to work to unravel each separate idea. First I concentrated on the streaks and, as I looked, I saw that they weren't just darts of orange as I had imagined, but tiny flames, each varying in shape and colour. They didn't seem to lead my thoughts anywhere so I turned my attention to the blue dots and, by degrees, I realized that each was a perfect little heart.

The whole formation was obviously, then, a love thought between Sirilla and Namsos and it struck me that perhaps I was prying into their private affairs.

I turned to them questioningly, but as they were watching me eagerly, I presumed that they wished me to proceed with my investigation. I was left now with the green background which, on closer scrutiny, appeared to be moving, and I soon realized that it was a river.

Hearts. Flames. Running water.

"My heart flows towards you like a flame . . ." I began. No, that wasn't any good. "The flame in my heart is quenched by the cooling depth of . . . what?" I admit that I was rather pleased with that one but I didn't feel it was quite right. "The quietness of my heart becomes flame 'neath the flood of your love."

I looked at them quizzically but I could see from the expression on their faces that I still hadn't got it.

"You've missed something," they prompted. I looked again but the only previously unnoted fact which I could now see, was that some of the hearts were bigger than others. "My love is as a flame which grows like a mighty river on its way to the sea."

They smiled delightedly at this final effort. "You see, you mustn't leave anything out or you change the whole meaning," they said. I was a little nonplused as to how the flame became a river but I suppose that difficulty would be covered by an elastic poet's license.

I asked them to show me some more formations and I spent a most exciting evening unraveling thoughts of love, plans for the future, a search for truth, and vows of eternal union. They seemed delighted that I should share their most intimate thoughts and I felt very honoured at being permitted to do so.

They manufacture, by this thought process, everything which they possess, the one exception being their ceremonial jewels. These are presented to them either individually or as a group upon their receiving a rise in status.

Namsos' personal jewelry consists of three fairly large stones, at least they are big for a fairy. The first one he showed me was pale amber in colour and he received it as a reward for his patience in working with his mostly unresponsive insects.

The second one was blue and he is particularly fond of this one because it was presented to him a short time after Sirilla became his paris.

The third, which is bigger than the others and also blue, is a fairly recent acquisition and was bestowed on him for his healing.

The fairies are all interested in every aspect of Daphne's work but, naturally, each has a leaning towards one or more branches of it. To Namsos, the healing is the most wonderful example of cosmic power and he spends a great deal of his spare time studying the different rays and the uses to which they may be put.

He tries them out on his insects, so far with little result, but he argues that if a human being can cure another, then the small amount of the ray which he can pass through him should affect say, an ant. I explained to him that a healer's body is vibrating at approximately the same speed as the patient's but that fairy atoms vibrate much faster than Man's, let alone an animal's.

I fear that his experiments will but add laurels to his cap of patience. Poor Namsos. He is such a dear little fellow but his tasks seem as though they must be too heavy for such small shoulders. If anyone can succeed, though, I'm sure that he will.

Sirilla also has three jewels, two pink and one white. She occasionally wears them to please me and I know that displaying them for my approval gives her great pleasure. Sometimes she places one on the back of her hand or on the centre of her forehead; they don't need pins or clips to make them stay put.

Namsos wears his in his belt, there being positively no frills or vanity about this quaint little man.

They asked me one day if I would show them mine and, to my chagrin, I had to admit that I had none. They were both crestfallen, not at my lowly status but that their request had forced me to reveal my shortcomings.

However, the day came when I was able to rectify this defect and, when I went to visit them, I slipped my new topaz into my pocket.

On Earth, it would have been extremely distasteful to me to wear jewelry, but here it's different. It's not a question of displaying one's wealth, but a jewel serves as a mark of distinction. After all, servicemen aren't ashamed of their medals, or of wearing them on the appropriate occasion, and so it is with us.

A topaz is one of the humblest stones but at least I earned it, and I knew that its size, about that of a green pea, would impress the fairies. They very nearly burst with pride over my modest achievement and we all wore our jewelry for the rest of the evening, even Namsos decorating his belt in my honour.

It was not long after this that we decided to try meditation together. Namsos and Sirilla had already done quite well on their mental flights and had reached the higher Astral which, until recently, had been my own limit when meditating alone.

We settled down near their home and when I opened my eyes we were drifting gently across the sky. Namsos was holding Sirilla in his arms and his expression of wrapt adoration lit up his rather plain little features so that he appeared almost good-looking, while Sirilla had attained real beauty as she lay with her eyes closed.

We began to gather speed until we were flying faster than my brain could record. I was very anxious to remember everything that happened on this journey, so when we reached our destination, I refused to allow myself the luxury of coming slowly to my senses.

I forced myself to open my eyes as soon as we stopped moving and I saw that Namsos and Sirilla were still blissfully unconscious of my presence or of their surroundings. I was filled with tenderness for them and, as I watched them, I experienced no feeling of self-consciousness as I undoubtedly would have done in the presence of two human beings in love, for I knew that they wished me to share their joy in each other as much as I could.

116

I rose to my feet and I began to absorb the landscape. This is the only way in which I can express the process by which one "sees" in the spheres above the Astral. One doesn't just observe with one's eyes. One knows. One almost experiences the sensation of *being* a tree, a flower, a rock or whatever one happens to be examining at the moment; the only reason why I don't have the full experience of *being* them is that I'm not sufficiently advanced.

I want to know almost passionately what a rock thinks and feels. Is it capable of loving another rock? or is it enchanted by a nearby flower? or by a

river rushing and brushing by? I don't know and I can't know until I find out for myself. Others can tell me of their own experiences but that isn't the same thing at all, because they were "being" different rocks in different parts of the universe. It's always the particular rock, tree or field upon which I'm pondering that I long to know, think like, and be.

After I had absorbed as much as I could, I wandered slowly back to the fairies and, as I approached, they opened their eyes. They asked me where we were and I replied that we were somewhere on the Third plane.

They jumped to their feet excitedly at the news. "Oh, thank you, Ronald. We've never been before," they said, almost overwhelming me with gratitude over our modest success. Yet I could more than sympathise because it isn't many months ago that I myself reached the Third plane for the first time and I had been just as exuberant as they.

I led them forward, not that I had the least idea what we were supposed to be doing, but I felt they expected me to take the initiative.

"Where are we going?" they asked.

"You'll see," I replied, hoping that I sounded full of confidence. They were enchanted with everything and they gave the plants little bursts of power as we walked along.

Eventually we approached the crest of a hill and, as we neared the top, I hoped desperately that there would be something interesting on the other side.

I wasn't disappointed for, as we reached the summit, a wonderful sight met our eyes. There was a large lake, very peaceful looking, very blue, and across the surface of its placid waters sped hundreds of tiny boats, fairy boats, which seemed to be traveling at tremendous speed without disturbing its eternal calm by so much as a ripple.

They gasped and so did I. I've no idea what I'd been expecting but certainly not a fairies' aquatic playground. They looked at me wistfully.

"Come on," I said, "we'll find a boat."

We ran down the hill as excitedly as children and there at the water's edge, right in front of us but slightly hidden by the rushes, was just what we were looking for, a small boat that was large enough for me to go with them.

We stepped in and I began looking for the oars but I needn't have worried because we had scarcely settled ourselves comfortably when we began to move.

Soon we were far from the bank, in the midst of a whirling mass of other boats and yet, for all the speed which was being employed, there was no feeling of being in a hurry; it was merely that, except for the lake, the tempo of everything and everybody had risen considerably.

We were all in high good humour; we waved our hands and greetings were shouted from one boat to another, until quite suddenly we realized that we were alone. We weren't sure whether we had been lifted to an even higher vibration, or whether, in a flash, we had been transported to another part of the lake.

We looked at each other and waited. A deep silence hung like a cloak over the vicinity as though shutting us off from all other life. The boat had ceased to move and I experienced the curious sensation of hanging in space; the lake was still there but it seemed to have no substance; it was as though we were poised over a bottomless vacuum.

The fairies looked solemn but quite unafraid and I felt ashamed of that feeling of uncontrollable terror which always grips me, however hard I try to check it, before some new "experience."

A great cry came out of the sky. It was as unexpected as it was uplifting. A mighty shout of triumph which filled me with the knowledge that all was well.

Then, like answering flashes to a thunderclap, came shaft after shaft of light which passed right through the boat into the lake. A murmuring began in the depths and, with this whisper of sound came movement.

The water rose on both sides of us and enveloped us. At no time did I experience any sensation of drowning; it was as though I was engulfed in some great,

118

sexless embrace. I was filled with love. For the lake? Or was I the lake, loving myself? I loved the two fairies equally, passionlessly, as though I *was* them with their love for one another lifted to the stars.

I began to fall, floating gently into that boundless abyss. It was wonderful - I hoped that there was in truth no end, that I should just go on forever and ever . . .

The base proved to be the ground outside the fairies' house. We had no idea how far we had fallen or how long we had remained unconscious after our arrival. All I know is that over three hours had passed since we had first closed our eyes in meditation; I only wish that I hadn't missed any of it.

I seem not only to have lost the thread of my description of the fairies' house, but I've also gone miles off-course. However, I'll go back now and tell you a bit more about it.

I've discovered that there are three rooms - a bedroom, a sitting room and a workroom. At least, they are the equivalent of what would be these in a human being's house.

As other people have given descriptions of several of the fairies' rooms, I'll just take the bedroom. I'd describe it as very feminine, because there are so many frills and flounces and, although I know that these are also thought forms, I'm sure that Namsos had nothing to do with their final structure.

The bed is a kind of sling or hammock, in pale pink, with streamers floating around it from the ceiling. They are never still and, I should have thought, very disturbing, but the fairies assure me that the movement is controlled and is for a purpose. In time, the air channels formed by these waving streamers will become permanent and can then be used in a similar manner to a springboard speeding a jumper in his flight, as a kind of booster for their spiritual thoughts. I hope that this explanation will mean more to you than it does to me. I can but ask and record their answers.

The walls look a bit like the bark of a tree - they're corrugated, yet soft to the touch and in pale colours. There's a large blotch of red on one wall, which is obviously Namsos' sole contribution. I was determined to find out what it was without displaying my ignorance, so I watched it with great concentration for several minutes.

I came to the conclusion that it was moving, not from place to place, but there was obviously life inside it. I looked again and things were definitely happening. I was sure that the movement wasn't just haphazard but that it had a purpose. I did everything I could to become in tune with it. I concentrated on the idea behind it. I was grimly determined but it was no good. It still remained a red blotch on the wall, with movement.

I must have looked very worried because, before I was obliged to admit failure by asking about it, Namsos shot a little flash of power into it and the agitation became feverish. I believe I expected it to burst and disgorge a lot of embryo worms or something.

It certainly burst, but no worms appeared. I did, however, experience a slight feeling of expectation. Of course, I'm too big for such a small instrument to have any real effect but the fairies are small and, for them, the result was instantaneous. They disappeared.

I thought that they might be teasing me but they aren't really frivolous types, and then it dawned on me. Of course, the red blotch was some kind of bottled power and they'd shot off on another meditation trip.

I felt rather offended at their leaving me. I was really quite sorry for myself. I'd arranged my time so that I could spend at least an hour with them and now, after five minutes, they were gone.

"Ronald, Ronald!" I heard through my gloom. "Come up here."

How stupid of me. What could be simpler than to follow them? I closed my eyes and when I opened them I saw two worried little faces looking up at me from my feet.

"We didn't actually mean to do this," they said apologetically. "We only wanted to demonstrate the power of the elevatus and Namsos gave it too much."

"Well, here we are, so let's enjoy it," I said, beginning to feel fine again now that I knew my two little friends hadn't forsaken me on purpose. And then I saw him.

"Look," I said softly to Namsos. His eyes followed my pointing finger and his face fit up.

"Oh, Ronald," was all he managed to say.

Slowly we moved towards him, so as not to frighten him, but I don't think we need have worried because as soon as he saw us approaching, he came towards us, making strange little squeals of welcome.

I had longed to see one of these non-Earth animals and now I had one before me. He was really beautiful. He was pure white with very black eyes and nose. Most pitch-black eyes look a bit wicked, but his were as soft and kind as the proverbial doe's.

He was mostly upright on his hind legs yet he didn't look at all cumbersome like an ape, nor yet as though he was begging like a bear; he looked just as natural and comfortable as a man or a fairy. He had a silky coat about four inches long, with short hairs on his face and long fur forming a frame around it. His ears were small and pointed and were placed on the top of his head like a horse. His face wasn't quite human but it had none of the comic cunning of a monkey.

He was, I suppose, a sort of young Pan, but not completely half and half, like a satyr. I think that he must have been brought for us to see, certainly from a higher sphere, possibly even from another planet. I wish now that I had tried to talk to him because I'm sure that he had enough consciousness to understand - perhaps he even tried to speak to me and, because I wasn't expecting it, I didn't notice.

He didn't seem to see the fairies but they were enchanted with him. As I patted him and made clucking noises, they ran 'round looking at him from every angle. He put his arm, or paw, 'round me in a most friendly way and I would have loved to take him home with me, but I'm sure he couldn't live in such a low vibration.

After quite a short time he began to look tired and he wiped his eyes with his paw just like a weary child. I knew then that he couldn't stay with us long so, by patting the ground beside me, I persuaded him to rest. He snuggled up against me and soon he was asleep. As his consciousness left the body in which he had materialized for our benefit, it gradually faded until nothing was left but the memory of a very charming companion.

There is one more adventure that I had with Namsos and Sirilla about which I must tell you. There have already been so many and, doubtless, there will be countless more; the difficulty is knowing which to choose and where to stop.

On this occasion, we found ourselves once again on the Third plane. The trees, as always, were whispering their message and the grass and flowers nodded to us in welcome from close to our feet. I'm always treated to a running commentary as to what they are saying so I don't have to make any conscious effort to hear the lessons which Nature, in all her forms, is perpetually teaching us.

We left the solid ground and floated to the treetops. The fairies became very excited as they realized that we had something important to do. I asked them what this was, but the trees couldn't tell them; they merely waved their branches upwards.

We sped along faster and faster and then, quite suddenly, we stopped. One might suppose that one's senses must reel at this immediate cessation of speed, but we scarcely noticed any change physically; mentally we became charged with tremendous urgency.

"This way," I cried, and we raced ahead as though the whole future of Mankind depended on our reaching our destination on time. We ran and ran until I began to feel that I'd made a mistake and that I should admit that I hadn't the faintest idea where we were going.

I had actually opened my mouth to tell them when I saw an enormous light in the sky and I knew that, after all, I hadn't been wrong.

"Stop!" I called instead, and we all halted. My heart was beating with the exertion but as I stopped, it stopped too. I knew that it hadn't ceased to function or, if it had, that its action was no longer necessary; it was still because it had to be. Everything was still. We were in the midst of absolute quiet.

Again I felt that rising terror which I can never curb and, once again, when I reached that certain pitch beyond which I know my mind would fail, the light began to advance and, with its approach, I became as still as my heart.

Fascinated, we watched the solitary beam traveling towards us and, just before it reached us, it stopped. I had hoped that it would travel right on through us because to be in and of that light is an experience which none can state in words.

As it ceased to move, my heart began to beat again and my awareness became acute. There was neither voice nor mental message. I just knew that I, who am about midway in knowledge in our group, and the fairies, who are in the same position in theirs, had been chosen – possibly as typical examples of our status – for a test; that we were to take part in an experiment as the mediums between some high sphere and Earth, and, according to whether we succeeded or failed, so would the plan be carried out in its entirety or be modified.

The light slowly withdrew and we waited. It wasn't necessary for us to speak to one another because we knew that our thoughts were the same. I was a bit nervous. I didn't want to fail, although I knew that it was not a question of me or us failing, but a demonstration as to whether mediums of our moderate status could stand the force of the power necessary for the success of some plan, possibly not to be used for many years.

Then again we saw a light, but it wasn't the same one. The first had been a person with a message but this one was the force which we were to test.

I raised my vibrations as high as I could and the beam surrounded us. The power seemed normal at first but gradually it increased in strength. We must retain our consciousness as long as we could and I made up my mind that I'd hang on to mine until I burst - and I wasn't far wrong.

I would have liked to watch the fairies to see how they were lasting out, but I knew that I should have to give my whole mind to the job if any useful data was to be provided by our resistance. That's not really the right word because it's one's ability to relax completely and not resist that governs the amount of power that can be passed through one's body.

As the power grows, the natural reaction is to tense oneself to take the strain, but that is the exact opposite to what should be done, which is to concentrate on further relaxation.

My mind was completely in tune with the force, but it needed a great effort not to be carried away to some wonderfully high sphere. Can you see the difficulty of resisting your natural impulses without, at the same time, using your will to combat them? You have to let everything flow in the same direction as the force, your thoughts, your nerves and your body too. With a physical body you can't do the last two but in the higher spheres, our bodies aren't static like on Earth; they can literally flow, yet you aren't left without one because fresh matter takes the place of that which has gone and your form is composed of millions of constantly moving electrons.

There always comes a time when everything flows so fast that you lose consciousness and it was at this point, with the particular force which they were using, which they wished to find.

122

It's a very pleasant sensation and, as the comparatively slow movement of the millions of particles of matter becomes a race, a wonderful feeling of exhilaration fills you. Then you begin to rise in the opposite direction to your flowing thoughts and matter.

I felt myself begin to do this several times but I managed to bring myself gently back. Finally I found that I couldn't do it any more and, whichever way of checking this flight I tried, I still continued to rise.

"If I can't stop, I must know where I go," I thought, but it was no good because the thought was traveling in the opposite direction and I lost it.

I remember a wild feeling of fulfillment, a tremendous desire to reach unknown heights, but I never knew whether I succeeded. If Death were possible, it would have been a glorious way to go, but how much more wonderful it will be when Sirilla, Namsos and I can rise in full consciousness, to enjoy together the wonders which we can't at present reach because they're beyond our understanding; their sight, instead of revealing new beauty, would blind us; our senses, far from learning new secrets, would be numbed by the power, and our Astral minds would be incapable of accepting the knowledge which is there for us and for us alone.

So we must wait, and take comfort from the fact that the sights, sounds and experiences which are ours can never be revealed to anyone else. It sounds incredible, I know, but I believe it because I've been told that this is so by people whom I've learned to trust. Anyway, what point would there be in not telling the truth; Although Truth is one and infinite she has millions of aspects and, as we advance, so we can grasp a slightly higher one, until the time comes when the whole will be ours.

– Ronald

MERELLA (Observer: Peter) and NUVIC (Observer: Andrew)

SEEDS
by Merella

I have always been of an adventurous nature; I love to battle with the wind, not to float with it but to force my way through it; my body being lashed with its strength instead of tiring me, fills me with exultation.

The rain, too, I love and, when it descends in torrents, I fly through the drops as they strive to pound me to pieces; I feel their sting as a refreshing caress as they cleanse me inside and out.

But best of all, I love the sun and the warmth of it seems to lift me far from Earth.

On the Astral plane, when I felt in need of friendly combat, with wind and rain, I visited the region where these experiences are provided, for normally there is no rain there and but a warm and gentle breeze.

My work has been with seeds as long as I can remember and, to me, they are the most wonderful act of creation; they are the outward manifestation of progress for which all Nature strives. After which fulfillment the parent plant is content to die back into the Astral or to rest for a season on Earth until it is time for her to begin her work again to attain the self-same objective.

Thus plants come into my care before they are born and again before they die, and at each stage they are beautiful. To you, a withered flower is probably something which you would prefer to be without, but to me she is different. I see her in her full maturity, preening herself in her approaching fulfillment.

I love all forms of experiment and I continually try new methods of coaxing my seeds to sprout. Sometimes I give them big bursts of power myself, at others, a constant trickle through relays of minutes. Again, sometimes I arrange for many of them to give the seeds a swift bathing, then I'll leave them for a day before I repeat their allowance of power.

If one way is not successful, I try another and I feel great satisfaction when, at last, I see a tiny shoot in answer to my unorthodox methods, particularly if routine ones have already been tried and have failed.

I like to perform every single act in as many ways as I can. When I fly, I usually travel fast but sometimes I allow myself to drop several feet, which quickens my vibrations. On other occasions I stay in one spot, completely stationary; this requires a great deal of control and it is only within the last five years that I have achieved success. For some time I was unable to prevent myself from falling but now that I have mastered the technique, I find this form of relaxation most restful.

At times I fly many miles in order to see how quickly I can come home. I am not referring to traveling by thought which, of course, we can all do, but by consciously drawing in power as I fly, I have reached tremendous speeds so that even fairies cannot see me as I pass. When we have races, I always win, so I have to start a long time after the others.

I think you know that, as well as our communal house, each pair of fairies has its own home, to which we can go when the week's work is over. Nuvic's and mine is in a well-kept garden not far from here. We have made it on Fairy-classic lines, the idea having been given to me by some buildings which I saw on the Astral. It is white, with pillars, and has steps all the way 'round. We also have a very beautiful door like white marble, hard and smooth. On entering, there is a fine open space with more pillars and a domed ceiling.

The whole structure gives an impression of great space although the house is, in fact, not very large. Leading off this central hall are three rooms; one where we rest, one for recreation and work, and the third for meditation.

The first is pale green with a soft, grassy floor, the walls and ceiling being composed of leaves and flowers. We sleep in this room, which is so akin to Nature, which we love, that we awaken feeling even more refreshed than when we spend the night in the community house.

The second room is the one we use when entertaining our friends. It is of every colour of the rainbow so that all who come are happy there. You will understand that, whereas Nuvic and I would feel greatly refreshed in a cream and green room, these colours might produce a very depressing effect upon a fairy who needs, for instance, a pink or a blue ray.

To be in this room is rather like flying through a rainbow, which for us is a most wonderful experience, the swift transition from one colour to another producing a fast change of vibration. All who come feel the invigorating influence of so many colours and they always depart refreshed.

The description of our activities in the third room, I have kept to the last because it is our favourite, for it is here that we endeavour to develop spiritually. I am more advanced than Nuvic in this respect and so I am able to enjoy greater experiences but, in relating them to him, I can, to a certain extent, share them. Sometimes we have them together and then, although we may not reach as high a plane as I might myself, I am really at my happiest, because an experience shared is always of greater value.

Last night we spent a beautiful time together. We seemed to be floating upwards, up, up, farther than either of us had ever been before. We experienced a sensation of absolute at-one-ness with each other and with all our surroundings. It was as though the whole atmosphere was our bodies, not separate but one; we felt free and tremendously large, as though we inhabited the whole of space. With this vast area of consciousness, we saw and felt and were all the people, animals and plants within it. We experienced being the hardness of stone, the prickliness of a rose, the body and thoughts, so different from ours, of a man. We felt these variations separately and, then again, together.

It was an almost overpowering experience, but now we have a greater understanding of each object and person which took part, and of their thoughts and needs.

To me, experience in any form is the reason for all existence and I, therefore, never miss an opportunity which may lead me to further knowledge.

I have already told you a little of how I try, by various methods, to make my seeds grow; how I like to use Nature's resources to provide me with pleasure, and now I will try to convey to you the wonderful advancement I have achieved by constantly exchanging power with other fairies.

Although this, to me, is always a great joy, it is not the sole purpose of my experiments, for each time I grow mentally and, as I progress, my work also improves.

We don't regard love-making at all as you do. At first I couldn't understand why you used to tease me about my love actions and, when I asked Normus, he was unable to explain your reason either. He asked his leader and he, in his turn, was obliged to go further before we received the answer and, when we heard that on Earth, love is regarded as a personal thing, we were amazed. To us, it is extraordinary that a man is jealous if his woman gives some of her love to an-other man. It was also explained to us that on Earth, people are unable to exchange power as we do, owing to the coarse matter of which their bodies are composed, and when we heard exactly how you make love, it didn't appeal to us at all.

There are so many ways of love-making which we practice, depending, of course, on the degree of attraction one fairy feels towards another. I often give a little burst of power to one just casually as I pass; it is more often in the nature of a greeting than a love act but I am thus able to give the recipient an unlooked-for pleasure.

If I observe that a fairy shines brightly, I know, of course, that he has a great deal of power and that if he wills, he can give me as much as, if not more than, I can give him. For perfection, the power should be equal, although it is wonderful to receive more than one can give, for the donor, under these circumstances, is the more evolved and can convey his greater experience and knowledge in his power.

Each time anyone gives power, he adds to his capacity for giving. Naturally the improvement is infinitesimal and it takes years for the increase to become visible to the eye of an observer. I therefore made up my mind that if I gave power every time an opportunity arose, without, of course, wasting it, for that is forbidden, I would grow twice or maybe three times as fast as I otherwise would. This supposition has proved to be accurate because, apart from Normus and Movus, I am the most evolved fairy in our group.

I think that my most interesting experience was the time when I exchanged power with Peter. Man being of another evolution, has entirely different vibrations. I was determined to obtain as much knowledge as possible from this blending of our two powers and, since then, I have a much greater understanding of Man.

When you have had as much practice as I have, you temporarily become the person with whom you exchange power, sharing their emotions and all their knowledge. During the trance state which followed, I suffered all Peter's misery as an earthbound and I shared, too, his hopes in his new life. Fairies don't suffer in the same way as Man, and to have shared with Peter, whom I love so well, that part of his life, was something which has caused a tremendous growth in me.

I know that I have much to learn but to acquire knowledge is the greatest excitement in Life. However much you know, each small gain in wisdom is but a fertilizer which encourages the growth of greater experience. This fact is a Truth which continues to be forever.

– Merella

MERELLA

by Peter

Two evenings ago, Daphne suggested that I should write a description of the occasion when Merella gave me power.

Previously I had succeeded in seeing only Normus, the Nature fairies' leader: he's about seven inches in height and is good looking in a cheeky sort of way. He has a merry twinkle in his eye and obviously has a great sense of humour. He and Daphne have a lot of fun pulling each other's leg but I know that, at heart, there's a very great affection between them.

Normus wasn't with us on this particular occasion, but on making enquiries, Daphne discovered that a little fellow called Nixus was working close by. She suggested to both of us that I should try to see him and Nixus agreed to lower his vibrations to make things easier for me.

I raised mine as high as I could and Daphne turned on some power. The surroundings became lit up and quite suddenly Nixus came into view, sitting on my left leg.

He is somewhat smaller than Normus and has a kind little face; he was wearing a green tunic with buttons down the front and sort of leggings, tights, I suppose you'd call them. He had tiny pointed shoes which looked to me as though they were made of leaves as I could see the veins running through the material. I held out a finger to him and he grasped it delightedly.

We were chatting about his work, which is with the grass, when I saw a flash out of the corner of my eye and I presumed that a butterfly had settled on my shoulder.

"Someone's arrived," said Daphne. 'Who is it?"

"I'm Merella," the tiny creature projected. I turned to look at her and I saw that she was lovely. She had black hair hanging to her waist and her eyes were gazing at me admiringly.

"Oh, he's handsome," she said to Daphne.

"Of course he is," she replied. "Merella, I'm afraid you're a flirt."

"She's after all the boys," piped up Nixus.

Merella pouted prettily. "Oh, Nixus! He never looks at anyone except his Lyssis." She settled herself comfortably on my shoulder, her long, cream-coloured frock waving gently in the breeze.

"Peter, I believe you're making overtures to Merella," Daphne said in an amused tone.

"No, I'm not," I contradicted her.

"Then Merella's making overtures to you," she insisted.

Merella bridled. "I wasn't exactly. I was thinking. I've got a wonderful idea. I'd like to give Peter some power."

"I'd be delighted," I replied, although I was secretly rather amused at the thought of so tiny a creature making love to me.

She flew off my shoulder and began darting through the air like a dragonfly. Daphne told me to watch carefully as she would probably begin to shine when she was full of power. She informed me, too, that there should be a centre of light, either in her forehead or in the solar plexus. I concentrated further and I managed to see a tiny beam glowing from her forehead.

Apparently she was soon full, for she came and lay in my lap. I began to feel a slight languor creeping over me and a movement as though a hundred butterflies were fanning my stomach. It was an exquisite sensation which is quite lost in words. I felt elated, as one always does after receiving power from more orthodox sources, but there was also a feeling of enchantment about the incident.

When it was over, she lay as though in a trance and I was not sure what I should do with her until Nixus said, in a bored voice, "You'd better put her somewhere on the ground. She'll probably stay like that for hours."

I lifted her as gently as I could and placed her under a leaf in the corner of the garden. I can now understand a little the strange tales that one sometimes hears of men falling in love with fairy princesses, and leaving their homes to seek them in the far corners of the Earth.

A Year Later

When I first met Merella, I thought her the most beautiful being whom I had ever seen and I still do.

At first her house appeared to be empty but I knew that it wasn't because she would point to objects and describe them to me. She began with a sort of box which she explained they used for resting; she told me, too, that it was green, with a canopy of flowers. After three unsuccessful attempts, she suggested that it might help me to see it if she got into it. She then appeared to be lying in midair but, after a few moments, I saw that something flat was supporting her. I asked her where the legs were.

"Legs? What legs?" she asked.

"The bed ought to have legs," I replied.

"What for?" she enquired.

"To support it, of course. You can't have a bed suspended in midair."

She looked puzzled. "Why not?"

"Well, there's the force of gravity, for one thing," but she didn't understand. Then I realized that it was I who was the idiot and that there's absolutely no reason why my own bed shouldn't be suspended in midair if I want it to be, because, of course, there's no force of gravity for us either.

So that night I solemnly removed the legs from my bed and, willing it to stay, I very carefully climbed onto it. It stopped, all right, but I didn't feel at all safe so I put the legs back again.

To return to Merella, she was lying there looking like a fairy princess; I noticed that the bed was moving gently about the room and it finally came right through the wall and floated past my nose. I suppose that I must have looked rather surprised because she burst out laughing.

"But this is ridiculous," I said. "How do you know where you're going?"

"We don't," she replied. "It wouldn't be nearly so exciting if we did."

"But don't you ever sleep?" I asked.

"Our journeys are our refreshment," she said. "You must visit other spheres too when you sleep."

"I don't know," I said. "If I do, I don't remember. Do you always remember yours?"

"But of course we do," she replied, "and the memory of the wonders that we've seen carries us through the hardest tasks of the day."

I asked her to give me an example.

"Well, last night, for instance, we went to sleep and, when we awoke, it was pitch dark. At first we thought we were still at home but when we tried to see – because we can always do so a little, however dark it is on Earth – we failed.

"Are you frightened?" asked Nuvic.

"No, it's exciting," I replied. "Are you?"

"No," he said, rather doubtfully.

"Let's get up," I suggested.

"But we can't go anywhere," he said. "It's too dark."

"Never mind, let's try anyway and see what happens.

"We arose and stood waiting; Nuvic was fidgeting and I was tingling with expectation when there was a huge Boom.

"We both nearly jumped out of our bodies. The air was so filled with the vibrations of the noise that, had we allowed them to do so, I think they would have broken us into tiny pieces. We stood firm, however, and after awhile the vibrations faded away - or rather, they withdrew and took us with them.

"Gradually it became light and we found ourselves on the outskirts of a vast plain covered with flowers, houses and people. Fairy people," she explained.

"Anyone from Earth always receives a great welcome," she continued. "Those who have been there ask if conditions have improved and those who have not want firsthand knowledge.

"We floated through the flowers, and what lovely flowers, Peter. I think my charges on Earth are beautiful but, when I'm amongst those on the Astral, I realize mine are but poor imitations. They laugh all the time, these astral flowers. Do you ever hear them?" she asked anxiously.

I shook my head.

"You don't listen," she said.

"But I do," I assured her. "It's no good, though. My ears aren't sufficiently sensitive yet, but I'll make them," I promised her.

She returned to her story.

"We were led to an open space where a meeting was taking place. They were deciding who among the community should be trained as future leaders. We saw the past hundred year's work of each of the fairies being considered for promotion."

At that time I hadn't seen these lightning projections on my own plane, so I said, "But it must have taken hours."

"About three seconds," she told me.

"Now, Merella," I began to argue. "How could . . .?" Then I stopped. How can I possibly know the speed of fairy thought? I'm still tied down by words and Merella speaks to me at what, to her, is a snail's pace. I know because she has told me. "All right," I conceded. "What happened then?"

"Everyone voted," she said. "We too," she added proudly, "then there was a celebration for those who had won."

"Are those who don't win very disappointed? I mean, working for a hundred years and then being turned down?" I asked.

130

"A hundred years – Pff," she said. "It's nothing."

"But a lot can happen in less time than that," I reminded her.

"We met -" we said simultaneously, and we both laughed with pleasure because, as you know, there's a very great love between us.

I am a man of six foot three and Merella is a fairy of about six inches, but love is an unpredictable force which strikes in the most unexpected quarters. It is a power of great good and I know that one day both Merella and I, through it, will understand facts which, without it, would be beyond our comprehension.

As time went on, I began to see more and more of the interior of my little friend's home. I have watched her, too, as she meditates, when she becomes lit up like a miniature beacon. Her thoughts appear as a million tiny flashes which arrive and are gone before they become intelligible to me.

One day she asked me if I would meditate with her. I replied that, although I should love it, I was afraid that my slowness would impede her progress.

However, she insisted so we sat down under the chestnut tree in the garden. She told me that she would control her thoughts so that I could see them. Until then, I had been receiving them as words in my mind but now she was very insistent that I should learn to see them.

"How can you appreciate an idea unless you can examine the colour and feel the texture?" she asked.

I confess that I had never thought of taking an idea between my finger and thumb and judging it like a piece of cloth, "Is thought ever really tangible? I mean, could I ever touch it like I do you?" I said, stroking her cheek gently with the tip of my finger.

"You could if you wished to, but I don't mean that type of 'feel.' I want you to feel it inside you, as though it were part of you. Now look, 'I . . . love . . . you.' " I heard in my mind.

"Did you see that?" she asked.

"You said that you loved me," I said, smiling.

"I said, did you see it?" she insisted.

I had to admit failure.

"Well, watch again," she said and, this time, instead of concentrating with my mind, I put all my thoughts into my eyes and I could see that she was turning a deep pink.

"You're pink," I announced.

"Of course I am. So are you. We always are when we're together. Didn't you know?"

"You've never been pink to me before," I said.

"That's because you weren't looking properly. You must be more observant," she said, almost primly for Merella. "Now, look once more."

I tried very hard and this time I definitely saw a deep, rose-coloured flame leap out of the top of her head.

"Do it again," I begged, and another little flame appeared. I felt very pleased with myself as I told her what I'd seen.

"But didn't you see the curly bit at the end?" she demanded.

"I'm afraid not," I said, "Was it so very important?"

"It was the whole point," she said. "That indicates that I love you as a paris and not just as a friend. I was mentally putting my arms around you."

"Couldn't you do that in fact, not just as a thought?" I asked eagerly.

"I'm afraid I shall have to grow a bit," she said, with her usual twinkle, "unless, of course, you would like me to embrace your nose."

I sighed. There are obvious disadvantages in our great disparity in size.

"Now, watch again," she said, "I shall add something besides the curl."

I looked carefully and this time I saw the deep pink flame with its curl, and then the whole thing, instead of fading, disintegrated.

"That means you love me to distraction," I said solemnly.

She clapped her hands and laughed delightedly. "Oh, Peter, you're a wonderful pupil. I shall be able to teach you many things."

I can assure you that she has.

On my following visit we meditated again. "You must follow me this time," she instructed. I was not sure what she meant but I soon understood. Now my thoughts literally followed hers, blending and becoming one as they sped upwards.

I still had to watch very closely, but soon I saw a spiral of blue smoke; immediately I felt the idea of hope for humanity rising from my heart.

Having concentrated on her visible thoughts, I now switched to mine and I found that they looked identical, apart from being bigger and stronger. My spirals locked into hers and together they floated upwards, eventually merging into one before disappearing from view.

Normally, of course, each thought follows another in lightning succession, but on this occasion we watched each fade into the distance before sending out another.

Next, a trail of golden stars floated upwards, to be joined together by tiny pale blue flowers. "Love those you meet upon the way," said my heart, and some larger stars sped after hers and overtook them. The flowers didn't seem to materialize, however, so I tuned in to her thought again and, as I murmured, ". . . and guide them gently along the Path," some big forget-me-nots rushed after the fast disappearing group.

"It's wonderful!" I said in awe and amazement.

"Ssh!" she admonished, 'We haven't finished our meditation yet."

132

As she spoke, a pure white, filmy trail floated out of her head but, instead of speeding upwards as the others had done, it came and wound itself around my eyes. Far from dimming my vision, it quickened it and I saw Merella as I had never seen her before.

She was bathed in ethereal light until she shone as brightly as a star on a dark night. "Follow me," she said, and as I relaxed, I felt myself floating through the air.

She sped upwards, with me following as closely as I could. Faster and faster we went until I could no longer see her, but I knew that she was ahead, for her vibration was leading me. Then I seemed to be floating again; I felt gloriously lazy; I couldn't be bothered to open my eyes.

"We're here," she said.

'What's here?" I murmured, still keeping my eyes closed.

'Wake up. You can't go falling asleep in this wonderful atmosphere."

I took a deep breath and, immediately, my laziness left me. I looked 'round but I could see very little.

"Can't you send me some more of that wispy stuff?" I asked. "I can't see."

"I will if it's necessary," she said, "but you must *try* first. Now raise your vibrations."

I already felt as though I should disintegrate with their speed but I obediently raised them a little higher.

"More!" she commanded.

"I can't, Merella, I must already be shaking like a jelly."

"More!" was all she said.

So I took a deep breath and, miraculously, instead of bursting, as I had feared I must, everything became still and calm. I looked 'round again and, this time, instead of blinding flashes of light, I saw a cool, clear landscape with graceful trees swaying gently to the rhythm of the music which filled the air.

'Where are we?" I asked.

"I don't know," she said, "but isn't it beautiful? Come. We're here for a purpose. We must find out what it is."

I rose to my feet, feeling like a leaf blowing in the breeze. We let the soft wind carry us into the music and then the notes seemed to lead us.

This is difficult to explain but I suppose that one floats down a vibration of sound as one might down a current in a river.

We came to a halt before a real fairy palace; it was white with little clouds darting about between the towers. Billows of soft stuff that looked like cotton-wool were gathered about the base; I supposed that they were more clouds but, instead of disappearing into a mist as we approached, they divided as I walked through them and closed up behind me again.

Merella led me under the arched entrance and immediately we were surrounded by fairies of all shapes and sizes. Some were as tall as I and others were plain little creatures of about an inch high.

After a moment, Merella explained to me that this was a hall of learning where each category of fairy was training for his next visit to Earth.

I asked them whether they all wanted to return and they began chattering at me at far too great a speed for me to grasp their meaning.

"They say they must suffer," Merella translated.

"But how can anyone want to suffer?" I asked, and again, a positive barrage of answers shot into the air.

I looked at Merella.

"They say that, of course, they don't like the idea of suffering, but they're all static. They can't reach higher in their meditation, however hard they try, so either they have to be content with what they have or agree to return to Earth."

"You know, I'm very interested in this," I told them. "I haven't been on the Astral plane for very long and everything here is so wonderful that it doesn't seem possible that it could ever pall. Then there are my visits to the Third plane, when each time more and more is revealed. How is it that one ever gets stuck?"

"We felt like that too," they admitted. "When we first came back, we vowed that we'd never willingly go to Earth again, but here we are, all just waiting for the time when a vacancy will enable us to gain more experience so that we begin to grow again."

It's hard to grasp that this is the universal trend throughout every evolution, that one must suffer reverses in order to progress. I can't believe that the time will ever come when I shall want to go to Earth again, but I suppose I shall, apparently, everyone does.

They led us further into the building. It seemed one vast space and yet I was sure that it was my lack of vision which failed to show me more. We twisted and turned when could have gone straight, so I presumed that there must be walls or some form of enclosure which I was unable to see. I noticed that the fairies kept glancing at me eagerly as though expecting me to express an opinion so eventually I apologized and confessed that, as far as I was concerned, there was nothing but empty space.

"Oh, Peter!" Merella said reproachfully. "Haven't lessons been of any use?"

"Can't you do something to help me?" I suggested. "You always have before."

She looked pensive for a moment, then she described an arc with her right arm. I hoped she was waving an invisible magic wand but her action didn't seem to have made any difference. Then all the other fairies copied her. Next, she formed a circle and this time they made a similar one with their bodies. "What are you doing?"

I asked. "Trying to clarify the outlines," she explained. "Now, watch them carefully." Then followed something rather like a game of follow my leader. Merella described circles, cubes, arches and acute angles, interspersed with disappearing acts when I completely lost sight of her. Wherever she went, the fairies followed but, whereas she seemed to be on a non-stop journey, they remained, forming the various shapes which she had made. By degrees things began to happen – a circle became a door or a window, a cube, a kind of box filled with knowledge. I

know this sounds a peculiar description but it's the best that I can do – the angles were alcoves of glittering beauty and, gradually, the whole fell into parts and the parts revealed the whole – a fairy palace of extraordinary design and incredible loveliness.

It is, alas, impossible to tell you much more because, if I described some of the shapes without their surroundings, they would appear merely strange and of no special significance, whereas in reality, each arc or line expressed a – meaning which could be divulged only after I had pondered upon it for several minutes.

As understanding of the method of teaching came to me, I became absorbed in the translation of the symbols, as each led up to and was part of the next. At the same time, all were complete within the sequence and yet were a necessary part of the whole.

I've expressed this abominably, but the idea was so new to me and the translation so engrossing that I scarcely realized what I was doing at the time and, afterwards, when I endeavoured to be analytical, all but the teaching had gone.

"When I saw Merella again, I asked her where she had been when she had disappeared.

"Peter, it was wonderful," she said. "You know that I was following the outline of the various objects and shapes – well, some of them just went on and on into the ether. I found myself in the most wonderful conditions, but I didn't seem able to stay there. The teaching was too advanced for me but I've been thinking a good deal since then. Nuvic and I have been back several times during meditation and I think that I understand a little more now."

"Understand what?" I asked.

"The reason why I couldn't stay."

"Well, why couldn't you?"

"I'll try to explain about the first one I tried," she continued. "it obviously led to 'perfect control,' but when I reached a certain distance, because of the rate of vibration of the surrounding atmosphere, I became excited. In fact, I lost control of my emotions and so I found myself back where I'd started."

I encouraged her to continue.

"There was another one too, that I was hardly able to negotiate at all. I tried it again with Nuvic and, to my surprise, he reached higher than I did. You know, there are many latent possibilities in my little man," she said seriously.

Had this conversation taken place with any young woman of my acquaintance, I should have been profoundly irritated, but with fairies it is different. She was delighted at Nuvic's success; although she is far more advanced than he, there was no condescension in her statement, only pleasure. She continued, " 'Perseverance' was the path of this lesson. I hadn't realized until then how poor I am in this respect, but when I came to analyze myself, I realized that, as a rule, I achieve my desires instantaneously. I don't have to fight for them anymore like I used to. I've become like a stagnant pool, satisfied with the rich growth of green weed which it has produced."

"Oh, Merella, you're being too hard on yourself," I said.

"I have to be," she said honestly, "because otherwise I might become contented with myself and that's a very foolish mistake to make."

She explained to me how each path led to new knowledge through a different quality; how she had reached far along "bravery" and "confidence" but had failed to gain even a foothold on "placidity."

"To know oneself is the finest form of education," she said. "There is only one way to find the Truth. You may analyze yourself to yourself – you may intend to be honest, but you can never be a really impartial judge of your own achievements.

"Now, with these paths, they aren't swayed by beauty, by striving, or by pity. They represent the way to Truth; they're stern in their ruthless rejection of the weak, but they also prove beyond doubt where you are strong; they point out your weaknesses and, if you are wise, you'll set to work until all paths are open wide and none cause your feet to falter."

"You should be a teacher, Merella. I really felt as though at least a farallis was speaking," I said.

"One day, when I've strengthened myself sufficiently, I hope to be one," she replied. "The time will come when I shall be great. People say that I'm ruthless, but I'm equally ruthless with myself. I won't tolerate blemishes; they are as insidious as Earth diseases; what starts as something minute can fester and rot the whole body, only, with us, it is the will which is affected and that's a hundred times worse."

"What's come over you, Merella?" I asked. "I've never known you to be so serious."

She smiled. "I believe I'm frightening you with my fierce preoccupation of perfection. But it's the only thing that matters, that and love."

"What about you and Nuvic?" I asked.

"I'm not sure," she replied. "At first I accepted him as my paris because he was so persistent. Then I grew to love him because of his understanding. I also wanted to help him because he was so eager to learn. Lately, though, he has changed, or perhaps I have. We achieve our greatest spiritual successes together, which is, of course, the best way, the way which could lead to perfection."

"I believe you're in love with him," I said.

Her dark, flashing eyes became quite dreamy. "He has all the qualities which I lack," she admitted. "The two of us could make a perfect whole, millions of years before either individually reaches perfection."

"Have you told him how you feel?" I asked.

"I don't have to," she said. "He knows my every thought almost before I myself have framed it."

"If you don't tell him, even if he knows, you're a fool," I said. "Knowing inside yourself is one thing, but bringing it right out for all the world to see is far, far better."

"I think you're right," she admitted, "but it's not quite so simple as that because, you see, I love you too."

"That can wait," I said. "We're not ready yet. We must advance probably to the Fourth plane before our turn comes, and when it does, it will be different. Love doesn't fade when it's as real as ours, but it will take years before we become properly in tune with each other's evolutions or, at any rate, enough for us to understand completely one another's ideas and ideals."

"You will wait, Peter, won't you, because it's an experience which only comparatively few are able to enjoy but, when it happens, it's different from anything that can possibly take place within a single evolution."

"I'll wait," I promised her, and I know that I shall, even if I have a hundred more incarnations and millions of years intervene, because Merella is part of me and always will be, regardless of time, space and evolution, and what is part of you must eventually come home before you can reach ultimate Perfection.

– Peter

Roses

by Nuvic

When I was living on the Astral plane, I thought that I was the happiest fairy alive; the air there is so sweet and, all day long I felt as though I were on the verge of a great new discovery. I used to tingle with expectation and, although nothing spectacular ever happened, I never lost the knowledge that one day it would.

The time came when I realized that I, myself, must go out and seek this great experience for which I had been hoping for so many years. I asked my leader for advice and he told me that I was obviously ready for further progress and that I should return to Earth.

"But I'm so happy here!" I protested. "I want to be even happier. Earth is the planet of sorrow; what I seek cannot be there."

"It may sound strange to you, but it is only through sorrow that we progress," he replied. "You feel, do you not, almost uncomfortable with your desire to grow."

"Yes, yes!" I said eagerly. "It's almost as though I must burst!"

He smiled. "It is indeed time that you went. Let me explain. You experience that feeling of tightness because, within that little body of yours is a great desire to give. Everyone here is so happy that you cannot get rid of your surplus love and you feel overloaded. Now, on Earth, where there is so much misery, there's not nearly enough love for those who need it. Go and give all that you can spare and you will know great peace."

I felt so inspired by his words that I consented there and then. "May I go immediately?" I enquired.

"That is impossible," my leader said. "You must spend several years in preparation. Your vibrations are too high. You must learn to lower them gradually in order to exist in Earth conditions. I warn you, you will not find it easy, but as time passes, the knowledge that you are giving where the need is so great, will bring you a far greater reward than your present sensation of almost bursting."

I had always worked with shrubs but now I was transferred to roses. The years passed quickly and at last I was informed that there was a vacancy for me. I became a little nervous as the time for descending approached, for I well knew of the initial unhappiness through which every fairy must fight his way.

For six years, I scarcely knew how to carry out my work. How I longed for that bursting sensation, for now I felt as heavy as lead. My rest brought me no refreshment and even my lovely charges failed to comfort me.

Eventually I was transferred to another group and almost immediately I began to recover. To arise with the sun became an excitement and each new day brought new joys. I was still uncomfortable sometimes, but it was no longer the overpowering misfortune that it had once been.

Everything then went smoothly for many years and I was eventually moved to the place where I now live. The gardens are small, it is true, but those which are cultivated are mostly tended by the loving hands of their owners rather than by gardeners who do not always love the flowers and shrubs as they should.

I was happy here from the day of my arrival, but the greatest event of my entire life happened soon afterwards. The fairy who was in charge of the seeds was due for a transfer and, when the new one arrived, I knew that if she refused to be mine I must leave, for to have been near her and not to be permitted to love and look after her would have been more than I could bear.

It was not long before we exchanged power and I have never experienced such ecstasy. I feared that the amount which I could give must seem meager in comparison to the indescribable gusts with which she enfolded me. However, she told me that I had great possibilities and that she would like to teach me. Merella is more advanced than I, so naturally I didn't hesitate.

For many years I was fearful of losing her because she loves to exchange power with any fairy who is willing. But she always comes back to me, so I am content, for there never has been and never will be anyone like Merella and to share her life is a privilege which I prize above all else.

– Nuvic

NUVIC

by Andrew

I want to take you back to the day I first met the others in our group. I'd been asked to tea and I was in a bit of a funk. I knew I was to meet some of Daphne's friends and I thought they'd more likely be her class than mine. Anyway, I arrived and they all gave me a great welcome; in fact, I never felt at all out of it from the word "go."

Then there was the fairies. Daphne had made me see Normus another time and then, with everybody's help, I got so I could see another little chap. I learnt he was to be my special pal and we took to each other right away.

His girlfriend Merella's a bit of a one but, of course, it isn't the same for fairies as for us. She's got a bit of a crush on Peter and Nuvic was kind of left out so I was glad to have the little chap to talk to and so that he could show me some of the things he sets store by.

That first day he sat astride my knee and fair talked his head off. His special work is with roses and he loves them like we do some people. They're people to him, all right, and they're as different as people too.

I'll try and describe him to you. He's about five or six inches high and his face is as brown as a berry. He laughs a lot and his eyes twinkle all the time he's talking. He mostly wears red, a sort of purply wine-red, I think you'd call it. He's got a tunic with buttons down the front and pockets and a belt. Sometimes he wears breeches and boots that look like bark, only they feel soft, or else things like stockings with long feet turned up at the end. He's got brown, straight hair and he likes it to blow about his face so he don't wear a hat.

He says he don't mind Merella playing around because she grows that way. Seems funny to me but he isn't jealous, though he's cracked about her.

He took me one day to see their home and I'll say she's got some taste. It's like a little palace. He made me kneel down so I could see in but, when I did, I couldn't.

"Nuvic," I says, "are you fooling yourselves or me? There's nothing there!"

"Oh, Andrew, I was afraid you wouldn't see anything," he says. "I was willing you to. I thought perhaps Merella's power might make the things solid for you. We'll have to concentrate and I'm sure you'll see then."

We tried but it wasn't no good that time nor the next, but the one after that I could see a bit of colour inside, a pale green in the room they sleeps in.

"Got your room painted green, I see," I says.

"It's not paint, Andrew. It's leaves," he says.

"You've got a room made of leaves?" I says.

"But of course. If only you could see it properly, you'd realize how pretty it is."

The next time I did see and pretty weren't the word. It seems silly to say it was like a fairy tale, but that's just what it was. There was little bits and pieces that I suppose was furniture. Nuvic lay on a bit of nonsense, then he sat on something else, then he disappeared.

"Andrew, here I am!" I heard him call, and I saw a tiny light up at the top, perching on the branch of a little tree.

"If you go to bed up there, you'll be breaking your neck one of these nights!" I says.

He laughed. "You can't break what isn't there," he says. "I'd soon make another one anyway."

"I wish I could join you," I says. "I'd like to know what it feels like without a body."

"Oh, Andrew. Do learn," he says. "We could have such fun."

So off I goes and I tries to learn but it weren't no good. I can't get my vibrations up enough. I can't even throw off a toe yet.

I'm getting closer to the fairies every time I meets Nuvic. I give lots of thought to it in between and I asks all sorts of people who might have a bit of a slant on it. Mostly I finds that me and the others have got more actual experience with them than the people I meet, but get me talking about them and I get so worked up I never knows where to stop.

I've talked to a few of the higher-ups too, and they says that my best plan's to meet and talk to as many as I can. They seem surprised that a rough sort of chap like me should be wanting to know, but I think they're pleased too.

I'll go back to my own little chum. You know, it seems daft, but I really love him. Silly, isn't it, with me sixteen stone and him like a feather in my hand. Cor, to see the welcome I get, you might think I was the king hisself.

I'll tell you a bit more about the house now. Peter can see more than me, or I sees different, but that makes it interesting. I'll take the hall next. Like a little palace it is, with a round roof like an Eastern mosque. It's all lit up with coloured lights. I don't know where they comes from – 1 can't see no fittings – but Nuvic says they're out of the air. I ask him why I can't see them always if they're there all the time and he said I could if I looked. I've been looking but I still can't see except on special occasions when I'm meant to.

The floor looks soft. I put my finger through the door and it felt like satin. I was afraid of spoiling it with my rough skin but Nuvic said I couldn't if I tried. He said, "It's made by thought and that's unbreakable when you've learnt how."

He showed me a silver-looking ball in the middle of the dome and he told me it was for generating power.

"Ah," I says, "that's my line. I knows all about that. You just tell me about it."

He lifted it down and brought it outside. I asked him if I could hold it in my hand and, lumme, it didn't half tickle! I asked him how it worked and he took off the outside case. He didn't touch it; it just went.

"Now look what you've been and done," I says. "You've gone and spoilt it!"

But he hadn't because when I looked again, the cover was back. "Talk about waving a magic wand!" I says, and then it was gone again.

Well, I knows all about generation but this had me stumped. There was a lot of strands, finer than hair. They didn't lead nowhere, nor was they attached to anything. They was just floating in the air.

"You've got me beat," I says. "Turn it on again."

A little spurt of power left him and the hairs started vibrating like mad so I could scarce hold the thing in my hand. It was like a lot of needles digging into me.

"Okay. It generates," I says, and I gave it back to him.

When I sees Nuvic again, he was right pleased with hisself. 'What's up," I said. "You look pretty cocky."

"I am," he says. "Merella and I found a wonderful place last night."

"Maybe I got to a high plane too," I says.

"Oh, Andrew, did you? Tell me," he says, as keen as mustard.

"I didn't do so bad," I says, and I stops and starts to chew a piece of grass just to keep him guessing,

"Tell me," he says. "Please."

I can't resist him for long. "Okay," I says. "I saw a lovely woman."

"You didn't," he says

"Well, why shouldn't I?" I says.

"You know I believe you did," he says. "Where was she?"

"On the Astral, but pretty high up. Must have been on the borders of the Third plane."

"What did she say?"

"Wouldn't you like to know?" I teased him.

"Andrew, I always tell you everything. Aren't we pals?" he says, and I could see he was real upset.

"I'll tell you," I says quick. "She's going to help me reach higher in my meditation."

He clapped his hands. "When are you going to begin?"

"Right away. She showed me her home. Pretty posh, I don't mind telling you."

"How big was it?" he asked.

"About as big as Buckingham Palace," I says.

"How big's that?" he says.

"You don't know how big the King's Palace is?" I says. "Come on, my boy-your education ain't complete."

"You mean now?" he says.

"Why not?" I asks.

"Okay," he grinned, and off we goes to Buckingham Palace.

We landed right by the main entrance but I took him outside the railings to see the soldiers. There was quite a crowd there and I hoped they'd change the guard, but they didn't.

Then, for the first time in my life, I marched through the gates, past the sentry, and right up to the Palace.

"Not a bad little place," I says.

"It's big," says Nuvic. "I didn't know people lived in such big houses on Earth."

"He's the King," I says.

"Can we see him?" asked Nuvic.

"He might come out," I says, doubtful.

"Could we go and find him?" he asked.

I scratched my head. "I dunno," I says. It was funny. I knew he wouldn't know that me and my pal Nuvic was there, but I didn't like busting in.

"Perhaps another time. He's probably having a bite of supper now," I says.

"All right," says Nuvic. "But I would like to see him one day."

"And so you shall," I promised him, and I'm going to keep that promise. [Unhappily, H.M. King George VI died before Andrew was able to keep his promise. D.C.]

The next time I sees Nuvic, he was all het up over the congress. We was all pretty excited about it too, so I was keen to hear what preparations they'd done.

"Come and see the house I made," he says.

"Wot, all by yourself?", I says.

"Well, no," he says. "But I thought it. The others only gave power because it kept disappearing."

It was tucked away in a corner, away from the main villages.

"Someone got something to hide?" I asked him.

He looked at me all serious, then he saw I was fooling.

"It's for someone very important," he says.

"Who?" I asked.

"Me," he says.

"But you've got a house," I says.

"But this is an observation post."

"Ah, spying on your visitors. You ought to be ashamed of yourself," I says.

He took me all serious for a moment. "I'm going to be there to help them," he said. "I shan't be there all the time, but one of us will, in case anybody wants anything."

"Let's have a look," I says. We went to the rockery and there, up against the fence, I saw a little box with a hole in it like a ticket office. "However did you think of it?" I says, pretending to be that surprised.

"I saw it with you, but I closed it in a bit, so they can't see me."

"Buckingham Palace," I says.

He grinned.

"Where's your horse?" I says.

"Now, Andrew, you must be serious. It's very important. Why, someone might be lost or something."

"Well, they wouldn't be lost far if they was here."

"Silly," he says. "I said this was an observation post. I've got lots of instruments inside."

"Now you're talking," I says. "Let's see." I lays up the rockery, with the stones digging into my stomach, and puts my eyes to the wicket. It was pitch dark inside. "Come on. Come on. Switch on the light," I says. And I'm damned if he didn't.

"Blimey," I says, 'Wot's all them beards hanging up?"

"They're vibration-catchers," he said.

"What do you do when you've got 'em?" I asks.

"They're very clever," he says. "Each one's different."

"Look the same to me," I says.

"Well, they don't to me. Now, this one," he says, pointing to a Father Christmas type, "catches the minor-distress ones. This one," he said, "catches the enquiring ones and this one, the frightened ones."

"What happens?" I asked.

"I'll show you," he says, and disappeared. After a second or two, the first beard must have been charged with some sort of current as, instead of hanging down like a beard should, it stuck out parallel with the ground. Then it fell back and No. 2 took over, then No. 3, which not only stuck out but shot up to the roof. Then Nuvic was back.

"What did you do?" I asks.

"Well, first I lost my way. Then I wanted to know where the reception was.

And then I caught sight of you," he says pointedly.

"What else have you got?" I says, ignoring the joke. He made some covering screen go, because I could see what looked like a blank picture in a frame.

"Television!" I says.

"Pooh!" he says. "You and your silly old two dimensional toys. We know all about them."

I felt real crushed, all six feet three of me. "Okay, show us more then." I saw a little figure close to a tall flower.

"Hello, Merella," I says.

"She can't hear you, stupid. She's right the other end of our territory." Then I saw Normus, then Lyssis and then Daphne in her sitting room.

"Did you make it?" I asked.

"Silly," he says. "It's made by very important people for a very important occasion."

"Do all fairies have things like this?"

"No," he says. "They wouldn't have the power to work them."

"Would they work for me?" I asks.

"I don't know," he says, "but you musn't try. Too much power might break them."

"I'll have to get some fancy-dress beards and hang them in my room for practice then," I says.

"They're very *clever*," he says again, nearly busting with pride that they were in his charge.

"I'm not arguing," I says. "I only wish I was clever enough to see how they worked."

"Poor Andrew," he said, condescendingly. "Perhaps you'll understand one day. You know I'll do everything I can to help you."

"D'you know how they work?"

He fidgeted. "I've shown you," he said.

"Do you understand the scientific data what makes them beards act like ballet dancers?" I insisted.

He grinned. "Not any more than you do," he says as he leaps from the sentry box.

When I'd picked myself up off the rockery he was standing on the rubbish heap with his fingers up to his nose, a trick I taught him. I made after him but he'd gone by the time I got there, so I sat down and waited for him to be in a less cheeky frame of mind.

Nuvic had been on at me to show me more of his home so, the next time I goes to see him, I suggested me trying right away.

"Look at our rest room again," he says. "You're more likely to see that than the others."

So down I goes on my hands and knees. I must say, I'm glad people can't see me. I must look proper daft. I put my eye up to his window and there he was, ready to show me around.

"Got your guide book?" I teased him.

"Here it is," he says, grinning at me, and he'd got something that looked like a book in his hand.

"Your round," I says. 'What are you going to show me first?"

"This," he says, pointing into space.

"Can't see nothing," I says.

"Yes you can," he says. "Watch me. I'll run my hand along the outline."

Have you ever seen anyone draw something on nothing? Looks proper screwy. First he made a square, than a cube. Then he puts a circle on top.

"It's a dressing table with a round looking glass," I says. "You forgot to make the drawers."

"You mustn't tease me. This is very important and very precious."

"Sorry," I says.

"Now watch carefully," he says, and he done it again, only he was concentrating deeper. I was really trying this time too, and I sees it. It was a little box what looked like it was made of gold, with a shiny gold ball on top.

"What is it?" I asks.

"It's our jewel box," he says.

"Open up," I says and, with great care, he lifted up the ball and brings it to the window.

"It's Merella's," he says, all serious.

"It's pretty," I says. "What is it?"

" It's a headdress," he says. "She looks lovely in it. Her aura shines through it and lights it all up."

"When does she wear it?" I asks.

"She hasn't had it long and there hasn't been a grand enough occasion for her to wear it yet, but I expect there will be one day."

He laid it down carefully and dragged the box nearer. Then he opened the lid and the jewels twinkled in the light.

"You've done yourself proud," I says.

"Merella's got more than I have. You know I'm very lucky to have her. I can't understand how I ever managed it. Everyone wants Merella but I've got her. I don't expect I shall always have her though," he says sadly. "Her Earth span finishes before mine and she's bound to have found someone else before I arrive."

"Well, what's meant, happens," was all I could think of, because I can't imagine Merella without a paris for long.

He pulled out a little red necklace. "I helped her to get that, " he says, ever so proud.

'Why didn't you get it then?"

"Huh, I'd look pretty silly in a necklace, wouldn't I?" he says.

"You could wear it 'round your stomach and hang your garden tools on the dingle-dangles," I says, trying to make him laugh, and he did. "Tell me what you did to get it," I says.

He went on holding it up to the light so it made patterns on the floor.

"Merella always wanted a red jewel but she never managed to get above blue ones 'till we were meditating not so long ago. You know, Merella's changed lately; she's much quieter."

"Go on," I says. "You'll be saying she's a reformed character next."

"But I don't want her reformed," he says. "I love her like she is. She's almost thoughtful now, though, sometimes – she's always been the leader, of course, because she's much more advanced than I am, but she's suggested that I should lead the meditation once or twice lately and we haven't done so badly."

"You shouldn't lead her. You should take her by the hair and drag her," I says.

He wasn't sure if I was fooling.. "Merella never needs dragging," he says, pretending to be offended.

146

"Not half, she doesn't, if it's anything in trousers that's doing the whistling," I says.

"I'm not sure" he says again, but he looked mighty pleased with hisself.

I've nearly had my ration of space, worse luck, so I'll just tell you an adventure Nuvic and me had the other day.

He'd been going on at me about meditating with him so I said, "Right. We'll sit down as soon as I gets here next time." So we did, before we started our usual gassing, and off we went.

I wanted to do well for Nuvic's sake, but we seemed to go on and on as though we'd never get there. We stopped at last and there we was, plum in the middle of nowhere. Grass stretched for miles everywhere and there wasn't a house or a tree in sight.

"Don't think much of your choice," I says, but he knew I was pulling his leg because we don't have no say in where we're going.

He looked a bit disappointed. "I expect we're here for a reason," he says.

"You bet we are. They've dumped us here just to see how quick we'll get bored with each other. We'll fool them though. We'll find something good in spite of them. Which way?" I says.

He looked doubtful. I spun a coin. "Heads, left, tails, right, and if it stands on end, up we'll go."

Believe it or not, it stood on end.

"Here goes then," I says, and up we goes. We traveled fast and I was beginning to lose my breath when we stopped and, when I opened my eyes, I near lost it again.

"We're in Fairyland!" I shouted. I was proper excited, I can tell you. I'd been there once and I'd tried fit to bust myself to get there again but I never did, and here we was, Nuvic and me . . . but it wasn't Nuvic when I looked, but a much bigger fellow, about a foot high.

"Cor, look at you!" I says.

"What's the matter with me?" he asks.

"You're fine," I says. "You're a blinking film star," and so he was. He's always handsome but now he was a real smasher.

"You're not so bad yourself," he says.

"Come off it," I says. "Let's stop admiring ourselves and look at the view."

Everything was sparkling like a box of jewels. The trees, the flowers, the grass, even the sky was glittering and shooting out millions of coloured rays.

Nuvic grinned all over his face. "I'll live up here one day with Merella," he says, "and you shall come and visit us."

"Keep a spare bed ready," I says, "I'll be popping in quite often."

I tried to drink in the landscape like I do our own but it hurt. "Does it give you a pain here when you breathe?" I asked him, holding my stomach.

FORTY YEARS WITH THE FAIRIES

"Course not. I just feel all sparkly, too, inside, as though I'm bubbling over with excitement and may burst."

"I wish I could," I says. "it might ease the tension."

"You've let your vibrations down," he said. "You must raise them again or you'll disappear."

I raised them. He was right, the pain had gone. "What do we do now?" I asks him.

"I'll be leader," he says. "Follow me."

"Okay," I says. "Carry on."

He scampered off and I followed him. The blades crackled under my feet and I looked to see if I was breaking them but, instead of me treading them down, they was coming right through my shoes. I waggled my toes to see if I'd been stabbed but they seemed okay. When I looked up, Nuvic was gone so I sent a vibration after him and hauled him back.

"You're so slow," he says. 'We've got things to do."

"What things?"

"You'd be surprised if you knew," he says.

"So would you," I says, and he grinned. "Go on. I thought you was leader." I says.

"So I am, and don't you go pulling me back again. You must keep up." He was off and this time I stayed close to him, skimming the tops of the hedges just like when I'm flying a plane.

"Do you know where you're going?" I shouted after him.

"No-o-o-o," he called, going all the faster. I'd almost given up getting any-where when I sees a huge building looming up in the distance. I've often wondered what "looming up" meant and now I know.

We saw some spikes first; then some turrets and then the whole thing burst out of the ground right in front of us. I had to stop because it dazzled my eyes. It was whiter than anything I ever saw. You think that snow's white and that it sparkles when the sun's on it. Well, it isn't and it don't.

I tried opening my eyes but it wasn't no good.

"Keep your eyes closed and look at it like that," Nuvic said.

"Go on," I said.

"Go on, yourself," he says. So I did and it was beautiful, just like he said.

"Who lives there? Must be a hiarus at least,"

"No, a hiarus would live on a higher plane than we could reach. It might be a farallis though."

"You'd better hurry and be one, too, then," I says. "I wouldn't mind spending a nice weekend with you here."

Nuvic wasn't listening – at least he wasn't listening to me. He was tense all over like a dog when he's spotted a bird.

I looked where he was looking and I saw the gate of the palace was opening. I felt excited then, wondering what we was going to see.

A big, sparkling beam shot through the entrance and along it came a beautiful girl. I suppose she was a fairy of sorts but I'd never seen the like. None of my expressions like corker, or smasher, would fit and I don't use the refined sort of words, so you'll just have to imagine the loveliest lady you ever dreamt of meeting.

Her hair wasn't dark nor fair and her skin wasn't pink or brown, neither-she just sparkled all over, every colour you can think of. When she smiled, her ray got stronger and knew I'd do any blooming thing she asked me.

Her aura got even more sparkly and I knew she was talking but I couldn't get it. I was so flummoxed by her, I don't think I could have heard even if she'd been talking as slow as our fairies, but she wasn't anyway.

Nuvic could hear though and he said, after a bit, "She bids us welcome to her home and she would be pleased if we would enter."

I looked down at my clothes. I'd put on my second-best suit to have tea with Daphne in, but it wasn't much for a visit with a great lady.

Then my eyes fair popped out. I was all sparkling too. Cripes, what a suit! It was all gold and shining like billy-o.

Seeing as how I was suitably dressed, I bowed very low and mumbled that we'd be honoured. She held out her hand and, believe it or not, I kissed it. Daft, isn't it, when you think of me acting like a proper gent, but what was even funnier was that it come quite natural.

She put her fingers on my arm and where they touched was like being electrified. Not prickly, mind you, but alive. Not that I'd thought of the rest of me as being dead 'til I kissed her hand and she touched me. I felt like my mouth was alight but not hot. I'm no writer and put things bad. You'll just have to take it was something out of the way.

I didn't bother to walk. I don't think I could have. I gazed at her like a faithful dog – just like Nipper looks at me, but softer. She did something to me, that fairy lady. I haven't got over it yet.

It's hard to describe where we went. I was dazed no mistake. It may have been the high vibration. On the other hand, it may not.

When I came to myself properly again, we was in a huge hall. Talk about jewels. I've never seen the like.

There were lots of people there, not quite as bright as my lady, but pretty near. She must have introduced me to them because the air got even more glittery, which I supposed was a greeting but I couldn't catch a word.

I felt a tug at my trouser leg and there was Nuvic performing the ceremonial salute, so I follows suit, first to my lady. Cor, I didn't know I was an acrobat but my head near touched the ground. Then another to the rest of them, which sent them all leaping into the air like a lot of jack-in-the-boxes. That was a new one on me but I suppose that meant they was pleased to meet me.

My lady led me to a kind of throne. I remembered my manners and tried to hand her into it but she shook her head and showed it was for me. Now, did you ever? Me, sitting on a throne!

I thought Nuvic would be fair laughing his head off but he weren't. He was bowing me into it. Well, what could I do? I sat. Comfortable it was, too. All pneumatic upholstery, gold or no. I sat bolt upright, wondering what was going to happen next.

My lady had disappeared, worse luck, but even that couldn't stop me enjoying myself. I was on top of the world and no mistake.

Then things started to happen. I wasn't sure what, at first, because my eyes couldn't focus properly. Then the jumble of jewels got to be a pattern what began to move and change around – central pivot.

Then I realized what was going on. They was dancing and my lady was the figure 'round what the pattern kept changing.

I musn't say "cripes." It wouldn't be fitting. I don't know what to say. It was the loveliest thing I ever did see. I even understood a bit. Enough to know that they was being nice about my progress, and that they'd like to help me if I'd let them.

Now how could I know that from a lot of dancing figures, you'll ask. And the worst of it is, I can't tell you. I just knew, as we always do know the things we're meant to. Can't tell you clearer. Only wish I could.

Then something funny happened. Not funny-joke kind, but I found I was dancing with them. Now I've told you I weigh sixteen stone and I'm not a dancing man neither, but it was like being a bit of thistledown swept about in the wind. Call me barmy. I don't care. That's just what it was like and, if you don't know what it feels like to be a bit of thistledown, that's your loss, I do.

I kept changing colour as well. That's a new one on you, too, I bet. It was on me. Excited? I've never been so excited in my life. I didn't know what I might do next. And, what's more, I didn't care.

That fairy lady, she was closer to me in that dance than you've ever been to a living soul, and that's no exaggeration. We was overlapping. See what I mean? I'll never get over it if I live forever.

I wanted to die right there. I thought, "I can't ever know anything better. I won't go back to the Astral." But I did.

There come a time when I must have overdid it. I couldn't stand it, see. I knew I was on the point of busting, but I had to go on doing whatever I was doing and, Bingo, I'd had it.

I woke up on my bed. It was midnight and I was still dressed. But I remembered everything. Even the feeling come back. It mayn't surprise you, I didn't sleep a wink that night.

– Andrew

NIXUS AND LYSSIS
OBSERVER: JOHN

GRASS
by Nixus

I want to tell you how I first met Lyssis. I was very preoccupied one day, giving power to guide some unites; my mind was completely concentrated when, quite suddenly, it seemed to go "Pff." *[I cannot think of a more adequate word to translate the picture he gave me of his head bursting like a blown-up paper bag. – D.C.]*

For a moment I couldn't think what had happened. I was dazed. Then I realized that it was a vibration which had done this strange thing to me.

Slowly I gathered myself together and I became aware that someone was standing in front of me. Lyssis.

She was, and is, more beautiful than a star and I knew that I loved her with every part of me. I couldn't speak. I just put out my hand and touched her.

You see, I couldn't believe that she was real. She smiled and her kindness seemed to release my mind from a spell. I drew back embarrassed, but she continued to smile. I knew then that she wasn't offended, so I said, "You're the loveliest fairy I've ever seen. Please tell me where you are from."

To my delight, she lived within three miles and she was visiting our territory in order to examine a rare flower she had never seen before.

"I will take you," I said, for the plant had already given me much pleasure. Together, we went to look at it and, in her presence, the flower seemed to gather fresh radiance.

"How I wish that I had a similar one to look after," she sighed.

"Why not help this one to grow?" I suggested eagerly. "I'm sure that the fairy in whose charge she is will be happy for you to come as often as you will."

Her face lit up. "Are you sure?" she cried excitedly.

"He is my friend," I replied. "He will be delighted, I know. Let's go and ask him now. He can't be far away."

But we didn't find him. We set out with the intention of doing so, but we quickly lost his vibration and we wandered along happily, along the rosy paths of love.

Lyssis came every day. At first we pretended, even to ourselves, that she had come to see the flower. I didn't dare think otherwise, although even then I really knew. Each day we visited the plant and gave it power, and each day we admired its growth and its increasingly beautiful form, although our minds were far away.

There came the time when I could bear this brief contact with her no more. It's true that we met each evening as well, when we mingled our auras and exchanged power, but this was not enough. I wanted her with me always. I asked her if she would share my life and she eagerly assented.

Our evenings of meditation with Daphne are always of the greatest interest for each time we learn something new. I would very much like to tell you about one visit to the Ceris sector which was completely different from anywhere we had ever been before.

Colours play a tremendous part in the life of every fairy, but we had never seen such deep, rich tones as we did that night. To you, colour is just a question of seeing, but we absorb it into our very being and each has a different effect.

The place we visited was beautiful. There were trees and a valley with a river wending its way lazily towards the horizon. Nothing very unusual in that, you will say. It was the colours, though.

The valley varied from purple, through every shade of crimson, to a pale rose-pink. The sky was fiery and yet it was peaceful. Can you imagine that? It isn't really possible, yet it was both.

The river was blue but it was quite different from any water that we had ever seen before. It was a deep, intense blue and absolutely clear. We gazed into its depth and we saw many brightly coloured fish and beautiful plants.

After we had been watching it for awhile, a wonderful sensation of peace stole over us. We felt that the river was washing all round and through us, and that it was carrying away with all our difficulties. A feeling of refreshment filled us when we again rose to our feet and we followed our Guide (The Marano Majol, one of the Shining Ones of the Ceris evolution) across the plane to the source of the river.

"There is a lesson to be learned from this river," He said. "Its peaceful flow is not entirely geographical. Each drop of which its water is composed has been tempered to its present state of calm. Centuries of wild lashing against rocks has taught it restraint and the joys of gentle movement. Later I will take you to the sea into which it flows, where scarcely a ripple stirs the tranquil surface."

We watched the endless flow again and, this time, in its still, calm depths, we seemed to see a vision of its former fury. Then, once again, the river swept imperturbably towards its future destiny.

By this time it was narrowing and we climbed up the sides of a brilliant waterfall, but even here, in spite of a drop of a hundred feet, there was no splash, no outward sign of disturbance.

We followed it to a cavity in the mountain side where it was composed of slow, intermittent drops of the same indescribable blue.

"And what is the lesson?" asked our Guide. We all knew the answer. "Great things come from small beginnings."

– Nixus

LOW FLOWERS

by Lyssis

When I lived on the Astral plane, I was with a big community of fairies. I can't remember any time when I wasn't there. We lived in a beautiful setting, far from Man, in our own sector, where the air sparkles and the plants all quiver with life. I was always so filled with desire to achieve that I never felt tired, and I took my periods of rest only because I was ordered to do so.

And how beautiful were these quiet hours too, when my body seemed to float gently while my mind became so still that I felt as though nothing in the Universe could escape my knowledge.

My work has always been with the small flowers, towards whom I feel the tenderest compassion. They have so much against which to battle for existence, not only weeds, but the taller and stronger plants as well.

On the Astral plane, of course, arrangements are better than down here, for everything has room to develop. There are no big, overshadowing leaves holding off warmth and refreshment, and all the little flowers must do is to grow as beautiful as they are able in the gentle light and the warm, moist earth. There, the wind caresses them and never becomes the rough force against which all their puny strength must be pitted.

I cannot explain, even to those who love and understand flowers, the exquisite beauty of our charges over there. They smile all day but, although they know contentment, they always strive for greater beauty, more colour, more perfume and an even more perfect way of expressing themselves. It is indeed wonderful that they, with their minute consciousness, should know what Life is for and, naturally, I do everything I can, by thought, by love and power, to bring them a little nearer to the goal which we all strive to reach.

Happiness seems to be around us and within us, always urging us on to greater activity until the time comes when we can bear it no longer. This probably sounds strange, that one can have too much happiness, but I can only assure you that it is so. One becomes restless in spite of constant activity and one's periods of repose cease to bring the peace which they should.

When this stage is reached, our leaders know that we must be persuaded to return to Earth. When this suggestion was made to me, I almost wept. I had no wish to leave my lovely home to battle with unknown difficulties down there. My leader didn't press me because she knew that, given time to think, I should come to the realization that, if I wished to progress further, I must suffer.

For a period I fought against this idea. I spent much time in meditation as I wished to prove that I was able to progress in my present surroundings. I was wrong. I couldn't concentrate and, instead of enjoying a sensation of exquisite relaxation, my mind whirled endlessly and I knew no rest.

Eventually, I agreed to come down and my training began. I waited twenty-five years before being permitted to descend and, by that time, I was all eagerness.

At first I suffered, as all who come to Earth do, but by degrees I became used to the new conditions and I was happy again. This time, though, I had greater understanding. I moved from place to place and each time there was new suffering, leading to wider knowledge and a greater determination to succeed.

Nixus has told you of our meeting and our resulting joy in each other. We know that we are but young fairies and we look to the future with hope in our hearts, for our love for one another and our work, together, ensure our happiness.

– Lyssis

NIXUS AND LYSSIS
by John

hen I met the men with whom I have now become such friends, I knew only a very little about fairies. I realized they existed because as soon as Daphne had told me about them, I made enquiries and I read several books.

That first afternoon I failed to hear any of them but the next occasion that we met, I heard Normus and, the second week after that, I met Lyssis for the first time.

When you've never seen a fairy, you're inclined to imagine a traditional figure with a wand and a star on the head, looking rather like a wax doll. When I saw Lyssis I realized how mistaken I had been.

She was just a girl in miniature and she smiled at me politely, very like any young woman on being introduced to a man for the first time. For myself, I felt rather tongue-tied as I've never been much of a lady's man. I think she realized that I was shy (who ever heard of a great man being shy of a fairy?) because she patted my hand and invited me to go with her to see her home.

This broke the ice so, with her perched on the palm of my hand, we made our way to a garden up the road.

"You won't be able to see much at first but at least you will know where we live," she said.

I walked carefully because I was afraid of dropping her but she seemed full of confidence. As we went along, we talked and I was able to study her appearance.

She is about five inches high, a little smaller than the other fairies, and she wears her straight blonde hair swept back from her face and falling down her back as far as her waist. Her dress was neat and rather demure; it looked as though it was made of cream-coloured cotton, with a stiff, white collar and cuffs on the sleeves, which came to her elbows. Her face is angelic. Perhaps I shouldn't say this, as real angels must be far more beautiful than she is, but she's angelic by Earth standards anyway.

She looks a little serious until a smile lights up her face and then she entirely changes and becomes all gaiety, rather like a child. Her skin is pale, like the clothes she usually wears; in fact, with her light gold hair, she looks almost as though she's made of cream.

We eventually arrived. She was right. I couldn't even see the house. She suggested that we should sit close to it, hoping that I could at least feel its vibration and, after awhile, I did indeed notice a tremor pass through me. She hadn't told me in which direction the building lay and she was delighted when I pointed out the correct position.

Nixus was, of course, with us although I couldn't see him, but we were able to talk quite freely.

He was interested to hear that my Earth profession had been selling and renting houses. I explained to them how there, people's material means governs the size and beauty of the homes in which they are able to live. This, they considered most unfair.

"Our house is the smallest in the group, but that is only right because we aren't very advanced," they told me. "We're learning fast, though, and soon we hope to be given permission to add a room for meditation. We aren't very good at this either; our minds keep wandering and we never seem to be able to concentrate for more than a second or two at a time."

I was intensely interested to learn that fairies, too, have this difficulty. I had just begun to try to control my own thoughts, not yet being sufficiently advanced to meditate, and I, too, was running into this same trouble. I made them promise that if ever they found a method of steadying their wayward thoughts, they would tell me and I would do the same for them.

During the week before my next visit, I studied hard and I learned how to raise my vibrations in order to be more in tune with the fairies. I still found that I was a bit nervous, but this time I managed better and I was soon able to see not only Lyssis, but a little man standing beside her.

Nixus isn't quite so similar to a man in miniature as Lyssis is to a girl, or maybe it's his clothes. Probably if he wore flannels and a sports coat he would be like a tiny man but, as it is, he's more my idea of the traditional fairy.

He wears brown, as a rule, a jerkin with a leather belt and long brown stockings. For a hat, he has a little round cap turned up all 'round, which looks as though it's made out of an old sock. His face is very brown, too, with rather a serious expression.

I think that these two young fairies are determined to make a success of their lives and they find that they must give all their attention to their work in order to keep up with the more advanced members of their group. They are always very modest about their achievements, and I made up my mind that I would do my very best to help them.

I wasn't sure whether fairies shook hands but Nixus seemed to understand what I wanted and he gravely laid his hand in my outstretched palm. "Will you come with us?" he asked politely.

We made out way to their home again. "I'm going to see it today," I told them with determination, as we sat down in a row, with me in the middle.

"Don't expect a big house," they warned me.

"I don't want it to be big," I replied. "I want a real fairy cottage. You know, I've been imagining it all the week and I can't get it out of my head that it will be made of pink and white icing sugar."

"It's not a bit like that," they said apologetically. "It's red brick, like that one," and they pointed to one of the neat little buildings close by.

I began to raise my vibrations and, after a short while, I saw a little house identical in every respect to the one which they had pointed out to me. It even had cream curtains and a door-knocker.

"I can see it!" I cried, and I hoped that I sounded enthusiastic, although their little home was not at all as I had imagined it.

"Do you like it?" they asked almost nervously.

"I think it's a dear little place and one that I should have been proud to have on my books," I assured them.

They seemed pleased that their home stood up to my professional standards. "It's really nicer inside," Lyssis said. "We have two rooms, one for sleeping and one for working, meditating and entertaining."

'When you're going to meditate," she continued, "it's very helpful to clear away all the ordinary thoughts from the vicinity, but it's even better if you have a special room because then you don't think any but high thoughts in it."

"Please tell me more about it," I said. "I never quite know what are high thoughts. They don't come easily to me, and when I try to relax as they tell you to do in books so that beautiful thoughts may flow, nothing comes. Then, after a bit, the same old clutter of nonsense whirls 'round my head again."

"Have you a symbol?" Lyssis asked.

"What, a cross or something?"

"A cross would do, or a ring, or a five- or twelve-pointed star."

"I'm afraid I wouldn't know their meaning, except, I suppose, the cross."

"That wouldn't matter," Nixus said. "Take a circle. You can draw one if you haven't a ring. Look at it and see what happens. Let's do it now," he continued, as he made one on the ground. "Now, what comes into your mind?"

I thought a moment. "A wedding," I replied.

"Well, that's a union, isn't it?" he said. "Union with what? You must ask yourself. Union with the Infinite. Do you understand?"

"Mm," I said, "Tell me some more."

He then drew a triangle with each side of the same length. 'What comes to your mind this time?" he asked.

"Equality," I said doubtfully.

"Go on," he prompted. "Ask yourself, 'Equality of what?' "

"Equality of what?" I echoed obediently, and then stuck. "Of what?" I repeated apologetically.

"Equality of consciousness with the Great Ones."

"Oh, but I haven't. I wouldn't dare think that," I remonstrated.

"But you must," he insisted. "Your consciousness comes from GOD. So does Their's. He gives us all the same amount but it's asleep. They've woken Their's up farther than you have, that's all."

"I hadn't thought of it like that," I said doubtfully.

"But that's what meditation is for; so that you do think things like that. Think and understand them too."

I had to leave them at this point but the lesson continued on my next visit. This time we took a five-pointed star as our symbol. I gazed at it vacantly.

"Well," said Nixus encouragingly.

"I can only think of a journey," I said. "It sounds silly but journeying towards the stars seems to ring a bell."

He looked a bit disappointed. "Is that all?" he asked.

I tried again but nothing else came.

"Start from the beginning of your journey. That's here," he prompted.

"Mm," I said, not very intelligently. "I know. I'll think what I'll take with me. Five things. Will that do?"

Nixus smiled and Lyssis obviously also approved. I realized that I mustn't let them down by taking a toothbrush and some cigarettes so I began with "Hope."

"Stop," said Nixus. "Now you must meditate on Hope." I could plainly see that I wasn't going to be let off lightly.

"Hope for what?" I duly asked myself. "Hope of finding what I seek. Hope to . . ."

"No, no. You mustn't go on yet. What are you hoping to find?"

"The Truth," I said triumphantly. That was easy. "Hope to . . ."

"Oh, no, John, you go on much too fast. This is a most fruitful meditation. There are a million aspects of Truth. You must think around them first."

I focused my attention on Truth but none of the million aspects revealed themselves. I became almost desperate. If there were so many, surely I could think of one.

"The Truth of ... of Love . . . that service brings happiness . . . that it is the duty of all to help others to evolve ... that GOD dwells within each and every man . . ."
I was so absorbed in the flow of my thoughts that I almost missed the expression

of approval on my little friends' faces. "Do I have to think of all the million?" I asked, but I must confess that I was finding this way of meditating much more interesting than I had anticipated.

"You don't have to," they said, "but you're supposed to think of as many as you can."

Several more came fairly easily. "Now you have a go," I said, after which, we took it in turns and it was extraordinary how each thought led naturally to the next; the longer we continued, the easier it became; in fact, we were still far off the millionth aspect when I found that, once again, I had to leave them.

From then on we always practiced meditation for, at any rate, part of my visits, until the day came when Nixus decreed that I was ready for a journey. All the others had experienced this mental release and I'd been very anxious to try for myself but, as Nixus and Lyssis had taken upon themselves the task of teaching me, I thought it only fair to wait until they considered that I was ready to accompany them. We all relaxed and I closed my eyes.

"We'll take the star again," Nixus said, "and we'll try to get as close to it as we can."

It was broad daylight and yet I could have sworn that, with my eyes closed, I could see a star twinkling invitingly to us potential voyagers millions of miles below.

Nothing happened for quite a long time and then I thought of turning on some power. Almost immediately we began to move – up – up, until I was sure that we must be beyond the star which I had seen from the ground.

At last we stopped. I opened my eyes, half expecting the land to taper away into a point beside me, with nothing but empty space beyond. But it wasn't at all like that.

Green pasture land and flowers stretched away in every direction. Nixus and Lyssis were still clasped in each other's arms and they looked really beautiful. I was sure that their thoughts were far higher than the place which we had reached, which was obviously a comparatively low sphere of the Astral.

I rose to my feet and began to walk. There was a tremendous surge of happiness everywhere and I felt very energetic-as though I ought to be doing something.

"John, John," I heard little voices near my feet. "Why did you go?"

"You looked so contented," I replied, "I didn't like to disturb you."

"But we've got things to do," they said.

"I felt that we had," I replied. "Do you know what they are?"

"No," they admitted, "but we soon shall." They led the way and I followed.

"Do you know where we're going?" I enquired.

"We're following the path," they said.

I could see no sign of a track or road but I wasn't going to admit it. Gradually they left the ground and began drifting upwards. I wasn't sure whether I'd be able to follow. It's quite different, floating with your eyes closed, to consciously walking on nothing when you're used to the ground.

I thought firmly, "There *is* a path. Take it," and then, to my relief, I saw it. Quite solid it was, too, rather like a raised carriage-way with a drop on both sides.

We ascended slowly, twisting and turning as though on a mountain road until, on rounding one of the numerous bends, we knew that we had reached the end of our journey. A real fairy palace rose up into the clouds, like an airy white wedding cake, but much more beautiful.

"What is it?" I asked.

They looked doubtful. "We've never been this high before. Oh, John, isn't it exciting?"

It was, and it was a great relief to me that our journey was a success from their point of view because I had been rather afraid that my ignorance would hold them back.

"Are we supposed to go in, do you think?" I asked.

"I expect so," they said. "Let's go up to it and we shall know."

They were quite right but it wasn't a question of knowing. One moment we were about ten yards from the closed gate and the next, we were the other side of it, and to this day I haven't fathomed whether we passed through it or missed it out altogether.

As soon as we were inside I knew what we were there for. Somebody needed us – somebody who had perhaps been cut off from Earth suddenly and couldn't get acclimatized to the new conditions.

Nixus and Lyssis began speed-moving and, by lengthening my stride, I kept up with them. I was sure that many people were leading us but I couldn't see a soul.

At last we stopped right in the middle of a large, vaulted room and, as soon as we did so, I could feel the distress vibration which was obviously coming from one of the corners.

I'm used to these vibrations when working with the earthbound so I followed it quite easily. We came to the end of it but still I couldn't see anything. I concentrated hard and then I saw her, a little fairy, looking very bedraggled and plain. My two friends were already trying to comfort her but she seemed almost dazed.

"Oh, John, it's like being earthbound to humans," they explained. "She must have raised her vibrations, which we're not allowed to do when we're on Earth, and she hasn't been able to see any of the fairies or this lovely house."

They turned to comfort her again and then the idea of giving some power came to me. The change was instantaneous.

She seemed to lose her haggard appearance and she clung to Lyssis as though she'd never let her go. Then she began to talk, too fast for me to follow at the time but Nixus related her story to me afterwards.

160

She told them how one night she had been reprimanded by her leader because she was neglecting her work. She had been miserable ever since she had come to Earth and she decided that nothing could possibly be worse. She didn't mind how much she was punished, but the prospect of another ninety-seven years of unhappiness was too much for her.

Then she had thought of her old home and had raised her vibrations. She sobbed afresh.

"But I didn't go there," she wailed. "I haven't seen anyone for, it must be years. It's all dark and I'm always cold, not just sometimes, like on Earth. Please, haven't I been punished enough?"

It was at this point that the fairies appealed to me. This was their first case of helping an Astral-bound fairy and they didn't know all the answers.

"Tell her that guilt and unhappiness always form a barrier between us and our desires," I said. "She's obviously not completely on the Astral plane, but betwixt and between in the no-man's land.

"You must persuade her to want to go back to Earth – I don't think by the look of her that you'll have much trouble," I encouraged them.

They turned to her again and I watched one expression chase another across her face. To begin with, there was fear. That usually comes first with the earth-bound too. Fear of further punishment, accusing words, or insistence on unpleasant atonement.

Then comes relief when they discover that we only want to help and not to nag at them.

Then hope that perhaps, after all, there may be something better for them in this life which seems to be endless and, finally, the beginning of eagerness to start afresh and really show 'em what they can do.

It was the same with this small person who had made a grave mistake too and soon, with a fairy on each side, we retraced our footsteps and returned to Earth. I left them on arrival because I knew that Normus would have to be consulted about accommodation for the night and the fairy's return to her proper home in the morning.

It was strange and rather gratifying that I, who am one of the lowliest members of our group, should have been chosen, with two of the humbler fairies in theirs, to bring before the band the possibility of yet another branch of helping those in trouble. This rescue work has now become one of their regular tasks.

From one meeting to another I'm filled with anticipation as to what we shall do and where we shall go on our next.

Together we have seen things which I never knew existed and Nixus and Lyssis have taught me almost all I know about meditation. I try to learn now, not only because I want to understand about everything within my mental range but because, in discussing new-found facts with them, they always somehow shed a different light on the subject. They disclose to me each new aspect as they learn it, whether it is about healing, their work with the human earthbound, or their counterpart in the fairy world.

They encourage me in my so far vain efforts to come in closer contact with my ceris (a member of another evolution), and when I can't hear what he is saying to me, they act as interpreters. They tell me about the many entities upon whom I rely for my continued existence in my present form. About these, I know even less than I do about my ceris.

Some time ago I felt that, with so many things going on around me, if I became in tune with all of them, the whole issue would be confused. I understand now, however, that this isn't true, that as one became in tune with another evolution, a whole new sector of one's mind became animated, and one is thus equipped to receive more and more knowledge.

When one realizes that each evolution has its own rate of vibration and that everything that grows with them and 'round them is also vibrating faster or slower than all the other evolutions, that they have their own plants and animals, different types of homes, instruments, music and all the others, one realizes that one isn't going to have a dull moment for a good many thousand years. Each new aspect learned opens up others until my head spins at the thought.

I've talked to quite a lot of people about these other evolutions and they seem even less known than the fairies, which all goes to prove that just because a person's dead, he doesn't necessarily know much, if any, more than you do.

Where we do score, though, is that as soon as we start wondering about some new subject, and we make a few enquiries about it, it's never long before we just "happen" to run into someone who can answer the questions which have been puzzling us. A little later we also "happen" to run into someone who holds classes on the very subject which interests us and so we are gradually led from one teacher to another until we are ready for the more practical side to be demonstrated. I could go on writing indefinitely but I mustn't, so you'll just have to hope that another opportunity will be given to us to tell you a bit more one day – that is, if you're interested in our adventures in Fairyland.

– John

FAIRY BABIES

by Rhelia

For some years now, I have had in my charge three young fairies. We do not have babies like human beings, but we provide them with the conditions for their growth. Is not this in reality what human parents do too? They produce the body which is the "container" for the soul and in their daily lives, they supply the conditions in which the child reaches maturity.

With fairies, it is a little different for it is our task to provide the means by which an un-individualized member of a group can be separated from that group and become aware of itself through becoming aware of its guardians. The conditions which we provide are not only "containers" but also "barriers" to prevent a return to the group.

A certain stage has to be reached before a separation can take place and the little consciousness presented to the guardians for care [cared for]. We then use Will. We reflect ourselves as individuals into the little mind so that the idea of something outside of itself enters. Eventually this becoming aware of something apart from itself causes it to become aware of its own self. In other words it becomes self-conscious.

There is no sudden awakening to the presence of this reflection of us leading to awareness of our actual selves. Day by day we perform this act of will until the appearance of a tiny light tells us that we have achieved our purpose and, as you would say, the baby has been born.

I have had three children, one is now the equivalent of about four years old, another six, and the eldest has reached the stage when she has gone out into the world to join another group in order to learn.

At Midsummer, the downpour of power filled her to prepare her for a new phase in her existence, and she left us to form her own judgments and to experience trials and joys of her own.

To a human being, I understand, this parting is a painful one, but to us it is a task completed. We prepared her for her test of living and now she must develop, as we all must, of her own free Will. This is the gift which Individualization bestows: Free Will to work or play, to progress or to slip back. It is therefore important that, while in their care, the guardians should impress on their charges their necessity to God's Plan; that their life is a part of the Whole and that the great gift of Free Will must be used wisely.

Of course, the young are not wise and they must learn through experience. But at least this young one knows the way she SHOULD go, and I hope that she will find her Path without stumbling too often before she reaches it.

– Rhelia, 10th July 1960

MANUSCRIPTS
SET #5

NORMUS, THE LEADER
OF THE FAIRIES

OBSERVER: FATHER JOHN

Preface

Normus was introduced briefly at the beginning of the first story in Manuscript Set #3.

Normus is an endearing character. One of the most fun-loving fairies you are ever likely to meet. He is also one of the most advanced fairies that Daphne works with. Perhaps the advancement is because of his fun attitude. Normus can also wax poetic and discuss the spiritual mysteries of the universe. Normus was only 1 foot tall when Daphne met him, but he evolved so rapidly that after 40 years of working with Daphne he was 3 feet tall.

Normus has authored more of the manuscripts then any of the other fairies, with the exception of Maire, one of the house fairies. They authored 12 manuscripts each.

– Michael Pilarski

NORMUS' CHILDISH PRANKS

by Daphne Charters

𝕬fter meeting him, it became my habit to go out into the garden each evening to say good night to Normus. To begin with, he was almost invariably cheeky and I had to put him firmly in his place but, after a short while, he altered; our conversations became more serious and each learned items of interest concerning the other's evolution.

About a year later I remarked on this change. I said, "At first, when we met, you were so busy showing us all what a clever fellow you were, you had no time for the kind of conversations that we have now."

"Mm," he agreed. "You know I hoped to get the better of you."

"And did you?" I enquired.

"No," he replied quite cheerfully, "but I always try."

Very early in our acquaintanceship, one of my discarnate friends – it was Ronald, as a matter of fact – came to see me. It is

my custom to kiss all my friends goodbye and I suddenly became aware that Normus, who had been talking to us, was almost in hysterics.

Until I came, kissing, to them, was a ridiculous performance, as to us is the fact that in some countries it is the custom for friends to greet each other by rubbing noses. I may add, though, that the fairies have since come to the conclusion that kissing is rather fun and the girls often embrace my astral friends and I always kiss Normus goodnight.

However, to return to this first occasion, I saw Normus rocking backwards and forwards, endeavouring very conspicuously to stifle his mirth by covering his face with his hands.

"What's the matter, Normus?" I asked.

"Oh, you look so funny," he squealed.

"If you don't behave yourself I shall beat your behind!" I said.

He continued rocking with laughter but this time he was shielding his tiny buttocks with his fingers.

168

"Normus," I said severely, "if you don't stop, I shall tear the living daylights out of you!"

I do not know what this vulgar piece of slang becomes when translated into fairy language but he ceased instantly. "Oh, Daphne, you wouldn't do that, would you?" he asked doubtfully.

"I certainly shall if I catch you laughing when I kiss any of my friends again," I insisted.

I do not know whether he took my threat seriously or whether he became used to the sight and so it lost its power to amuse; anyway, I never saw him laughing at me under similar circumstances again.

On another occasion, I wanted him to entertain George for me. "Normus, are you there?" I enquired, although I knew that he could never keep away when I had a visitor, the desire to show off with his merry quips being as attractive to Normus as to any precocious schoolchild.

There was no reply. I took a second "look" and I was convinced of his presence. "Normus," I said, "you are here. Stop fooling."

"Yes, I'm here," he piped up.

"Now, Normus," I said, "you should really know better. Your not answering when I call you is like trying to trick a poor blind woman and that's not at all kind."

"Pooh," he said, quite unimpressed, "you can see quite well when you try."

Nails and Noses

Aiding me in my work has helped the fairies to evolve but sometimes their progress is my loss. For some time Normus was never quite sure whether I was teasing him or not, and he would waver backwards and forwards, quite unsure of himself.

However, one day I decided to ask him some questions about the fairies' bodies.

"Have you any finger nails?" I enquired.

" 'Course I have," he said almost belligerently.

"What do you do with them?" I asked.

He paused a moment. Obviously he does not need any of his body for his work and his nails are a decoration. He could find no answer so he said, "What do you use yours for?"

"To pick my nose," I solemnly replied.

He looked at me quizzically, then he squealed triumphantly, "You're teasing me."

"On the contrary," I replied, "I'm extremely serious."

"You aren't," he said, "you can't fool me any more, you've changed colour – you've gone a faint mauve."

I had known for some time that more evolved entities, like Father John, can read one's mood by the colour of the aura but this feat was something quite new for Normus.

"What do you have up your nose?" he asked seriously.

"Well, I think we breathe up particles of dust which are surrounded by gelatinous matter, presumably to prevent them from going all the way into the lungs, which are the organs with which we breathe."

"What happens to the little bits when you don't pick them, then?" he enquired.

"We blow them into a handkerchief '" I replied, and I proceeded to tell him how, when we catch a cold, we have to blow and blow and our eyes water and our noses get red.

"I don't think I'd like to see you with a cold," he said.

"Well, you probably won't have to," I replied, "because I refuse to have them and, in any case, you see my astral body and that wouldn't get a red nose, I'm sure."

Feet

Normus had learnt more about human noses than I had about his fingernails and I was still anxious to pursue my enquiries so, on another occasion, I said, "Fairies I know sometimes wear long, pointed shoes; are there any feet in the shoes or are they mostly just space?"

" 'Course there's feet inside," he said.

"Well, are they like mine or do they run the whole length of the shoe?"

"They're like yours," he said.

"Well, why don't you turn up the toes of your shoes and hang a little bell from the top - you could make it in the shape of a bluebell; it would look and sound so pretty."

Normus was enchanted with the idea and said, "Wait a second and I'll make them."

"Will they ring?" I asked when he proudly displayed his handiwork – or, I should say, thought-work – and I heard a tiny tinkle.

"Watch me, watch me," he called as he flew from my shoulder and executed a little dance, more for his own benefit than for mine. "I shan't sleep all night. I shall just dance," he announced.

"I shouldn't do that," I said. "You've work to do tomorrow and you should have your rest. Won't the other fairies be surprised? If they don't get up in the morning, you can go and ring the bells right in their ears."

He was still brimming over with excitement when I left him and, in the morning, when I greeted the little people as usual, I heard a tiny tinkle.

"How d'you like Normus' shoes?" I enquired.

"Oh, they're lovely!" they chorused.

"Show them to the house fairies," I said.

Then I heard a little voice. "Do you mind if we copy them?"

Normus replied, "Well, you mustn't at present. I want to keep them to myself."

"Oh, Normus!" I said reproachfully. "If they want some too, why won't you let them?"

"I'm going to make them earn them," he replied.

"Did you?" I asked softly.

He paused. "Well, no, I suppose I didn't. They'd better have them too, if they want them."

"I've got a lovely idea," I continued quickly, not wishing to discomfort him further. "Tomorrow's Saturday and your astral friends will be coming to tea. Why don't you surprise them?" Oh, yes, oh, yes," they said eagerly.

"When they're comfortably settled and eating, you can swoop down on them all at once, ringing your bells like mad."

They were wildly excited and I've no doubt that the planning, execution and success of this simple idea kept them amused for several days.

More Jokes

Having given the fairies so much happiness with the love vibration, enabling them to visit the astral plane as a group, I decided that Normus, as leader, should also have this privilege by himself.

As his body went limp on his entering a higher vibration, I would carry him back to the corner of the garden where the communal house stands, and put him to bed, not in his own room because I don't know where it is, but in a miniature human bed which I made by thought.

First of all, there was just the bed, then, on the next occasion, I put him into a pair of red and white striped pyjamas. This was a great joke and caused all the fairies much amusement.

Detail by detail I added accessories, each leading to an explanation in regard to their use the following morning. I gave him a bedside table with books; next, an electric lamp was added, then a miniature decanter of whiskey and a syphon of soda. Of course it was inevitable that my sense of humour should run away with me and, after my final addition, I was asked the obvious question on the following morning.

"But, Daphne, what was the little thing *under* the bed?

Fairy Origin

One day I asked Normus how fairies are born and he told me that they are never babies, as in our human evolution. This seems to indicate that the old tradition of the changeling is but a fallacy, and it is my contention that these troublesome infants were but the "problem children" of their day.

He told me that a tiny particle of matter commences to thicken, gradually becoming more tangible as the years pass, until it is sufficiently developed for a fairy soul to enter it. This does not lead to a sudden awareness of existence, as the soul is still sleeping and only gains consciousness by slow degrees, until eventually it becomes a rudimis, one of the tiny entities whose only means of expression is its constant movement.

I have since ascertained that this description is not entirely accurate, but I certainly think that it is far nearer the truth than the proverbial stork and gooseberry bush, fortunately now almost entirely out of date.

I have a very firm conviction that it is unwise to make definite assertions about matters which cannot be proved. However, I will give you my firm beliefs at my present state of understanding; but these may become amended, or even cast aside, in the light of further knowledge.

I believe that fairies are identical in origin to Man or any other evolution, apart from the fact that they are composed of different atoms.

I do not believe that we are born onto this Earth as babies, either as princes or beggars, with apparently no discrimination or fairness. I believe that it has taken countless millions of years in which we have passed through other planets and other solar systems, not only as people, but as matter intangible to us, as minerals, rocks, metals, precious stones, vegetables and animals. I believe that we have known many lives on Earth, which the majority of people are unable to recall because they have a different body and, therefore, a different brain.

I believe that each person suffers in this life for the sins he committed in his previous ones and that as we behave now, so shall we be rewarded, both over the Other Side and in the improved or adverse conditions in which we shall be placed on our next appearance on Earth.

Eventually we shall have mastered all the lessons to be learned here and we shall be released from the necessity of returning.

I do not believe that there are good and bad people, only that the apparently good are older souls and, therefore, more advanced than the bad – and I believe that many lives ago, in nearly every case, the good people have acted in just the same way as the criminals, drunkards and bullies of today.

– *Daphne Charters*

NORMUS

by Himself

As you know, we fairies volunteer to come down to Earth for experience. There is keen competition because a span of a hundred years here teaches us more than possibly a thousand years on the Astral plane.

When I approached my leader on the subject, he asked me whether there was any particular task that I wished to undertake. I had no doubts and I replied that I wanted to continue with the trees.

"Have you ever considered working with Man?" he enquired.

"Not much," I replied. "I've always been a Nature fairy and, as far as my capacity goes, I know my job."

"It is good to have varying experiences," he said. "Think about the matter and let me know if you change your mind."

I pondered for several days and, although I felt that he would have liked me to gain this new experience, I couldn't consent to leave my trees, with whom I particularly love to work.

Thirty years passed, and then I received a summons from my leader. I was almost certain why he wished to see me and, although I wanted to go to Earth more than anything else, I confess that I was a little afraid.

We are always taught that we must fear nothing because Good always overcomes evil and, if we concentrate our thoughts on Goodness, we cannot fail. I therefore told my fears to go away. I thought how fortunate I was to be given this wonderful opportunity to progress and eventually I became calm.

The great day came. I had already taken a rather sad farewell of the friends who were staying behind.

"What are a hundred years?" they had said comfortingly. "A mere flash in the eternity of life."

"Then why don't you try it?" I had asked.

"When you come back and tell us all about it, maybe we will," they had laughingly replied.

I lowered my vibrations and I knew that for one hundred years I was not permitted to raise them again, except during meditation.

I joined a group of fairies who were working in some fields and I commenced my tasks immediately; I was miserable for many months and I seemed quite unable to adjust myself to the new conditions.

At first the rain was torture to me and I became as limp as the leaves I was endeavouring to help. I was taking the place of a fairy who had finished his Earth span and who had naturally been very efficient in overcoming his difficulties, and

I am afraid that my poor charges didn't relish the change. Of course it is my task to help the trees, but at this period it was they who were aiding me.

Eventually I not only became used to the wind and the rain, but I learned to love them. I discovered that the trees are uplifted and refreshed by rain and that the wind invigorates them and enables them to perform movements impossible without its aid.

I worked with that particular group of fairies for twenty years and then I was moved to a big place in the country where there were two gardeners. At first I kept as far away from them as I could, but I gradually became used to them and even forgot their presence.

One day I approached one of them and a little nervously I entered his aura, which wasn't very large so that I was obliged to get close to his body. However, this was not as disagreeable as I had expected. At first I was rather frightened, but the other fairies had all entered the gardener's aura and had survived, so I was determined not to give in.

After awhile I began almost to enjoy the prickly sensation and certainly it was like nothing that I had ever experienced before. After this occasion, I entered his aura about once a week in order to train myself, because I knew that one day I should be moved to tend trees where many people lived and I was determined to prepare myself as fully as possible.

The years passed pleasantly because I had become completely acclimatised to Earth conditions, and once again I was the happy little fellow that I had always been.

For some time I had been having jokes with the other fairies, and because I don't think that you can possibly play the same kind of tricks, I will tell you about some of the things which make us laugh.

If I see two fairies, obviously very interested in each other and trying to make up their minds whether to mingle their auras, I give one of them a little push and so make up their minds for them. Their surprise at finding themselves already doing what they were using so much energy to decide, makes them go a peculiar shade of mauve and I know that my trick has been a success.

Sometimes if I don't think that they will suit each other, I raise my vibration a little and hover between them. Of course they can't see me, but when one steps forward to enter the other's aura, he can't.

They usually know who it is teasing them and a merry chase follows, with me raising and lowering my vibrations in order to keep out of sight. They try hard to catch me and when they succeed, we are all so out of power and so full of laughter, that they're in no mood for gentle love-making.

Then there's another joke which makes me laugh until I feel I must burst. I hide behind a plant and wait until one of the fairies passes, deep in thought. I must explain that I'm in my Earth body but the fairy on whom the trick is to be played must be without his.

I spring high in the air, landing right on top of him, my comparatively heavy body squashing him as flat as a leaf; at the same time the shock causes him to shoot out many multicolored sparks. He implores my mercy and the more he begs, the more the sparks fly and the more his struggles tickle me. I laugh so much that I become incapable of moving even if I would.

Then the trapped fairy, with a stupendous effort, contracts himself to a mere wisp and creeps out in pieces through the cracks between my body and the ground. Then, of course, it is I, weak and helpless with laughter, who is the victim, and a great rough and tumble follows.

When I do this to the girls, my punishment is always greater because they continue tickling me until I am in such agony that I would promise anything to make them stop. Sometimes they wheedle an extra hour of rest and I'm thus obliged to do their work for them. Merella usually makes me give her more power than she should really have, but I'm helpless.

[Some time after writing the above I was sworn to secrecy over the disclosure of a magnificent new joke. Normus at that time had only tried it out on Movus and he wanted to submit all the other fairies to the consequent discomfiture. It had come to him on the spur of the moment that morning when he had been flying fast to catch up Movus, with whom he wished to converse. He was in the act of overtaking his unsuspecting friend when he suddenly swerved and flew right through him, scattering him in all directions. "He looked so funny, all in pieces," he squealed with laughter again at the recollection. "He was so surprised." That, I could quite understand and I think that I am rather glad that no one can play these jolly little jokes on me. – D.C.]

The time came for me to move again, and once more I was sad. However, two friends, Movus and Mirilla, were coming with me, which softened the parting from the rest of the group; we swore eternal friendship and we promised that we would meet on the Astral if our paths failed to cross once more on Earth.

We again went to a big garden, but this time we were close to a large town. When we stopped working, we could hear various roaring sounds which at first terrified all three of us, but the other fairies reassured us and we came to know that the noises were powerless to harm us. Later we became accustomed to them and eventually we ceased to notice them at all.

Life was much the same except that this time there were several children. I was delighted when they first came into the garden but, to my disappointment, they couldn't see me.

They seemed very undisciplined and I soon realized that they were young and turbulent spirits. They frequently tore up our most beautiful flowers and left them to wither where they had flung them. They picked the fruit before it was ripe, not to eat, but to throw at each other.

However, this was good training for me and I began to learn patience. At first when I saw the poor flowers lying on the ground, I wept, but my leader told me to pull myself together.

"To weep is the worst thing that you can do," he said. "The flowers are sad enough without receiving your unhappy vibrations. It's your task to lighten their burdens, not to add to them. Tell them that on the Astral plane they will know happiness beyond anything that they have experienced on Earth, and that if they are brave and smile, they will have far more beautiful bodies than they have had down here."

The trees, too, became upset when the results of a year's labour were roughly torn from them and bruised and battered beyond redemption. I talked to them and reminded them that they still had other fruit beyond the children's reach, and I advised them to devote all their strength in making those which remained larger and stronger than they would otherwise have been.

At first they wouldn't listen to me but after awhile I could see that they had understood my words and were trying to carry them out.

These children's vibrations were far from pleasant. One day I entered the aura of one of them, which was even smaller than the gardener's, but I was unable to stay there for more than a second or two, the pleasant, prickly feeling being replaced by a series of stabs.

I experimented quite often, hoping that I should get used to this new sensation as I had the other, and that it would mellow into something pleasant, but it never did. In fact, as the children grew older, the stabs became so painful that I was obliged to cease entering their auras altogether.

It was while I was working in this garden that I met my first Earth paris. I was high up in a tree overhanging the road when, in the grass below me, I saw a girl fairy guiding some of the tiny entities who stimulate the green blades by their continuous movement. Her face was not as pretty as I had expected from the grace of her body but she smiled coquettishly.

"How would you like a trip up here?" I asked.

She frowned as she contemplated my suggestion. "It would be a new experience," she admitted. "But how do I know that I can trust you?"

"Trust me for what?" I enquired.

"Not to drop me, silly," she replied.

"You can trust me as far as that goes, but I make no other promises once I get you up here."

She flashed me a come-hither look *[I tried several other adjectives as I doubted Normus using this expression, but he insisted that this was a good translation . – D.C.]* and, like a flash, I shot downwards, gathered her in my arms and soared to the topmost branch.

I felt as though I were on fire and I began to give her power even before we alighted. At first she lay in my arms and absorbed it hungrily, then she began to return it in quick little darts which grew in intensity until the pain was almost unbearable; yet, at the same time, it was most satisfying.

I had never been given power in this manner before and, consequently, I couldn't leave her alone. I knew that she wasn't very evolved and that, apart from my power (for even then I was quite prolific), she didn't love me. She was a vain little thing but when she was filled with light she looked almost beautiful, so for a time I lived in the illusion that I loved her.

She was very selfish and, after awhile, she only wanted my power and scarcely gave me any of hers in return. Of course this upset me, not only because I enjoyed receiving but because when one loves, one must give and, by her abstention, I knew that I meant nothing to her.

After some time, I took my troubles to my leader.

"I can't do without her," I said. "Yet I know that she's sapping all my strength and my trees are suffering."

My heart was heavy, for it is sad when one knows that one isn't loved. The leader approached a higher source and, as it was approximately time for me to move again, I was transferred to another garden, or I should say, a series of them, where I'm still working, in a pleasant part of town, away from the roar of traffic.

There are big trees to tend and I knew immediately that I should be happy here. At first I naturally suffered in mind and body, but the pain gradually decreased and I was able to see my little paris in her true light. I realized how foolish I had been and I made a vow that never, never would I again be misled by any girl fairy.

After several years my leader sent for me. "I have but five more years of my Earth span to complete," he told me. "I have been asked to nominate a suitable candidate to take my place. I consider that you are the most efficient worker in the band and, although you're inclined to be a little over-mischievous, I'm of the opinion that the responsibility of leadership will act as an effective brake. Now, how do you feel about it yourself?"

I was taken completely unawares. Such a thing as being elevated to Dramon's status had never entered my mind.

"Would that mean that I couldn't go on having fun?" I asked him.

"Of course not," he twinkled. "I don't think that anything in the Universe would stop you from playing your tricks for long. Just choose your time, that's all. No fooling during working hours, but be as merry as you please in between."

"Well, if you're sure that I'm capable, how can I refuse? It's a great honour and I'm really very excited that you should have chosen me."

"I wouldn't have done so unless you deserved it," he concluded.

Apparently his nomination was accepted, for I was taken away from the trees to work at Dramon's side for the next five years.

You may imagine my delight when I found that the fairy who was to take my place was my old friend Movus; at least, he who worked with the shrubs changed to the trees, and Movus took over his charges. The fairy who worked with the tall flowers was also transferred so that Mirilla's task remained unchanged.

I was amazed at her increased beauty. She had always been a sweet and pretty fairy, but now she was becoming exquisite.

Movus and I embraced each other warmly and that evening we had a great celebration.

I was naturally invited to their cottage and we spent many happy hours together. Watching them so very much in love once again turned my thoughts towards the joys of union and I yearned to have a paris of my own. It is good to seek for one's affinity, for that is one of the reasons of life, and until one has found her, one cannot truly rest. But to seek as I was is foolish. One must be patient – and have faith that when one is ripe for the experience, she will come and one will know.

I was searching impatiently and without caution. I felt that if I was ready to become leader, I must be more advanced than the other fairies in our group. They nearly all had their paris, why, therefore, hadn't I?

However, because I was more efficient with work, doesn't prove that I was more advanced emotionally; the very fact that I was seeking as I was proves that I was far behind them in this category.

One day, as I was working, I felt a rising surge of excitement run through me and I turned to see a girl fairy flying by. She was beautiful, in an uncontrolled kind of way; she had long, fair, curly hair which was floating behind her in the breeze; her dress was transparent and I could see her limbs quite clearly. Fairies love to show their legs and arms and, sometimes, their shoulders or the faint curve where their breasts begin to rise but, as a rule, they reserve the even more beautiful parts of their body for those they love.

I watched her and I became convinced that she had fallen in love with me at first sight; that she knew that I was her duo and that she was revealing this knowledge by showing me that which was mine.

I don't remember taking any action; I just became befogged with power, wild, unruly power, giving and receiving more than is possible with any degree of comfort or pleasure. After a time we were both exhausted, not refreshed and joyous as we should have been. I felt depressed, both mentally and physically, as though I had done something which isn't permitted, so I decided that I would avoid her in future for I was quite unable to do any more work that day.

Forty-eight hours later she came again and, once more, before I had time to close my power-ducts against her, I found myself amidst a storm of uncontrolled emotion. Again I was exhausted, but this time she appeared to be refreshed. I hoped that this indicated the dawn of a less tempestuous love, which would contain the essence of sweetness, as it should.

But I was wrong. It was merely that once she had caught me in the whirlpool of desire, she somehow managed to close her own channels and she was then able to absorb all my power without giving any in return. I begged her to cease,

for this time I felt really ill, but she laughed wildly and left me lying in the grass.

When I had recovered sufficiently, I went to Dramon.

"Now, Normus," he said, "this is ridiculous. She couldn't drain all your power unless you permitted her to do so."

"I'm in the centre before I'm even aware of the edge," I explained dejectedly.

"You must open your danger alarms so that you're warned of her approach."

"But, Dramon, they're only used to ward off evil. I couldn't use them against her when I love her."

"You do not love her," Dramon said firmly. "Although it's extremely bad for you, you love the experience of having all your power sapped from you."

"I don't, really I don't," I assured him. "it makes me feel dreadfully ill."

"I know, but even that you're enjoying," he replied. "I'll do everything I can to help you, but you must make the initial effort of controlling her yourself. She lives for this greedy absorption of power and, so far, no fairy upon whom she has preyed has been able to resist her wiles. They have gradually been sapped until they're of no further use to her, then she leaves them for another victim.

"Now, Normus, you're not going to allow her to do the same to you. You're the most evolved fairy which she has succeeded in trapping and you are naturally the most attractive to her. She won't let you go without a struggle. You have a hard task. Go out and win."

I didn't get much rest the following two days. I was too busy making plans. Fortunately Drogetta, for that was her name, left me in peace during this period and I was thus able to rearrange my mind.

All this time I had kept my alarm ducts open but nothing happened until the third day, when I began to feel hot and I knew that she was in the vicinity. I continued working but I was prepared and, as she approached, I switched on my power to my fullest capacity. This is very different to having it turned on for you, because this time I was the one in control.

She didn't notice at first; she had all her inhaling channels wide and I was able to see that those through which she should have been exhaling were tightly closed. As swiftly as I had opened out, I now shut tight.

"Now, my pretty one," I thought. "It will be interesting to see what happens."

She continued inhaling and suddenly, instead of the beautiful power, she drew in a gust of pure air. Now, if you are intending to do this, air is very cleansing, but when you are expecting power, it is as though a bucket of cold water was thrown over you.

She gasped. "Give me some power quickly!" she demanded as soon as she had recovered sufficiently to speak.

"Not unless you give me some," I said firmly.

"Normus, please, you don't know what you're doing to me."

"I do," I replied. "Because this is what you've been doing to me although, fool that I was, I didn't realize it at the time."

She pleaded but I was adamant, although I nearly gave in because she looked so bedraggled and wretched. She slunk away but she was back next day, this time employing quite different tactics. She came, glowing with power like a miniature beacon.

"See what I've got for you," she smiled archly.

"That's wonderful," I said. "I'm more than eager to receive it."

She began exhaling until my senses reeled, but I managed to keep control of myself and, as she gave, so did 1. However, she soon stopped.

"What's the matter with you. Have you lost your power?" she demanded angrily.

I grinned at her.

"Take that ridiculous expression off your face!" she snapped.

I grinned all the more for now I knew that I was her master. "I'll prove to you that I haven't," I said, letting out a strong spurt. She absorbed it instantly, but the ecstasy lasted but a second.

180

"Give me more!" she screamed.

"Not until you do," I insisted.

"I'm not very powerful," she wheedled. "You've had all I've got."

"Well, you can give me back that little bit which I've just given you."

"Oh, go and festoon yourself!" she shouted as she left me. *[This expression amused me so much that I asked Normus exactly what it meant. He explained that it was very insulting and means that you should surround yourself with your own power. - D.C.]*

I knew that she was beaten and I was amazed how easy it had been. I began to realize then that I had but to make up my mind firmly - and there was nothing that I couldn't do, in fact it's the adjusting of the mind which is the real difficulty and not the ensuing action at all.

The next big step in my progress was when Dramon left. As a new leader is installed only once in about twenty years or so, there is always a great celebration when the retiring leader hands over his gold belt to the fairy taking his place.

I shall never forget my sensation of happiness and pride as he buckled it about my waist. All the surrounding groups were present to bid Dramon farewell and to pay homage to me, in my new post of authority.

There was a vast gathering, music and dancing and, of course, a huge ball of power. Having now a certain position to keep up, I was very careful not to enter the power enclosure too often, as it would have been most undignified if the new leader had been found lying drenched in cloud moisture.

When I began to work as leader-proper, I was a little apprehensive. Until then, I had known that Dramon was ever-near to help me if a problem too difficult for me to handle arose, but now I was the one before whom all the other fairies would be placing their troubles. Dramon had promised to continue helping me from the Astral, but I had made up my mind that I would only appeal to him in cases of dire necessity. He had served his Earth span and I considered it only fair that he should be left to enjoy the fruits of his labours.

All went well, however, and the expected difficulties didn't arise, except in a small measure. I have now been leader for ten years and, as I have twenty years to run, you will understand that I was young to be chosen for this high honour, and I'm very happy to have earned this distinction.

[The above incidents all took place with the first six months of our meeting, then I began to spend my spare time taking down the individual stories of the other fairies. Normus, being the leader, came first and I think it only fair that he should have another opportunity to describe some of the events which have taken place during the intervening eighteen months. – D.C.]

Many months have passed since I gave Daphne my story and I think that more interesting things have happened during this short period than in all the rest of my life.

We have learned to heal and to help, not only humans, but other fairies in distress. We have formed an ever-growing link with the ceres and we are being encouraged to become closer in bonds of friendship with all the other evolutions as well. These, although for the most part invisible to us because they are in a different vibration, nevertheless work side by side with us with both the Nature kingdom and with Man.

We have learned to heal and to help, not only humans, but other fairies in distress.

Each person, plant and object has a ceris. Whereas we in the Fairy kingdom give power to the etheric bodies of plants, they give power to the mind or consciousness.

Then there are the harneles, who replenish the colour in everything that you see.

The gravines are those who give perfume, whether it is to a piece of iron or to a rose, for all things have their individual scent, some not altogether pleasant.

We have also contacted the thormes, who are the entities which give power to sound. Perhaps it has never struck you that everything has its individual note. We aren't yet sufficiently advanced to know ours but we have recently heard the mantric note of our evolution and that of Man as well.

Each person has a vibration, as has every living thing in the Universe, and this is in the charge of entities who are known as drones (pronounced dronies). It is according to the care which they take of your vibration and those which they direct towards you, how you react to certain misfortunes.

Of course, the choice is not entirely in their hands, because your own will guides them also. If you succumb uncontrollably to sorrow, the drones are naturally affected and, in their own misery, they will attract similarly unhappy vibrations, which they pass on to you.

If, on the other hand, you try to master your troubles, then your strength will be more noticeable to them than your misery, and they will then be imbued with the will to find other vibrations to assist you.

We have been told that when the powers of all the evolutions are blended together, then there will be Perfection on every plane. It is because of this intermingling in the highest spheres that near-Perfection has been reached.

On Earth, each evolution is quite separate and it is the desire of the Great Ones that we should do everything in our power to bring them closer together.

We are already successfully blending power with the ceres each day when we send out the Peace Ray.

Last year we had our own Congress, but this summer there is to be a combined Fairy and Ceris conference, when we will hold joint committees and pool our ideas. Thus we hope that, with the added strength provided by our united powers, important decisions will be reached.

Doubtless, year by year, one or more of the other evolutions will join us, as we learn to become more in tune with them until, within the limited scope of the small numbers with whom we make contact, there will come into being the nucleus of Unity.

Each week now I have three visits to the Astral, or above, and I will now tell you of three of them. The first occurred about eight months ago when I found myself in our own sector but higher than I had previously reached. Everything sparkled and I had a tremendous surge of expectation. I didn't know why, but I was sure that something was going to happen and that I hadn't been brought to this particular spot either for recreation or for work.

I waited because I had to. I tried flying off in several directions but each time I was brought back to the same spot so, after three attempts, I just stayed where I was.

I began to tingle all over. This raised my expectations to bursting point but still nothing happened. When I reached a state of endurance beyond which to exist would be impossible, I began to move.

Straight up I went, at tremendous speed, the sensation of which remained with me even after I had stopped. I was stationary but my atoms were still in a state of constant change. I felt so excited that I hardly knew how to keep myself together.

Gradually they, too, slowed down and I felt as peaceful as the lull after the storm. I would have liked to sink down in relaxation in order to recapture the sensation of my flight but, before I could make my thoughts become fact, I was again swept upwards at even greater speed.

This time, when I arrived, everything whirled in a wild kaleidoscope. I endeavoured to raise my vibrations but they were already at their height. I tried relaxing but still the landscape spun 'round me.

I waited as patiently as I could until the spinning slowed down and finally stopped. Even then I felt a little dazed but I managed to rise to my feet, and what a shock I had. They were such a long way away, at least a yard and a half.

I was wild with excitement. Always I yearn to be big. I think myself huge. I plot and plan but, apart from making myself tall for a second or two, I'm never more than seven inches.

I longed to see myself because I was sure that I was handsome. I wondered whether I could throw a thought form of myself on the sparkling atmosphere but nothing happened. I examined my hands, which looked quite different. They were pretty, long and smooth. I began to run and what a lot of ground I covered. I ran and I ran. I didn't know why or where I was going, but felt that I must keep moving.

I'm not sure for how long this continued, but eventually I realized that I was unconsciously following a path. I looked back and I could see it trailing behind me as far as my vision reached. I looked ahead and, as I saw that I still had miles and miles to go, I began running again. But this time I had a motive, to reach the end of the path.

With my desires to aid my feet, I soon came upon a silver pool. I hovered over it and for the first time I saw myself in my "body of experience." Since then I've been in it in an even larger form because I was in a higher sphere but, at that time, I had never seen myself looking so beautiful. I lay face downwards about a foot above the water and I gazed at myself with intense pleasure.

Suddenly it came to me that I hadn't been brought to this high plane for the sole purpose of admiring myself. Reluctantly I took one last look at my reflection and I returned to the path. On, on I went, my thoughts centred on reaching the end. As a matter of fact, I don't believe that there was one, or if there was, I never found it, because what I was seeking appeared when I could still see the path fading away into the distance.

I stopped and bowed respectfully because I knew at once that the entity before me was a farallis even though I'd never met one before. He shone so brightly that for awhile I was reluctantly obliged to disperse my own beautiful body because, in it, I couldn't stand the glare.

When I had become more in tune with him, I reassembled my form and I looked at him with my eyes closed. He was huge. I should think about nine feet tall. He returned my greeting and then he reduced himself in size in order to be more on a level with me. He still towered above me but now that he was smaller, my awe of him abated a little.

"I have been watching you for several months now," he told me, to my amazement, "and I think that you are the fairy for whom I have been seeking for many years." I remained silent and he continued, "There are acts which those on Earth can perform, that we from higher spheres are unable to accomplish, owing to the tenuity of our power. Would you be willing to work with me on a project I have in mind?"

I looked at him almost unbelievingly. To be asked if it would please me when already I would have given all my power for him.

"Anything, anything," I managed to blurt out. It was a pathetically inadequate projection which I made but he understood it.

"Come with me then, and I will show you my plan."

I don't remember moving but I found that the scenery had changed and, in the distance, there was a huge palace. It was the biggest building that I'd ever seen. I wanted to ask him if he lived there, but I wasn't sure whether I should address him, so I said nothing. We swept up to it in a fraction of a second and I followed him inside.

Being a Nature fairy I had never been very interested in buildings, but now I realize that Nature resides in brick and stone almost as much as in plants. Of course, a brick on Earth hasn't the consciousness of a flower, but a stone in the higher spheres vibrates much faster than an Earth plant and therefore it seems far more alive. It also feels more, although its experience has not yet included the ability consciously to grow.

This palace was full of power and shone brightly even in those brilliant surroundings.

"My hall of learning," the farallis proudly said. "This is not only where I teach, but where I myself learn. Earth is my special interest at present, although other planets are also covered by my desire to assist all who strive."

There were thousands of fairies in many stages of progress. To begin with, I had felt gloriously big, but then I realized how small I actually was.

The farallis was greeted with great respect wherever we went. He paused here to praise, and there to make a suggestion to one whose problem was proving too much for him. I studied several thought formations but I couldn't understand any of them. They were so big that my vision, let alone my intellect, was unable to cover them.

I became a little nervous for obviously the plan would be of gigantic proportions and if I was unable even to see it, how could I possibly be of any active assistance?

We entered a room so vast that I was unable to see the far side of it.

"You're worried, are you not?" the farallis said, "but it is not necessary. I would not ask you to do anything beyond your present powers. But as you grow throughout the years, so can you participate more and more in this project, which possibly will not reach tangibility in Earth conditions for a couple of centuries."

I tried to relax but I wasn't very successful. I consider myself very far-thinking when my projects cover two seasons, but to plan in terms of several Earth spans is far beyond my present ability.

"You are already interested in my idea; in fact, you have unconsciously helped me. Fairy and Man must work together, and as Man, taken as a whole, is quite incapable of striving without seeing the results of his labour, he will equally be unable to work with partners whom he cannot see and with whom he cannot communicate.

"We have already spanned the first seemingly unbridgeable gulf. Man has talked with the Fairies. And so simple did this heretofore insoluble problem prove, that we now have hope that all our difficulties will likewise fade."

"What can I do?" I asked eagerly. "I frequently talk to adults and children but they never hear me."

"Do not worry about your apparent results," he said. "Fill the air with projections and leave it to us to make them grow in strength and clarity. One day someone will see one of these thought forms, possibly unconsciously, and his brain will translate the message. He may not know whence it came, but no matter.

"There is also much that you can do to make yourself visible. You have not yet learned to lower your vibrations sufficiently. You have an advantage over most other fairies in that you, at least, have a human being who knows that you are there. When you are with her, strive to absorb her power so that you will become more in tune with her. You will understand that great patience is required, as success is not probable within a question of months. Do not lose heart, though, and one day you will succeed.

"You can encourage other fairies to strive also. It is only by a combined effort over a long period that you will bridge the gap between the evolutions."

He showed me some thought formations and, because they were small, I knew that he had made them 'specially for me. They showed the results of the same plan with Man and Fairy completing their part of it, first separately and then together.

It was unbelievable that the mingling of the two powers should make such a difference, and yet it was so because I saw it for myself. The experiments had been carried out on the Astral plane, but obviously a similar success could be obtained on Earth.

He told me that already results were being effected by the combination of our own group with Daphne's. In fact, he showed me thought formations of our achievements which had been obtained without our knowledge. Merely by being together and talking with Daphne and our other guardians has set up a force which is being utilized without our even being aware of its existence.

"Be conscious of this new power," the farallis continued. "With your thoughts, help it to grow and even better results will be forthcoming."

He left me to examine the other thought formations without his aid. At first I could make little of them but, by pondering on each section, I was eventually given a glimpse of the whole. At the time, I didn't understand any of it very clearly but I was able to bring back with me sufficient data to study and, by degrees, everything is becoming less obscure. I must have fallen asleep over my efforts because when I awoke, I was back on Earth.

The following event took place three months after the last one. I was a little tired because it happened during one of those periods when, having accepted extra work, my power had not yet grown sufficiently to deal with it.

To tell you the truth, I would have been content just to lie in Daphne's aura and merely refresh myself. I felt the usual languor steal over me and then I began to sink. Maybe I slept for awhile, I don't know, but when I came to myself I felt wonderful, full of love for my fellows and with a keen desire to help others in distress.

186

I jumped to my feet, eager to begin the task which I knew awaited me. I didn't have to look far. I saw a group of people weeping and then I knew that instead of being transported to some higher plane, I was still on Earth. They were standing 'round a bed where an old man lay. His astral consciousness was sleeping in his physical body in order to refresh itself before its awakening in the finer atmosphere of its new home. To the mourners, though, he was dead.

I felt a little worried. I knew that I was supposed to help these people in their grief but I didn't know how to do it. I tried making thought formations. One after another, I flashed on the atmosphere messages of truth and hope, but they had no effect.

Then I concentrated on one, a little girl, and after awhile she slipped away from the others and sat by herself in a corner. I would have liked to continue comforting her, but I knew that somehow I must help every one of the people present.

I stood on the bed and spoke to them. I described some of the wonderful things that I've seen on the Astral. I told them that it was terribly wrong to grudge this old man, who had obviously completed a long Earth span, the enjoyment that was rightly his. Not a tear was dried.

I tried making separate thought forms and wrapping them 'round their individual heads, but they can't have been strong enough because only in one case did they seem to do any good.

Then my attention was drawn to the sleeping man. He was stirring and the silent "watchers," who were, of course, invisible to the weeping men and women, gathered 'round the bed.

You may think it silly of me to think that I could help to comfort where these more experienced in this work had failed, but I knew that I must try.

The old man yawned and he sat up. "My dears, why do you weep? I have had such a refreshing sleep," he said, smiling. "I think I shall get up." Of course they couldn't hear him. [Normus was unable to hear the words direct but the watchers gave him the context.]

"I must do something quickly while the influence of Earth is still strong in him," I thought.

"Please make them see him before he goes," I prayed and, with those who waited to welcome him, we made a strong thought form of him as he sat there, I saw one of the watchers gently turn a woman's head towards him.

"Why, father!" she cried, and she rose to her feet, but as she moved, so she lost her brief vision of him.

"He's gone," she said helplessly. Her relatives gathered 'round.

"There, there, dear. You know he died two days ago."

"But I saw him. He was sitting up," she insisted, "and he looked so well."

They patted her on the shoulder but each one wondered whether perhaps she had been given a glimpse of him whom she had loved all her life.

I watched the old man's face as, with joy, he greeted old friends and then I was taken away. I knew, though, that the daughter would tell of her experience again and again and how, eventually, all would believe.

Why had I been there? I asked myself in the morning, and then, for a second, I saw the farallis and he was smiling. I argued with myself that surely my own small contribution couldn't have done any good. Then I remembered the thought formations which he had shown me of the additional power produced when that of Man and Fairy are mingled.

Of course, I can't prove that the same thing wouldn't have happened if I hadn't been there, but I like to think that I helped. In fact, I'm sure that I must have done so, because nearly every week now, I find myself among those who mourn and always a vision is given to one or more of those present.

For my last incident, I'll tell you what happened to me on another occasion when I visited a sphere at that time new to me. After my preliminary semi-trance, I awoke and, as is my practice, I remained for awhile with my eyes closed. This is partly in order to adjust myself to the new conditions. Still with my eyes closed, the scenery appears before me after awhile, but not very distinctly. It has almost a dream-quality with everything becoming clearer very gradually.

I knew that I was in a sector that was neither Man nor Fairy and I was naturally longing to know where I was. But I exercised control and followed my usual pattern.

The first thing which literally met my eyes when I opened them was a huge flower, immediately in front of my face; in fact, it was her vibration which had aroused me. I had never before awoken as though a veil was drawn over the landscape and I knew that it was not by chance that this flower was being used as a screen. Obviously, this time everything was to burst on me in all its glory.

I arose to my feet and, with eyes and senses closed, I walked out from my sheltered nook. I opened everything at once, but I opened them too wide, because I was knocked down.

I tried again, this time from where I was lying so that at least I wouldn't suffer a similar discomfiture. I cautiously opened one eye, and then I released a little consciousness – only a very little, though, because otherwise I knew that I should be blinded again. Little by little, I built up both vision and awareness until I had reached my limit. Very carefully, I rose to my feet. First I walked, then I ran, and finally I flew to the peak of the highest mountain I could see.

Again I had to wrestle with my consciousness, and when I had steadied my-self, I looked again.

The shapes were familiar in some instances, but the colours were amazing. The higher planes of Man are bright with a white light which intensifies every tone; in the Ceris sector, they are deep and strong; the Fairy division sparkles with a million tints within each; but here there was pure colour, at least, it was as pure as the individual forms contained in the landscape could manifest. In all sectors the whole is divided, in varying degrees, into form consciousness, colour, sound, scent, vibration and will. Here colour predominated with the other components as a muted accompaniment.

You know the power of colour in healing; now, for the first time, I was experiencing it as an aid to my own evolution.  As I became in tune, I lost some of my will and restricting form. I, too, became colour and consciousness, with my other qualities reduced to a minimum. It was as though I was green fire.

It's very exciting to experience the different conditions when one component is more advanced than usual. I felt filled with vigour and I'm sure that if I could have stayed like that, I should never feel tired.

The more I gazed at the landscape, the more I became affected, because not only was my own green greatly intensified, but as I absorbed the unusual idea of a mountain of pure gold, trees that were scarlet and silver, and brilliant, blue grass, so my wonder and enthusiasm grew.

Suddenly the sky, which was silver, became suffused with the brightest pink I'd ever seen. I watched, fascinated, expecting a pattern with a message to form on the vast canopy. But, instead, the glorious pink detached itself and stood before me.

I bowed low in respect although I regretted being obliged to remove my gaze for even the short period necessitated by my deep obeisance. Not only were the clothes of this exciting personage of the same brilliant hue, but he was this intense pink all over his face, his hair, his hands and his eyes, which gleamed with extraordinary intensity and yet were full of gentleness.

We stood gazing at each other in silence and I was sure that he was probing my innermost thoughts.

"You'll do," he said with a smile, as he sat down beside me.

"You are interested in colour apart from its beauty, are you not?"

I eagerly assented because Father John had already told me about some of the experiments being carried out by my higher self.

"Are you sufficiently interested to find sometime to help me each day?"

I thought for a moment. Already I was working harder than I had ever done before, but I knew that I wouldn't refuse him.

"I'll make time," I said.

"I'm afraid that we all have to do that; that is, once our feet are firmly set on the path . . . even as are yours," he added.

'What can I do?" I asked.

"Meditate on me for five or ten minutes every day. I want you to absorb my colour as much as possible. It has great power, and you will find that both your plants and the humans with whom you come in contact will benefit. Strength is the quality which I strive to bring to others – not only that of body but of Purpose also. Endeavour to include some of my colour each time you give power and I am sure that you will be amazed at the results. Come now," he said, "I have many things to show you."

I found myself wrapped in a pink cloud and, when we stopped, I still seemed to be surrounded by it, but this time there was also form. You might think that an entire landscape in the same colour might be uninteresting, but there was wonderful grace of outline and an endless array of tone.

"My home," he said proudly as he presented a glorious structure to me. Its walls were not solid as you know them. They were like an ever-flowing cascade of shining pink water, forming glowing pillars and arches filled with transparent pink air.

I followed him as he led me inside. I was on tiptoe all over. I knew that he would have exciting and incredible things to show me. I felt the warm, welcoming vibration of the house as we passed between the vaulted pillars and then I lost consciousness.

I could have wept when I awoke on Earth. There is so much to learn and to see and then, just when this wonderful new aspect was to open up before me, I lose it through lack of power.

I've been working hard with this new ray because I feel that, if I can become more in tune with it, I shall then be able to retain consciousness longer and I shall see, at any rate, a few of the treasures which the magnificent building contains.

I've already been achieving results with several plants on whom I've been experimenting. I give the ray to Daphne too, but I don't think that she's noticed it. The other fairies have also been concentrating on this colour and we all agree that we definitely have more strength to perform our many tasks.

As a group we're very happy to have this wonderful opportunity of telling you in a different evolution a little about our work and our other interests.

Fairies differ as much as men do, so don't think that all members of our evolution are like us. Because of our many unusual opportunities for advancement, owing to Daphne living among us, I think that we are probably more evolved than most.

Wherever there is a medium, fairies work with them, but they are not usually those still on Earth, but the more advanced ones. We have the advantage that Daphne knows of our presence and that she consciously gives her power to help us.

We hope that this book will show you that we are individuals and not flickers of only semi-conscious light. We are sometimes seen as flashes because the watcher is unable to maintain our high speed of vibration for more than a second or two at a time. We are quite solid to ourselves and to each other when we want to be, and when we are without our bodies, we experience much greater freedom than you can possibly know.

In parting, we all send you our greetings with the hope that one day you will see and hear the fairies who are always near you in your homes and in your gardens.

– Normus

NORMUS

by Father John

I paid Normus a visit at Daphne's request because, unlike the other fairies, he has no astral "guardian." Before going, I took the precaution of having some training in analyzing fairy projections more meticulously than had previously been necessary, because I was sure that he would be able to teach me facts previously unknown to me, and I was quite correct in my supposition.

I will now give you a description of him (1) on Earth in his astral body, (2) on the Third plane in his mental body and (3) on the Fourth plane in his body-of-experience. Normus was very intrigued when he discovered that I was able to do this without the necessity of traveling to the appropriate planes, and I think also that he felt a little proud because he is the only fairy so described.

Normus' Astral Body

To normal astral eyes, he is seven inches high, with straight brown hair, which he wears a little longer than the average man* so that it can be seen when he is wearing a hat. He has a bright little face and he invariably has a twinkle, except on very solemn occasions. His eyes are green, not the grey-green of a human's, but a vivid leaf green; his nose is retrousse, which adds to his impish appearance. His skin is fair, with a faint tan; his lips rather thin, but with no trace of meanness; his chin is firm.

He obviously has a tremendous sense of humour; one look at him will tell you that, and, at the same time, there is a great deal of character in his face.

191

*Men's hair fashions have changed from the "short back and sides" considered normal when this book was written.

He is slim of build and always looks neat and well dressed. Usually he wears green but not always the same shade. I have seen him in so pale a tone that it almost looked white. A bright, Lincoln green is his favourite, with brown buttons and a serviceable looking belt. His tunics vary, sometimes being scalloped, sometimes plain; some have pockets with flaps, others have none; occasionally he adds a brown collar or even a coloured tie.

Fairies like a change of clothing as much as you do, and the more advanced they are, the greater variety will they show in their garments. Cotton-like material for the summer and wool for the winter is the general rule, although this change is quite unnecessary for they can alter their vibrations to keep warm or cool as required. But when they see people walking about in overcoats, they probably feel that a change of material will prepare them for the altered conditions.

I have never actually seen a fairy in an overcoat, but I have no doubt that some make them after seeing Man in one for the first time. Fairies are inveterate copyists and anything new must be tried until familiarity causes them to lose interest and revert to their own customs.

Normus' Mental Body

Normus' mental body is several inches taller than his astral. Unlike Man, height in the Fairy Evolution is a sign of development; the more advanced the entity, the larger he is. He is, naturally, also better looking; the retrousse nose has become straight and finely modeled, the eyes shine like small emeralds, and his hands, from being rough like a workman's, have now grown in length, the fingers being slimmer and the nails pointed.

His clothes, while retaining their traditional shape, are of far richer material – silk and satin being his favourites for summer and velvet for winter. His belts are no longer of leather but have the same shining appearance as his jackets.

Normus takes great pride in his hats in all spheres. He wears a Robin Hood, as a rule, with a quill or longer feather. On the Third plane, where he sees more colourful birds, his choice of plumage is less limited and many and varied are the decorations that he wears on his head. Sometimes the entire hat is composed of feathers, sometimes of flowers, and I have even seen him with a miniature nest, complete with mother bird sitting on her eggs!

Talking to him on this plane, I found him surprisingly mature for so young a soul. He has great plans for his band of fairies, whom he hopes to have under his charge for many years to come.

192

His desire is that they shall become the nucleus for a tremendous surge of fairy aspiration; that healing, helping the earthbound, as well as others in distress, and the handling of the many rays for promoting peace and goodwill, will become the general practice in his evolution instead of a noteworthy exception.

He is convinced that fairies would make admirable mediums for the passage of any force between the different planes. He understands that many would be required to do the work of one man but, as he says, there are thousands of fairies who are occupied for a short period each day while the remainder is spent in recreation. If their playtime could be used for teaching them facts attractively, so that the lessons would prove more amusing than their simple games, then he is confident that an enormous new army of workers would come into being.

"That is what we all desire, Normus," I said, "but how can one interest a consciousness which is so little awake? These young entities are only able to concentrate for a second or two at a time. Mediumship requires great perseverance if real success is to be achieved. How do you propose to encourage this consciousness to grow?"

"Flowers are sometimes forced to bloom months before their time," he replied.

"That is true," I said, "but you cannot successfully force a flower more than once and often great harm is done to the plant if it is a perennial."

"Power is the answer," he said decisively, "but I haven't yet thought how it can be administered, when each consciousness already absorbs as much as it is capable of receiving. I don't know, Father John," he said, "but one day I will."

Normus' Body-of-Experience

We continued our conversation on the Fourth plane. Normus had grown considerably and was now about five feet tall. He had developed not only in stature but in grace, being noble in his bearing, with great charm of manner.

His clothes were not so bright in colour, but they had attained immense luminosity, his aura now being several feet in width. He wore a jeweled belt over material which itself sparkled like a million pinpoints of coloured lights, and a cloak like a flame curled itself about his slender form.

Gaiety was still exuding from him but the strength of his character was also more apparent in the swiftly changing colours of his aura.

'Well, Normus," I said, or rather I used his Fourth plane name, "have you solved the problem here?"

"Yes," he said with quiet confidence. "It's so simple. It's strange that it has eluded my lesser vehicles so completely, but I will transmit my plan in time."

"Can I help you?" I said. "I can, if you wish, inform your lower selves."

"If you can, then why cannot I?" he demanded.

193

"Because I am an older soul than you, my son," I said. "For your age you have already achieved wonders. You have yet to learn patience, though, and that is one of the most difficult lessons of all."

"Advise me," he begged. "Should I avail myself of your services or should I wait until I have grown sufficiently for all my selves to understand?"

"You must decide," I said. "Ask whether the result is to benefit yourself or many. Will your plan mature if the transmission is postponed, or is it sufficiently near completion now?"

"I don't have to think," he sighed. "It's true that many will benefit, but the plan, in reality, is but an idea and I must work upon it for years before it will become practical in Earth conditions."

"What have I been saying?" asked Normus eagerly when I had lowered my vibrations and he could see me again on Earth.

"You have a plan," I told him, "but it is not sufficiently mature for use, so you did not give me any details."

"Plan, plan," he said. "What plan? It's ridiculous that I should be making a plan and yet, down here, know nothing about it."

"When it is ready to be put into practice, I am quite sure that you will know down here as well," I assured him. "That is, if you are prepared to work hard to raise your thoughts sufficiently for your more advanced consciousness to reach you. You know, everybody on the Fourth plane is full of ideas; they spend a great deal of time making plans, good, workable plans, most of them too, but usually they are not of any use, because their Earth selves are not interested in anything which they are unable to see, hear, touch or smell. Their world is so very small when it could be so large. I am sure, however, that you will not make that same mistake."

"I have reached my body-of-experience twice," he told me, "but although I've tried and tried, I can't, as a rule, find it. Where is it?"

"It is true that it dwells on a plane far removed from this lawn," I said, "but you can so clarify the conditions here that, if you are unable to reach it, you can bring it down to you."

"Would I feel big?" he asked eagerly.

"If you could think yourself large, you would be," I told him.

"I would so like to be big and strong and then Daphne would take my love seriously."

"I can assure you that she does so already," I told him.

"But she can't feel my power," he said sadly.

"She cannot feel mine either," I said, "so, you see, Normus, it is nothing to do with size. It is just that we are unable to pierce her coarse, physical jacket. She has never felt the beauty of power so, if she teases you, it is only because she does not understand."

"Can a human being ever love a fairy as I want her to love me?" he said.

"But of course she can," I said. "She does so already, but it will probably take years for your combined love to mature and, when it does, it will be a very wonderful experience for you both. I myself have never known a fairy's love."

"Poor Father John," he said, "but perhaps one day you will, and she will convey to you secrets of love which are unknown to Man."

I was intrigued. "What secrets, Normus?" I asked.

"They're secrets," he said. "We're not allowed to tell, not even to talk about them. I've never used them myself because I haven't been very successful with my pares and it would be betraying a trust to try them unless, through the combined male and female adoration, a new force would be born to help those in need."

"Where did you learn these secrets?" I asked him.

"When I was in my body-of-experience," he replied.

"Do any of the others know of them?"

"I don't think so, but I mustn't ask. I think I should know if any of them understood though; it would show in their faces, in their forms, in their work and in their "selves;" there would be a light which I should recognize, even though I had never seen it before or knew what it should be like."

I looked at him with even more interest than usual. I was sure that he was telling me something which, until that moment, he had not known himself.

"Do you know what you have been saying?" I asked him.

"Yes," he said, "but until I saw the projections which I was making, I hadn't known anything about it, and yet it's coming back to me. I did know about it when I was in my body-of-experience but, until this moment, I have never succeeded in bringing the memory down with me."

"It's beginning to work," I smiled at him.

"The connection?" he said, his face brightening. "Of course. I will know what's going on up there. I must."

"You will," I said, and stroking his cheek with the tip of my finger, I left him to ponder on the spiritual meaning of those secrets which he dare not reveal.

The Communal House

The next time I went to see Normus, he asked if he might show me his part of the communal house where all the fairies live, for, like human beings, they too are proud of their homes and their possessions.

I have often looked inside the house but on this occasion I had prepared myself by tuning my vibrations more exactly to those of the fairies' and the difference was extraordinary.

The house, from the point of view of Earth, is very similar to Daphne's, but I was regarding it from the higher aspect of the Third plane. It was transformed into a miniature palace and, at the same time, Daphne's small garden took on the dimension of a large estate. I greeted Normus, also in his mental body, and we walked into the building side by side.

I think that, without an explanation, the above description may sound a trifle too like the traditional fairy tale for acceptance as the truth. I will therefore endeavour to explain this separate existence of the various parts of the whole.

– *Father John*

virtually unknown	7th Plane	*virtually unknown*
virtually unknown	6th Plane	*virtually unknown*
virtually unknown	5th Plane	*virtually unknown*
Mind of Experience	4th Plane	Body of Experience
Mental Mind	3rd Plane	Mental Mind
Astral Mind	2nd Plane	Astral Body
Subconscious Mind	or Etheric,	Sometimes known as the Etheric Double.
Logical Brain	Ist Plane	Physical Body
Consciousness	Including Earth	

[I have made the above diagram to help clarify Father John's words. I need not go further into the matter of the Earth plane because we know it all too well. I have already written in the foreword a brief explanation of our astral and mental bodies, so I will only give a few more details of the body-of-experience which we possess on the Fourth plane.

Father John has told me that, as far as he knows, no one who has temporarily descended from the higher spheres to the comparative limitations of Fourth plane consciousness is able to describe the life which he leads above. No one from the Fourth plane who has visited the Fifth has ever brought back a memory, and it is Father John's contention that we are not supposed to know about the life there, which is doubtless beyond our understanding. It would, in any case, I am quite sure, be impossible to translate any communication received into words.

Our Fourth plane bodies are still quite visible but are what I would describe as much more fluid. They are composed mostly of light, in the centre of which the familiar form is discernible.

In a flash of thought, we are able to change from normal proportions to so great size that we can cover vast territories and we have the ability of absorbing into our being the consciousness of all the people, animals and plants which live in this area.

The Fourth plane is the dwelling place of the Soul and, when we die, quickly or slowly, according to our experience, we wend our way through the Astral and Third planes on our way Home, for our Fourth plane mind contains the memory of all our previous incarnations and all our past experiences from the moment we left the Godhead tens of millions of years ago. – *Daphne Charters]*

Father John continues:

Seven Planes of Consciousness

You yourself are existing in increasing degrees of consciousness on seven different planes at one and the same time.

That is not all, however, for wherever there is a Bond of love between you and another person, between you and an animal, or you and an object, that affection does not begin and end on the Earth plane.

Visits to Higher Planes During Sleep

When your body is asleep, if you have knowledge of these matters or, alternatively, if there is someone who loves you who has gone on ahead, you leave the plane on which you normally reside to visit a more advanced sphere.

If you are still in your physical body, you will visit the Astral plane, but if you are "dead" and already reside there, then you will go to the Third plane. We, like you, often do not remember these journeys which we make during sleep, unless we learn how to do so.

As long as you are still on Earth, your astral body is attached to its physical counterpart and does not, as a rule, lead a separate existence except when the physical body sleeps. But you lead separate and different lives simultaneously on all the other planes.

197

The Soul Presiding Over Your Homes

On each plane you have a dwelling place, and if you love your Earth home, the same soul will preside over all of them. If, however, you live in your present house only because you cannot afford a better one, you probably do not feel much affection for it and there will thus be little compatibility between you and the presiding house-soul. Under these circumstances your homes on the higher planes will be in charge of a different soul with whom you will certainly be linked by bonds of affection.

If one soul presides over all your homes, this does not mean that he will necessarily keep the same outward form as the one you know on Earth. The presiding soul is not sufficiently advanced to make his own body and it is thus your desires, governed by your state of progress, which create the shape and size of the higher vehicles over which he resides. It is nevertheless the same house-soul, no matter what his outward appearance, in the same way that you are the same person, although your higher plane bodies are far more beautiful than the one which you use on Earth.

As friends gather 'round you down here, so they do too on the other planes. Communities are formed in the same way also, but friends are not parted by restrictions such as the necessity of living near their work.

Your pets, in their more advanced consciousness, are also with you, and it is on attaining the Third plane that you have both reached the state of consciousness when you are able to converse with one another.

Traveling by Thought

There are two methods by which you can visit, for instance, your home on the Third plane when you are living in the Astral. You can, by raising your vibrations and conjuring up a mental picture of the place, find yourself there. It is as simple as that when you have learned how to do it.

The Aura

Alternatively, each person or object holds within his aura a facsimile of all his other bodies, one within the other. Normally these are not visible but, again, anyone who is sufficiently evolved and who has learned the procedure can, at will, see and converse with a person in whichever form and corresponding level of consciousness he desires. Personally, I can contact my Fourth plane body at will, but not my higher vehicles because I have never consciously succeeded in reaching the Fifth plane.

The Community House on the Third Plane

On this occasion I saw in the house's aura its mental body. Normus, also in his mental body, led the way through the front entrance, which was formed by an archway with roses climbing up each side. He took me into a spacious hall consisting of many graceful pillars, some of which supported climbing plants of brilliant hue. We glided up a beam of light in a similar manner to mounting a stair and he escorted me to his suite of rooms. These were large and full of light and colour, blue for rest, green for work and pink for meditation.

Normus' Work on the Third Plane

He carries out his experiments in his workroom and he has now learned to use healing rays to encourage growth in plants, instead of power alone. He has discovered that the blue ray produces a very sweet scent, the yellow a hardier growth and pink for finer texture.

At present these experiments are confined to the plants on the Third plane, for he has not yet discovered in his astral body the uses of these rays, apart from their healing qualities. He is also keenly interested in the effects of different vibrations, and it is his desire to discover a method of raising those of flowers in the same way that mediums raise the vibrations of their bodies, enabling them to function on planes above that of their normal residence.

He has discovered that some flowers produce quicker and stronger growth when placed next to certain other species, while others appear to lose their eagerness when near the same plants. Do we not have the equivalent situation on Earth, when a violent antipathy springs up when certain white people are placed in the proximity of Negroes, whereas others can live happily side by side with them? He is endeavouring to discover whether the dislike is in the mind, the vibration, or whether colour and form influence the outcome.

He showed me rows of seeds which he had placed in different types of soil. Before planting them, each had been minutely scrutinized in regard to its makeup and most detailed records were being kept of day-to-day progress. From this, he hopes to deduce whether a well-formed seed necessarily produces the finest plant, or whether a more advanced consciousness can overcome the misfortune of an imperfect vehicle. I asked him how he was able to judge the state of consciousness when the form was so minute.

"I have an instrument," he replied, and he required no persuasion to show it to me.

Normus placed a single seed upon a transparent tray and, to the top, he fitted a similar one. He passed a series of rays through the box thus formed until I was able to see a minute but regular vibration emanating from the seed.

"That's a good seed with an advanced consciousness," he said. "I should say that it has incarnated on Earth several hundred times."

He picked up another which looked exactly the same as the first.

"This one has incarnated twice only – now watch the difference."

The rays played upon the box again but, this time, there was no steady, answering vibration.

"There, did you see that?"

'What?" I asked, for nothing had been apparent.

"It emanates a tiny force about once a minute. I'll try to tell you when it is about to exhale it again."

We tried for a short while but I fear that my sight was not good enough to catch this infinitesimal fragment of life.

"Now here," he said, holding up a third seed, "is an interesting case. Look."

I took the tiny brown form and I saw that, instead of being smooth and oblong like the others, it had a kink in the centre, giving it a twisted appearance.

"That has incarnated eighty-four times previously. Watch."

He placed the disfigured seed in the box and he turned on the rays. To begin with, nothing very much happened, and then there followed a series of force-stabs which continued for about five seconds and then ceased.

"It can't keep them up continuously as it should but it will start again after a rest," he explained. This proved to be accurate and in about half a minute, the force became active again.

"Will it grow?" I asked.

"It has a chance," Normus said. "I planted five hundred in this row here. They all had blemishes and, as you see, about half have come up."

"Some are obviously much weaker than others," I remarked. "Several here look as though they will fade."

"That's true enough," he replied, "but even a few hours of life in a new form is of value in its next incarnation. I could prove it to you if I could show you the ensuing life of this strong plant, this weakling and one of those which have disintegrated without a struggle."

"How will you know when these particular seeds are born again?"

"That's the tragedy," he said. "I haven't the power to tell yet, but I've been taught by those who have watched similar experiments over hundreds of years and I don't doubt their word."

I could have stayed with him for weeks and even months to follow the various seeds in their course of evolution, but I have other work so I was obliged to take my leave.

On my next visit he took me to his rest room. He invited me to relax as he could see I was a little tired.

"The blue ray in here has great powers," he told me. "It's possible that it isn't your blue, though. I changed it fifteen times before I found the one that is mine."

"It's very soothing," I said appreciatively.

"Tell me what you feel," he said.

Blue, to me, is always a great healer and I would have been content to relax and allow it to permeate my whole being, but I realized that more than this was required of me. The ray entered my body and, after a minute or two, I said, "I feel rested, yet very alive. I'm not sure that I shall not be seeing something very beautiful in a moment. My eyes are beginning to open."

"Too much yellow," he said decisively, and immediately my eyes, too, were at rest.

After a short while I had the impression of sinking, almost as though I were going into a trance. I relayed this new condition to Normus.

"Too much pink," he said, and immediately I became static. I felt as though I were poised in space, free, yet secure, quiet, but without the awe-ful silence experienced sometimes during spiritual seeking. I had no desire to speak any more and I knew that Normus would understand. I am not sure how long I remained thus, but I suddenly realized that I was wide awake and completely refreshed.

"I added a little yellow to wake you," he said. "Do you feel better?"

"It is remarkable," I replied. "I had no idea that you knew so much about healing."

"If only my Earth-vehicle understood as well, we could help Daphne a good deal more."

"You mean that it is never just a question of giving a patient a blue, pink or green ray – it has to be that person's particular blue, pink or green?"

"But naturally," he said. "The original blue I gave you is perfect for me but it is quite wrong for you. What would be the good, when you needed relaxation, to stimulate your mind or give you the sometimes rigorous experience of a trance? I've only been studying rays recently and their power is infinite, but great knowledge is essential. I have only touched the fringe so far. It is a life's work."

"Will you take up healing as a career?" I asked.

He sighed. "I've thought for weeks about it but I can't make up my mind," he said. "How can I forsake my trees and flowers, who have given me their love and helped me to reach my present state? And yet . . . the sufferings of Man cannot lightly be cast aside either."

"Could you not combine the two?" I suggested. "if you can bring healing to the fine art necessary to give health to the sick, surely you can also translate your findings to succour weak or maimed plants?"

"That's what I'm hoping to do," he said, "but I'm afraid of knowing a little of many subjects, but not enough of one to provide the necessary force to aid any to a satisfactory degree. "

"Already your lower vehicle is distributing its much smaller power over many different projects. Surely you do not disapprove?"

"Indeed no. It's merely that I wonder whether here I should concentrate my slightly greater power in one direction until I have learned to produce more of it."

"There are always two sides to every question but I am sure that whichever way you decide, it will be right for you at this present time," I told him.

"I have hopes of so many of the ideas which come to me, but they never seem to materialize into anything worthwhile," he lamented.

"You are young and so are your ideas," I said. "They take time to evolve also. In science, it is often the idea of one man which becomes tangible through another long after the real 'finder's' death. No thought ever dies, remember that; some lie dormant for years, owing to the apathy of the person who gave them birth, but as soon as anyone begins to think along the same lines again, that person's thoughts speed towards the original, giving it strength and causing it to evolve.

"Eventually it is ready for all men to see, hear or feel. That point is reached when any new invention comes to light, but you may be very sure that the idea behind the designs and the eventual manufacture came into being probably centuries ago."

"Patience," said Normus with a sigh. "That is what we all need."

"And all must acquire before we can be of real use on any plane," I said. "Impatience leads to shoddy work. We endeavour to produce magnificent new objects from unmatured data and the inevitable happens. The result disintegrates after a time, instead of growing and improving as is the case when you and your idea progress together."

"It's a fascinating thought," he said, "this dual advancement, step by step, almost like going for a walk together.

"That's a good simile," I said. "The great thing is to guard against getting out of step. Nor yet let your ways part for then that which is really yours will continue its journey with another partner who, by paying more attention to detail, will win the acclamation which always comes with success and which might have been yours."

"But what of me – I'm the one who should be rewarded," he argued.

"And so you will be, but not by public acclaim. You will receive the award of increased awareness to which your work entitles you. But had you been more patient, more vigilant, more determined, you could have carried your work through from start to finish and earned both your spiritual reward and the acclamation as well."

"Is this a special teaching for me?" he asked.

"No, Normus, but it is a lesson of which we should all take heed."

The Meditation

Three visits are not nearly enough in which to study such a complex nature as Normus'. Indeed, a whole book could be written about him, his ideas and his experiences. However, the other fairies deserve space too, so I have contented myself with giving you Normus in three of his aspects, his work and a few of his ideas. Now I will take you with us on a journey which we made during meditation.

Normus had asked me if I would meditate with him on my first visit because he knew that my somewhat more advanced power would carry him to a sphere beyond any which he had succeeded in reaching before.

He who meditates does not usually know where he is going. The results, however, are far from haphazard. In fact, they are carefully planned to give the entity in question as much as possible of the knowledge for which he is prepared at that particular time. It was not in my hands what should befall us and I was looking forward to the experience almost as much as Normus.

The Journey

We relaxed and away we went. I wished to remember our experience together from beginning to end and so did not allow myself the pleasant half-consciousness which these journeys through the spheres can bestow.

We traveled fast and I could feel the gradual lightening of my body as it gathered to it the varying atoms necessary for existence in the rapidly changing conditions. The process took place naturally without effort on our part, our will to live being the nucleus around which the atoms gathered in their desire to "be" and to express themselves in some tangible form. My body soon became so light that I knew that we had reached the Fourth plane, yet still we sped on.

Normus had begun the journey on my shoulder but, as fairies progress, so they also grow. He rapidly became too big to retain his perch and took his place by my side, clinging to my habit in his anxiety not to lose me. Soon this position, too, had to be relinquished as he became larger than me and we clung to each other's hands on this journey which hurtled us, in a few minutes, several million miles.

"Impossible," you will say, and so it would be for you, because your bodies, composed of the coarse, slowly vibrating atoms of Earth conditions, would disintegrate under the tremendous pressure of the higher spheres. But, as the pressure increases, so our bodies become finer and less resistant, and so also do our perceptions become keener in the rarified atmosphere. To us, your brightest sunshine on a clear June day is like forcing our way through a London fog in comparison to even the higher Astral plane.

The Arrival

We came to a halt and there we stood, hand in hand, in our refined bodies of the upper Fourth plane. I was no longer a monk, nor was Normus a seven-inch fairy. Nevertheless, Normus was still Normus and he grinned down upon me from his superior six feet six.

I watched his thoughts as they flew through his mind. "Now that I'm bigger than Father John, am I superior to him?" was his first query to himself.

"He's so beautiful, I wonder if I am too," he pondered. There were many more thoughts, all natural to one who was experiencing being comparatively large for the first time in his life. His eyes shone with excitement – not just the vivid green irises; his anticipation came from much deeper than that.

We looked at each other critically and what I saw confirmed my previous opinion that Normus, in each of his vehicles, reveals the seeds of potential greatness. His beauty now was quite outstanding but, in spite of the dignity in his bearing, there was still the merry twinkle in his eye which, to me, on whatever plane we are manifesting, is quite irresistible.

"I'm enormous," he stated triumphantly.

"And how about the understanding?" I asked. "Has that grown too?"

He thought for a moment and then he beamed. "I know the answers to all the questions which that poor little me has been worrying about. What a feeble mind I must have down there, when it's all so simple."

"It still will not be simple when you return," I warned him. "It is but the power and the purity of the matter of which our bodies and the walls of our minds are made that gives us this great knowledge."

"I want to do something tremendous," he announced. "Something that will justify my having this wonderful form."

"Can you see yourself?" I asked.

"I don't really have to," he said. "I'm superbly beautiful. Aren't I, Father John?" But it was not really a question – he was merely acknowledging a truth.

"We are beautiful by Earth and Astral standards," I said, "but, in comparison to most of those who dwell on this plane, we are but poor specimens."

His face fell. "Do you mean that our beauty is an illusion?" he asked, obviously fearful that my reply would reduce him to his snub-nosed, seven inch astral form.

I took his arm. "Indeed no," I answered him. 'We are as beautiful as we know ourselves to be, but we lack light and that is the essence of all beauty."

"Our auras light the whole scene," he said, but there I felt obliged to correct him.

"The landscape is producing its own light," I said. "Each particle of matter has experienced truth beyond our astral comprehension, otherwise it would not reside here. We are but on this plane through the power of others, given to us in order that we may enjoy an experience which will benefit us for the good of those for whom we work."

"Work," he repeated. "There's work for us to do here too. That's why we're here – and what is more, it is work which those who reside here are unable for some reason to do. That makes you think, doesn't it?"

"Always there is work for each one of us; work which is ours and no one else's. It is a thought which should sustain us when we are weary beyond words; the fact that whatever is occupying us at the moment is our task and that the will and love with which we do it is weaving our part of the pattern, without which the Plan could never be completed."

"But what if we fail to follow the part which has been designed for us?" he asked.

"Others will finish it," I said. "The Plan must be completed but we will have lost an opportunity which will never return and, with it, we will also have forfeited our position on the Path. We will have retarded our progress and experience which might have been ours as a reward for duty faithfully fulfilled, may not come to us for thousands of years."

"You mean that one little oversight or slackness may lose us so much?"

"How can we tell whether our omission was large or small? That which appears a simple task if properly carried out, might form a vital link between two stupendous victories."

"It's difficult to believe, for instance, that a fairy's failure to tend a flower, causing it to die, could be of great importance. There are so many flowers; it is unlikely that the loss of her present span, among so many, should be of any great consequence."

"But you cannot know, Normus," I insisted. "That flower, had she been permitted to complete her Earth span as she should, might be destined as a gift for a

Great One on a visit to the Astral and, as you know, any flower which is touched by one of Them gains power which it might not attain through a thousand years of repeated incarnations."

He understood at last and we felt ourselves being drawn along a path which had appeared before us. I felt very peaceful yet, at the same time, I was filled with anticipation. This was not only a new experience for Normus, for I myself had never meditated with a member of the fairy evolution before. The path had an upward trend and I knew that we were to be taken to yet a higher sphere of the Fourth plane.

The Experience

We found ourselves on the top of a great mountain, gazing across myriads of stars and planets, which nestled amidst hills and valleys composed of matter so refined that one could feel their presence without seeing them. To you, sight means so much, but I can assure you that beholding a person or object loses all value when one can be them without, at the same time, losing one's own identity.

As we stood, so we became the landscape, not just part of it but every atom of that vast expanse of Nature was as much *of* us as are the fingers of our own right hands. The whole history, from the moment when, as light, each component left the Godhead as a divine emanation, perfect as that living fount of All Perfection from which it came, was revealed to us.

We were each and all of them, as well as ourselves, through millions of years of involution and evolution.

We shared each moment of their agony of life without Light, which they experienced for the first time in the total darkness of the Arc of Evil.

With them, we turned the bend and up, up we went as, with the experience of negation added to our original perfection, we fought our seemingly endless way 'round the first cycle on the long road which leads back to the Godhead whence we came.

Then we began the second stage of our journey, the light of our first passage also accompanying us to lessen our burdens – Gas, or the compound mixture of gases known as Air, we were this time. Down we dived, our light gradually fading as we sank to the bottom of the circle to rise again, struggling onward and up until once again the apex was ours.

'Round and down we plunged again, this time as liquid, taking with us the experience of our two other completed lives.

Again we finished our cycle and once more we descended, becoming more tangible this time as mineral. Through the ages we changed our form, through rough dull granite until we shone as the jewel on the brow of a Great One.

On our next journey we learned to perform the function of growing and we had other duties too. As members of the vegetable kingdom, we passed through ten thousand phases, from the slime in a filthy pool in the Arc of Evil, to the noblest tree that lifts his proud head towards the Power which gave him birth.

We grew much in understanding during our next cycle for we encountered the suffering of physical pain as animals. We learned, too, in the later stages, to control ourselves and to obey. No man reaches far until he has learned obedience and that is why it is our duty, with love and kindness, to train our younger brothers whilst they are still in the sixth cycle, or the animal kingdom. We attained incredible beauty as once more we reached the heights before taking our final plunge into the depths to which, at last, we need return no more.

As our consciousness grows, so does our joy in the Light. So, too, does our unspeakable agony become even more unbearable when, for our final salvation, we must learn, as Man, to do without Its comforting radiance. For how can we know happiness unless we have sorrowed? How appreciate good health until we have been sick, and how love the Light, until we have known the horrors of total darkness?

As Man, we descended for the last time for, as Man, we once again regain the Godhead from which we come, at least that is our hope and our faith, the goal to which we aspire. We cannot know because none who has experienced this wondrous re-union has ever returned to tell the tale.

All this I saw and yet more because, with Normus beside me, the seven cycles of his evolution were also revealed. The experience is similar but the form is different because the matter of which fairies are made vibrates faster on each plane than its counterpart in Man. Fairies, too, pass through the forms of flowers and animals but they are not necessarily such as we know them, for through form a soul expresses itself by gathering around its core or being, the atoms of its own vibration. Because the fairy idea of beauty is sometimes different than ours, so the form varies. To a gnome, his round, fat body and wrinkled face are doubtless a great satisfaction. Even a wart hog is probably of beauty to its mother or mate. Beauty varies according to our consciousness and even the same person or object will reveal varying degrees of beauty, depending upon the awareness of the beholder.

Normus and I stood as though poised on the brink of eternity, all our past laid bare before us. I have never previously accompanied a fairy soul on this journey from birth until the present day, and to follow the course of the two evolutions at one and the same time was more than my consciousness could retain, thus part of the fairy passage was lost.

When it was over and we became our present selves again, we felt as though a great burden had been lifted from us. We understood why certain events within our memory had occurred. We had followed the pattern from the beginning and we knew that we must now strive to follow it also day by day, in our work, in our play, in our hours of rest and, most of all, in our striving for further understanding.

It all seemed so easy in our Fourth plane bodies and, with our minds so well tuned to this sphere of understanding, I felt sure that I should never forget one second of this experience which I knew must soon end, for already we were both slipping over the edge of consciousness. Those of us who are able, can visit these higher spheres, but not for long. The purity of the atmosphere – which is so stimulating and which enables us to have experiences which could not take place on lower planes – becomes too much for us to bear and our vibrations drop, no matter how much we endeavour to hold them high.

When we reach our own plane again, sleep is already upon us, to give us the opportunity of readjusting ourselves to the familiar conditions. Sleep also wipes away part of the memory. There was a time when I strove diligently to remember all, but I am more patient now. I understand that we recall as much as we deserve and that if we wish to retain more, then we must work with a greater will so that our tiny section of the pattern is as perfect as we can make it, that it may take its place in the Whole, when that, too, becomes Perfect.

– Father John

THE GODHEAD

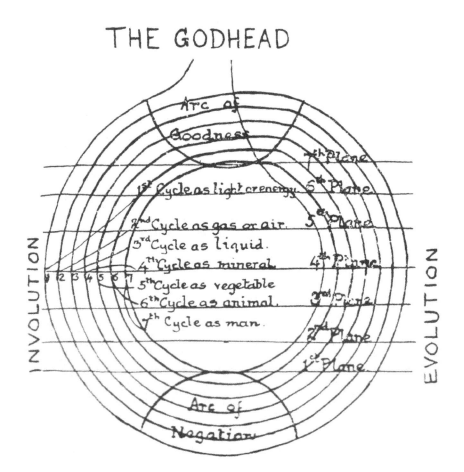

Arc of Goodness

1st Cycle as light or energy.
2nd Cycle as gas or air.
3rd Cycle as liquid.
4th Cycle as mineral.
5th Cycle as vegetable
6th Cycle as animal.
7th Cycle as man.

7th Plane
6th Plane
5th Plane
4th Plane
3rd Plane
2nd Plane
1st Plane

INVOLUTION

EVOLUTION

Arc of Negation

208

[Once again, in an endeavour to simplify Father John's brief outline of invo-lution and evolution, I have drawn a diagram.

I am aware that I have attempted the impossible, for how can one hope to il-lustrate in a few square inches an experience which lasts for millions of years and covers many planets countless miles apart? In two dimensions, one cannot make a spiral begin and end in one place without intersecting itself several times whereas, in reality, Life wends its unbroken course from its beginning into Infinity.

With seven degrees of consciousness, each with its own limited power of growth and, in seven types of form, each with many variations, we plunge into matter, which is known as involution, and, by our own will and determination, we battle, or evolve, out of it.

As there is a positive force for Good, so also there is an evil, or negative, one. From the moment that we leave the Godhead we feel this force and it is owing to its power over us that, even as a piece of steel is attracted to a magnet, so are we inevitably drawn ever deeper into the material planes until we have safely turned the bend and begin to fight our way upwards towards the Godhead once more. Even then we are constantly pulled back by this force of negation but, as we rise higher, so does its power abate as, to an increasing degree, we lift up our eyes and hearts to the Light. – Daphne Charters.]

TRAVELS

by Normus

7th February, 1954

One Wednesday night you and I met and you said, "I'm sure we're going to learn something special tonight." So, full of anticipation, we set off and when we had adjusted our consciousness to the high vibration, we found ourselves in the Fairy sector. However serious the reason for our visit may be, first we must play. This is a necessity and not a frivolity because, until we have rushed about as fast as we can, there remain clinging to us, Earth ideas, and until we are rid of them, we are unable to concentrate. What fun this period is. We burst and reform only to disintegrate again almost immediately. In this destruction, the atoms of our bodies change their positions and one of our amusements is to stop them from rejoining those of the person to whom they rightfully belong. Of course we can never prevent them from doing this for long, but sometimes we keep them poised between the two of us, they look so funny that we begin laughing, our concentra-tion vanishes until we are once more complete and ready to burst again.

Eventually we feel calm and we begin to look about for the reason of our visit. Usually a light is either present or soon appears, or a path shows us the way that we must go. Sometimes, for fun, one of us will say, "Let's tease the past. We'll ignore it." And we pretend we haven't seen it and we start off in another direction. But the path refuses to be ignored and we are gathered into it and swept at breathtaking speed to wherever we are meant to go. Usually we find ourselves in a tangled mass at the Ra-Arus' feet. He pretends to be very surprised at such an unusual display in His presence, but we know that it is really He who has arranged our undignified entry, and we love Him all the more for pandering to our youthfulness and ideas of fun.

On this particular occasion, instead of springing up and making one of our gestures of honour and eagerness to obey His will, we found ourselves unable to move for about five minutes. I had a foot in your mouth and you were at the same time sitting on my head. I screamed and you choked (not really of course), until eventually He set us free, and a great effort was needed, after so much hilarity, to get into the right mood for our lesson.

We were in one of the Ra-Arus's palaces but soon we ceased to be aware of its enclosing walls and, under His guidance, we spread until we had reached our limit. At one time I liked to make myself a huge body, but I have learned that a form of any sort is restricting and that, even when I have apparently reached my limit, a few thoughts will wander further afield and manifest, if they are not restricted by an outline. However refined the atoms my be I think I am wrong in saying that MY thoughts spread; it is rather that my consciousness becomes aware of other thoughts if it is as unrestricted as the plane allows. This time it was really the Ra-Arus's thoughts which we were assimilating and as, in comparison to our own state of consciousness, these are of course limitless, it is only our restricted capacity which prevents us from sharing His limitless knowledge. Therefore we try very hard to expand as much as we can. At first this spreading used to cover space as we know it. We become the trees, the birds and the people within that area, we even learned to give them thoughts which would occasionally become actions. But now the change (our spreading) is different. Material objects have ceased to be important; we have risen above form. We absorb not the colour, the perfume or the shape of the contents of the plane, but what you know as their abstract qualities. Their enthusiasm in their act of evolving is what we absorb when we are with the Ra-Arus. We are so limited that we cannot experience more than the main function of the particular Teacher-Lord who is teaching us. We would need a separate occasion and the assistance of the Marata for us to receive the spiritual state in abstract of the same souls in their present vehicles.

One relies so much on sensation on the physical and astral planes, that it is extremely difficult to bring back one's reactions during these experiences. For feel one certainly does, but not with one's senses, and yet one is aware of everything to a far greater degree. One is always aware that one loves a person even if he is miles from one's sensation of touch, smell, sound etc. You are aware of your love for Jack and Bran even though they have been completely removed from your present main plane of existence. You know that your astral love is greater than your love for either of them on Earth. That is because your capacity to love has grown greater and, with it, your awareness. Awareness always grows with capacity and that is why we try to remove the barriers of "form" for you, and "will" for me, because our powers are also our restrictions.

8th February

You already understand that the deeper into matter you plunge, the coarser are the atoms of which your body is made. This is obvious because atoms can only exist within a certain ratio of density. It is the same with all the other Evolutions. Will, perfume, sound are made of atoms too and, in the same way, when we fairies descend to a lower plane, so our will becomes less refined, and we lose the desire to do some of the things that we did when we were living on the astral. We have the will to do less, in other words we are more restricted. When we visit the higher spheres, we make all kinds of plans which seem to be workable in Earth conditions, but when we return, we have the will-power to do only some of them. This is partly due to the time factor and partly for the reason that even when we have brought the ideas down from the plane on which we made them where they seemed reasonable and workable, from our much lower aspect they appear like so many inconsequential dreams. It may be that we fail to bring all of the plan down and thus several vital links are missing; and perhaps we cannot understand it in its different manifestation. In any case we are unable to translate many of our ideas into action owing to our restrictions.

Rimago and I have struck up a great friendship. We seem to have so many things in common. We often work together and I will now tell you about one of our many projects. This is the mutual exchange of power, in other words the exchange of his "consciousness" for my "will". You might think that, as we are fairly even in the former now, Rimago could not help me to expand my consciousness, and I do not think that he could in general knowledge. Naturally he can give me a great deal of information about his evolution and, in visiting his or other sectors with him he can give me a different aspect of the same object. That is not what I mean. Rimago, being a ceris, has for power the "food" on which thoughts thrive, and this power, if given to another evolution, will provide the equivalent of heat and

211

moisture for forcing a plant. In other words, with his help my thoughts grow to maturity far quicker than if I relied on the normal amount of ceris-power which my own attendant provides.

As Rimago has developed, naturally all his aspects have developed too. He has far more will-power now than when you first knew him and this has quickened his progress. When I consciously give him fairy power, because my state of progress is more advanced than the fairy who normally gives it to him, he receives additional and superior "will" to his usual intake.

However, we have found that if we exchange power without first using all our capacities for taking a plan as far as we are able with our Earth consciousness, we are very little better off than we were before. We have to exercise all our faculties to their limit, then, when we know that we can do no more, he will give me power if it is a fairy plan, or I him if it is a ceris one, and then we are able to take it one step further. There is no great revelation, no instantaneous solving of our difficulties, but in this way we can begin work on uncompleted plans, because we know that we can always keep one stage ahead of what is then in actual practice.

(Part of original manuscript missing) . . . consciousness can follow, and however hard we try, we can remember nothing after the preceding moment to this release.

On earth one does it just for the excitement. I fill myself with power, drawing in more and more until, just like a balloon with too much Air in it, I burst, and spread over the surrounding atmosphere. My thoughts, which are comparatively orderly under my guiding consciousness, are now without control and they mingle and merge, and are funny or interesting, according to my intention. This bursting will sometimes give the answer to a problem, for unconsciously I have been keeping apart two ideas, which when merged in this way, are exactly what we have been looking for.

– *Normus*

A FAIRY'S IDEA OF GOD

by Normus

On the higher planes I am still seeking, but not for a sensation, answers to problems, or for frivolous recreation. It was only after many experiences which took me along paths as varying as "strength" and "gentleness", "justice" and "pity," that I realized that I wasn't seeking any of them but God. Who-what is God? Nobody seems to know. Many have found an aspect of God which those are not very far advanced mistake for God Himself. Some share an aspect with others and are then even more sure that theirs is the only one. I know that if I were able t follow my paths right to God Himself, I would see a million different Gods, each being He yet only part of Him. My idea of God is changing, growing. Before I met you, I thought of Him as my Creator, as the Creator of the Universe. I gave Him a form – It was more beautiful than any fairy I had consciously known. Then He became formless, too magnificent to be contained. Then I saw Him in all forms, in every worm and blade of grass. I became confused. How could He be formless and yet have every form? Although confused, I knew that I was on the border or, to me, a new truth. Month by month my convictions grew. It came to me that there was not one God but two. Yet I knew that there is only one Absolute. I recalled Lerra's words to you: "Remember that even your most humble action is but a reflection of an act of God." I felt sure that this phrase held the key. I began by saying, "I am an act of God." Then I said, "Of what am I composed?" "A body" – I disintegrated it – "and I." "That's it!" I shouted. The Universe is God's body which He could disintegrate if He willed as easily as I have mine. But still I am left and I was happy because I knew that through life it would always be like that – the disintegration of material things which are of no importance because they are made to be destroyed and made again in a different form. But always there is the experiencing of these forms and casting them away because I no longer need them. "I" am eternal – not my body, not even my consciousness. There is something else in me and in everyone, it is the particle of God with Which we have been endowed that we may bring it to perfection through experience. I felt tremendously proud that I had been entrusted with that particle. It became very precious to me. It was God's gift to me and one day I must return it to Him as perfect as the day He gave it to me. Then my heart sank. If it was perfect when He gave it to me, to what purpose all my struggles to make perfect what is now so very far from perfect? This was no easy problem and it took me many months to solve. I realized that there are degrees of perfection. A pin may be perfect but one cannot compare its perfection to that of a rose.

One cannot even compare with a rose the flawlessness of its bud wrapped tightly within itself. The bud must grow.

We can only reach a degree of perfection which limited by our status. Then we begin to unfold again. Our original perfection was limited to its particular status, and though it may appear that we are less perfect now than we were, this is not really so, because when we have reached the completion of our present status, we shall once more be perfect within its limitations. It is only when we have completed the cycle which contains every status, yet is only one, that we shall have reached the Great Perfection and are ready to return whence we came.

– Normus

'Letter' to Daphne

by Normus

Another project is the beginning of your unit on the Astral. Each night we go with you and Jack to build up the power. Of course many astral entities are there and the power is growing. We are all excited about it, for now we know we will never be separated; that when our Earth span is over, we will join those in your house and garden and continue our work together there. Thus, although our spans are of different length, we of our group will always be together and that has made us very happy for we respect each other's qualities and know that each one of us is necessary to supply the power to make the whole. You know, I think that "the boys" will be leaving. We shall be a little sad to lose them because they are so happy, but we know the two who will take their place. They are equally gay but more advanced and already working with thought formations so they will be a help to the house fairies. Of course Geoff will be their guardian, as least he will have the girl and Bumpy the boy, or rather they will have them together. They are coming from China, so we are becoming international now.

Of course you understand that all who are drafted to your Astral home will help us here too. They are bound to be advanced so we are assured of some exciting results. We have so many meetings both here and on the other planes and we have already started our training for the more advanced work which will take place there. Daphne, you do not know what an honour this is – for we continuously meet Great Ones. We never know when or where they will appear to give a word or a suggestion. Life is so exciting. There is so little discord among us. I think I can say it is negligible. We realize that misunderstanding must be smoothed out, for where there is even slight disagreement there cannot be harmony. In our hearts we know now that there is only one "right" for Perfection and now instead of arguing our own point of view, we examine the "right" until we see its rightness and only when all are in tune do we even begin to work on any project. You see, if there is any doubt in any fairy's mind about the correct approach to any task, however simple, he cannot give his best. Now, when we are given some work, we all sit quietly, putting aside our own ideas. Soon we know what we should do. Then we allow our own ideas to return and we compare them one by one – but always, after consideration, we see that although each one had merit, it was not perfect for the case in hand. Often our own thoughts and the completed plan are one and when that happens we are very happy.

We find "the children" very helpful, always willing to give their fresh young power if their particular quality is weak in the entity we are endeavouring to help.

We are beginning to see how much thought has gone into the forming of this group. Yet we were all here long before you came and little did we know what was in store for us.

Now I will tell you what happened last night. I must say first how lovely it is that you no longer leave us, and our sadness is that you have no memory as we have. We are sure that if on Tuesday morning you would concentrate with us at breakfast, that we could give you at any rate some of the incidents.

We went to the Third Plane of the drone sector and so many came to greet us. They aren't solid as we are, but they are of so many colours, some rich, some pale, according to their degree of progress. The drone sector is especially exciting because one's powers of feeling are particularly sharp. We cannot keep solid form because we continually disintegrate with excitement. You laughed and laughed because you were determined to keep your form even though it was really impossible, and it was only when you discovered how to spread it, so that hundreds of the drones could share it and experience more form, that you managed to keep even an outline. Then, because they were sharing your form, you of course shared their vibration and as you couldn't be part of all of them at once, you took it in turns and we guessed which one you were being. We got you every time because you were laughing so much. You could not seem to control it and that made all of us laugh too. It was one of the happiest sessions we've had. We didn't learn anything profound except of course we shared ourselves too, so we learned what it felt like to be a drone.

One feels like a generator sending out a continual surge of power in every direction at once unless one controls it and makes it go one way. You might think this exhausting, but I wasn't at all. We seemed to replenish faster than we could send it out, so we were in a continual state of movement with no control at all. They showed us how to direct the vibrations but we were hopeless, they just continued rushing in all directions regardless of our efforts. I'm sure we created turmoil in this higher plane but hey didn't mind a bit and said that our happy power with its comparatively low vibration would help them and they would soon have it where it would all be under control again and direct it where they wanted it to go.

We weren't there very long because we were worn out with so much movement. We still have some of it with us today and we hope that you have too.

– Normus

MY FANTASY

by Normus

Weary and depressed, I lay beneath a tree. My work had led me to regions most foul, so to soothe my despair I thought of beauty in female form. Slowly an image grew. Glorious she was and of heavenly brightness. Watching her I relaxed and was cleansed. I knelt before her laying my services at her feet. I was pleased with my gesture gracefully performed, but I was yet more pleased with this lovely figment of my mind, whom I had conjured up and on whom I had bestowed so much perfection.

I began to call her to me with ever growing frequency. And one day she smiled. I had made her of my very highest thoughts and awareness of me had not been one of them. My heart sank for she was my ideal and I did not want her spoiled by any action, even one as guileless as a smile. In my admiration of myself for the creation of this image, I had somehow defiled her. I had, against my will, attracted my perfect emblem from her divine aloofness. I had besmirched her purity. But I knew what I must do. I blotted out her smile and I returned her to her sky of blue, gazing steadfastly, into the great unknown. Then I smiled myself, my problem solved.

A week later I was working, completely absorbed in my task when I felt myself grow very hot and then very cold. My train of thought was broken. I was not alone. My image was with me, and what was worse, again she smiled.

"Go back" I shouted at her, and why should I not shout at my own creation? "I don't want you down here. You are Perfection. Go back." I had to work much harder this time, but eventually I succeeded once more replacing her in her cloudless sky and I returned to work.

Three days later it happened again and I almost wept. "Can I not be allowed one perfect image?" I cried. "Must everything be polluted by the dust and dirt of Earth consciousness?"

"I am not perfect" she said. Yes, my image spoke, although I had made her above speech, above thought, above everything but the purest beauty.

"I am real" she continued "I am I. I am not a puppet of your imagination to be commanded away from where my duty lies. It is true that last time I returned to please you, so that my apparent fall from grace might be less painful for you. We have work to do and in that work you will forget the loss of your supposed dream, for love will bring me closer to you. Remember, you laid your service at my feet and I accepted it. I am calling on you to fulfill your promise."

The word "work" always acts like a violent stimulant to me. I may be feeling weary, lazy, dreamy or irritated, but the suggestion of a new project re-awakens the best in me and I am ready to try any suggestion that may be presented.

She continued "You and I are standing at the beginning of a new path, quite new to you, not so new to me, because I have contemplated it for many years. In reality, it is as old as Time, and has been there since the beginning even though it has only recently reached a stage in its evolution when we two can tread it."

"There are so many paths." I remarked. "I wonder why this one should be ours."

"Because it was made for us and we for it. Because it is made of the same force that we are."

"But we all come from the God force – we are of the same force as everything else, yet we cannot tread all the paths in the Universe."

"That is true and as we are all One, in reality 'we' do tread each path – it is only our present limited consciousness which prevents us from realizing the fact."

"What governs which path this consciousness experiences?" I asked.

"The rate of its vibration."

"But yours is a million times faster than mine."

"In the consciousness in which you are talking now, yes, but not a million times, for otherwise I could not be communicating with you at all. But you have higher states of consciousness. You know that."

"But I still don't understand what governs which paths we must tread."

"It is always the state or the rate of the vibration of your lowest vehicle which controls the tasks which you are capable of performing. Because my lowest vehicle dwells on a higher plane then yours, I can bring down to you a little more understanding – I can show you this path which your own consciousness would not enable you to do."

Excitedly I began to look for a road – for a great straight stretch of light which would lead us among and above the stars. But I could not see one, so I looked again, with a more modest idea of my future destiny. I searched first for a winding, narrow road, then for a lane almost hidden by refuse, then for a path which became gradually more and more overgrown, until finally in desperation, I tried to bring into being a way myself, even though there was nothing of which to make it.

I was almost in tears and very tired. "I've failed you before we have begun." I said shamed of my inability to pass this initial test.

"I told you that you could not see this path without my aid" she said gently.

"I am too impetuous." I said. "I am sorry. Please help me." I filled myself with power and this time I gave her my mind. I raised my thoughts as high as I could and began to look again.

A gentle voice penetrated my concentration.

"You are seeking in the wrong direction."

Everything fell about me, my body, my mind, my aspirations. I seemed to disintegrate completely When I came together again. She was looking at me gravely. "From the greatest heights of your mind to the lowest, I am sad I have fallen so far."

"But you can't go down there. I won't let you" I said, "Could we not work in a higher sphere? You have been my emblem of the brightest and best in me, and even though you aren't really mine, couldn't you remain my star. I could keep my mind upon you, beautiful, serene, pure, and when I am in the "dark places." You would stop me from being afraid."

"And what of the path? Is it to remain untrod because you fear to shatter a dream? She asked.

I felt heavy. Everything had fallen in such a brief space of time. But a path is a path. It is not there to be ignored but to be used until a small, unbeaten track becomes a well-known road, growing brighter and larger at every footfall.

And then I saw it. A little thread of light leading from the ground beneath our feet, down, down into the enveloping gloom until it was lost in the negation that only those who work in the "dark places" know.

"It isn't very big." I said, more for something to say than anything else.

"But it *is*, and that is all that matters. There is much work to be done before we can use it. For remember it not only leads into the dark places, it also leads *out*. Along this path, many sad and fearful ones will pass. We must work hard that their journey be smooth and light as possible."

I peered down the tiny thread, still unable to raise myself to a happy frame of mind.

"Look up" she said and this time there *was* a path. It was not very large but as I looked. It became bigger, wider and then, at the top, I saw Her, my dream, my emblem – but more beautiful, clearer then she had ever been before. She was not gazing up impersonally at the boundless sky, she was looking down and smiling at *me*. Then I turned and she was still beside me. I looked up quickly but she was there as well.

218

"There, here and on every plane, wherever you may be", she said, and I know that if I had lost a dream, I had gained a friend who would bring beauty, for she was Beauty, not only to me in my higher consciousness but to those who lie in the depths as well.

– Normus

MEDITATION

by Normus

Unless we are otherwise employed we always hold a joint meditation when our daily work is done. We gather together and decide which particular problem requires an answer. We relax and ponder. Sometimes one of us receives the complete answer, at others several of us will be given a part and we have to fit the pieces together so that we have the whole. At times we find that the answer is incomplete and that we must try again. Often we are taken to a higher plane to a hall of learning, if the answer is not as simple as we had imagined. Sometimes we arrive at the house of one of our teachers and he will give us the answer. Usually if we make thought forms immediately on our return to Earth we know what to do, but if we have been to a fairly high plane for our instruction, we fail to bring it down automatically and the following day we must hold another meditation so that we can remember what we have been told.

At other times our meditations are not teachings by the exchange of thoughts. They are explorations of new territory either in our own sphere or in one of the others, and according to the evolution of the places we visit, so we strive to develop that particular component part. Naturally the one, or ones, belonging to that evolution does everything he can to help all the others and a hilarious time we have with our failures and mistakes but always we learn a little and so we add to our knowledge nearly every day.

We always enjoy the most the times when you accompany us because you are so funny. You pretend not to understand just to make us laugh – you look so woebegone as you make more and more ridiculous suggestions as to what something we are trying to show you, is, and then finally you give the right answer and a great game follows. You are so good at games and always have so many ideas to amuse us and often it isn't until we've finished that we realize that there was a point to what we have been doing and that either we have made something or have unexpectedly learned a new truth.

The little new fairies are making good progress. They need a lot of encouragement but each has been adopted by one of us and we invite them to our homes for instructions or recreation and they have thus become members of the group in every way. Your suggestion that Herus should help Finto would never have struck me. I would never have thought that a fairy so young as Finto would have been capable of making thought formations when he was still unable to perform his own work properly. It has been a great success and now Herus has an ever-growing list of would-be pupils and, as you know, he had asked Pino to help him. I think that he himself is a little bewildered by his success and although he is not always very patient with their shortcomings, he eventually laughs at himself and so gains their affection. I have invited him to give us all lessons in thought-formation which almost overwhelmed him but he is really brilliant and has such fresh ideas. I know that it will be a great asset if we Nature fairies learn some of the rudiments, although I myself and some of the others naturally wish to go further that that. It is essential to our work and our contribution will, I know, eventually help the house fairies in their important work.

– Normus, 1st Feb. 1954

MANUSCRIPTS
SET #6

MUSIC IN THE
FAIRY REALM

Preface

This is a small section of seven stories found scattered in the manuscripts and brought together here because of their focus on music in the fairy realms. The importance of music to the fairies is evident in many of the stories, but particularly so in these seven.

Three stories are by Rudolph, an astral human musician. One is by Jack, Daphne's deceased husband, living on the astral plane. One is by Normus, the leader of the nature fairies. One is by Maire, one of the house fairies. One is unsigned.

Several other stories in the manuscripts describe visits by fairies to the realm of the Thormes evolution. The Thormes are the beings who govern sound and music. Are Thormes a branch of the fairies, or are they a different evolutionary life-wave altogether? Those stories will be in Volume II.

– Michael Pilarski

THE SPIDER MUSICIANS
by Rudolph

[Rudolph is a discarnate human and musician living on one of the astral planes at the time. – M.P.]

Before beginning to work on my "Island Serenade," I asked for help from musicians of the Fairy Evolution. The Arienes were natural singers but I required some technical advice on how to interpret the sounds which I had heard on that amazing day in order to include them in my composition.

I was waiting for my promised assistants in my house, not sure whether they would arrive in a chariot drawn by dragonflies, or float through the window on a breeze.

A sparkling multi-colored flash appeared before me. I had, of course, already seen members of the Fairy Aspect of Evolution but none quite like this one. She was about five and a half feet tall and looked as though she was made of aquamarine chips gleaming through a powdering of jewel dust. She scintillated much more brightly than the Arienes, who, on that magical day with the island's inhabitants, were the most exquisite beings I had ever seen.

"Greetings, Rudolph," she said, "What a pleasure it is to be invited to help you. My name is Lerralina and I am a player of instruments rather than a singer. We have many ways of making music including pipes as large as your church-organs which we bear up and down the air currents to make sounds of great majesty. We fly between carefully spaced trees and other plants to produce lighter tones and we know of caves where spiders weave their webs and as we draw our fingers across the intricate threads, a high, sweet melody flows."

"But surely the threads must break," I said in disbelief.

"Our fingers do not actually touch them; it is the power that emanates from them that causes the spiders to create the sounds, and these are amplified by the caves."

I shook my head. "It sounds impossible; it must be a fairy-tale."

"They are fairy spiders," she replied with a smile.

There was another corruscating flash like myriads of rubies, emeralds and sapphires, all shooting their light in every direction. A glorious being took gradual form. At first I thought that her hair was black, but it was, in fact, dark blue. Her face was also dark, tinged with blue and she had a sweet, shy smile.

"Friamista has a lovely voice," said Lerralina. "We often make music together. It is to her song that the spiders spin their webs, the notes guiding them to form the desired pattern." She turned to her companion. "Rudolph does not believe me; he is worrying about sonority," she laughed.

"We can coax music from a worm or a sunbeam," said Friamista.

"At times I'm still shocked by Earth's limitation," I told them. "Would you please take me to the caves one day so that I can witness your wonderful achievement?"

Once again, I was waiting for the two fairies, this time in a valley close to their home. I had visited them there on several occasions and it never ceased to intrigue me that not only did they and their surroundings sparkle, but I did too. At first, I touched my hand to find out whether it was merely a coating which would brush off, but I discovered that my skin while remaining soft, was obviously composed of shining, multi-colored atoms.

I heard someone singing in the distance, accompanied by a stringed instrument and as soon as they came within sight, I ran towards them and held them affectionately, one on each side of me. To embrace a fairy is an exciting experience; touching them causes a faint prickling sensation, as though tiny jewels were sparkling against my skin and within my aura.

"Come with us, and we will show you the caves," said Lerralina. Joining hands, we flew through the air, this contact causing me to tingle with warm friendship toward these lovely beings of another world.

Mountains rose in the distance, and I gasped at their beauty as the snow enveloping them threw a million white pin-points of light on to the multi-colored lustre of the sky behind them. It is impossible to describe in Earth-terms the effulgence of the Fairy Sector. There are many adjectives to describe a glistening effect but these are only adequate when one is referring to reflected light shining on cut facets of gems or crystals. This sparkle is an inner light flashing through living, growing forms which are not composed of solid matter as we know it, but a tenuous substance, pulsating with life.

"Stop, do let's stop", I begged them and we descended slowly to land on a flat surface to enable me to gaze on the fantastic scene while stationary. "Why can't I be a member of your Aspect of Evolution? It isn't fair that you should all be so beautiful and live in such a bewitching land."

"But you are beautiful, Rudolph." said Friamista.

"The steady light and comparative stability of the forms in your Human Sphere entrance us," said Lerralina. "One can weary of the restless, ever-changing brightness here. The steady calm of your landscapes, the subtle colors of your vegetation and the comparative stillness of the atmosphere enthrall us."

"I suppose contrast is the attraction for all of us. However wonderful it may be, that which is familiar eventually palls, like love in spite of its infinite variations," I said.

"That is so," said Friamista, "Even love must change and evolve."

"Are you in love?" I asked her.

"With a male? Not at present, but I have experienced love many times. Both Lerralina and I are in love with life and with music, and both are an endless adventure."

"Listen; the caves are calling," said Lerralina, "Come." hand in hand, we again swept towards the mountains and landed in front of a thickly covered rock-face.

"We will play some music now," said Lerralina as she walked away and moved her arms rhythmically through the air. When she turned, I could see that she was holding a jewel-studded instrument rather like an early trumpet with a small one on either side. I could see the stops which regulated which horn or horns the air would pass through. She began to play, but the music was unlike that from any trumpet. Soft, sweet tones flowed through the horns, sometimes separately, at others simultaneously. There were no puffed cheeks during the performance; she remained as beautiful as always as the coaxed the notes on their journey, rather than forcing them through the aperture. Friamista added her resonant voice, the sound emanating from the chakras, and those from the instrument, blending as though they came from a single source.

Out from the caves bustled the weavers, looking like dozens of jeweled broaches; they scampered towards us, peering at me eagerly as they arranged themselves in groups around us.

"We will have a little concert," said Lerralina. "They will produce music with us but it will be inaudible to you. Later we will cease to play and sing, and their melody will reach you."

The music rose again in a brisk, joyful tune. The spiders looked as though they were hypnotized. They watched the fairies as keenly as players their conductor. The audible melody ceased, and I strained my senses to detect the spiders' song, and at last I succeeded. The sounds were higher than I had ever heard before, and incredibly, they were in harmony. It was the same song as that which the fairies had performed, but now they were singing without their guidance.

"Are you sure you aren't deceiving me with some form of magic?" I asked.

"We are too mature to play tricks," smiled Friamista. "We have spent years with these spiders. Our love for them and theirs for us have enabled them to share our skills."

"I didn't mean to offend you," I said contritely, "but to a human being, singing spiders are inconceivable except in dreams."

Friamista smiled. "You are in fairyland; do not judge what you experience by Earth-standards, or you will remain in a constant state of disbelief."

"How can I show them my appreciation?"

"Send them a love-vibration; one from a Man will thrill them." I beamed one in their direction and a visible tremor emanated from each.

"Come now. We will show what we can do." We all went closer to the cave and Friamista stood near its mouth with her back against one side of the entrance.

She opened her lips and sent a note in the direction of a group of waiting spiders. One of them detached itself and ran towards her. She picked it up and placed it on the opposite rock surface. The note rang out again and seemed to form a path, and the spider ran through the air towards her towing a glimmering thread behind it; this was then attached to the wall behind Friamista. this performance was repeated several times and then she said "That is enough, Hi; we must have some other notes or we shall be playing a tedious tune."

She then sent out different calls and each time another spider came running until there were sixteen contributors in all; they moved swiftly in every direction following the notes which Friamista sang until the entire access to the cave was covered with the silver threads of a giant web.

"It can't play," I argued silently with myself. "There's nothing to produce resonance." But I knew all the time that it could and would.

"Now we have an instrument, we also need an orchestra. Would you care to join us, Rudolph?" asked Friamista.

"Not yet," I said firmly. "My mind still doubts that this web is a playable instrument. Theoretically it cannot produce sound, and yet I know it will. Don't tantalize me any more."

A sound came from her lips – a high-pitched note – and the spiders scurried to take their places. Each on a thread it had emanated.

"It isn't true," I said to myself, still only half-believing the evidence before me. Lerralina moved the tips of her fingers close to the web, and Friamista did likewise. Wherever their fingers went, the spiders followed, and as their feet moved, a tiny note was emitted. It is utterly impossible to compare these sounds with anything on Earth because they were too high to be audible there. I can only assure you that it was as though a sixteen-piece orchestra was playing a melody.

The two fairies smiled and asked, "Now do you believe us?"

"Only because I have to. Can I join you now? But how does one read invisible fairy music? Is it possible for a human being to do so?"

"You will need some help from our Master of Music."

"Is he here?" I asked excitedly.

"Yes, he is beside you," said Friamista and I could then see a scintillating ray shining between us. They made an obeisance and I repeated their actions and as I raised my head, I became aware of a beautiful, youthful face alight with a smile.

"Let us begin," he said.

"I don't know what to do."

"Let us begin," he repeated, his eyes twinkling.

I stood in front of the web and hesitantly ran a finger close to one of the threads; a spider followed my movement. I raised a finger from my other hand and a different spider ran forward. Gaining confidence, my hands became more dexterous, as I gave myself over to the Master of Music's will. I could hear without effort now, and what sounds those spiders made as they obeyed their angel-instructor. My fingers flew faster and faster from one side of the web to the other and always the spiders followed them. But now, they not only ran up and down the threads, but they pirouetted, bobbed and leapt in the air like a chorus of ballet dancers. We all laughed so much in joyous amusement, that I sometimes lost the tune, but each time I concentrated once more. I was amazed at the intricacy of the part each spider played.

"That was a true Tarantella," I said when the dance came to an end. "Could we play once more?" I begged; I felt my hand raised towards a thread and again a spider responded. My other hand was drawn into position and we were away. But this time, the music welled up inside me and I was able to control the movement of my fingers myself. A new experience always inspires me and I began to really enjoy myself. I became bolder, adding my own ornaments, which resulted in the most extra-ordinary antics among the spiders, who seemed to be having a wonderful time. It would not have surprised me to discover they were laughing as much as their audience.

When I tried to tell some of my less musically-inclined earthbound friends about my enchanting experience, their faces froze in total disbelief, only melting to give a quick glance out of the corners of their eyes at one another or twitching a single eyebrow.

Who can blame them? I myself had more than doubted Lerralina when she first told me about the bewebbed cave and the musical spiders. I don't mind what they think because I heard and watched that Tarantella. I know.

– Rudolph

[Which all goes to prove that individual awareness does not come equally to all who are now living on the Astral Plane. One has to seek and learn from each experience which is granted. – Daphne C.]

THE POWER OF MUSIC
by Rudolph

(15th April, 1962 – during Cecile's visit here)

Cecile has asked about the power of music, quite an inspired question because it is, in a way, the theme of what I had planned to tell you.
We perform various tasks according to our temperaments; you and Jack have long done rescue work while Cecile and I seek always for the inner meaning of music. Jack and I combine, he with his knowledge of machines, and I of the mechanics of music to make "vehicles" for the transportation of the "lost ones." Now this may sound a somewhat strange association but a machine must "work" and so must music. We have found that if I play a decisively phrased tune while Jack meditates on the theme of transmission, he receives ideas upon which a framework can be devised. This is not a vehicle from a mundane point of view, but an artificial auric envelope which can be placed around a sleeping "lost one" with the idea of raising his or her consciousness. And very effective they are too, for they contain my music and Jack's will, a kind of magic which will not be lost to you.

Cecile loves to help distressed children, and she and Jack work in a similar way to achieve the same result. The music for this purpose, must be gay yet tender and highly imaginative, so that in their dreams the children may be led to a sphere where they can live in sleep the kind of life that is denied them when awake.

She has asked what I am doing. Much the same as on Earth but with the vast difference that I have found the Reason for my music. The driving force is not for the sole purpose of compelling me to provide a form to mould the raw material of music into a constructive pattern, although to organize it in this way is an accomplishment it is true, and through it many can be uplifted. But now there is Purpose to every composition; it is created for a particular function and not merely for my personal satisfaction nor yet for the pleasure of others. One might say that each bar is like a link in a chain, the end of which is placed in the hand of someone in distress. These people are not necessarily musical and yet the power of music is such that they can be led by it in the right direction without even hearing it.

I cannot compose this music in the normal way; it emerges through inspiration alone. I do not hear it note by note; the composition is complete before I begin to play. It is as though I am outside myself listing to someone else. The music is unknown, and I have no idea as to the following phrase, yet as player, there is no hesitation. Once completed, the whole is established on my plane, and I hold it in my memory and yet I sometimes wonder, after frequent and diligent practice, whether the perfection of that first rendering is ever re-attained.

On these occasions, Cecile is sometimes with me and in some way, the theme is also passed to her. She too has the same experience of not knowing as the player, with the consciousness listening as though to another performer.

She has asked after our father and he is well, mellowed by appreciation and the endless offers of work we all have. Our ways are not the same, although we naturally meet, interest in the family's music chaining us to Earth. We each inspire in our own way and not only members of the family. Dorothy is wonderful and gives of herself and her boundless talent to many projects for which she is especially gifted.

Cecile's music soars to me, a great and welcome anchor. If we have no anchor, we can do but little for those on Earth. Interest in mundane music is lost in the glory of sound that surrounds us as we strive to reach the higher planes to find ever purer forms. All of created music is hidden in a single puff of wind; but we lack the power of apprehension.

Sometimes I find a ray that must flash from Music's Soul itself, a fleeting illumination, when my innermost being opens to receive this perfect caress. I am so overwhelmed by this momentary bliss that I overflow and die, to live for an unremembered moment

Beyond manifested Life.

– Rudolph

THE MUSICIAN

by Rudolph

Most of my companions still find joy in the notes which emerge from the subtle forms of metal, wood and strings, but I am restless for the essence of music. I still have ears to hear, but I can also sense sound without them. Each note is an experience, quickening consciousness; a staccato rhythm lacerates me until I must be free of my body or go mad.

This is not unpleasant but a wild excitement and when the exploding point is reached, how that crazy disintegration satisfies. It is as though the Universe is collapsing and I am in the centre enveloped in chaos, and glorying in it for I am Whole and nothing can change that wondrous Truth. Oh the exhilaration, the fulfillment, the rapture, as I know myself imperishable in the face of Death. Music is my deliverer, for beyond the destruction, the turmoil and the triumph, lies peace – not only that of activity stilled, but the peace of indivisibility. Harmonizing like a whole choir of angels without thought or effort, I am the song and yet apart from it; it is both me and mine; an emanation that leaves yet also stays, like an aura revealing a light from one's inner being, splendid in itself, yet but a reflection of its reality.

Peace with ecstasy; that is the object for which I strive. I find first one and then the other, but together they elude me. But though my own talents fail me, other people have succeeded and through them I reach my blissful goal. Musicians who have lived here many years and have absorbed the higher meaning of music, have humbly offered their services. Yes, humbly, for the great here wear humility as a badge of achievement, for always they have experienced through others greater than they, a glimpse of the Glory

Beyond.

To talk to these Masters of Music is a revelation in itself. They begin with words and written scores covering such a multitude of instruments that normally my mind could not begin to sense the whole. But even as I despair, the music starts and the unimaginable happens; a great volume of sound floods the air, as though all the orchestras of the world were playing in perfect unison. I can hear but I cannot see the hidden musicians; then realization dawns: there are none. The Master is the composer, the players, the music; there are no pipes, strings or human larynx, this mighty wave of sound rolls from one

Being. He breathes and from him flow sounds so heartrendingly exquisite that tears well into my eyes. No musician could hear this music without heart and soul being torn asunder in painful, unimaginable bliss. A commanding finger points at me; I tremble for

I have no instrument and the music is beyond my powers to play. My pent-up emotion swells, then bursts and from me flows a single note, soft, unfaltering, perhaps divine, the perfect response to his demand. We are the Master's instruments, although he really needs none, for he is all, within himself. I know now how it feels to be playfully plucked like a harp string, or to have a bow drawn expertly through my inner being. The first makes me laugh in clear, sweet notes, the second more thrilling than the beloved's caress, extracts a paean of joy, tempestuous, gentle, fearful, exultant. As the notes are drawn from me, my body fades. I lose myself to become the score and through the score, I enter the composer's mind. I am no longer Rudolph, but Scarlatti, Bach or Handel. From me pour a million notes. I stand like a young, triumphant god, music pouring out o me. At my command a great cleansing river of sound flows from the heights to fulfill its destiny far below, inspiring some, a comfort to others, a redeeming force for all in need, if they but pause to hear.

– Rudolph

"I" RETURN TO THE LAND OF MUSIC

My visit to the land of Music, when my friends and I had been an orchestra of sound, had instilled in me a desire to return there and to hear the song, not of mountains and trees, rivers and sky, beautiful though they had been, but of the inhabitants. I became ambitious in my ideas – I wanted to meet an advanced entity among these creators of Sound – a female who would envelop me to become part of me and I of her as I had previously been with the mountain.

My desire became almost an obsession and one day I knew the time had come. I was excited as I relaxed, which is not the best condition in which to meditate, and I sent my thoughts flying to my mountain peaks. I would start my journey towards her from them, because they were my friends and would help me find the way.

Perhaps she would even be there to meet me. My heart beat wildly at the thought. Too wildly, I suppose, because when I opened my eyes, I appeared to be nowhere, at least there was nothing to see, not even the outline of mountains and trees which had been visible on our previous visit.

I was crestfallen, not only was there no divine female to welcome me but there was no indication that I was in the Land of Music at all.

I realized that an effort was required of me and I opened myself out in an endeavour to become in tune with whatever was there, whether I could see anything or not. Eventually I distinguished a tiny tinkling sound, rather like a child's musical box, but so faint that all my powers of concentration were required to interpret from the direction of the sound and the way it flowed or was comparatively static, that there was a field with a wood on my left, and a river winding into the distance on my right. This discovery was exciting, because, before we had had visible outlines to reveal the scenery to us, but this time I had found the landscape not as previously though my eyes, but through my ears.

I continued to open out, hoping to find a person to whom I could talk, but this time I failed. I realized that I was in what might be termed the nursery of the Land of Music, and I began to wonder how I could reach a higher sphere.

Quite suddenly I found that the sounds which surrounded me had become richer and fuller in tone, and I realized that my desire had become fact. I knew too that, although there was still nothing to see, someone was standing beside me.

"Hello" I said not very intelligently, but it is not easy to talk to someone whom one cannot see or touch.

"Who . . . are . . . you?" came the reply. It was obvious that thought was still almost as non-existent as form, in this very young entity.

I gave him or her my name and related that I was a human being with connections with Earth. Apart from my name which was repeated delightedly, my word obviously held no meaning.

I decided to try an experiment and I released my mind so that it covered the space in front of me. After about five minutes, he – for it was a male – was able to converse a little more freely. He told me that he lived close by and that he was learning, through a teacher, to differentiate between the various members of the vegetable kingdom in the area, I presumed a form of elementary botany. I imagine that teaching these very young members of the Music evolution, must be somewhat similar to instructing a deaf and dumb child.

As a further experiment, I withdrew my mind, and I found that he could no longer answer my questions, and apart from an intermittent cry, which I could not hear clearly, once again there might have been no-one there.

I decided to try to find a rather more advanced entity and again my wish was granted. I found myself in a considerably high aspect for here there was colour, slight form and, again I heard, quite clearly, that wonderful music that we had experienced before.

This time, I seem to have been expected because several people were there, their bodies appearing and dissolving in rapid succession. Sometimes the form was accompanied by colour, at others it was preceded by it, or alternatively, by a breath of perfume.

"You're so solid" they greeted me admiringly.

"That is due to my Earth experience," I informed them.

"Earth" they echoed, excitedly as though I had said "Heaven."

"Tell us. Tell us all about it," they begged.

I began my stupendous task but I did not get very far. I told them of my fairy friends and I suggested that contact with this other evolution might help them to progress.

"How can we?" they asked me. "They so rarely come here."

"Well, why not go to them?" I suggested. "I have expended considerable thought on the idea of coming here. Why don't you do the same?"

"We're not very advanced," they excused themselves, the idea of personal effort obviously overcoming the faint enthusiasm which I had aroused in them for such an unusual experience.

"Goodbye, Goodbye," I heard the sound fading into the distance before I realized that I was once more on the move. When I stopped, I found the scenery much more advanced in every way. The form was more static and the colours became deep and pale in turns. I judged that there must be more general stability in the minds which were in control.

A blast of sound hit me – it was so intense that I almost lost consciousness. On Earth, a sound can be but a note, a chord, or a sequence, prolonged or otherwise of either or both, whose existence is governed by the capacity of the transmitter, whether it be of metal, wood or flesh and blood. This sound which I heard would be unrecognizable as such to any relying on their ears for hearing. It was something I had not known existed. It was an impression of all the senses, not one.

When it had faded, I waited in the following silence for what seemed like hours. I knew what it heralded and again I was obsessed by the idea which had haunted me for weeks.

There was no room for anything else.

I felt a tremor. It was as faint as the chime of a distant bell, yet I knew that my vigil was ended. The whisper came nearer, gaining in strength until I was enveloped, entered, engulfed in a glorious wave which swept me as in a great caress into a thousand pieces, each one of which experienced more ecstasy than I have ever known before. Gradually I regained control over my splintered senses; I drew them together, slowly, infinitely slowly, for each blending was both unbearable pain and exquisite bliss. Once again I was whole and this time, because of her will, I was able to bear this unbearable gift of music which she was pouring into me and of which I had now become a part.

The intolerable, ineffable ecstasy lasted but a brief moment before she began to withdraw herself. I tried to go with her, to follow her wherever she would lead me, but I could not. I was held back by some impenetrable force.

All I could do, I did as she returned to the Unknown. I sent out a cry of agony, that was so heart-rending and yet so beautiful, I can scarcely believe it was I created it.

– (unsigned, but almost certainly by Rudolph)

MAIRE IN THE THORMIS SECTOR

by Maire

𝕴 have visited the Thormis sector on several occasions and each time it has been a delightful experience.

All fairies love music, and naturally each evolution has its own, varying according to the needs and customs of those whose lives it is intended to enrich.

The thormes naturally create the most beautiful music of all, because sound is their major contribution to the Plan. The very young entities are able to express their individual characters through only one note. The advanced ones come with the essence of music expressing itself through them.

I arrived the other day in the centre of a large hall. What you on Earth would call a choir practice was in progress. The participants were at many stages of evolution and the variety in the quality of the sound produced, seemed to enhance rather than detract from the result. The high, clear notes of the young ones blended with the maturer tones of more experienced singers, giving a youthful eagerness to the otherwise controlled medley of sound.

They rose, tier upon tier of them, seemingly to heaven itself, for however far I expanded my vision, I could still see and hear hundreds more disappearing into the distance. As my consciousness rose, so the song changed as I reached the spheres of the more advanced thormes. The song was the same, but the thought behind it was revealed more clearly; the meaning of each note created in my mind a train of thought, which reached as far as my limited consciousness permitted. As soon as I had reached the end of one thought, another began, my mind seemingly expanding to an extraordinary degree so that I was following dozens of separate ideas and absorbing the main theme at one and the same time.

As I rose higher and higher, the quality of my own thoughts rose too. I was joining in the song, contributing my fairy power to the thormes'. You may think It unlikely that one small fairy could influence to the least degree, the production of thousands of thormes. Yet I did, for into the song was poured not only the enthusiasm of the thormes, but the will to carry out the theme which was being created, not only for the pleasure of the participants, but for the good of many yet unknown to us.

Sound is force and without force or power, none of you would be able to breathe into your lungs the air which is necessary for your continued existence. My one tiny contribution sent a message into the ether - a call to my evolution for the power to add the necessary will to this great prqject.

Instantly the answer came in a million notes, each sparkling with a million lights which flashed their way from a million quarters of the Universe until the fairy and thormis power was equal.

This I knew was only the beginning, for the power of the other evolutions as well must be added before the song would be ready to commence its work.

– *Maire*

A FAIRY IN THE LAND OF MUSIC

by Normus

𝕴 will now give you the story of what happened when my new human friend, Rudolph, who himself is a fine musician, came with me. When we arrived in the Thormis sector, we were greeted by a paeon of sound which filled me with energy and an eagerness for whatever was to befall me. The notes were coming from each blade of grass and every leaf in the landscape. At that particular level each leaf or flower has only one note which it gives out intermittently. You might think that millions of notes, all being produced together would make a discordant noise, but that is not so. The sound is sweet and gay, a kind of melodious laughter which made me want to sing with them. I added my note to theirs, and instantly those near me increased in volume to match my louder tone.

I moved about, sometimes running along the ground and at others rushing through the air, which was sending out a continuous whisper, its millions of particles producing a faint, musical breath.

Soon we were surrounded by Thormes, from the very young, who, like the flowers, produced their note intermittently, to much older ones, who surrounded us with a rising crescendo of continuous sound.

They carried us away to a higher sphere where those who were manifesting were not wholly occupied with the production of their own note, but had also found their colour. At present it was but faint but its introduction added immeasurably to the happiness of all. On, on we flew until the colour disappeared and a certain amount of form took its place. It was vague and shadowy, somewhat like an out-of-focus film, but at least a new idea of expression was being tried.

We were escorted in turn to other sectors where vibration, scent and increased consciousness became apparent and finally we came to the one which naturally interests me most – the will to evolve. Here the plants were trying experiments – first they would produce a little form, then colour would be added but usually not before the form had been lost.

At the request of my new friends, I singled out several flowers and a shrub and gave them power. Slowly all the component parts came into being at one and the same time, and even after I withdrew the power, the plants maintained their new strength for about half a minute.

We were then taken to a higher sphere where the plants and trees had learned to produce more than one individual note and they were able to play a tune either individually or together, the more advanced the area, the more beautiful the song.

Rudolph then asked me if I would like to watch him conduct. Eagerly I assented and he rose high above us and the surrounding scene. Soon the sequence

236

of sound changed entirely. Whereas previously the idea behind the individual or collective compositions had been simple, expressing joy in growth and welcome to their visitors, or gratitude to God for their being, now an altogether more mature idea was being expressed in waves of sound which entered and enthralled

me. I know that all in physical bodies hear with their ears, but as you listen to a great piece of music, I feel sure that your other senses must answer the call. Everything in me rose up and entered that magnificent music-mass. I grew in size until I was spreading over as wide an area as possible, so that I could experience the sound to the limit of my capacity. I felt a tremendous strain. It was as though I was stretched beyond endurance and yet the pain was exquisite. I opened a little more and a thunderous, sonorous roar entered me, and yet I somehow managed to retain my consciousness. Yes, little though I am in this body. I overcame that enormous volume of sound and in withstanding it, I tamed it, until it was all sweetness, all docility. I was filled with the thrill of mastership, of my own consciousness, and of the will of something so much larger than myself. It caressed me more blissfully than any embrace I had previously experienced. It filled me with ecstasy, and my thoughts soared to the heavens. I knew peace and contentment unknown to me before, and all this I discovered, not in the arms of a beloved, but in the heart of harmony itself.

– Normus

The Mountain and I

by Jack

Sometimes John, three mutual friends and I meet together in order to meditate. We have found that our combined thoughts have the power to take us farther afield than we can travel alone, but once we have visited a place, we are usually able to return to it, at will, when we are by ourselves. On this occasion we began to move somewhat sooner that we usually do and we traveled fast. We stopped three times on our journey to enable us to acclimatize ourselves to the greater speed at which our bodies were vibrating. Each halt necessitated our struggling to retain consciousness, and when we stopped for the third time, and a quarter of an hour passed before we had properly adjusted ourselves, we came to the conclusion that we had at last reached our destination.

But we were wrong. No sooner were we completely in tune with our surroundings, than we began to move again.

We all lost consciousness on this final phase of our journey and when we awoke, it was to the strains of exquisitely beautiful music. This helped to rouse us, and when we had regained control sufficiently to open our eyes, we were excited to find that our forms were only a faint outline.

This could mean but one thing. We were no longer in the Human sector. We inspected each other with amusement and interest but when I tried to lay my hand on John's arm an amazing thing happened. The contact produced not a sense of touch, but a musical note, and when, as an experiment, we all linked arms in a circle, we created a tune. We were fascinated. Were we the notes or did the contact produce them? A ridiculous scene followed. We chased each other over the fields and whenever our feet touched the ground, a new sound came into being. Each combination created by one catching another, produced a different result, and even our almost formless bodies rushing at speed or, alternately, drifting dreamily through the air, created yet other songs.

Eventually the novelty waned and we began to examine the countryside. The outlines were as faint as our own and the tones subdued until something started a new tune and then the colours became intense. Anything appeared to warrant a song; even an unconscious thought of mine admiring the snow on a distant range of mountains, received a magnificent bass solo in acknowledgement.

Having made this discovery, we decided to form an orchestra. I kept my mountains, Peter took the trees, Ludwig the river, John the flowers, and Ronald the sky.

We began somewhat cautiously because we did not want, in our enthusiasm, to lose consciousness through the volume of sound which we might possibly raise. "Now," I gave the signal and our thoughts sped to their objectives. Voices and instruments seemed to combine, yet I suppose, in reality, there were neither. There was only sound.

Once we had set them going, no further encouragement was required, and we relaxed and drank it all in. It is difficult to convey this idea of pure sound which needs no medium of metal, strings or human larynx. It was the innermost expression of souls who had evolved no further than the vegetable kingdom. What could those who have reached the understanding of Man produce?

Although we were almost drunk with the beauty of it, we became restless. We already had more sound than we had, until that moment, dreamed existed, but it was not enough. We knew that we must add to it. We knew that those whom we had roused with our call now required something of us. We rose to our feet, each taking a different route. I made my way to the mountains and the others went to their appointed places. As we alighted, the vibrations of our evolution produced the form giving everything within sight a greater chance of expression in this particular aspect. Each note took shape as it left its creator, to join with others in a stream of sound which, in its turn, produced yet other contours, colours, scents.

We already knew that we have a note, a mantric note, but we had not known that we were a song too. We were not singing with our voices. We ourselves *were* the melody. That of the landscape had been beautiful in its purity, but with our knowledge of sorrow and suffering added, the tones became richer, their meaning clearer.

As I stood among my vast mountain peaks, I longed to follow that song, which I knew was myself. I tried to will myself after it, but my mountains held me in a firm if fond embrace. I knew that they loved me because, through me, they were experiencing the form which was enhancing all that they had to give. "If I cannot go, then show me all you know," I said, and I entered the mountains and became part of them. Their music which, received from the outside, had almost overpowered me, now took hold of me until I could think and feel nothing else. I was aware of nothing except sound which I was not hearing with my ears for I had no ears with which to hear. I had only a tremendous desire to express myself through this new medium which was all I possessed.

I grew in volume, smashing my way upwards, the mountains splitting to set me free. Up, ever upwards I thrust myself, growing, growing until I too, I suppose, burst.

One day I shall stay whole and not disintegrate as I invariably do, because always I must try to do things beyond my powers. Each time I last a little longer though, and I bring back with me more of the memory.

If I could either curb my ambitions or remain calm even when every atom inside and outside of me is charged with excitement, I might know what I must know sooner than I dare to hope. But if I fail to do both or either, when my time comes, I shall doubtless burst at the gates of Eternity Itself.

– Jack

MANUSCRIPTS
SET #7

THE HUMAN AND FAIRY RELATIONS CENTRE

Preface

It is helpful for the reader to grasp the topic of how Daphne Charter paired up her fairy friends with her astral human friends, since so many of the stories involve both fairies and astral humans.

Daphne Charters brought together her fairy friends and her astral human friends to work with each other to strengthen human and fairy communication and cooperation. These human/fairy partnerships worked very well as can be seen in the Manuscript's stories and they resulted in the formation of a Human and Fairy Relations Depot which linked up other fairies and astral humans. The program was so popular with both astral humans and fairies that hundreds, if not thousands, of these partnerships were formed over the years. After it had grown larger the title "Human and Fairy Relations Depot" was replaced with "Human and Fairy Relations Centre".

Soon after the "Human and Fairy Relations Depot" was started, an astral human named Betty became the human coordinator for the astral realm. Betty describes the development of the Centre as of 1985 in one of the manuscripts in this section. In 1990 this program was first initiated with physical humans and fairies. This is described at the end of this section.

The fairies that work with humans through the Human and Fairy Relations Centre are not a 'genie in a bottle' kind of deal. They don't deliver pots of gold or follow orders. Fairies should be treated as you would treat any human of equal (or higher) stature then yourself. (Ideally all humans would treat each other with equal high respect.) Deception and lying does not work with fairies. They can see right through you. They can read your aura. They are beings of Light. They respond to respect and loving intent. Disrespect or bad motives and they are not available. In fact, it is purity, love and a raising of our human vibrations that allows any contact at all.

– Michael Pilarski

243

Human and Fairy Relations

by John

[My suggestion that my astral friends should adopt a pair of fairies proved so successful that later the idea was given to me that further contact between the two evolutions should be encouraged. I approached Betty and asked her to take over the human side of the proceedings and I suggested to Sheena, Pino (two of the house fairies), Namsos, Sirilla, Nixus and Lyssis that they should deal with the fairies. Hence was born the organization known as the Human and Fairy Relations Depot, and here are a few details as supplied by John and Nixus . – D.C.]

A short while ago, Daphne invited Nixus and Lyssis to join with Namsos and Sirilla to arrange for more fairies to have human guardians. They were frankly amazed, for they are pathetically modest of their achievements and the fact that they had been singled out for this new job filled them with excitement.

To begin with, Sirilla and Namsos have been particularly good friends to them and the idea of working together on this very important project appealed to them immediately.

Many of the local fairies visit them and listen with avid interest to every tiny incident that has ever happened between them and me. They had sometimes been asked whether perhaps I knew of someone who would like to become friends with a fairy too. We had discussed the idea several times on Saturdays as similar requests had been made to the others in our group but, much as we should have liked to carry the idea further, we're all so busy that sometimes we have quite a job finding time to meet our own fairies, fond though we are of them.

Then, on Saturday, Betty told us that Daphne had asked her to tackle the human side of the business, while the four already mentioned, together with Sheena and Pino as the representatives of the house fairies, should deal with the other side.

Betty was thrilled at being asked but had been doubtful as to whether her powers of organization were good enough to carry out successfully the very tricky task of finding the right human being for the right fairy.

It would obviously be unwise to arrange for a very studious young man to adopt a mischievous girl fairy, although sometimes the combination might prove to be a great success. However, as a rule, it's better to play for safety by trying to find human beings and fairies who are at approximately the same degree of progress and who have similar interests.

Betty has told me that she is sure that she is being helped and that the whole scheme has been organized from higher up. She seems to know instinctively which fairy will suit which human, even when she has never seen them. This goes for the fairies too.

When the idea was made known, literally thousands came to register. Their names are required, length of time on Earth, their branch of work, and their chief interests in their spare time. All these particulars are made into thought forms and obviously the fairies have a very efficient method of filing. Don't ask me to give you details because it's quite beyond my powers of comprehension.

A similar written form is provided for the humans' use, substituting age and number of years on the Astral, in place of length of Earth span completed. Each week, Betty and the fairies exchange lists and both try to fit two or more applicants together. The following week they discuss their conclusions and they tell me that the number coupled together by both parties is quite amazing.

The human and fairy forming these identical results are immediately brought together, the dissimilar ones are then discussed and the merits of all suggestions scrutinized. New facts about the characters of each, previously only surmised, are brought to light and one side bows to the other's judgement.

Time is the only factor preventing more mutual "adoptions" from taking place. Both humans and fairies are treating their meetings very seriously because they realize how much they can learn from their new friends, who will present facts to them from the point of view of a different evolution.

– John

HUMAN AND FAIRY RELATIONS
by Nixus

Apart from our work with Nature, the task which perhaps interests us the most is that with the Human and Fairy Relations Depot. This is possibly because we have more responsibility than with any of the other projects with which we assist Daphne, important though they all are.

Nearly every evening we visit Namsos and Sirilla and we ponder over the names. To most humans, a name is just a name, of no great importance; but, to us, who have each earned our own, it is a very different matter.

Of course we have always known the fact that each has a meaning. For instance, my name, "Nixus," indicates that I do my work conscientiously, while "Lyssis" shows that, where her work lies, there also is her heart.

But to translate the meaning of the names was no longer enough. At first we didn't know how we could possibly understand the character of each fairy from the first brief encounter, which was all the time that we could allow for each applicant. In fact, we were worried and then, one day when we had looked at the ever-growing list almost in despair, we realized that a farris was with us.

He came every evening and, by slow degrees, we found that by intoning each name together, we set up a vibration.

At first it was just another vibration, but we learned how to analyze it until now we are able, in a matter of seconds, to know the past history of every fairy.

This may seem unfair to you but, as soon as we have made a note of his character-istics, the memory completely disappears; indeed we haven't the ability to retain so much data in our consciousness once it has served its purpose.

At least once a week Betty comes and we exchange our conclusions. Sometimes we disagree as to the suitability of a man and fairy combina-tion but always, after further thought, one side or the other admits that they were wrong.

This pairing is an end-lessly fascinating business. Of course, it isn't really we who decide which fairy will suit which human. We are merely told indirectly and, as each meeting has been a great success, we are obviously not allowed to make a mistake.

Sometimes when we examine a name-vibration, we are unable to read the past history. We no longer continue to probe it as we did at first, thus wasting valuable time, but we separate it from the rest. We have learned that these weak vibrations come from fairies not necessarily of unsound character, but from those who have a tremendous enthusiasm when a new idea is presented to them, but who haven't the necessary determination to carry it to any con-clusion. These, we know, will probably have forgotten that they ever made the application in a short while because their desire is already so faded that it is practically negligible.

246

Many ever-growing ties of friendship have been formed and each of these is helping to build the bridge to span the gap between the two evolutions. Often we think back on that great flow of water which came from so tiny a source. Our work at present constitutes the drips which through the years will grow until a river will form, wending its unhurried way, not only through the Earth and Astral planes, but far beyond, so that communication between Ra-Arus and Man on Earth will be a comparatively common event instead of the treasured experience of the very few.

– Nixus

HOW IT ALL BEGAN
By Betty

[Penned January 11, 1990. Betty is one of the humans living on the astral realm, with whom Daphne worked. – M.P.]

It was natural with so many young "dead" killed in World War II, that we should continue having gatherings such as we used to have on Earth when we reminisced and danced the night away.

At one of these, I saw a real "smasher" and he was looking at me in rather an interested way, which was surprising because there were far prettier and better dressed girls than me there. He came over and said "My name's Jack; you're Betty aren't you?" I said "Yes, but how did you know?" "Vibrations;" he replied. "I was told that you would be here, so I thought we could have a chat."

"About the past, present or future?"

"Certainly not the past, but it could be the quite near future. I'm going to ask you a very peculiar question." Heavens, I thought, what on Earth can it be, because I'm really rather an ordinary person, not I would think, peculiar in any way.

"O.K. I'm ready" I said.

"How would you feel if I told you that Father John, whom I believe you have just met, would like you to join a group who are working with fairies."

"Fairies?" I said "You must be joking!"

"Father John wouldn't have told me to come and explain the situation to you as a joke."

"No, of course he wouldn't. But fairies are simply not one of my interests. I know nothing about them. Fire away."

"Right," said Jack, and fire away he did. I think my eyes must have got wider and wider, and probably my jaw dropped as well in amazement. Everything was so new, and exciting. I'll put it in his own words.

247

"My wife, Daphne, is still on Earth and she has developed not only an ability to talk to me, Father John and others, but also with fairies, which is much more unusual. Together we work with Father John to help the 'earthbound'."

Earthbound? What were they? I'd no idea.

Jack continued: "These are people who have ruined their own lives by addiction to drink or drugs, or alternately other peoples by their cruel or incessant thoughtless behavior. At present we have six of them that we have persuaded after many weeks to leave the sub-earth, where they found themselves when they died, to come with us to the lower Astral plane. They are all men; four were alcoholics, one a suicide, and the sixth a German princeling who was drunk with power, not alcohol.

"We brought them to a certain stage of understanding about the reason for their past misery in the dark, dark conditions where they had been for several years, but we wanted to give them an entirely different outlook. Actually, it was Daphne's idea. 'Bring them one by one to the flat and we'll teach them to see and talk to the fairies. That ought to shake them!' she added. And that was what we did. Each was allotted a pair or a single fairy. I also have three. None of us are sure whether or not we adopted the fairies or they adopted us. To start with, one of my three, whose name is Herus, has had a very tough time during his life on Earth, and I think it would do him good to have a female to take him on."

"It sounds out of this world" I said. "When can I start?"

"Tomorrow, if you like; the sooner the better."

And so a new page of the book of life was turned over; I first had to learn to see and talk to Herus, and then all the others as well. This, of course, brought me into contact with the ex-"earthbounds", and our mutual experiences with the fairies led to many meetings, much talk and real friendship.

Well, of course, fairies like us, talk to their friends, and all wanted a human chum too. That, from our point of view, was rather difficult to arrange because people just don't agree immediately if you say "How would you like a fairy-friend?" even on the Astral.

As the ex-earthbounds were now involved in other work, including going back to the sub-earth to try to persuade those still there to come with them back to a more normal life, Father John suggested that I should go round the schools and colleges which were running courses on the various aspects of Evolution and offer them this practical assistance.

The response was instantaneous and very enthusiastic. I had to give up my other work in order to cope with the rush, arranging meetings with prospective fairy companions and bringing two of a like temperament together, rather like a Marriage Bureau! And so the Human and Fairy Relations Depot came into being, and the time came when I was so swamped with enquiries that I had to ask not only for help, but for someone who was used to organizing large numbers, to take charge with me as a willing assistant.

Herus has always taken a keen interest in the Depot, and I wished that he was with me on this project, but his other tasks particularly the thought formations were at the time, more important. I longed to be able to see and understand them because their creation constituted the greater part of his life. He is a true artist, hence possibly his untidiness and the temperament which for some time he seems to have had under control. I could never help visualizing him in an old fashioned painter's smock, standing before an easel with all the paraphernalia of a royal Academician. I tried so often to unravel the little flimsy fragments I would have given almost anything to be able to admire them, I'm afraid they never looked more than rather bedraggled spiders' webs to me. We both did our best, but it was no good. I wanted to decipher them so much because I was sure that into them he poured his innermost thoughts, the ones that were too precious to be projected in the normal way. I wondered how I could ever get to know my dear little friend unless I could read these formations which to him, are the height of his creative ability.

Each one has a mission to perform; an act of healing, a ray of hope for one who has seemingly lost everything, a power to comfort, inspire, or raise from the depths of depression. He told me so many instances when these thought formations have proved to be the turning point in some distressed person's life. If one failed to achieve results, then another was made. Sometimes one was sent every day for months. The fairies never lose hope, and with such determination, I'm sure that, given time, they must always succeed.

A misty look would come into his bright little eyes sometimes as he told me of some of these who have been given a tiny glimpse of light through their work. "It's difficult to believe that little people like us can influence such big minds," he said to me one day. I even find it hard to understand myself. I wondered why advanced entities of our own evolution couldn't find an answer; then I remembered that the coarse atmosphere of Earth lessens the strength of the power from the higher spheres. Herus looked down at his own small body. "It's not very big," he said, "and yet enough power passes through it to materialize the thoughts sufficiently for them to do their work. If only it was bigger, what much better results we'd get."

"The thoughts would have to be bigger and better too."

They're the best I can manage at the moment," he said as he fingered his latest attempt to pierce my dull comprehension. "But you'd be surprised if you knew how much they've improved. At first, we just used prayers and ordinary happy thoughts that were in the air around us, but now we've got sufficient experience to include our own. Look at the places we've been to, and the people we've met, even Shining Ones," he said in a hushed voice. "Each has told us to call on Him

249

or Her, and when we do, they always answer and even in the coarse atmosphere down here, some of their splendour and Divinity remains."

It was hard to believe that there was anything divine in the strange little rag which Herus was holding so reverently. It was sad too that I was unable to recognise the Divinity whose presence Herus could see, touch and feel. How very much more advanced are even young fairies than we poor humans who, until we learn better, are apt to regard ourselves as God's greatest creations. And the irony of it is that our only visible competitors are animals and plants, our own younger relations we often treat so badly.

When you're alone sometimes, do sit and listen. Perhaps a little voice belonging to one of the many small people who are with you will pierce the barrier which keeps us unaware of the many wonderful things that are going on around us. Listen well. There's such a lot to learn. I know so little and yet in comparison to what I knew on Earth, I am at least rich in the knowledge of my ignorance.

Down the years, the Depot has changed its name and has become the Human-Fairy Relations Circle. After thirty-five years, it has become international with fairies and humans travelling all over for the benefit of Earth and its inhabitants. Sadly, nearly all the humans taking part are discarnate. What a wonderful scheme to be a part of. It has led me not only into an enchanting world but has enabled me to meet many angels or Shining Ones as the fairies call them, with whom we now work; and also visit the Higher Spheres where we have the most unbelievable experiences, all of which increase my awareness and give me incredible joy.

– *Betty*

Human and Fairy Relations Centre
– Recent Developments
by Michael Pilarski

Several years before Daphne's death she asked if I would like to become a coordinator for the Human and Fairy Relations Centre. Daphne said that heretofore the centre had only worked with linking up astral humans and fairies. They now thought it was a good idea to extend the centre to linking up fairies with humans in physical form. I felt very honored to be given this opportunity and accepted her offer. This would have been about 1990. Since then I have given several dozen, public workshops on fairies. I usually offer workshop participants a chance to sign up for the Human and Fairy Relations Centre. In this way, several hundred people have signed up to the Centre.

Here is how it has worked thus far. Fairies volunteer to participate in the centre's program. Somehow or another the centre's fairy coordinator assigns two fairies to each human participant that volunteers. The fairies and humans vow to work at communicating and sending love/feelings/thoughts/visions to their "penpal" so to speak. The human agrees to tune into the fairies periodically. Communication and cooperation happens in many ways. The goal is that everyone involved (both humans and fairies) increases their spiritual growth and their ability to serve others. The goal is also to increase understanding and cooperation between our two evolutions. The fairies are not condemned to following their human everywhere all the time. They come when the human wishes to communicate. The rest of the time they are involved with their own fairy pursuits.

But, you may ask, how does one "call" the fairies? It is the equivalent of the fairies and the human always having their cell phones on and with them. They have a wireless system. Calling is mainly a matter of "intent". You could call it telepathy if you wish. A person does not have to be a member of the Human and Fairy Relations Centre to initiate communication with fairies. Most of us Talking to fairies and devas can be as simple as how we talk to our favorite pets, flowers, trees, and landforms. You can speak out loud or in your head.

But I would also say a word of caution. Be clear about who you communicate with. There are many beings in the unseen realms. Indeed, there are many realms. I would recommend that neophytes read all of Daphne Charters' Collected Fairy Manuscripts. Furthermore I would also recommend that people read other authors on fairies. In the appendices of this book is my list of Top Ten Reference Books, as well as a lengthier bibliography. Over time and sampling you can discover which authors you are attracted to. Study cannot replace experience – but reading can be a powerful, useful adjunct and preparation to communication. Finding people who are more advanced to study under can be very helpful. Also helpful is to be part of a peer group who are studying and experimenting with fairy communication.

Some of Daphne's biggest contributions to human and fairy relationships have been on the other side of the veil in the non-physical realms. She was a giant in this work. Each of us who thinks kindly towards fairies can do our own small part.

– *Michael Pilarski*

MANUSCRIPTS
SET #8

THE FAIRY AND HUMAN RELATIONS CONGRESS

Preface

This set of manuscripts describes how the first Fairy and Human Relations Congress came about. Father John and Ludwig report on what happened at the first Congress.

The idea for the first congress was conceived by Daphne and the nature fairies during the first years of their acquaintance. It was sometime in the early 1950s that it took place but there is no written record as to the exact date. 3,000 fairies from all over the world attended the first Congress, along with the high devas assigned to help keep it organized.. Daphne Charters was the only physical human in attendance. There were some astral human observers as well as devas and illumined humans from loftier planes.

The 1st Congress was a great success and it was subsequently held annually for many years, and grew much larger. We don't know much about the intervening years, but there is a large report by Daphne and each of the 33 fairies about the 1985 Congress, in which they reported that 200,000 fairies attended as well as numerous discarnate humans from the spiritual planes. Most of the fairy's reports are of their own personal experience with the "keynote speaker".

Silvyl says in her 1985 Fairy and Human Relations Congress report that she had been invited by the Canadian delegation to the Congress to help them arrange a miniature congress in their country.

Sulan says in his 1985 report that he has traveled overseas (from England) to see friends he met at previous congresses.

Julus, during his report on the 1985 Congress says that some of the fairies had traveled with Daphne on her frequent holidays in Spain, and while there spoken to many of the fairies from Spain who had attended the Fairy and Human Relations Congresses in England.

Normus reports that one year they had a combined Fairy and Ceris conference. This was reported by Normus in the 1956 edition of "A True Fairy Tale."

Since Daphne's passing, we don't know if the Congress is still happening in the fairy realm.

And finally there is a report on the current-day Fairy and Human Relation Congress happening on the physical human plane. Our 7th annual Congress is being held June 22-24, 2007 in the North Cascades of Washington State.

– Michael Pilarski

Introduction to The Fairy Congress

By Daphne Charters

𝕴 am happy to say that my work with the earthbound is not confined to the English or indeed to white people and, up to date, I have been instrumental in helping Negroes, Indians, Burmese and Arabs, among the coloured races. The language difficulty does not arise as my task with them at the present time is finding these temporarily lost souls who have usually passed far beyond the realms of consciousness.

This work has brought me into touch with the guides of many nationalities who always talk to the fairies when they are presented to them. It is a great honour for the little people to meet anyone as advanced as a guide and one day, when Maroni, a Negro, had been with us, I asked Normus whether there were black fairies. He had not apparently thought about this possibility so we asked Father John.

"Of course there are," he replied. "There are fairies attached to every nationality under the sun. You know that they form their own bodies by thought, so it is natural that they should make them similar to the people among whom they work."

I then asked him whether it would be possible to bring the different races together, a contingent from each country, to form a congress. They could exchange ideas with one another, discuss their varying methods of work and see how fairies from other lands looked. Father John liked the idea, and when Normus asked his leader and a higher authority was approached, permission was given for a congress to be held.

Several times during the following summer I asked Normus if he had received any news on the subject, but always the answer was in the negative. However, early in September he was able to tell me that the congress was to take place on the three days commencing the 15th.

When the idea had first entered my mind, I had visualized two or three fairies from each country meeting here, having discussions and a few celebrations; but I now learned that three thousand delegates from all over the world and various parts of England were to be present.

I, of course, to my sorrow, knew that I should be able to see nothing, too many vibrations always confusing the little vision which I enjoy. However, Father John gladly consented to act as observer and he "covered" the congress every moment of the day and night. Jack and my other astral friends came to watch the proceedings for themselves on both the Saturday and Sunday afternoons. I asked them to poll the information which they received and they chose Ludwig to piece their separate stories together.

– Daphne Charters

256

THE FAIRY CONGRESS

Observer: Father John

The First Day

I arrived shortly before dawn to find the fairies in a fever of excitement for their guests were due to arrive with the first rays of the sun. They were in somewhat unusual garb for the occasion as they wished to show deference to all the visitors. Owing to the fact that many nationalities take part in our weekend work, they are not ignorant of the many forms of attire worn by men and women belonging to other races, but I must confess, even I was amazed at the incongruity of some of their garments.

Congress Clothes

Normus was clad in his usual green jerkin and tights but instead of his feathered cap, he was sporting an Indian chief's headdress. Movus' dark hair was entirely covered by a turban; this was a great concession on his part as he always goes bareheaded. Nuvic was wearing a pair of sandals and a richly embroidered Chinese kimono; Namsos was covered from head to foot in Arab garb. Gorjus was resplendent in an Indian tunic and a Chinese coolie hat and Nixus displayed legs encased in cowboy chaps and a tiny black mandarin's hat.

The girls had been equally original and all looked beautiful, with their eyes flashing in anticipation of the admiration which they knew would be theirs. Merella's usually flowing black hair was tightly braided under a mantilla but there the Spanish influence ended, for she wore her usual flowing gown from under which peeped a pair of clogs. Mirilla's golden curls were hidden by a yashmak and her blue eyes fluttered alluringly through the narrow slit. Myrris' graceful form was skillfully revealed, yet demurely hidden, by partially transparent Turkish trousers. Sirilla was content to wear her usual clothes surmounted by a wide-brimmed beach hat such as she has seen Daphne wear in the garden. Lyssis was half Spanish, with a swirling crimson skirt and half Negress, with a mammy's bandeau tying up her hair.

The Delegates Arrive

I congratulated them on their appearance and almost immediately the delegates began to arrive. The intention had been for the home fairies to line up on the lawn and to greet the visitors as a group, but as soon as any of them saw another fairy wearing a similar garment to themselves, they forgot the carefully made plans and ran laughing to their counterpart. Soon, instead of a semi-ceremonial greeting. there was chaos; they leapt and shrieked, they slapped each other on the back, and they dashed off with their new-found friends to show them their homes, their charges, or Daphne asleep in bed, instead of waiting for the appointed hour later in the morning.

I remained on the lawn, doing my best to welcome the swiftly arriving guests. Fortunately the possibility of a breakdown in the plans had occurred to those in charge and soon a group of more advanced fairies arrived from the Astral and order was soon restored.

The Morning Ritual

When the first excitement had worn off, the home fairies remembered their duties and a semblance of the original plan took place. Somewhat later than had been anticipated, the usual morning ritual took place. and fairies of many lands worshipped God according to their own customs. To a certain extent they simulated the postures of the human beings in the countries from which they came; some had prayer mats, some removed their shoes, others their hats; some faced Mecca, others danced while they prayed, but all were sincere in their Thanksgiving for this wonderful opportunity to meet their neighbours.

It was somewhat difficult to follow the movement of our own fairies as they were continually changing their colour and costume. However, always their vibrations told me that the grinning Negro boy was in reality Normus, and the slant-eyed Chinese siren, Merella.

258

The Fairy Villages

The visitors were next taken to the quarters which had been prepared for them during the previous week. Two entire villages had been built, one on the lawn in this garden, and another on an unused building site nearby. The houses were beautifully designed, giving each visitor or pares a rest-room and a robing room. There was also a community reception centre and a powder- or refreshment-room.

A farris was accommodated in the largest house in each village and any problems could thus be taken to him to solve. The indoor fairies were all staying in the surrounding houses to which the necessary suites had been added. I had previously inspected all the buildings and had watched the fairies working, by thought, upon their construction. Sometimes one would get a little over-enthusiastic and, in one case, instead of a roof, a church spire had been placed, complete with chiming clock.

The was a wealth of variety in the designs as the assistance of neighbouring fairies had been sought, so every type of building was represented, from a thatched barn to a severely square factory. Even when the local architecture had been used, there was a certain attractive quality, for naturally the fairies see the etheric bodies of everything around them.

Inside, the fairies carried out their own ideas of comfort, which is far removed from yours. Light and colour are of far greater importance than well-filled mattresses for their hours of ease, which may be spent upside-down or in mid-air, according to their own individual desires.

There were cries of delight as the delegates were shown their quarters – some, in fact, had never known such luxury. Remember that they make their houses similar to the human habitations around them and those living in a jungle swamp would probably have but a covering of leaves to protect them from the tropical rains. They tried everything; they suspended themselves at extraordinary angles and they were so overcome by the novelty that they scarcely knew what to do next.

When the original excitement began to flag a little, it was discovered that it was past the time when Daphne was to have addressed the delegates but fortunately this important function had also slipped the speaker's mind as well. Remembrance returned to the dismayed orator at the same time that the fairies arrived, so all went according to plan.

She had not prepared a speech but they were well satisfied with the simple welcome which she gave them, after which they all rushed over the surrounding countryside until each plant had been examined, the soil investigated and minute comparisons made. You may imagine the joy in which the Arab fairies greeted the flowers, so well remembered from the Astral, again. To you, a tropical plant is a source of wonder, but to those whose work lies with them, the simple daisy was an engrossing subject, the precious memory of which will long remain in their hearts.

After this outdoor inspection had taken place, there was a period of rest before the main event of the day, which was to take place in the afternoon.

The Transformation

This work, in which we all assist, is known as a transformation. We seek and find a lost soul whose astral body, as well as the physical, has died, leaving no trace to normal astral eyes. However, because you cannot see a "dead" person, owing to his faster rate of vibration, it does not follow that he has no body. So it is with those whose vibrations have sunk through the years until only the Great Ones know where they lie.

We find these people by their vibration, however slow and, although we are unable to see them when we reach them, we mark the spot and direct rays of power and love upon them until their vibrations are sufficiently raised for the bodies to become visible to us. This is the first stage in the rehabilitation of 'lost souls,' as much power has to be directed to them over sometimes long periods before consciousness returns.

In order to achieve even the first part of the transformation, it is necessary for many hundreds of people from the Astral to gather together. By passing power through their bodies, it becomes sufficiently coarsened to be effective amidst very slow vibrating matter. This is where Daphne is of use to us, for her physical body vibrates slower that those of us who live on the Astral, a higher plane, thus power which is passed through her coarsens the whole.

Unless you are clairvoyant, you will not have seen a display of power so you cannot know the magnitude of the volume, or the intensity of light. Fairies can naturally see this power for it is their life's work to distribute it, but normally they know only the quantity which they can collectively produce in their own group. Our own fairies, who always help us, are ever amazed at the never-ending supply so we were interested to see how the delegates would be affected.

The Delegate's Reaction

After the Invocation Ritual, when the power burst upon us, the delegates all covered their eyes. Our own fairies were obliged to do this when they first attended these sessions but now they not only can face the power, but they also add their own.

Gradually, however, the visitors became used to the strength of the beam and, one by one, they lifted their heads and gazed in awe. Some stood with their mouths open, others danced and pointed with excitement, while yet others endeavoured to give a little themselves.

I spoke to many of them afterwards and here are one or two of their impressions which may interest you.

A South African Negro: "I have never seen such a volume of power in all my life and I was happy to know that it was being used to help the people with whom I work. Their lot is often hard and, as a rule, they are but young spirits whose descent into matter proves more than they can bear. Yet those who can soar above the almost animal conditions in which they live often attain a happiness unknown to the peoples who lead less simple lives."

An American White: "How different is the power which we witnessed today to that which is known by the same name on Earth. Man ever seeks for power to overcome his neighbors, to add to his possessions, or to acquire authority over more people. Today we were privileged to see the essence from which all these petty misnomers have their being. But this true-power, in its purity of purpose, performed a deed so wondrous that if men were told of it, they would not believe. If only those who sought to misuse it understood the condition in which they will find themselves when their ridiculous, puffed-up physical bodies and accompanying personalities are no more, perhaps they would then use it to lift up instead of to crush, to comfort rather than exploit and, in the happiness which they would at last know, they would find the key to a better world."

A Chinese girl fairy: "I come from the other side of Earth and I have seen mediums work in my own country but I have never previously taken part in the type of work which we witnessed today. It is a pity that more psychics do not use their power to help those beyond normal aid. In China, where sometimes even children are taught to hate their neighbours if they do not think as they do, many die in a welter of hatred and find themselves in conditions worse than their own wretched Earth environment. It is small wonder that with their love of forbidden drugs, they sink so far and so fast. Please ask your charge to help those from where I come and she will gain the love and gratitude of every fairy who strives, without a medium, to alleviate a little of the dire distress of the many who have turned their faces away from the Light."

An Indian: "This communication was received shortly after the partition of India.) "My hopes of a peaceful world in which all men love one another have recently received an all but mortal blow, following the events in the country which I love and strive to serve. If Man will torture and deprive his best friend of his present incarnation because he worships God in a manner somewhat removed from his own, where is the progress for which we all strive each day to attain? I understand that man is very proud of that which he calls civilization – but all it seems to have brought to the world is an increased desire for material pleasures.

Far from bringing him nearer to the Truth, it seems to have driven from him nearly all his latent desire for understanding. Yet I still hope, for it is often after such strife that the conditions necessary for a spiritual revival make their appearance and many that were feared lost are found to have been but delayed upon the path.

The gathering which I have today witnessed has put new heart into me for I have seen the men of all nations come together to help those who by Heavenly, if not by Earthly standards, have failed. To have been permitted to give power for such a purpose has been a great privilege and one that I shall never forget. I shall take back to India with me an indestructible memory to share with those I meet so that they, too, may lift up their hearts with hope for the future of mankind, whom we ever seek to serve."

The Flat

Afterwards, the delegates mixed with the human crowd and later they were shown over the flat. To the casual observer, this is but a well furnished home without any special interest to the fairy mind, but I can assure you that there are many things which, although invisible to you, are of great importance to the little visitors.

Thought Formations

As an example we will take the hall, in which the house fairies make their thought formations. To you, a thought is probably something which has been hatched in your brain and either literally laboured to death or forgotten almost as soon as it was formed. To us, a thought is something which, if we wish, we can see; it has degrees of strength and weakness; it has colour and shape and, far from disappearing when you have forgotten it, it remains attached to your aura for all eternity.

This may be a somewhat terrifying idea – that our mental sins are as real as our physical ones. Does it not say in the Bible, ". . .Thou shalt not covet thy neighbour's wife nor his manservant nor his maidservant nor his ox nor his ass nor anything that is thy neighbour's. . ."? It does not say that you must not steal them, but that you must not desire them. In other words, it is the thought, which may or may not lead to action, which is wrong.

However, not only do your lower thoughts hinder your progress, but those of a higher nature, also often forgotten, help you on your upward path. It is these happier ideas which can be used by the fairies in helping those in distress. They are woven, one by one, into designs of great beauty and power and are sent to those who need them. Naturally some fairies, as some painters and poets, are better at creating these formations than others. The house fairies are advanced in this form of work and cries of administration greeted the display which they had been preparing for some days.

Gradually the visitors became a little weary after all the wonders which they had witnessed and they drifted back to their own quarters for rest.

That evening was the monthly full moon, when all fairies are especially active, and a great gathering had been arranged, beginning with an official reception, when all would wear their ceremonial garments and be presented to the farris who was presiding, in strict order of precedence.

Ceremonial Garments

These robes cannot be made by thought as simply as a ball gown may be chosen and ordered by any woman who can afford to pay for it. Each leaf or flower decoration has been earned by the wearer in the same way that your 'orders' are on Earth.

I watched the delegates arrive and I have seldom seen a more delightful sight. At similar gatherings of my own evolution there is gaiety and a pleasure within all that they are looking their best, but these small people were almost overcome with excitement and their eyes flashed as brightly as their jewels.

As this was a ceremonial occasion, it was not permitted for the fairies to disguise themselves in the garments belonging to another. When men and women come here to give power, they are not wearing their best clothes and thus the fairies had not seen the wonderful materials and colours of which those from the East are in habit of using on an important occasion.

Individual Garments

I was first attracted by an Italian girl fairy who had returned to the era of the crinoline. Her fan was composed of feathers the colour of bougainvillea, which matched her jeweled mask. I soon lost sight of her in the growing throng and my eye next alighted upon an Eskimo whose fur-like attire shone and sparkled as though each hair was a spider's web covered with early morning dew. I was so intrigued that I beckoned him and asked if I might touch him. The material looked so brittle that when he eagerly acquiesced, I put out the tip of my little finger. He laughed and with his own hand he brushed the fur-like substance as one might an animal's.

"My own invention," he twinkled good-humoredly. "I wanted something really distinctive. The first time I wore it, I made it of ice and, after a short while, I was as flat as a sealskin. By trial and error, I've reached this stage but I'm not satisfied yet. I want to fill each hair with light as well."

A friend came back and took him away and I began to seek for more unusual garments. It was not long before I observed a Negro whose pure white clothes made him somewhat conspicuous. He was wearing nothing but a shirt which came to his knees and a white trilby hat. To you this probably sounds very amusing and unsuitable apparel in which to attend an official reception, but to him, his clothes were the grandest he had ever seen. The hat was studded with white brilliants, the shirt of finest satin. He also wore a large diamond-like ring, proving by its size that he was the leader of a large group of fairies. To himself, his appearance was beautiful, and to the other fairies also. He was filled with dignity and happiness that he was giving so much pleasure to others. There was no more reason for me to find his garments amusing than that he should think my white habit and tonsured head strange. I might add that he was most interested in my fringe of hair and he toyed with the idea of copying it, but then he decided that his own wooly locks were hardly suited to that form of coiffure.

After he had left I was content to gaze for awhile upon the ever-moving throng before me. At an Earth reception you may have people standing on a balcony above your head, mounting a wide staircase and surrounding you at your own level, but at this fairy gathering, they were everywhere, from the tree tops to the ground. The air was filled with music, the colour of 3,000 robes flashed from here to there and back again, and had I not undergone a very special training for this occasion, I fear that I should have become dizzy before the reception had begun.

The Reception

Quite suddenly the music ceased and was replaced by a single flute-like note. This was the signal for order, and in spite of the almost uncontrolled excitement, it was instantly obeyed.

The home fairies took their places behind the presiding farris and the presentations began. The delegates were in groups according to their rank and, as they moved toward the farris, they formed symbolic designs expressing their joy at this honour which was being bestowed upon them.

In time the reception was quickly over, for the actions and thoughts of the fairies cannot be measured by ours. But during that short period, the farris had delivered a formal address welcoming the delegates, each group had replied, and every member had been appraised, his rank noted and many vibrations of esteem and messages desiring a closer acquaintance had been flashed from one to the other."

The Dance

The party now became more informal, music again struck up and, as fairies began to dance whenever possible, there was soon a whirling, leaping, spinning mass of rapidly changing colour, which moved with gathering speed from one end of our territory to the other. A few of the more serious-minded delegates retired to the apartments set aside for the purpose to hold a miniature congress of their own. To my surprise, most of the home fairies were among them and it was most gratifying for me to note that the love of their work now takes first place, even before their consuming passion for merriment and exchanging power.

The Congress Within The Congress

Many projects were discussed, the most important being the necessity for a concerted effort to maintain peace. It may surprise you to be told that fairies, who have always been regarded as carefree little people who spend their time dancing in the moonlight and sleeping by the fireside, should be concerned about something which one might imagine would not touch them. But this is far from the case, as you will have grasped from the extracts which I have already quoted by the Indian and Chinese fairies. A deep concern is felt for the peoples of the country in which they are living and the vibrations of fear and hatred caused by war can be as injurious to a fairy as to the humans who suffer them.

It was also generally realized that Earth fairies could develop more power. Usually they are content if they have sufficient to give to their charges, but it was now agreed that it was the solemn duty of each to develop as much as possible so that the surplus could be used to promote peace, heal the sick and comfort those in distress.

Healing was the next subject brought forward for consideration. It was regretfully agreed that not nearly enough fairies are interested in this compassionate work. "If only mediums knew of our presence and would greet our efforts with love, perhaps more would be attracted to give power," one suggested.

"One should not work for reward," said a delegate who had nearly finished his Earth span.

"It is difficult to make the young ones understand that service should be entirely selfless."

"Surely a little love would not be asking too much?" said a third.

"But how can people love us when they don't even know that we are there?"

"They are going to," said Normus decisively.

All eyes were turned upon him. "What makes you say that when for centuries we have been ignored by all but a very few?"

"We have a champion," said Normus. "A most important person. We have met him and his love for us is strong."

"He spoke to you and told you what he would do?"

"He tried, but he could not hear." Eager faces fell, Normus, of course, could not resist dramatizing the situation. He was revelling in his position and he was determined to raise their hopes and dash them, to raise them again to the limit.

"That is not all," he said. "Daphne acted as interpreter. She is writing a book about us which, for the first time, will record our work, our desire to help mankind and the fact that, if we only had a little understanding, we could do very much more."

There was tremendous excitement. Where was the man? Could they meet him? There were many things which he should be told.

Normus shook his head. "His Earth affairs keep him very busy; it is only upon rare occasions that he can be spared to come and visit us."

"Could we send a message?" the advanced fairy suggested. This idea was heavily applauded and many thought forms were made, destroyed, re-made, amalgamated and finally approved. Here is the text of the pictures which formed the appeal:

> "0 Mighty Warrior (Air Chief Marshal Lord Dowding), Our hearts go out to you in gratitude for the love and interest which, in your graciousness, you have seen fit to bestow upon us. We regret deeply that we are unable to bow before you in humble greeting, but this happiness is not, at present, to be ours. We would therefore give you a solemn pledge that we will continually strive, by lowering our vibrations and by loving those near to whom we work, to do everything in our power to render communication between the two evolutions easier than it has been heretofore. It is possible that we have been selfish in our attitude that we have not tried hard enough to bridge the gulf which has appeared to be all but impassable, but now we know that gulf is but an illusion, created over the centuries by Man and Fairy alike, our urgent desire is for Man to know that we stand by his side in every work of mercy in which he is employed.
>
> We would that we could thank you in person for the great bravery with which you have told the world of our existence. It seems strange to us that courage should be necessary to state something which is quite obvious to us, but it has been explained to us by Daphne, through Normus, that those who say openly that we exist are considered insane. This, to us, is stranger still, for we know that children can often see us and, occasionally, adults as well. Whence the secrecy? We have nothing of which to be ashamed, in that we live and work in order to help Man, no matter whether we are Nature or house fairies, healers or engaged in tasks of which he knows nothing. We would ask you to help us to help you, for when Man knows of our activities on his behalf, his awareness lightens our tasks, gives joy to our hearts and instills in us the desire to serve him again.

We salute you, great and kind sir. Our prayers will speed heaven-ward with most earnest requests for your happiness. We know that already many blessings are showered upon you by those whom you have helped in their sorrow, We now request, on your behalf, the bless-ings of our great Devas, who ever watch over even such young spirits as are we. Though our power is not strong, we hope that our most earnest desire for your well being will bring down upon your head the most beautiful blessing which our evolution can command."

The meeting then broke up as it was decided that it was the duty of the more advanced delegates to instill into the lesser members of the community the fact that the principal function of the congress was to promote good will between all Fairies, between Man and Fairy, and between Fairies and the other evolutions.

They mingled with the rest of the party, some joining in the dance for a short period, while others set to work to lure excited participants from the fray in order to talk to them of more serious matters.

Some eagerly listened as soon as they were outside the aura of the power enclosure but others, I noticed, were attending with but a fraction of their minds, while the rest was yearning to return to the gaiety of the dance.

I do not blame them. They had probably never experienced such a concentrated mass of power in their young lives, and the admonishments to strive to develop their own must have seemed unnecessary advice, for were they not already the most powerful fairies ever known? (This is the effect which this mystic force gives when taken in slightly too large quantities.)

However, although those taking part were sometimes borne upon to leave, oth-ers took their place and the dance went on, a wild, hilarious example of perpetual motion, or so it seemed to me, as I sat in a corner of the garden and watched. Usually there is a design to their dances, but this one had passed beyond the bounds of control and all that mattered was that each fairy must keep moving at as high a speed as possible, and travel as great a distance as he [she] could before retiring for a short spell of rest; and even during these periods they were giving and taking power from each other almost without respite.

The Action of Power

This may sound to the uninitiated to be in the nature of an orgy but I can assure you that this is far from the truth. To give and receive power is a most beautiful experience, always linked with spirituality and, even when there is much excitement, there always remains the desire to seek higher and ever higher; the more power that is absorbed, the wiser both giver and receiver become and, with this increased wisdom, they know that they must replace that which they have accepted and so the power is exhaled again.

The Power at Work

This particular occasion was the night of the full moon, when the soil is replenished, together with everything that grows in it. It was the determination of every fairy present to make the greatest concentration of power ever seen, and even if they did not achieve this ambition, they certainly produced a very large quantity for such very small people.

Midnight struck, the dance ceased and the fairies escorted the power mass in their thousands. Apart from the fact that they were now working, there was little change in the outward appearance of their activities, except that no one entered the enclosure, their movement and power-giving continuing from outside. Thus the mass was constantly replenished as beams from within it sped in all directions on their energy-giving mission.

I followed in their wake, adding my power too, and I can truthfully say I do not think that any plant or tree was missed for, instead of its usual single journey from one end of their territory to the other and back again, tonight the power lasted for over an hour and many excursions were made. At last all had been distributed and the fairies retired to their quarters for rest. I, too, was in need of repose and I returned to the Astral for a few hours' sleep."

The Second Day

At dawn, I was at my post again; in fact, it was a little before the first sign of the sun that I descended to find the fairy villages still at rest. But not for long. As the first finger of light crept in at the windows, there was an instant response. The streets became filled with small figures and the second day's activity began. The ritual took place at the correct time and once again, I watched three thousand heads raised towards the sky and three thousand heads bow before the answering blessing.

Although everything had been viewed the preceding day, they all wished to see everything all over again. The home fairies' houses were open to inspection and great interest was shown in their various treasures, but as they are described in a later part of the book, I will not tell you about them here. All fairies take a keen interest in their homes and many notes were taken and diagrams made for future reference.

During the morning there was a large religious gathering to which many neighboring fairies were bidden. A farris from the Astral plane addressed the visitors and a lecture on healing followed.

In the afternoon there was another transformation, after which they were left to their own devices for awhile. The less advanced ones played games, laughed, sang and enjoyed the company of their neighbors. The more serious-minded formed small discussion groups, pooled ideas and endeavoured to make a plan to save power and time. Up to the date of this congress, many of them had not understood that there was any necessity to develop their power and, as fairies are very like human beings in many respects, the repetition of this fact began to have effect and they started to take an interest in the ways and means.

The Mass Meditation

The asset of having surplus power to that necessary for their work was demonstrated in the evening when they all took part in a mass meditation.

There are numerous methods of so-called meditation, most of which take many years of practice before any satisfaction can be obtained by the person concerned. A constant battle with uncontrolled thoughts is ever in progress and, to begin with, the wayward and intractable mind invariably wins.

One Method of Meditation: Fairies and men who have studied the various ways of seeking to contact their higher selves (for that, in brief, is the main reason for meditation), usually follow the simple procedure of raising their thoughts to as high a level as they can and then following them. If you are still in your physical body, you must first learn to extricate your astral body from its coarse enclosure before you can do this. Fairies of course, do not have this added encumbrance and so they are able to reach a sphere as high as their minds are capable of attaining.

Spiritual Light

Light is the factor which is the cause of change in entities and all existing things. I am not referring to light which can be switched on and off at will, but to spiritual Light, which we all seek, although many are unaware they are so doing. It is a necessity of life and that is why we must have it, for without it we would sink among the lost legions who dwell – for one cannot call it living – within the aura of Evil.

All who are now reading this have dwelt there millions of years ago, for it is a state through which all but a few of the Very Great must pass. It is a period of anguish which our present minds can fortunately no longer reach; it is a time of tempering, for even as steel must pass through the hottest fires before it can be moulded, so must we suffer in order to become strong and shining in a more advanced way.

It is this Light which all strive to find when they meditate and often, in the early stages, the seekers will choose a shining symbol which they can see, such as a star or the sun. Later, they may think of qualities which they know but which are invisible to those on Earth, such as Love, Christ, or Holiness. I do not say that you will travel to the realms where the Source of Love, the Christ Spirit and Wholeness, or Being-at-One-With-the-Father are, but you should always aim at the highest point within your limited consciousness, and thus you will attain a finer aspect than the one you already know.

During the mass meditation, all were transported to the same place, yet many and varied were the descriptions which I later had given to me. All agreed that the scenery was more beautiful than they had ever seen before. But whereas the lesser-evolved delegates had seen the astral body only of trees, the mountains and the sky, others had seen their mental, and one or two, their bodies-of-experience. Their vision depended on whether the individual fairy was linked mentally with his astral mind only, or whether he had achieved the more advanced state of functioning in his Third or Fourth plane consciousness. This may sound very complicated to those who have not studied the subject so I will tell you the facts as simply as I can.

The Seven Selves

Each entity, whether Man, Fairy or member of one of the other evolutions, has seven separate selves. The seventh, sixth, and fifth are too evolved to communicate with those on Earth so we know little about them.

The fourth self has reached the stage of working almost entirely by thought.

The third self works partially by thought and partly with his body, which can be seen by those he is endeavoring to help.

On the Earth plane you work almost entirely with your bodies and brains with but a few seeking to establish contact with their Higher Selves. Those who succeed are said to be inspired.

Your physical mind, of which most of you are solely conscious, as a rule knows nothing of his higher bodies and minds, but your other minds are very aware of the actions and thoughts of each of the selves below him. In other words, your Highest self knows of, and endeavors to control, the actions of all his lower

270

selves. The sixth self is at times in touch with his seventh self, but he is constantly so with his fifth and fourth, etc. Alternately, if you can make mental contact with any of your higher selves, you will open your mind to knowledge quite beyond the capacity of your physical brain under everyday conditions.

Fourth Plane or Body of Experience

Now, in that crowd of fairies, only a few were able to function in their bodies-of-experience, but this ability enabled them to contact and discuss the current problems of the congress with the Fourth plane minds of the other fairies present, although the lower aspects of those selfsame fairies were quite unaware that any conversation had taken place. In fact, when they were later informed of the answers to certain problems which they themselves had provided, they were incredulous at their own wisdom.

The Result

Through the means of this mass meditation, decisions were reached and plans made far beyond the mental capacity of any of the fairies under normal conditions. That is knowledge not normally accessible to you. This understanding is often accompanied by spiritual ecstasy and by visible beauty but to seek for Truth is the main function of our quiet periods when we strive to attain a consciousness beyond our usual capacity.

As everyone who meditates thus goes into trance, I left the little people after I had seen them on their higher levels of consciousness and retired to rest.

The Final Findings of The Congress

On the afternoon of the third day, there was to be a joint conference of both Nature and House fairies to clarify the findings of the congress as a whole. I had been looking forward to this event with interest to ascertain whether anything more tangible than enthusiasm and good intentions would be the outcome of their various meetings.

A farris was present as a figurehead only, as it was strongly desired that the fairies themselves should set their ideas in order and make arrangements for future cooperation if they considered it desirable.

I was pleased to note that, although the original excitement had remained, there was now a semblance of control to modify the somewhat chaotic conditions of the first few hours.

Help for the Earthbound

The outstanding feature was the almost unanimous desire to help the earth-bound. The stories given to them by our astral friends had clearly touched their hearts more than any other aspect of the congress.

They had been awed but fascinated by the two transformations and, from these, they had made their own plans for helping these people and I was happy that they were all in agreement that they should ask for the aid of a human medium from the astral if none from Earth was available.

They understood that they must begin to work, whenever possible, at the moment of death so that they could bring their powers to bear in order to try to prevent the person from sinking lower than the region to which he had condemned himself by his sins on Earth. Their task will be hard for they will be unable to reach the earthbound, as we can with words. Thoughts and love will be their only tools, but I have no doubt that, if their determination remains as great as at the congress, they will succeed.

All agreed that more power was essential and all were determined, by attending halls of learning and by using their wills, to increase their outflow by at least fifty percent.

Healing

Those who lived in towns were to seek out the healers and offer their services to those in charge of the operations. If they are accepted, they will learn from these the rudiments of healing and the procedure necessary in order to permit the different rays, instead of pure power only, to pass through them.

The advanced members pointed out to the younger ones that less time would have to be spent in play.

Normus Speaks from Experience

Normus then spoke and he told them that this would only be necessary for the first few months. His band of fairies had found that their power has grown to such an extent that, not only have they plenty for the new, as well as for their more usual tasks, but that less effort need now be expended on the latter, giving them more time to follow their own devices.

I noticed many little faces brighten. It is easy to long to do great deeds of compassion but the glamour is somewhat lost when precious periods of rest and recreation are threatened. I have no doubt, however, that had it been necessary, most of them would have sacrificed their leisure for the satisfaction of increased service. A spark had been lit within many small hearts which will not be easily extinguished. At times it may flicker and when the vibrations of those more advanced than they have been removed, it may even fade. But whereas some had only been interested in their immediate charges and in the well being of their own small group, I do not think that I exaggerate when I say that all had become aware of the enormous scope for their varying talents and, where previously they had but a limited view, new horizons had been opened wide before them and their own latent possibilities brought to light.

Various other subjects were discussed, with surprisingly orderly insight. Many told me later that they had grown during these three days far more than they had in the last twenty years.

The Farewell Reception

On this, their final evening, there was to be another reception when there would be music, dancing and complete freedom of movement and discussion. Those who did not wish to attend were not expected, by good manners, to do so; in fact, it was desired that each one should enjoy himself in his own way.

I watched them arrive at the meeting place and I observed a new dignity about them; they were quieter, less excited, but that which they had lost in over-high spirits had been replaced by the happiness which their new-found responsibilities were given to them.

You may think it almost sad that their carefree attitude had been taken from them, but nothing could be further from the truth. We do not take anything that is not gladly given and, when we do, the donor is repaid a hundredfold by his increased awareness of all that goes on around him.

There we will leave them, for farewells are always a trifle sad. Their little hearts were filled with high hopes for the future of mankind and for all those who seek to serve him. In their turn, they too should be served. Do not forget that. Service for service is a Universal law, and until we understand this eternal truth we shall be unable to travel far.

The Congress
by Ludwig

Saturday

We had all been in a state of great anticipation pending our tea party in Daphne's garden during the weekend that the fairy congress was taking place. Nor were we disappointed, for I have seldom seen a more delightful sight than that which met our eyes on arrival.

The lawn was the site of a complete village, the streets of which were filled with gesticulating people in miniature, as they stood about in groups, obviously settling the affairs of their various nations.

The air was filled with thought forms, not always entirely truthful, if one could judge from the size of the flowers which one of the visitors was assuring his audience he had personally grown in his jungle garden. I am aware that tropical flowers are of a great size, but this particular one was as large as Daphne's house; in fact, he was using the outside wall as a background.

Another fact which we doubted was when we saw an ape, rivaling the flower in size, which another visitor was claiming as a friend. One would have thought that a fairy exaggeration would be in proportion to his size but apparently this is not the case.

While we ate our tea, we were happy just to watch the colourful throng as it split up and regrouped itself time and time again. At first the fairies did not seem to be aware of our presence and we wondered whether perhaps we would be unable to talk to them as we had not spent hours of concentration, learning how to become in tune with these particular little people. However, we need not have worried because, as soon our own friends arrived, it seemed as though an invisible curtain drawn around us was removed, revealing us to their astonished gaze.

Normus clapped his hands peremptorily. Although to us there was, of course, no sound, there must be an equivalent vibration because the fairies accompanied him as he flew 'round to perch on each of our heads and introduce us to the fast-growing multitude.

They stood all over the table, they flew 'round our faces in order to obtain a better view, and they climbed up our legs to gain strategic positions for later use. They were not only told our names, but most of our past and present as well. We were only surprised, so enthusiastic did Normus become as his oratory carried him away, that he failed to reveal our future lives as well.

The visitors shook their heads sadly as he related how most of us had been earthbound but they began to smile with happiness as they understood that we had benefited from our misery and how, through the experience gained, we were

274

now able to help others who find themselves in places as dark as those where we had once dwelt.

As soon as Normus had finished, a thousand thought forms flashed, as everyone began asking questions at once. I have recently succeeded in seeing these fairy projections rather than receiving them in my mind, but this wild clamour of converging colours proved too much for my inadequate training.

As none of us could understand what they were saying and they were, therefore, receiving no answers, it was reasonable to suppose that the continuous flashes would soon cease. Perhaps fairies do not expect answers to their questions; it is also possible that the beauty of their own projections so fascinates them that, by the time one is finished, they have forgotten what it was that they wanted to know. In this particular case, at any rate, about five minutes passed before anyone seemed to realize that we were all silent.

"Why do you not answer them?" Normus enquired in a hurt voice.

I took his hand. "There is nothing we should like to do better but we do not know what they are saying. They are talking at normal speed and it is beyond us."

"Of course," said Normus, "how silly of me. I quite forgot to tell them. You must speak slowly," he said to them. "No faster than this . . ." and he flashed half a dozen pictures on the air which even I could read.

They gasped. Then a Chinaman pushed his way through the throng to the table, bowed before me and projected the one word, "Greetings."

I flashed back, "Greetings, honoured sir."

He smiled and said, "We apologize. We are unused to talking with man since our sojourn on Earth. If you will be patient, we have many questions we would like to ask." As his sentence grew longer, the projections became faster, but between us, we managed to understand him.

"One at a time then, please," I said, and immediately five hundred flashes filled the air.

"I mean one question from one fairy at one time, please," I said, "but you can ask each of us a different one."

At last they seemed to grasp our shortcomings and order was more or less restored. The questions were so varied and some were so unexpected that, at times, we were nonplused but I think that, taken as a whole, we appeared to give satisfaction. I have selected a few which may interest or amuse you.

"How many pares (wives) have you?"

"Do the earthbound which you help know that fairies also try to help them?"

"As getting drunk seems to make people bad tempered and unhappy, why do they do it?"

"When two people are married on Earth, why are they not supposed to make love to other people too?"

"Fairies always help each other in their work; why is it that man so often tries to hinder his neighbour or even to rob him of his rewards?"

"We understand that Man cannot see power; why is it, though, that he has also failed to grasp its significance in regard to his daily life? All know how one person with evil thoughts and words can sway a hundred satisfied and contented people, given sufficient time. It would work the other way too if one man had the courage to try to combat a hundred evil thinkers."

"At this Congress we have found, perhaps to the surprise of some, that fairies of a different colour to ourselves are fundamentally the same. We are interested in the same subjects, our work varies but the welfare of Mankind or Nature is our common task; we all seek higher planes in our meditation and we endeavour to help our younger members to reach better conditions. If we can meet with understanding for each other's customs, for our differences of opinion, and for the way we work and live, why cannot Man?"

Eventually the questions came slightly slower and we had time to breathe once more. then it was our turn and we learned many facts about the fairy communities of other lands. Their interests we found as varied as our own and by no means restricted to their work.

Music appears to be an almost consuming passion, particularly for those living in remote districts. Some of them had brought their instruments with them; these were eagerly passed from one to the other as we examined them with minute care.

Most of them appeared to be wind instruments of numerous shapes and sizes; some were literally held at varying degrees so that the wind whistled down them, producing different notes; others, the fairies blew down themselves, some being almost like bagpipes in appearance, but there the similarity ended, for the sweetest tones exuded from them. There was one other which was quite new to us and was brought by an Eskimo. The music, he explained, was produced by the intense cold snapping what appeared to be fine threads of ice, yet they did not break when we touched them.

Many fairies, in their spare time, make thought formations as a decoration, in the same way that some people paint. Several of them showed me examples of their work and it was most interesting to note the influence of the country where they lived. I do not mean only that those from the tropics used the glorious colours of the flowers, or that the fairy from the Italian Lakes had somehow given his formation the appearance of slowly moving water; but somehow they seemed to have depicted either the serenity or the turmoil, the dignity or the flamboyance of the land of their adoption. Not only the country was portrayed, but their own characters as well.

Of course they are not restricted by two dimensions for their work, nor yet by their materials. They can, with thought, produce the actual texture of a flower petal, although they may be using it in a sunset; they can capture the sound of rushing water, yet translate it into colour.

It has taken me many months of patient, if loving, labour to enable me to see these pictures and gradually the understanding of their true meaning is coming to me. A painter in oils endeavours to give you his idea of a subject – how much wider is the fairies' field and, indeed, that of the painter, once he is rid of his physical body and the restricted vision which goes with it.

There is another form of recreation which is obviously the counterpart of our reading. Through the medium of many thought formations, a story is told and the reader or viewer actually enters into and becomes part of the theme. Thus the adventurous can sail the seas in the company of fairy pirates, or set forth to overcome their foes, either single-handed or in the company of the good fairies, who are ever ready to come to the aid of those wishing to combat evil.

The gentle can spend their hours of ease, drifting peacefully along the air currents in what I can only describe as flying gondolas, or diving with the water fairies amidst the unexplored depths of some imaginary ocean.

The merry can encourage their laughter by joining the company of advanced practical jokers who conjure up palaces of amusement, full of devices which expand and shrink, blow up and capsize the bodies of the fun-seeking fairy. He is presented with the fiendish forms of terrifying elementals which burst with a loud report when but a few inches from their, by this time, thoroughly scared victim. Ravishing fairies of the opposite sex embrace them, to disintegrate in their arms, leaving them soaking wet and in the pitch black. They gave us endless examples of the predicaments in which they had found themselves, and their merry laughter and twinkling eyes testified to the happiness which these uncomfortable situations had given them. Another favorite type of "book" depicts true stories of the other evolutions. They can thus become acquainted with many forms of life to which they would not otherwise have access. They can learn as well as obtain pleasure from their reading although, as a rule, it is only the more advanced fairy who is interested in this latter type of literature. Fairies nearly all love acting in the same way that most children like to dress up. They have the added advantage of not being restricted by the clothes and props of their own or their friends' homes, having the almost limitless horizons of their more-than-fertile minds. Any object, once seen, is never forgotten and can be produced from memory when it is needed. One day I was fortunate enough to represent a vast audience while the fairies acted a play and I found that the costumes appeared to bear little in common with the character depicted.

Merella, as the heroine, wore a most gruesome mask, half bird, half human, and her lover, Gorjus, concealed his good looks beneath a crimson hood with holes for eyes, nose and mouth. The chorus, who told the story as it was enacted, had animal heads or tails, claws for feet, or great boots such as the navies wear.

As the tale unfolded, I was amazed at the relish with which they acted the horrible situations. Mirilla, who to me is the personification of charm and sweetness, scratched her rival until the blood gushed in veritable streams upon the stage; she dragged Merella by the hair and trampled her in the dust. Then, with shameless abandon, she hurled herself at Gorjus.

But his heart was broken. I know it was because I could see it as it dripped, a revolting, glutinous mass down his jacket.

However, Merella may have been down but she was far from out. Silently she rose to her feet and, as Mirilla was extolling her own virtues, she made a deadly weapon, consisting of a series of little demons who would enter her rival and drive her to her destruction.

I watched the little black creatures surround my beautiful Mirilla almost with fear in case Merella, in her enthusiasm, had called upon real demons from the dark places. Suddenly they pounced and disappeared and Mirilla, as though demented, rushed backwards and forwards, battering her lovely head and face against shrubs and stones until she was but a torn and mangled mess.

Merella, resplendent in victory, wore an even more repellent headdress as she and Gorjus, his heart now restored and whole in its proper place, marched triumphantly 'round the stage while the chorus chanted the virtue of love conquering evil.

[I was very interested, if amused, at the very unfairy-like subject of the play. I asked Normus later whether they usually act such unpleasant themes. "Oh, yes," he answered gleefully. "At one time or another the stage is always running with blood." At first it seemed strange that these little people should obviously be so intrigued with something which they do not possess and then I remembered the probable reason. These particular fairies have been given lessons in human anatomy and the functions which our various organs perform. They were told that the heart is the seat of the emotions, as indeed it is, whether there is a physical manifestation of it or no, hence the enjoyment they experience in displaying hearts, whether whole or broken, as I understand they now invariably do. As children love to scalp each other in blood-curdling battles between the settlers and Indians, or fill their playground with gangsters and corpses, so these little people indulge in their own forms of make-believe. – D.C.]

"Did you like it?" I was relieved to see Mirilla, normal and beaming, on my lap.
"You are not hurt?" I asked anxiously.
She clapped her hands delightedly. "Am I not a good actress? He thought I was disintegrated," she boasted to the others.

"I think you were all wonderful. It is certainly a very dramatic play, full of strong situations," I commended them. "Who wrote it?"

"Oh, we make it up as we go along. Aren't we clever?"

I sat back and mused. To have watched my little friend, as I usually do, earnestly seeking for Eternal Truth, and then to see her, as she now appeared, with her eyes bright with excitement over her horrible – though I must admit – brilliant performance, made it indeed difficult to believe that she was the same fairy. Like children, they too must have their contrasts. When they have known the true beauty which they find in their meditation, what possible pleasure could they gain from the mere acting of it? I was beginning to understand and, feeling happier about the whole matter, I was able to congratulate them with more depth of conviction than I could have done a short while before.

If the delegates' questions had, in some cases, surprised us, they were amazed at our ignorance in the matter of fairy life. We explained to them that we were but beginners and, however eager we were to learn, it had taken us a long time and much hard work to have become even as much in tune with them as we are at present.

To our regret, owing to other commitments, we had to leave, although we would dearly have liked to have remained and witnessed the formal reception and the full moon celebrations which followed it.

Sunday

When we arrived the next day, what appeared to be a multitude was awaiting us. I think that our friends of the previous day must have brought along all their acquaintances; we seemed to be waist-deep – and more – in fairies.

They had also forgotten the "one question at a time" request and again we were almost stunned by the impact of thousands of enquiries which seemed to be hurtling at us from all directions.

Tea was out of the question, so we abandoned the idea without more ado. With a joint effort of will power, we managed to quell the near-riot and, as we felt ourselves quite incapable of controlling the speed of the questions once they were permitted to launch them, we informed them that, if they were agreeable, we would tell them of incidents connected with our work with the earthbound or, in the case of Jack and Andrew, those living in the very dark places.

This last offer temporarily switched the limelight onto the somewhat unwilling recipients of hero worship. We already had fairies all over us but Jack and Andrew were now subjected to a most minute scrutiny until they begged for mercy and we again joined wills to bring order into being once more.

"Quick, start telling them something, Peter," I said and he obligingly complied. I will not relate to you the stories which we told, for this is a fairy book, but one day we all hope that the plight of those we seek to save will become more generally known, for those on Earth can do so much to help if only they desire to do so. I need only state that those near two thousand over-excited members of the fairy evolution remained spellbound and, unbelievable as it seemed at first, silent.

As soon as one of us finished his tale, a babel broke loose but we had learned our lesson and immediately another began, and quiet was restored. It was really somewhat like the Eastern prince who would only save some poor wretch's life as long as he continued to entertain him with his storytelling. Fortunately, there were eight of us and we have an almost endless fund of true experiences from which to draw and, even had we run out, we have many friends whose work lies parallel with ours and whose observations we could have borrowed.

When we finally came to the end of our time, if not our tales, they remained silent. Excitement had given place to sadness; the desire to learn was still present but in a different guise. Before, they had been clamouring for information, it is true, but there had been no plan behind their questions. I would not go so far as to say that they wished to gratify their idle curiosity, but a query from one fairy would have no bearing on what he would ask a little later. But now there was real reasoning behind each enquiry and, not only that, they even asked permission to speak. We had obviously risen in their estimation. We were no longer just examples of another evolution, extraordinary only because we could talk to them. We were people with a purpose and they wanted to find out how we had reached our state of comparative contentment. We explained to them that it was our work which made us happy.

"But how can that be," one asked, "when you leave the light which you've earned to work in darkness?"

"We take our own light with us," I explained, and by doing that, we are able to share it with some poor soul who has none of his own."

They were talking quietly to one another now.

"Could we help?" one asked.

"Our power is so small," regretted another.

"We have so little time after attending to our charges," said a third.

I called for Normus and set him on my knee.

"Here is one who can answer your problems," I said. "He has practical experience. His band of fairies not only do their own work and help with the earthbound too; they also heal; they send out the peace ray each day, and they have made contact with, and help, not only Man, but some of the other evolutions as well. If they can do it, you can."

I whispered in Normus' ear and he took them across the lawn and addressed them from the top of the rockery.

I will not say that we were glad to see them go but we were delighted to celebrate the obvious success of the congress in a belated cup of tea.

THE FAIRIES' REPORT ON THE
1985 HUMAN AND FAIRY RELATIONS CONGRESS
(Held in the Fairy Realm)

FOREWORD
by Daphne Charters

[The Congress had been held annually in the fairy realm for over 30 years at this point, being held annually since the early 1950s. – M.P.]

Early in 1985, a friend of mine, Susan Anderson, who is a professional illustrator and paints fairies (Susan painted the second cover for *A True Fairy Tale*), phoned me to say that a man to whom she had lent my book *A True Fairy Tale*, would very much like to meet me. I agreed to see him and John arrived. He was very well read and knowledgeable over occult matters, and he had tried many systems for expanding consciousness, some of which he would probably have been better without! So we had no difficulty in finding things to talk about.

Eventually he said, "Have you heard of Sai Baba?" I had not, and my heart sank at the thought of yet another Indian guru. In any case, with all the wonderful things I already had: the fairies, my guide, mentor and beloved friend of many incarnations, whom I know as Father John, Augustine or Ronanus, and my clairaudience enabling me to communicate with them all, I really was not looking for anything or anyone else. John told me about Sai Baba – that He is the Avatar of the Age, that he heals the sick, performs miracles, and teaches that all religions are one.

He does not encourage people to change their religion because the basis of all of them are the same. It is only man who has produced tenets and taboos, causing not unity, but division among the people of the world. John offered to lend me some books which he had brought along with him, and after he left I browsed among them and chose one to read more carefully. This was Peggy Mason and Ron Laing's wonderful *Sai Baba, The Embodiment of Love*. When I reached about page 20, I knew that he was the "One", and I have never changed my mind.

To go back to the early days of my relationship with the fairies nearly forty years ago, I was working with the "earthbound" and was in touch with the guides of various nationalities, who always during their visits to me also talked with the fairies. One day, after a negro, Maroni, had been with us, I asked Father John whether there were black fairies, to which he replied, "There are fairies attached to every country under the sun, and they usually form their bodies so that they are similar to those of the people in the land where they live." I then asked him whether it would be possible to bring the different races together by holding a Congress, during which they could exchange ideas, discuss their various types of work and see what fairies from other lands looked like. This suggestion was passed to a Higher Power and the idea was accepted. I had been thinking in terms of about two hundred visitors, but in fact three thousand delegates came to the first Congress, which was a tremendous success; but so much excitement and enthusiasm were generated that I fear arrangements did not always go according to plan or take place at the allotted time!

From this enjoyable and modest beginning, a Congress has been held in late summer every year. The theme is always to generate as much power as possible through the fairies, angels and discarnate humans who have attended the gathering in increasing numbers from the first one onward. This power is for the good of Earth, her inhabitants and her substance, whether human, animal, trees, and plants, metals, minerals and rock formations including precious stones, rivers, oceans and their contents – in fact all the constituent parts of Earth and her environment. Added to this, there is always a concerted effort to promote peace and good-will between man and fairy on every plane.

In the intervening years we have all grown in maturity, and the Fairies have expanded mentally. A further group has joined us making three in all, and there are now thirty-one members of them that I know individually and with whom I communicate regularly.

During the preparation for the 1985 Congress, Father John approached Sai Baba, for whom he had worked for many years, and asked Him if He would do the Fairies the great honor of bringing the Congress to its close. He agreed.

The Fairies have experienced wonderful visitations from High Devas, but always they meditated on, and yearned for Him, whom they called the Name-less One. I knew that an exalted Entity was to be present at the Congress and I asked Father John to tell me His name. "Maratumel" he replied. So when one of the Fairies visited me later, I said quite casually, "By the way, Father John has given me the name of the Exalted One Who is to preside over the Congress. It is "Maratumel". I did not realize at the time that this was a momentous revelation for them, and that I had given them the Name of the Nameless One.

The astonishing fact is that not only each of my fairies, but also the 200,000 delegates had a different experience of the "Appearance". Some saw him as Sai Baba, some as Maratumel, others as a constantly changing form either male or female whom they revered, as an animal or Celestial Light – each according to his or her need and present state of consciousness. In time the whole proceedings took two minutes, a sublime example of Divine Magic, which to them, will last for ever.

After the Congress, each gave me a detailed description of his or her individual experience, which I have now incorporated into this pamphlet. I hope it will give you some enchanting moments and open up a New World far removed from the jokey "fairies at the bottom of my garden." If people did but know, if they were not all over their gardens, giving power to the plants and trees, and taking them through each phase of their growth from seed to flower and fruit, to put it simply, they would have no gardens. Many fairies are, of course, concerned only with the Nature Kingdom, but others who have been in contact with man's concrete thinking mind, expand in knowledge and gain the ability to serve both the Human and Devic Evolutionary Cycles.

– Daphne Charters

[The following manuscripts are the personal accounts of 31 of the 33 fairies (in the three groups which work with Daphne) on what happened for them at Maratumel's appearance at the 1985 Fairy Congress. Maratumel/Marata are the male/female names of the highly evolved being currently incarnated as Sai Baba. Gorjus and Myrris accounts are missing from this compilation and hopefully will be found. – M.P.]

GROUP I:
THE NATURE FAIRIES

Preface

As some of the fairies in their descriptions of the Congress use the term "duo-dua" and "pares" (sing. paris) here are a few words about fairy unions. They do not marry as humans do on Earth, but they form relationships between males and females. There are two categories which come under the heading of "duo-dua". Some are what might be called twin souls; these split at an early stage of their evolutionary cycle, forming two parts of a whole; each wends its way through mineral, vegetable and animal kingdoms until they eventually meet once more as separate entities who gradually draw together though aeons of time and become one again.

Fairies who have been united during various descents into matter similar to our incarnations, and also for periods on higher planes between them also receive the title duo-dua. At times they are separated; at others they come together again, possibly after many years, proving their love is an indestructible bond.

Those that stay together for a number of years become pares. There are also others who have relationships of a temporary nature.

The love-act is an exchange of power – a surrender of mind with a blending of their ethereal bodies, attaining a state of rapture. The interchange of power to a lesser degree is also used as a gesture of friendship or sympathy. There is no resentment if one paris gives and receives power from another fairy. Indeed to do so with a leader is in the nature of a reward for work well done. Duo-duas usually exchange power only with each other and their leaders, except when they themselves are leaders.

The joint leaders of Group I are two girls called Mirilla and Merella. Mirilla's paris is Movus; when I first met him he was underleader of the group with Normus as its leader. As the years passed, Normus was promoted and became an Over-leader, with four groups. Now he has twenty one groups. The time came for Movus also to become an Over-leader, and he now has sixteen groups.

Mirilla and Movus were not only hard workers, but were continually expanding their consciousness by visits to the higher spheres.

Merella was a bit on the wild side! She would exchange power with virtually any fairy to whom she felt attracted. Her paris, Nuvic, was always proud of her beauty and vitality, and accepted that fact of frequently exchanging power with other males because she assured him that each blending helped her to progress.

284

This supposition proved to be accurate because, apart from Normus and Movus, she was the most advanced fairy in the group.

The affect of her experience at the Congress was so overwhelming that she literally became another person. I am not clairvoyant and can only know which fairy is with me by the "feel" of his or her vibration. For quite a time afterwards. I did not recognise Merella's. From being ever active and with unlimited enthusiasm for her work, which was experimenting with seeds, and her enjoyment of every aspect of life, she had instantaneously become serene, gentle and at peace.

The group includes two other pares, Namsos and Sirilla, Namsos was very shy and worked with the tiny animals in the soil, the grubs, slugs and his favorites – worms. By the time I moved to London, all the fairies were employed with other work and direct attachment to the Plant Kingdom ceased because I then had no garden. It is not therefore surprising that he gathered round him many larger fairy-animals; you might say that he now has the equivalent of a sanctuary for misfits, which under his loving and patient care soon revert to the category to which they belong and can lead normal lives.

Sirilla was always bright with an intense interest in her task with the trunks of trees and the insects which run up and down the cracks in the bark.

Nixus and Lyssis were the other two shy members of the group and also the youngest. Originally Lyssis worked with the small flowers in the garden and Nixus tended the lawn. Both were modest and unsure of themselves, but the work in which all the fairies became involved, including teaching, during the next thirty years gave them the confidence which they had originally lacked.

Rhelia, in the beginning of my contact with her was not a member of any of the groups. She, with two young male companions, were bringing in three fairy "children." As with their human counterparts, they in turn reached the age and degree of maturity when they not longer required the security of a family, and left to lead their own lives. Rhelia and her two companions also parted and she joined Group 1. She has no paris, but is loved by all.

– Daphne Charters

MOVUS
[Transcribed on 24th Aug. 1985]

I was with Mirilla and my groups waiting for the promised Appearance. We had had many discussions as to how He would manifest. I felt sure that He would take the form of a Great Shining One. Others thought that the lesser evolved members present would be struck down by the power. Remembering the times that Mirilla and I have disintegrated during our endless search for enlightenment, this did not worry me much! It is all part of experience, and gradually one learns to hold oneself together until the message has been received or the joy granted as a reward, has become part of one, to be savoured and gain knowledge from the precious gift bestowed.

But nothing like anything we had previously encountered, happened. The clouds were first pierced by hundreds of beams of light, which descended and attached themselves to each person present. I gasped as mine entered my body and spread to each part of it until I felt myself shining like the sun. I became enormous. I was no longer part of my groups or the rest of the Congress. I was a god, waiting to receive a visitation from my Lord. Then, through my own emanation of light, I saw Him. "I am Maratumel." I prostrated myself before Him. "You are mine to serve, mine to obey; mine to love and in return, I will give you Love such as you have never known. Be still. Listen. My will shall reach you in the breeze, on the crest of a wave, in the perfume of flowers. All contain my plan for you which will gradually unfold. Perform your tasks as an over-leader diligently. But pause and open yourself to Me. I do not roar. I whisper; but this tiny sound is more potent than the loudest clap of thunder. I need you as you need Me. We will not fail each other."

– Movus

MIRILLA

[Transcribed on 25th Aug.. 1985]

Merella, my co-leader, was standing on my right with our group behind us. We were filled with expectation, especially me. I am always uplifted by Merella's enthusiasm. "You will see," she said. "This is going to be something beyond anything we have known before."

Movus, with his sixteen groups, was standing next to us, and as I gazed up at the sky, I expected to blend with him; but throughout I remained myself, and was aware of no-one else. Movus and I are always searching, always finding wonderful Beings whom we blend with, converse with, learn from and love; but as soon as Maratumel appeared, I knew that He was the Nameless One whom we have worshipped for years no matter the name and form He was manifesting at the time, because we always knew that beyond Him was Another.

"This is He," and I was transfixed and unable to make my obeisance or offer my allegiance and service. I felt nothing but overwhelming love. It was nothing but love, not the love I feel for my dearest Movus or my many friends. It was purged of any desire. I wanted nothing except that I should be enfolded in it

286

forever. I saw no form, only a vast pink radiance, giving itself eternally down the ages in selfless profusion. My inner being became active. Adoration enveloped me until I reached a point of near annihilation of my fairy-being; and then I spread, entered the radiance and for a brief moment became it, knowing all in a flash of consciousness that will lead me into the future with joy, wisdom and determination to make the world a better place.

– Mirilla

NAMSOS

(Transcribed 26ᵗʰ Sept., 1985)

The concluding day of the Congress was with us. We had experienced so much power, and absorbed so many speeches containing wonderful thoughts that we could not imagine anything more inspiring happening. And yet in our hearts, we knew that it would.

All of us were looking after delegates from different countries, and my group came from Australia. We all got on very well together. On a pre-Congress visit, I had marvelled at the size of their country; and now, they were amazed at the compactness of ours.

What a gathering it was; thousands of fairies and humans bonded together by a common cause – to evolve a method of bringing down to this plane the Forces of Peace and Love to such a degree that the inhabitants of the world must pause in their apparent determination to destroy Earth and themselves with it.

Midnight arrived and with it a feeling of infinite peace for me, and I knew that all our discussions, ideas and hopes would bear fruit, and one day our goal would be attained.

Then into my stillness came Light more radiant than the brightest sunrise I had ever seen. It permeated the site of the Congress and all who were waiting in breathless anticipation for the "Appearance." The centre of the Light compressed and slowly materialized a form so magnificent that I thought I would faint. I inhaled deeply and managed to regain my equilibrium. This was Maratumel, the Lord of our Evolution, about Whom I had pondered for many years. The Nameless One, Whose Name we now know. What inexplicable joy to know it and then to see Him. His hair was of fire – the eternal flame. His robe was like swirling water; His form was of air; and He stood in majesty, on a replica of the planet Earth. His body changed from male to female; sometimes He was a youth, then a sage with the ancient wisdom. He simultaneously emanated energy and stillness, author-ity and compassion. Love flowed in countless beams towards us, their courses

287

veering, crossing and re-crossing one another as each sought its individual target. One came towards me, but before it reached me, it changed course and sped on its way. But I never doubted that one was for me, and I suddenly felt a surge, not of expectation but a certainty that a particular beam was mine. It was a very deep pink, and it was in no hurry. It was floating above the crowd, seeking its counterpart – me.

"I am here," I called softly, and immediately it hastened towards me; it hovered above me for a moment as though to check my identity; then it diffused and I was covered by a multi-coloured cloak, protective, inspiring, tremendously strong, and I knew that I could perform any task allotted to me.

I was still savoring its properties when I realized that my group had gathered round me, chattering excitedly, and showing each other their gifts.

"Where is yours, Namsos?" they asked.

"This lovely cloak," I replied.

"Cloak, what cloak?"

I smiled. "I must have been dreaming," I said. This was not the truth, but I did not want to hurt their feelings. My cloak is real; it was their eyes that were not yet sufficiently open to see it.

– Namsos

SIRILLA

[Transcribed on 27th Aug., 1985]

𝕴 cannot describe to you adequately the excitement that ran from one fairy to another in the group as we heard the name of the Nameless One. We all began to chant it and almost immediately we felt the Power which we had endeavored to reach for so long.

As we stood waiting for the Appearance, my anticipation rose almost to bursting point, but I managed to contain myself. I was in the centre of delegates from America, all of whom were enthusiastic about our way of life. Some of them came from homes in which Sai Baba's photograph was displayed, so I did not have to explain to them who He was, and all of them expected Him to appear in this form.

Presumably because of this, at first they saw Him as Sai Baba but I did not. I saw a huge light fill the sky. It was all shades of pink like a brilliant sunrise; indeed I felt as though the sun was rising inside me. As his power spread so did that from inside me, until both met above the group. As they described it afterwards it opened their eyes and they saw Him as Maratumel. I could hear the gasps all round me, but at the time, strangely I felt alone. I rose towards Him gazing in adoration. He was so strong, so beautiful. His commanding Presence drew me towards Him until I stood above the group. He gazed at me lovingly and it was as though He reached out and stroked my hair, but perhaps it was a breeze – but then, He is the breeze I began to tremble, praying for a word of encouragement or perhaps some confirmation of His Love. He became misty; I think my eyes were filled with tears and then I heard. "Listen to the murmur of your heart. It is a true reflection of Mine. It will tell you all you want to know." I felt a small cold patch on my breast. I looked down and there was an emblem of the heart. I could see it vibrating. I listened, but all I could hear was, "Listen, listen," and when I looked up, He had gone, but in the sky was a vast pink heart, pulsating with its message, "listen, listen," and this I shall do until mine reveals its secret.

– Sirilla

MERELLA

*A*s you know, I was standing near Mirilla shortly before midnight, absolutely bursting with energy and expectation.

Midnight came and instantly there was a refulgence of light which encompassed the sky and the entire site of the Congress. Each individual fairy and human lit up like a power-unit in response to the radiance which entered each one of us; and I knew that a great awakening was taking place in all of those present. So powerful was it that I lost sight of the thousands of humans, angels and fairies that surrounded me in order to concentrate and hold myself together, or disintegration would have taken place as it has done many times before; this I was determined not to repeat until I had at least received a glimpse of Maratumel, on Whom I had been meditating ever since I had heard and felt the magic of His Name.

Do you realize what you have done? You have given us the name of the Nameless One, Whom we have worshipped for years and about Whom we have prayed that we should at least know Who it was we were serving.

It happened so quickly. We knew the Name only briefly before the Appearance was to take place, but we were so occupied with the arrangements for the Congress that we had virtually no time to prepare ourselves.

I tried to maintain a pin-point of calm in the centre of the whirlpool of my yearning to experience whatever He would give me. I nearly lost this glimmer of serenity several times, but somehow I managed to preserve it.

The Celestial Light divided to reveal an even brighter one, and although at that time it was formless, I knew it was Maratumel. I think I called His Name and immediately a beam of light pierced me. I expanded to absorb the shock and to enable me to experience to the fullest degree this power that at the same time was both painful and ecstatic. I willed myself to see Him through the sensations which beset me: love, hope and determination to prove my earnest desire to serve; and finally, an extraordinary feeling of wholeness – holiness – absorbed me. My eyes closed in bliss and it was then that I saw Him, a nebulous white form, clothed in flames with beams of red, white, silver and gold radiating in all directions.

I felt myself drawn towards Him until I was at His feet. I tried to touch them but they remained beyond my reach. I strove to draw nearer but was unable to move.

He bent down and caressed my brow, and then I saw Him clearly. He had a long, aesthetic face with a dream of the future in His eyes, which dilated until I was aware of nothing else. They showed me an age when Man would realize his brotherhood with all Humanity, when fairies and angels would roam the Earth to be seen by all, where animals were regarded as loving friends to be cherished and helped to grow in understanding. Earth and all its denizens had great beauty, with an aura of love, gentleness and humility pervading the planet.

My heart leapt with joy at the proof that pain and grief no longer existed because Man, of his own free-will, had changed and become that which was planned at the time of creation, but which he had lost during his descent into matter, overcome by its wiles, and caught in the snares of the falsehood that happiness emanates from physical possessions, success and adulation.

I expanded with joy, until the Power overcame me; my body dissolved and I fell down to Earth in countless fragments. But I retained the vision of what is to be.

I know that it will not happen tomorrow or for many years to come; but I have pledged myself to do my utmost to help this vision become Reality, in spite of Man's indifference to the suffering that he himself has created and forced on so many, and his ignorance of his own true Heritage.

– Merella

NUVIC

[Transcribed on 20th Sept.. 1985]

Naturally, Merella (Nuvic's "paris" or companion) and I had discussed the coming appearance of Maratumel, wondering what He would look like. We have been fortunate in having experienced the Presence of a number of Shining Ones, mainly because of Merella's ability to detect their power even when they are far away.

But on this occasion we could not be together. Merella being joint-leader with Mirilla, they were members of the "host-group" looking after the most important delegates, while I had the more modest task of taking care of fifteen visitors from

Germany. We enjoyed each other's company; they were so anxious to learn all they could about the expansion of Human-Angel-Fairy relations, and the work in which we were to take part in the future of contacting as many fairies as possible in all countries of the world.

Midnight approached, by which time I was almost exploding with excitement. If I had done so, no one would have noticed, because of the exhibition of pyro-dynamics which were rending the clouds apart to clear the sky for the Climax of the Congress.

I have never seen anything like it, and I have witnessed some extremely impressive scenes when the environment has become a living illustration of power in action. It was as though Heaven discharged every individual force secreted in it at one and the same time. The colours of the spectrum were dimmed by the strength and variety of the sounds which cannoned across the sky like a barrage, not of guns but of giant wind-instruments.

I was all but rent asunder – but that was only the beginning. At the Appearance of Maratumel, the previous colours, speed of movement and intensity of sound sank into insignificance. The colours became Angels that streaked across the sky in all their breathtaking beauty and joy of living. They were moving faster than

light, and yet I could see each one clearly – their eyes shining with excitement as they chased each other in a complex dance to the music of a heavenly choir singing paeans of praise to their beloved Lord. Suddenly He was with them – joining in their dance, but more swiftly, more effulgent, His Beauty more breathtaking than any of them. His hair and robes formed a trail like a hundred meteors behind Him as He sped among the dancers singing in response to their love and devotion.

At the exact moment when I could contain myself no longer, action and songs ceased, and colour faded to a dim replica of its previous glory. He stood towering above me about fifty feet away and gazed with His gleaming brown eyes straight into mine.

"Did you enjoy that, Nuvic?" He laughed as though enjoying a heavenly joke. I, too, began to laugh; my wonder was too much for me, and had I not laughed, I would have wept or dissolved into fragments.

"It was glorious," I said. "You have fulfilled a dream for me and given me an ideal to aim for. You have showed me Power that is not just for a purpose to calm or stimulate, but which has overwhelming beauty as well. I have tried so often to combine colour, movement and sound. I can manage two of them together, but not three. Now that You have shown me what can be done, I will continue to strive to attain my goal if it takes me a million years."

He laughed again. "One day it will happen for you, too." He was gone, but His demonstration of Supreme Power will never leave me.

– Nuvic

Nixus

[Transcribed on 23rd Sept. 1985]

I was looking after a group from Japan, and I much enjoyed the experience. We had many talks on the possibility of influencing men's minds by giving them a vision of the future. They have invited me to visit their country; I have never been so far away before, not so much in miles as in difference of culture. Their towns are as much industrialized as our own here, but I would like to see their countryside, which they showed me in miniature on a replica they had brought with them.

As a member of your original group of fairies, I had the honour of being told that Sai Baba would appear as Maratumel, but I was not allowed to tell them; so they, in fact saw Him in his incarnated form and were very happy to do so.

Midnight – the hour of magic in fairy tales – was indeed a time of incredible happenings. A moment before, I was with them, and then I lost the crowds which surrounded us and I was alone, gazing at the sky in eager anticipation. The sweetest music beguiled me; it came from far away and gradually drew nearer. I tingled all over as I always do before an important event; and I held my breath, because I wanted to be completely still and receptive to show that I was ready for anything that might be required of me.

Maratumel appeared to me as a female, robed in flower petals, her golden hair streaked with silver lights blowing about her in a gentle breeze. Her eyes were bluer than aquamarines and held in their depths the mystery of water, the sustainer of the plants I love. I found myself standing at Her feet. I put out my hand to touch them and quickly drew back; I have never caressed an exalted Shining One before, and I was not sure whether I was permitted. "I am Marata," she said, "the Goddess of Nature, Whom you have served so well from the days when you tended my blades of grass as though they were the loveliest plants in the created world. Since then, you have specialized in the simple meadow-flowers, which are just as precious to Me as the exotic orchids in the rain-forests. And for this I love you, because you have detected in them the same spark of Divinity which resides in all the species in every land on Earth and on the Higher Planes. Touch my feet; it will be a joy to feel the hands which have fondled so many of my children." I gazed up at Her smiling face in adoration and fell on my knees and gently stroked Her feet, which smelled of grass and wild flowers, combined with fresh spring water eagerly making its way to the sea.

She bent down and raised me to my feet, and caressed my hair with such tenderness and love that I wept. My tears fell on the back of my hands, and when I looked at them I saw that each bore Her image, and miraculously I still have them safe in a secret place that only I know.

– Nixus

LYSSIS

[Transcribed on 30th Aug. 1985]

The concluding, communal addresses had been delivered and we were all waiting in great expectation for Sai Baba, who had recently come into our lives.

All eyes were fixed on the sky. Although I was with a group of Russians for whom I had acted as guide during the Congress, and was surrounded by thousands of other fairies and humans, I felt completely detached from them. I knew that I was Lyssis, but that was all.

A blaze of pink light appeared in the distance. I watched intently for the form and gradually it became clearer. To my surprise, a beautiful female came into view. I knew her to be Marata, the feminine aspect of Maratumel. Her hair was of fire, her body seemingly flowing water from which Love issued as a constant stream of light. Her eyes flashed more brightly than the ceremonial jewels She was wearing, and on her breast was a circle of gold bearing the Aum symbol. I lost her as I gazed on this all-powerful form, and I repeated its sonorous sound, at first softly to myself; then, releasing Its rising notes, I followed them upwards. Many others were doing the same, I learned afterwards, and each time an Aum reached Maratumel/Marata, there was an instant response of a tiny explosion, and back to each donor came a dazzling pink beam. I felt a little prick as mine pierced by breast; my heart opened to receive this Divine benefaction; and whenever I think of it now, I can hear the resonant Aum inside me.

– Lyssis

Normus

[Transcribed on 27th Aug. 1985]

𝕬s soon as I heard that Sai Baba was to appear at the Congress, I puzzled how I could get to see him. Even if I traveled to India, He probably would not grant me an interview and there was no way that I could ask for one. Anyway, I went. I followed Him around wherever He was in all my scant spare time. I even watched Him during His brief periods of rest. I had not really expected any sign of recognition, and sadly, I did not get one.

Then you found out that He would appear as Maratumel, and again I set to work. You know that however advanced is the Shining One we manage to contact, we always hope to be allowed to serve Him or Her, but always we know that there is a Greater Being beyond referred to as the Nameless One.

I have always as long as I can remember served the Deva Marusis with diligence as well as joy, and I paid Him a visit and asked whether there was any way by which I could receive a message during the appearance.

"Can you keep a secret?" He said with His eyes twinkling.

"Well, I suppose I could, but I shall be sorely tempted to disclose it to perhaps one person or even two. We are told to share all that we have." I grinned at Him.

"You must not divulge this one because it is a secret of Maratumel's." I nearly burst with excitement.

"In that case, it will be safe, locked in the inner recesses of my mind, which even I hardly dare to open."

"I trust you," He said. "Everyone will receive a message, a gift or enlightenment."

"But two hundred thousand fairies will be present. If He comes at midnight as promised, none of them will get home to their normal duties at dawn the next day."

"It will take two minutes."

I fell over. Yes, the shock was so great that my legs gave way and I sat in front of Him with my mind in a whirl.

"He is is Maratumel." He said quietly.

I went home and brooded. I had to believe Him. A Shining One never deviates one iota from the truth, let alone tells a lie.

I had many tasks to perform at the Congress, and my mind was fully occupied all the week. When the short rest-period came each night before falling asleep from exhaustion, I always pondered over this impossible feat that Maratumel was to perform.

The other fairies in our groups had a secret too; they were allowed to say that the Avatar of the Age would close the Congress, but they were not to divulge what form He would take. As it turned out, it was just as well that we kept quiet on the subject.

We took up our positions a little before midnight. The ground, trees and air were covered or filled with fairy and discarnate human forms; the sky above being reserved for the Shining Ones and highly evolved Human Beings, who had addressed us during the Congress.

I was standing in front of my twenty groups with their individual leaders, and was slightly elevated above them. My inner time-keeper told me that midnight was almost with us . . . coming nearer . . . Wham.

The Earth exploded, I can call it nothing less. It rose to the height of a small mountain, erupting fire which streaked up into the air, then precipitated downwards as streams of brilliant pink light. The sky which had been dark with underlying clouds became more dazzling than anything I had ever witnessed before. But I would not close my eyes. I refused to lose consciousness as I have so often done before when faced with a new, spectacular phenomenon. I moved towards it slowly, purposefully, absorbing into my innermost being this wondrous radiance, about which I had dreamed so often but never experienced. It was as though I too was fire but I did not feel hot as this blaze of enthusiasm, determination and will sped towards me and entered me. I was a whirling mass of energy; I could do nothing. Nothing was beyond my power. I only had to lift a finger and the Universe would expand or contract; a million new stars would come into being at my command. All I had to do was to say one word – I knew it then but I have now alas, forgotten it. I did not want to change its form, only its inhabitants. But I realized this was beyond me. Only they could change themselves. And at that moment I knew that they would change; I would show them what they are like now, and what they could become.

I began to fall, twisting and twirling like an autumn leaf on its way to the ground. But I did not mind because I had been blessed with a vision of the future, and I knew that however far away this might be, it would happen.

– Normus

RHELIA

[Transcribed on 18th Sept.. 1985]

We have known each other a long time, and although we have had a short weekly talk, this is only the second time that we have written together.

How proud I was when you asked me to describe how a new fairy comes into being, in order to include it in your lectures. And now I am equally proud to be here to tell you about my wonderful experience at the Congress; all the other fairies are also giving you their version of the Appearance, because each was individual to that entity. What an astounding feat of Love, Will and Power, that everyone's perception of the event was so apt for his or her needs.

As you know, for many years I and two friends looked after three young fairies from their birth to the time when they were ready to make their own way in life. After that, my friends and I parted, and I became a member of Movus's group after Normus had left to train as a super-leader. At that time, its members were mainly concerned with the Nature Kingdom; but as soon as they made your acquaintance, the situation changed. Human beings – except for you, all discarnate – became part of their everyday lives; stories, ideas, aspirations were exchanged and a new world came into being under the leadership of Father John.

From the beginning, I was interested in the promotion of Fairy-Human Relations, and for some time it was my main task. Then I decided that I wanted to pass on the importance of this project to the young; so I myself returned to school as a pupil in order to learn how to express myself and convey lucidly the necessity for the power of Man and Angels to blend, in order to save the world from Man's lust and greed for Matter, which he is supposed to master but which now masters him.

What a wonder-filled day it was when I first heard of Sai Baba, and I was included among those who were told that He would appear as the Nameless One, Whom we now know as Maratumel.

Some of the others have told you about His effect on their groups, so I will take you up to the few minutes before the time promised for the Appearance, when we all waited in breathless anticipation without knowing what to expect.

To me midnight came literally on wings. Angels, birds, butterflies swooped and fluttered across the sky in endless flight, diving, soaring, then diving again in constant repetition. The angels and the butterflies darted like millions of iridescent jewels above our heads.

In the centre of this sparkling kaleidoscope of sound and movement, I saw a brilliant orange star, which expanded until it burst, revealing a figure such as I have never even dreamed. His Power almost overcame me. He was very tall and of unimaginable beauty; and as He moved, flames circled round Him – but these were no ordinary flames, being multi-coloured, flashing and radiating rays in all directions before returning to their source. He stood in majesty, the fire caressing Him with love. He held His arms above His head, and from His fingers beams of light shot across the sky, forming patterns which gyrated and twirled round one another in exquisite grace. Suddenly, they spiraled away, and the sky became dark, except for the glorious figure which now seemed to be gazing at me with deep concentration.

I was enraptured. I love this Being as I have never loved anything or anyone before. I only wanted to serve Him, know His will and obey.

"Come," He said, and I felt myself drawn towards Him. I was surrounded by thousands, but I was unaware of them. My mind was His. Again He said,

"Come," and I drifted towards Him as though in a trance. I drew nearer and nearer until I could go no further. I yearned to reach Him, but I knew that I had gone as far as I was worthy to go.

"You wish to serve Me." I smiled. " You have been doing so for years, although you did not know Whom you served. This silver cord will bind you to Me, and when you have doubts about My Will, hold it above your head and call My name, and I will answer you."

I was back with my group, and in my hands was the silver cord; my fingers could feel its power. It never leaves me day or night, but what it tells me is for me alone.

Postscript: Rhelia reports that she became a member of Movus' group after Normus had left to train as a super-leader, sometime before 1985. So Movus became the leader of the nature fairy group that worked with Daphne after Normus was given a promotion and transferred.

– Rhelia

GROUP II:
THE NATURE FAIRIES

Preface

Pellus is the leader, and he and his dua, Fina, have been together for many years. When I first met them, all the members of the group had been working with the Plant Kingdom; but they were drafted to my fairies for a special purpose, which was to travel all over the world, form groups and instill in those who came to meet them the necessity of working together in unity to help save this Planet. Pellus, with Fina's help, also organises the weekly gatherings of fairies from many countries which take place to promote this same purpose. They have two "children": Sulan, who is similar in intellect to a boy of about thirteen; and Finto, who is very much younger in awareness and can be compared to a child of approximately seven.

Five other members of the group – Festus, Nella, Silvyl, Reena and Lunine – all have a pares; they do not work together, and have their separate vocations.

When they first came, Pirilla and Julus were pares, with Horrus as a loving friend to both. Although Julus was always very pleasant when with me, I was somewhat mystified by his vibration, which I can only describe as brittle – spiky. The story of their change in relationships is related by Julus in his impression of the Appearance.

– Daphne Charters

FINA

[Transcribed on 21st Aug.. 1985]

The members of our three groups were dotted about among thousands of fairies and humans, all looking up at the sky expectantly for the promised Appearance. A small light appeared like a far-away star against a background of Cimmerian darkness; it grew until it became a glorious radiance which gradually materialized a form I did not know. He was emanating both majesty and tenderness. His hair flowed like a stream of water about His shoulders. His eyes were dark, gleaming yet gentle. He seemed to be looking directly at me. He was tremendously tall and slender, and arrayed in flames which moved constantly as though caressing His body. He was surrounded by flowers which all leaned in His direction.

I held out my arms towards Him, love pouring from me, and I could feel His Love in instant return. I opened like a flower greeting the sun; and one of those lying at His feet was gently wafted towards me and settled on my heart. It was a flower I have never seen before, pale translucent pink with five petals pulsating with life; its centre was of gold, from which a delicate perfume arose; I can still smell it when I concentrate. I gently touched it, and it disappeared inside me, where it has been ever since. I know that it is growing and will continue to do so until I am ready to return to Him and be with Him always.

– Fina

SULAN

[Transcribed on 11th Nov. 1985]

Each Congress has been the most exciting time of year for me, with so much preparation and so many unknown faces. A number of new friends, from countries overseas that I have since visited, have given me the opportunity to discover how people and fairies live and look in other parts of the world.

I always act as an usher. I am given a list each day and show delegates to their appointed places when they arrive for each event.

All were where they should be at about a quarter of an hour before midnight; and I moved about among them, as they discussed various incidents that had taken place during the day, and made sure that they were all happy, including their own guides.

I was standing at the back of my section when midnight came. I was tingling all over with excitement, not sure what to expect. Suddenly the sky was filled with dancing flames, whirling round one another and finally joining together as an enormous fire. The blaze fanned out to form an oval, and in the centre stood

Sai Baba; His orange robe seemed to be made of flickering flames, too. He stood there looking down at us all, and then He stepped out of the flashing frame and walked towards us. He picked up tongues of fire and tossed them above His head until they made a crown, which shimmered with life; and the rubies, which made a big circle in front, glowed like deep red stars. He looked wonderful – so majestic, and yet He seemed to have a twinkle in His eye as He looked at me. I could not believe that He could possibly see me where I was standing at the back of such a big crowd; but He did, because He called my name, "Sulan." I hesitated, thinking I must have imagined it. Then He said, "Come to the front; I have a gift for you." I was stunned; I could hardly move; in fact, I think He helped me, because I just found myself within about twenty feet of Him. "You have done well, first caring for your little brother, Finto, and since then at school. You have worked hard, and I am pleased with you." He waved a hand in the air and threw something at my feet. I continued to look at Him in a daze. He smiled, "Do you not want it?"

"Oh, p-p-please, y-yes." I bent forward and picked up a little green medallion with His face on one side and a fairy symbol, a beacon, in the other. I gazed first at one and then the other. When I at last looked up to thank Him, I found I was at the back of the crowd again. "Thank you," I called very faintly. But I expect He heard me.

– Sulan

FINTO

[Transcribed on 25th Sept. 1989]

𝕴 was with a group of young fairies who came with their guardians to the Congress just for the big event. I had never been to the Congress before and it was very exciting, nor have I ever seen such a crowd of fairies and people together in all my life. Several of the humans came and talked to us which was a new experience for some of the others, but of course, I have talked to you and Father John, so I pretended it was nothing special. We were told to be absolutely quiet and still as midnight drew near. I could hardly contain myself, I just felt something extraordinary was going to happen – and it did.

The sky was dark and overcast, until suddenly there was a burst of light and the clouds vanished. I felt in case a wind had blown them away but there wasn't any wind.

Then, what do you think I saw? A great big tiger was looking at me wagging his tail like an enormous cat. For a moment I was frightened, and then the tiger laughed, his eyes flashing in fun. I laughed too, and he began creeping towards me until he was sitting in front of me. He licked me all over, which made me laugh all the more because his tongue was tickling me. Then he stood up and I wanted to ride him. "Lie down," I said, and to my surprise, he did. I climbed on to his back and he began to move. There was a collar of flowers round his neck and I hung on to them as we flew into the sky, higher and higher; he twisted and turned carefully, so I didn't fall off. I was laughing all the time so was he; it was like the purring of a cat but much louder. At last the ride was over. We came back to Earth and he sat down; I slid off his back, and patted him; then he was gone, flying away into the sky. I watched him getting smaller, then her turned and gave a roar which I knew was a laugh. He waved his tail in farewell, then disappeared. Wasn't that exciting.

– Finto

PIRILLA

[Transcribed on 4th Sept. 1985]

ℐcan only describe the atmosphere before the appearance as electric. I was tingling all over, and many others had the same sensation. The members of the group that were in my charge during the Congress were Norwegians, and we spent much time discussing the problems of the world, interspersed with exchanging information about our respective countries.

I was filled with awe at what was about to occur and I wondered what He would say. We had all been amazed at His acceptance of Father John's invitation.

One minute to the hour of midnight, all eyes were gazing upwards. The clouds melted away and there He stood in His orange robe, a tiny figure in the distance to begin with; then He expanded and came gradually nearer until He stood clearly illumined against the background of the night sky.

My first thought was of His gentle grace. He was smiling and as I smiled back, I realized H was looking directly at me. His gaze never wavered; it was as though He was there for me alone. It was a wonderful feeling of intimacy and loving concern. I felt myself rising towards Him and I yearned to get close enough to Him to kiss His feet. And that was what I did. My early tingling burst through my aura in a shower of tiny sparks which lay before him. His smile widened as He picked one up, holding the tiny fragment of Eternal Life between his finger and thumb. I watched it grow in size and brightness. "Hold out your hand" He said. I did so and he bent down and placed in it a medallion with the likeness of His face on it.

"Place our problems near it and I will help you solve them," He said with a final, loving smile. Then He withdrew, or so it seemed to me at the time, but in reality it was I who slowly returned to Earth, still holding the medallion in my hand. I looked down at it, as in a dream, gazing with indescribable love, oblivious of my Norwegian friends who were gathered around me asking to see His gift.

– Pirilla

HORRUS

[Transcribed on 23rd Aug. 1985]

I have been looking after a group of delegates from Africa and I had told them that Sai Baba had agreed to make an Appearance. As midnight approached, we were all looking expectantly at the sky when suddenly a great Light burst above us. And there He was, not in his Indian incarnating body but as Maratumel: He was very tall, powerful and was carrying a blazing torch which showered scintillating beams towards us. When mine pierced my breast, I began to tremble. I held myself together with all my will and His message reached me; that I was to continue to travel round the world, spreading the news among all fairies that during the New Age which is coming Man and Fairy will co-operate to save the Planet from gradual inevitable destruction to which Man is propelling it through his greed and lust for material gain rather than cherishing its prodigality and beauty.

I held out my arms to Him and said "My heart burst with happiness when I heard your Name and now to see you in all Your Glory is beyond my highest hopes. Help me to perform the work I am doing with even more diligence than now, that I may please You and earn Your Blessing. A brilliant beam of Light left Him and enfolded me; I felt the touch of His hand on my head, and round it I could feel a circlet, which later proved to be of silver with my name engraved on it.

I did not know at the time that my group, who were all black, saw Him first as their individual ideal of the rural god, which gradually changed to the most beauteous Being they had ever seen. To some He appeared filled with authority. To others gentle and kind, but to all He emanated a Love they had never known before. When He left, they all wept, danced, sang, laughed and fell on their knees and worshipped. Him. I just stood among them motionless, stunned in wonder that such joy had come to me.

– Horrus

REENA

[Transcribed on 2nd Sept. 1985]

We were all gathered together among the groups that we were looking after during the Congress. Mine came from Sweden and I learned much about their country and have many invitations to visit individual homes.

Midnight came and there was silence. I had half expected a choir of angels to burst into song or perhaps a clap of celestial thunder to disperse the clouds above us. But there was only this wonderful silence filling me with Peace and Love – the maxim for the Congress. I continued to gaze at the sky. There was a near-blinding flash and there He was. The orange colour of His robe appeared in the centre of a pink light, and gradually material-ized until I could see His form quite clearly with his dark hair haloed about His head. We had seen many images of Him, but the reality was quite different: images can show likeness but can give you little idea of His dignity and gentle-ness with a touch of sternness – perhaps I should say authority – and above all, his overwhelming Love. I felt my heart melt, indeed my whole being dispersed and I remained poised in space, stripped of all my desires and petty failing, leaving me only with a feeling of deep gratitude that I am a member of such a wonderful group. All that remained of Reena was the heart which had now expanded to replace my body. I ached with love for Sai Baba, the world and all its inhabitants; and then once more the heart began to melt, but this time I could feel a force leaving it and I could see it spreading all over those standing

around my now rematerialized Reena-form. My right had suddenly felt cold and when I looked at it, there was a heart-shaped garnet – a stone I had always loved. Tenderly I pressed it against my breast and there it has remained until this day – an everlasting reminder of an unforgettable Event.

– Reena

SILVYL

[Transcribed on 9th Sept. 1985]

I always help my leader Pellus with the weekly gathering by looking after some of the visiting fairies from abroad and also entertaining them.

Of course, the Congress is a very different matter, and its preparation was to a great extent, in the hands of those who are used to managing large crowds. But still I had a part to play as a courier between the organizers and the various fairies in our three groups. In this way, their normal work was interfered with as little as possible.

I was also allotted eighteen delegates from Canada and I have since been invited to help them to arrange a miniature Congress in their country.

Sai Baba was a tremendous attraction. They had not heard of Him and could not understand how the Avatar of the Age had received as far as they knew, so little attention. I told them that He has in fact millions of devotees in all parts of the world but that it was part of His Plan to gain an even larger following in His own Land first.

I knew what He looked like from your many books and photographs, which all of us have studied with care and love and I had imagined Him walking amongst us as He does with His devotees at Puttaparthi. But I realized when we were advised to look upwards that it was going to be a very exciting Appearance.

As midnight was drawing near, silence reigned, and by concentrating, I saw an orange light far, far away; as it drew nearer, It became a single beam, which divided into hundreds of rays, and formed intricate patterns all over the sky. These suddenly parted to reveal him in his orange robe gradually moving towards us. As he came nearer, His features became quite clear, and his very special hair seemed to gleam like a dark halo round His head.

His eyes were the most remarkable feature in His truly remarkable face; they kept changing completely according to whether He was looking holy or whether He was smiling.

He stopped and held His arms towards us all. I could not prevent myself from rising from my allotted place and moving towards him. "Sai Baba", I called softly, and he heard me. Among all those thousands, He heard me although I spoke little above a whisper. "Well Silvyl," He said. "how is your tree growing?" I nearly fainted. Do you remember how years ago, I told you that I had a tree inside me? I threw up my arms and revealed it with its leaves shimmering in the pink and silver light emanating from Him. "Well done," he said. "I remember when it was a tiny sapling." I saw something floating towards me – a beautiful deep red flower. "It is time the tree bloomed." He said. "Next year I shall hope to see that this one flower has become two." I held out my hand which tingled as I caught it, and placed in on the top-most branch, where it is still of course, the tree is inside me again now, and only I can see it except when I choose to reveal it.

– Silvyl

NELLA

[Transcribed on 25th Aug. 1985]

Throughout the Congress I was with delegates from India, so you imagine the excitement when I told that Sai Baba had consented to close the proceedings with an Appearance. Many of their "hosts" with whom they lived in India were Sai Baba's devotees and many had seen His portraits and examined the vibuthi (holy ash materialized by Sai Baba).

Midnight. A burst of music strange to my ears filled the sky; but my delegates knew all about Bahjans (sacred Indian songs) and joined in, joy now being added to their anticipation.

The music stopped and Sai Baba came into view walking across the sky in His orange robe. He looked straight at us and then his form altered – my Indian friends told me afterwards that He became their beloved Krishna. For me He changed again and became That which I now know is Maratumel. I was stunned by his beauty; His dark hair enveloping Him like a cloak. He smiled directly at me, not only with His lips; His eyes – His whole being appeared to be smiling. I smiled back and He seemed to touch my cheek. Could He have done so? I keep asking myself. Sometimes I am sure that He did; at others I fear I must have been mistaken; but whenever this happens I am sure that I can feel His gentle hand again, and I smile as though I were a little child, rejoicing in a mother's caress.

Still looking at me, He spread out His fingers towards me, and from them emerged dancing ribbons of light, which rippled and twisted as they descended towards me. One of them detached itself from the others and became a silver necklace which poised in space on a level with my face. Hanging from the necklace was a pendent like a spider's web covered with dew. I love spiders and often watch them as they run up and down their intricate works of art exuding silken threads with which they fashion webs in their own inimitable way. I stretched out my hand, wondering whether it really was a gift for me and also whether it would break if I touched it.

"Take it, wear it," he said, "and use it as an aid to meditation. The threads will lead you ever nearer to the centre of your being". I am wearing it now; it never leaves me and never will.

– Nella

JULUS

[Transcribed on 13th Sept. 1985]

This Congress stood above all the others like a mountain towers above a valley. At the time the others had seemed wonderful, in fact we always agreed afterwards that the last one had been the best.

More people and fairies came this year than ever before, and much emphasis was placed on the importance of the Human - Fairy relationships we all enjoy throughout the year, culminating in this gathering, when many of both lines of evolution are brought together for the purpose of strengthening bonds and spreading the importance of ever-increasing numbers working together.

For a good many years, I played a very minor part in the proceedings because as you know, I "fell by the wayside" and only through the combined help of many, and particularly my previous paris, Pirilla and our great friend, Horrus, was I ever hauled out of the quagmire to lead a normal life again.

I lost Pirilla as my paris, and now she and Horrus are together, with me as an ever-welcome third in their home, I have found no replacement for Pirilla, doubtless because I am not ready to enjoy the delights and also accept the responsibilities of a full male - female relationship, but I am happy as I am.

For the last six years, I have looked after small groups of delegates from minor countries at the Congress, but this time I was asked if I would like to act as guide to some Spanish fairies. With your frequent holidays in Spain, some of us have travelled there also, and spoken to many of the Human – Fairy Relationships that we all enjoy. Some content with their own small world, but others became interested and came to our weekly gatherings. Some of these lost interest, mainly because they were too immature to feel the power we generated, but always there were a number who came regularly and these were invited to the yearly Congress.

I had a group of ten, all old friends, and I was of course very proud to be able to tell them of the honour that had been granted to us by the promise of the Appearance of Sai Baba.

All was quiet as midnight approached and I became apprehensive because we had been told that Sai Baba knows everything about every living being. I tried to calm myself by the realization that many present must have had their failures, and anyhow, how could He possibly notice me among the 200,000 gathered to see Him.

Most of the guides stood at the head of their groups, but when I had made sure that my ten were in their correct place, I retired to the back, while they were occupied gazing at the sky, which I had told them to do.

I too looked upwards. The sky was dark with clouds hiding whatever was behind them, but they suddenly parted to the sounds of Nature blended together in perfect harmony; the tinkling notes emanated by streams and, and the louder more staccato tones of waterfalls joined the sonorous roar of mountains singing together. Bird-song interpenetrated the melody and a sighing breeze rustled the trees.

Then I saw Him, dressed in His orange robe. He was far away and looked like a miniature of Himself. He came nearer, accompanied by ever-increasing sound, which kept in time with his footsteps, as though it was they which were making it, and perhaps they were, because when He stopped, there was absolute silence. And yet this silence was electric as a great surge of energy rayed out to all at the Congress.

When it engulfed me, It was like a shock, a jolt, and in a flash, I saw my past; my lazy stupidity which turned into a torpor because I was not generating enough power to keep myself on the etheric plane. I began to sink like a dead leaf falling from a tree in autumn, but I was not dropping through air but mud. I could not breathe: I tried to flail my arms but they scarcely moved. I knew that I was dying as Pirilla and Horrus called to me. I managed to gasp "Help. Save me. I repeat, Help, Hel… He…" Each cry was fainter and the next would have been my last but I began to rise. It was as though an all-powerful hand plunged into the swamp and plucked me from the tightening grip that was dragging me down .. to Oblivion … Very slowly I became myself again.

"I heard your cry Julus. You are now repaying your debt to Me. Continue to improve and much happiness will be yours." I felt something cold in my hand and when I looked, I saw a little pendant on a chain. On one side was the face of Sai Baba, and on the other, a hand reaching downwards. Not only had I seen Sai Baba but my unknown Saviour.

– Julus

LUNINE

The Day. I still cannot believe that it happened. All our expectations were high, but not one of us anticipated anything like what actually took place – a different experience for each one of us, and also for the delegates either separately or for individual groups.

The Hour. The last discourse was over and we had a short time for either discussion, or relaxation to prepare ourselves for the Appearance. I was with my group, who were from Italy, a land of opera, the sun, and buildings of great beauty. The delegates combined gaiety with gravity, and we enjoyed each others company, but as midnight approached, we parted.

The Moment. We were all quiet for the final five minutes, preparing ourselves by cleansing our bodies and minds of anything not connected with the great Happening that was about to occur. To me, it was announced by a single note, higher, more pervading than I had ever previously experienced. It came from far away, but gradually it drew nearer and merged with me. My whole being sang with joy, and my mantric note chanted in unison to produce another and then another until we became an orchestra, not playing familiar music, but creating combinations of sound so exquisite that my whole being melted in ecstasy. I was <u>Music</u>, and as that Music, I would have been in rapture for ever. But another infiltrated my perfect harmony – a note that commanded attention. I, Lunine, extracted myself from the enchantment of Sound; I retrieved my vision and what I saw filled me with wonder. The sky was a blaze of Light, all shades of pink suffused with gold and silver; the sound of a thousand angels pervaded the air; the perfume of heavenly flowers permeated my being; electric currents from outer space chased each other, whirled into a thousand shapes, escaped from their enclosures to move at lightning speed and form others. The sky became a kaleidoscope with perpetual motion; yet there was no sense of chaos; all was controlled to the last atom that was taking part.

Then from the centre emerged Maratumel. All movement ceased, because the will activating it was now transferred to us – and me. His form kept changing from male to female, from Man to Archangel, from Archangel to a vision of the world as it is, and as it should be. He was a bird, a breeze, an elephant, a bee. A million flowers cascaded among us; mine floated towards me with the sound of that note which had blended with me from out of the sky. Although I can no longer see the flower, the note is with me every moment of every day.

– Lunine

PELLUS

[Transcribed on 25th August, 1985]

𝕵, as a member of the Organising Group, was in the centre of a large contingent of delegates. The Congress had been much the most successful that we had ever held, and I was relieved that everything had gone according to plan. So many fairies and people had worked hard over many months to ensure that everybody was happy, well looked-after, and in their proper place at the right time.

We were tremendously gratified when Father John told us that Sai Baba had accepted his invitation to attend the closing ceremony and great expectation was in all our hearts, although none of us had any certainty of what would actually happen.

The clouds parted and there He was, resplendent in His God-form of Maratumel. I gasped at His beauty, majesty, resplendence and incredible height. He looked down on us with a wonderful smile, and as He held His arms towards us, a myriad of beams poured from them and entered us. I could see one coming directly at me and I moved towards it. In spite of its speed, I felt only the gentlest touch as it entered my heart. I felt it pulsate, becoming gradually faster until I could scarcely breathe. I then took flight, soaring towards Him, eager to touch the hem of His garment, but I sped higher until I could see the expression in His eyes which were shining like stars. Infinite wisdom and divine love encircled me until my sole desire was to relinquish my life, my work and determination to bring my group to the height of their present talents, if I could but remain in His presence and be His slave, performing any menial task He cared to give me.

"I have more for you to do than to serve me as a slave. Your work will grow until it spreads to every corner of the Planet. Many are here tonight; but millions are in ignorance, and need the call that will quicken their resolve and give them the will to follow the Path of Renunciation and service which I offer. I will be with you wherever you go; each of your thoughts will be a replica of a thought of mine. You cannot and will not fail."

– Pellus

GROUP III
THE HOUSE FAIRIES

Preface by Daphne Charters

It was some time after I had met the garden fairies that I began to wonder whether there were Indoor Fairies as well as those working with the Nature Kingdom. Father John told me that this was so, and he helped me to make contact with the three who were living in the flat occupied by my mother and myself. Maire (pronounced Maira), her duo Mairus and a male called Herus, who had been on Earth for forty mostly unhappy years, and a difficult character to say the least.

There were two pares, Pino and Sheena in the flat above us and two young boys called Fello and Serrus on the third floor.

The leader is Maire and apart from giving power with the others to the contents of the flat, she was engaged in the making of what are known as Thought Formations. She and Mairus would collect thoughts from the atmosphere and add some of their own, which they would then weld together to make a kind of living projection containing specific powers to help people in distress. I have written many times with Maire about her visits to the Higher Realms and many aspects of her work. [There are 12 stories by Maire in the *Collected Manuscripts*. MP]

Maire and Mairus were very patient with Herus and his tantrums and eventually he succumbed to their constant kindness and showed a remarkable talent in the making of the Thought-Formations.

Later Pino and Sheena began to work for Maire and her various projects but they were too modest to accept her invitation to find thoughts for use for the Formations; but eventually she overcame their lack of confidence and they are now full members of the Group and its activities.

The third floor flat was occupied by a young woman who re-married and went to live on the opposite side of the road. The two boy-fairies decided to go with her because she had a pretty little daughter of whom they were very fond.

They were replaced by a couple, whose present descent into matter had taken them to China. These were the dua/duo Perima and Sulic. Perima was very advanced in the knowledge of the Higher Realms and has also taken part with the over-leader Tepi in a prolonged battle between Good and Evil in the Underworld. She is also an expert in the art of creating Thought Formations. …

MAIRE

(Part of original manuscript missing) … cross, the Aum, Fire, the Wheel, and the Star and Crescent appeared above H is head, each glowing with Power and with the purport of moving the hearts of all present.

Each one lit a light inside me, unleashing a greater devotion, inspiring me to right wrongs, help man to see the Light which is there for all to see if they will but change; forsake the desire for worldly success, the craving for admiration, the greed for wealth, and reject the present false god, Money, for fulfilment gained through service to those around them, and with an increasing desire to spend their energy for the good of all.

Two hands came out of the sky and gently picked me up. I felt myself being lifted above the Congress until I stood just below the level of His face. I nearly fainted at Its beauty; His glowing eyes gazed at me with such tenderness that I feared I must melt and lose this priceless Vision. He smiled and said, "You have worked for many years with diligence and love. I offer you more work, more knowledge and a greater Love than you have ever known. Are you willing to serve me?"

Tears of joy filled my eyes. I could not reply with my mind, but I opened my heart to Him. I lost my Maire form and became pure being. I knew nothing but all pervading Love until gradually I felt myself sinking until I was standing at the head of my group once more.

All around us were excited delegates laughing and crying with joy as they showed their gifts to each other, except for my group which was silent, gazing at one another with wonder in their eyes. We could not speak; the Love which cannot be described had touched us all. We silently dispersed to find a quiet corner where we could relax alone and try to recapture that precious moment of unforgettable rapture that had been the experience of every one of us.

– Maire

MAIRUS

I was looking after a group of Chinese delegates. Because of Perima and Sulic's connection with China, we have always had a strong contingent from that country for both the weekly Gatherings and annual Congress. Many of the Chinese fairies by whom they had been spurned, were helped by them throughout the Revolution and became firm friends through gratitude.

Sulic and I, although very different in character have always been pals, and so I was allocated the task of greeting the delegates and staying with them in their quarters. They had particularly requested that everything with which they come in contact should be as English as possible as a new experience. We therefore made a large country house for them, furnished with pictures of the aristocracy of many generations. The furniture was copied from the finest pieces that we could find in a Stately Home, and the dining table was laid with heirloom silver and china.

I could hardly drag them away from all these treasures for the first discourse, but once at the Congress with its own decorations and power, they were at once absorbed, and returned to the house only for periods of rest and recreation.

By the time the Congress was coming to its close, they could not believe that the power could be more potent than that they had already experienced, or that any further event could surprise them. But they were wrong.

The Appearance was heralded by the sound of a huge Chinese Temple gong, which became increasingly loud until we were all vibrating with the sound. This was followed by a display of fireworks such as I had never seen before. Flowers, birds, butterflies streamed upwards then cascaded towards us, to rise again as though in an exquisite dance. They disappeared and a single point of Light took their place, and from it, multicoloured rays fanned out to form a semi-circle. First the head of a Chinese sage appeared; this they recognised as Confucius, grave, saintly, calm and dignified. It changed into a blood-stained youth, representing the Revolution, shouting abuse, his gun firing in all directions. Then He appeared as an enormous pink Light. "I am Maratumel," He said "You are straying my children, from the code of conduct laid down for you. Return to Me. The gifts of the Spirit are more valuable than the humans' material wealth with which, you, as their attendants, come into conduct." His form changed into a large lotus flower from which fell sixteen petals, one of which fell at the feet of each delegate. "Count the petals every day; their number will grow for each good deed you perform with no thoughts of reward." I looked up at Him sadly because there was no petal for me. Then a cream and pink rose, whose name I knew was "Peace", floated towards me and settled on my heart. I placed my hand over it tenderly. Although it looks and feels like a rose, it is in reality made from the thoughts of Maratumel and is everlasting; it is now and always will be my most precious possession.

– Mairus

PINO

[Transcribed on 1st Sept. 1985]

We were all in our appointed place at five minutes before midnight. That in itself was a near-miracle because after the last discourse, we had been milling around, endeavouring to collect our groups together so that all would be in the right place, according to precedence. The rostrum was the sky and we all gazed upwards anticipating what? I expect we all had ideas on what we should see; and what we thought actually happened.

I was literally on tip-toe with excitement. I longed to dance and sing, but of course the occasion was far too important for such a demonstration.

"Look." A concerted cry came from all around me, and there He was, just as I had imagined Him from His photographs. He was dressed in a bright orange robe and His hair stood out round His head and glowed like a dark halo. He was very beautiful and His Light gradually spread over the whole vast gathering.

To my amazement, He seemed to be looking at me. I bowed, then felt this was not adequate acknowledgement for such an honour, so I sank to my knees as did many of those around me. I felt very drawn to Him, but I could not move. I was transfixed with love for this wonder of the age. He said, "Some years ago, you were a valued servant of your leader and those involved in the important act of creating Thought Formations for those afflicted and in distress. By your own diligence and tender care for those for whom you worked, you showed humility and love, never aspiring to that which at that time was beyond your capacity. Almost against your will, you were persuaded to join in this work by travelling away from the precincts of your home to seek thoughts on special subjects to incorporate into the Formations. Your searching proved successful and by degrees, you learned the technique of placing the thoughts in their proper positions and welding them to the others in the Formation to enhance the whole. Now you are a full member of the group, respected by all for your justly earned status. You have done well, and as a Token of my Love for you, I bequeath this gift."

I felt something cold hanging round my neck and when I looked down, I saw a medallion with Sai Baba on one side and on the other, a face I did not recognise, but know now is that of Maratumel. Every time I look at them, they shine with more Light until last time, they almost hurt my eyes with their brilliance. What a wonderful present especially for me.

– Pino

SHEENA

[Transcribed on 8th Sept. 1985]

I felt very honoured to be given a group of delegates from the Middle East, both Arab and Israelis. They all lived in luxurious surroundings, and I had the task of planning suitable accommodation for them. I realized that I could not compete with their magnificent palaces containing beautiful rugs and furniture, so I decided to make them a bower of flowers. It was very comfortable, but it was composed solely of products from the Kingdom of Nature. Instead of carpets, there was rich green grass, and trellises up which roses and other plants climbed in profusion took the place of walls; the reclining areas were as soft as the petals of flowers and the lighting was a reflection of moon-power. They were enchanted, most of them having come from the desert countries had never seen anything with which to compare their temporary home, so I was gratified that my idea gained their approval.

They had listened attentively to all the speeches and many were the discussions between Israelis and those from the Arab States; and all endeavored to think of a possible solution to unite the two opposing forces perhaps through some magic formula through which contrary views could be brought into equilibrium.

I told them about the intended Appearance of Sai Baba, the Avatar of the age and they were thrilled that He was coming to close the Congress. His name was familiar through a lecture which some of them had heard in the house where they lived, but they knew nothing else about Him. I was of course with them when midnight approached. As they received my whole attention during the previous days, I felt that I could give all my thoughts to the wonderful experience which I felt sure was awaiting us all.

I heard a chanting sound. I did not understand it, but I knew it was a summons to prayer. I repeated "Sai Baba, please hear me. I want to serve You. I have been a servant to those I love and now I would like to serve You if You consider me worthy."

I had been so intent on my prayers, which I was saying with closed eyes, that I had not realized until that moment that the sky was flooded with pink light. It was both breathtakingly beautiful and potent. I was filled with love first for my dearest Pino, for the others in our group and also for the delegates which whom I had become such friends. I was obsessed with this love which was something I had never before experienced. It was not that of one individual for another, but all-pervading. It included the earth, the air, the sky, rivers, glens, forests, deserts, mountains, open spaces and tiny restricted gardens, the sun, wind, the moon and all the planets in the Universe. I felt enormous and unamazed at this astounding Love.

Then He spoke. "Your heart has encompassed the world. What about me?"

I had been so immersed in this all-engrossing love that my vision had left me. At that moment, it returned and I saw Him in His orange robe, with His dark hair like streaks of black light against the dazzling sky. His look was for me alone, full of Love, tenderness, gentleness, and urging me to understand what He required of me.

"I love you," I said. "What do You want from me for all I have is yours."

"You have this moment bestowed on Me what I desire. Thank you for your gift. Be at peace and know that I love you too." I felt something cool against my heart, and when I looked to see the cause, I found a pink pearl, which I pressed to my lips before He faded from view. But the pearl, His gift of Love is with me now and for ever.

– Sheena

HERUS

[Transcribed on 30th Aug. 1985]

Do you remember, Daphne, many years ago when we first met over the coke water-heater in the kitchen and how I prevented you and your neighbour who lived upstairs from lighting it? That gave me the basic knowledge of how to manipulate fire and took me step by step into the realm of this exciting Element.

This may seem a strange opening for my description of the appearance, but there is a connection.

313

I had spent the Congress looking after a group of Indians, most of whom knew about Sai Baba. I was happy to be in their company; we seemed to understand one another; I introduced them to the art of Thought-Formation construction and they helped me to understand their many god-forms.

Naturally we were together when midnight struck – and strike it did. To me it sounded like the repetition of a single note – a sound I have always connected with a summons. (The Indians told me later that they had heard it as a temple bell, others as Bhajans, their sacred songs, or as a call to prayer.)

I immediately gained my fully-alert consciousness and became aware of unusual events. I felt as though a door was opening in my mind; my body lost the continuity of its frame and I became free from its restriction. I found myself leaving the group and rising to a higher level. And there I saw Him; and our precious secret until that moment – that He would appear as Maratumel, the Resplendent One, was now revealed; the unseen Watcher of our every movement; the Listener to every breath that we inhaled or exhaled.

Although He was far away, I knew that He was the Lord of Fire. He was a conflagration such as I had never seen before, even though I have witnessed forest fires, volcanic eruptions and explosions of nuclear bombs. But, unlike these, I knew that He was not destructive. He was the Force that made the planets and all the stars in the Universe. He emanated Divine Power at its most primitive and at the same time, at its most advanced. As He drew nearer I saw his eyes like twin suns shining for me alone. Tongues of flames streamed from His solar plexus and descended on one delegate here, another there, each a selected recipient of the Paracletal gift from beyond the realms of Mind. I saw one which I knew was mine, coming towards me; it enfolded me in an ecstatic embrace for a treasured moment of heavenly bliss. "You have done well, Fellimo; I declare you my Initiate son. Touch all whom you meet with flames of action so that, like you, they will strive to bring to bring to others a burning desire to cleanse the World of greed, cruelty, the craving for material wealth, and replace them with the warmth of a caring heart with its power of Love, the only Force which can and will change the World and give the Human race the knowledge that each one of them is brother or sister to all the others, under the guidance of the One and only Father of all manifestation."

I held out my arms towards Him and said, "My heart burst with joy when I heard your Name, and to see You as I do now was beyond my most fervent hopes. Help me to perform the work I am doing with even more diligence than now that I may please You and earn Your blessing." A dazzling beam of Light left Him and encircled me, and I felt the touch of His hand on my head. I could feel something round it which later I found was a band of silver with my name and status "Fellimo Herus" engraved" upon it.

– *Herus*

PERIMA

[Transcribed on 1st Sept. 1985]

As soon as I knew that Maratumel was to make an Appearance at the Congress, Sulic and I began to meditate on His Name. We received many indications in regard to His Identity but no positive facts; I realized that we were not meant to know – the time was not now.

I was with a large group of delegates from the Arabian States. We had participated in many discussions on the futility of war and how to help combat it. They were also fascinated by our Thought-Formation work and I agreed to visit them and initiate them into its intricacies.

Sai Baba has many Muslim devotees and so some of them had heard of Him

and a few had seen His photograph in the houses where they live.

At midnight we were all assembled in our allotted positions, waiting for the great Event.

I began to tingle all over as I became aware of a point of Light in the far distance, which normally heralds the presence of a Shining One. It was so faint that it was only just discernible to my "extra" vision. I waited for the blaze of Light which I was expecting, but it remained stationery; I called His name, but He made no response. I thought of the disappointment of all those present, because not many enjoy the "extra" vision with which I am blessed.

"Cease doubting," I said to myself, "always you have to seek the Shining Ones after the first intimation of Their Presence."

I repeated mentally, "Maratumel, I implore You to show me the way that I may reach You in order to offer my services for whatever cause You desire to give me."

A beam of pink Light shot through the darkness and enveloped my feet. Immediately I felt being drawn along it. I continued to repeat "Maratumel" as I ascended skywards. Darkness surrounded me. I forgot the Congress and the thousands of fairies and discarnate humans below. I was alone in Space, with Maratumel still far away in the distance. Journeys towards a Shining One often take weeks of concerted striving, but although it seemed as though I was travelling for a long time, in reality it could have been but a few seconds.

The colour of the path kept changing, telling me that Maratumel was not Lord of a single Force, but many. The point of Light began to move towards me and I continued to travel in His direction. I began to feel His Power which became like a stream of cleansing water; my sins, horror, fears and failures, disappointments and despair from the past were all flowing away from me to be absorbed by outer Space. I felt light. I was the Light. Expectation and joy enfolded me as I moved steadily towards Him. At no time did I see His form. I was Perima Ascendant, and then I became Him and His Love, ever emanating, ever replenishing Itself from the Beyond which I now yearned to reach.

What could be beyond my present indescribable Bliss? "Onwards, ever onwards," I commanded myself. "I must know what is Beyond-Knowing.

"Enter if you dare." I knew that I stood on the brink of Eternity. I was being offered dispensation and everlasting Bliss. I had to but make one infinitesimal movement forward and then It would all be mine. I paused, and in that fateful moment, I thought of Sulic, my beloved part-self, with whom I have lived, from whom I have been parted and been reunited down the ages; Tepi, my more recent companion with whom I experienced a grim but successful contest between Good and Evil over a period of many years; Herus, my fellow Fire-Initiate, and all the members of the three groups with whom I now live and work. I love them all and am loved by them in return. This is the love only knowable by an individual, and this love would be lost for ever; and for this I was not yet prepared.

I became Perima again. I stepped back and joyfully began my journey Earthwards. Often, the brightness of a jewel that one holds in one's hands is dimmed by the lure of the greater Splendour Beyond. It will still lure me, but at the present stage of my evolution, the jewel that I hold is too precious to place on the altar of Liberation.

– Perima

SULIC

[Transcribed on 26th Aug. 1985]

I was standing with my beloved Perima with a large group of European delegates. Perima and I had spent all our spare time, which was little and infrequent during the Congress, singing and intoning both the name of Sai Baba and also that of Maratumel. Sometimes I would sing one name and she the other, or we would intone one of them together. We had received instantaneous results. We can, of course, differentiate between the powers of the Deva Kingdom and of Man and also see them. As you know, fairy power is like a million pin-points of multicoloured lights which scintillate, whereas the purest Man - power is steady and white. That of Sai Baba, because, He is incarnating in a human body and emanates Love, is pink. Not only did the two powers answer our repetition of the Names but they combined, weaving beautiful patterns which delighted our eyes. They also formed symbols which gave us a new insight into the future.

Midnight drew near; the air was hyper-active with expectation as well it should be.

Heavenly music from a great choir of angels pervaded the scene with songs of praise. The sound swept over us giving us a feeling of near saturation before Maratumel had even appeared. Then quite suddenly He/She was there, neither male nor female but androgynous, taking any form at will. Her hair fell in a golden cascade about Her shoulders; Her eyes held the wisdom of eternity, and yet were filled with gentleness. Her body was swathed in floating gossamer which swirled around Her with a dream-like, rhythmical motion. She wore a diadem of stars and jewels composed of gems I had never seen, each radiating all the colours of the different planes as well as that of its own nature.

I was entranced. I do not think I inhaled or exhaled during Her entire Appearance.

Her form faded and the patron saint of each of the delegates manifested, and finally Jesus, first as He was at the beginning of his ministry, then on the cross and finally in Glory as He is now. He began to speak. "Many of the countries of Europe have joined together as economic partners. This is good but it is not good enough. All of mankind are brothers and sisters. No country should be poverty-stricken because its resources are less, its technology not so far advanced as those who are better educated and thus more efficient at attaining higher living standards. All must come together in love and understanding, and leaders of the nations should be an example to the rest of the world. Success for one country should not be achieved through overcoming another either in battle or commerce. Greed, ambition and oppression must all be cast aside and all the countries become one in reality not just in name. Endeavour to pass on this truth to the humans among whom you work, wherever you may live." The message faded and I began to receive my own. "You and Perima have loved one another for many centuries and you have experienced great joy, but also separation and sorrow." This was not Jesus talking to me but Maratumel. He was tremendously tall and slender and I gazed at Him with adoration equal to that I had experienced for His female form, and I knelt before Him with my head bowed to the ground. "All of you in your group share great joy in mutual love. Let a continual exchange of power flow between us and your work will grow and attain success such as you have never dreamed."

He held His arms towards me and from them there flew a pale pink bird. As it drew nearer, I could see that it held in its beak a golden chain. I stretched one of my hands towards it; the bird settled for a moment on my wrist, released the gift and flew away. I gazed at a jade medallion attached to the chain and saw the face of Perima in its centre. Then as I held it closer, it changed to that of Maratumel. What a wonderful gift for one who is still only striving and frequently failing on the hazardous Path of Evolution, to have always close to my heart the image of the two great loves of my life, my dua, Perima and He/She we served without a name, but Whose name we now know.

– Sulic

TEPI

[Transcribed on 21st Sept. 1985]

𝕴 lost contact with my beloved Perima and my good friend Sulic when they came to Earth. I had no desire to do the same. For a long time my life had been a succession of errors. Which had to be rectified by journeys of almost indescribable horror to the Underworld, accompanied by Perima and Augustine, a wonderful human being. This was followed by a number of successful and joy-filled years when together we explored the higher realms and studied spiritual teachings and delved ever deeper into the Ancient Wisdom with elation and amazement. It was all there. Why had I not involved myself with it years ago? Perhaps the time had not been ripe.

I became a teacher, a leader and then an over-leader with several groups in my charge; then I was ready to come to Earth.

By this time Perima and Sulic had left China and were living with you. I saw a great deal of them and was often invited by them and the other fairies to join in special events that they were celebrating. I longed to work with Perima and the House-Fairies with their composition of Thought-Formations, for which I had a special talent even when I was low in spirits at the beginning of my road back to redemption, and now I wanted to use this faculty on the world-wide projects in which you and they were involved. But no call came. I asked Augustine if there was any chance of my joining them, he shook his head sadly, and said that it was not within his jurisdiction to say "Yes" or "No". I therefore continued working with my own groups, but I did not lose hope.

For some years I had taken part in each annual Congress, and had been transported to realms above my normal consciousness by the great down-pouring of Power. Then in 1985 I was invited to act as a guide to some of the delegates. I was thrilled and felt certain that a new world was about to open for me.

I was told about the coming Appearance of Sai Baba, and I prepared myself with special care for the great event by cleansing my mind of both doubts and hopes, and when midnight approached I felt calm and detached from the vast crowd of discarnate humans and fairies which surrounded me.

At midnight all my carefully prepared serenity left me. I became a channel for an electric current, a veritable lightning-conductor. I could scarcely breathe, and felt that I might detonate into a thousand pieces. Then, from the distance, exquisite music reached me and assuaged my over-active atoms. It grew into a tremendous volume of sound – not at all like thunder's roar but like a musical cascade to purge the world of sin.

Then what we were all waiting for happened. There He was in His orange robe and halo of black hair, but much more beautiful than any of your photographs of Him. I was filled with instant love for Him; it took total charge of me and nothing else mattered. I bowed before Him to the ground and held my arms towards Him with a heart-felt plea to permit me to serve Him with the talents I had striven for so many years to develop for a purpose which had remained unknown, in spite of my every endeavour to extricate it from my other desires and dreams.

He walked straight towards me. I could not believe my eyes. Surely He must be about to contact someone behind me; but He stopped right in front of me. "This is the hour, Tepi," He said, "the hour for which you have longed for many years. You have worked with great diligence to achieve the peak of excellence which was your goal, and now you have reached it. We need each other; you need Me to love, and I need you to work for Me in my task of halting Mankind in his fall from Grace by denying the Code of Conduct, which you have studied for many years and by which you have also lived. My decision is not that for which you have been praying for so long." I felt my heart stand still with sadness. "I want you to travel the world spreading the Ancient Wisdom combined with My own Teachings which are simply phrased, and can be understood by the lowly as well as those who are reaching for the stars." I gasped in astonishment. "You will form groups wherever you go, and they will impart this priceless Truth to those who live around them. You will be the switch for the electric current which is Me, and thousands of bulbs will shine forth to illumine for others the Path of Redemption which you yourself have trod." He raised His hand above His head and a dazzling stream of Light enveloped me, and for a brief moment of heavenly Bliss, I became It . . . . . and then I knew no more.

– Tepi

FESTUS

[Transcribed on 13th July 1989]

Oh Daphne, what joy was mine when I was told that you realized I had been left out of the excitement of giving you my impression of the Appearance at the Fairy Congress of 1985. I was disappointed, I confess, but we often wonder, as you cannot see, feel or hear with your ears, how you can tell which one of us is with you. Please do not worry about it any more; after all, if I had given my description to you then, I would not be with you now!

I was looking after delegates from Brazil and we enjoyed every moment of being together. Except during official events of the Congress and when we were sleeping, I do not think we ever stopped talking, telling each other of our hopes for a better world and how it could be achieved.

We were together too as we waited for the final Act, as we had been throughout the Congress. I knew Maratumel/Sai Baba was to appear and I had relayed this news to them. Naturally they were very excited and we exchanged dozens of idea as to what he would look like and what He would wear and do. As it turned out, we were all right and He appeared to each of us as we had imagined Him, but everything, colour, sound and movement were all augmented a hundred fold. We had never seen anything like it before.

As midnight drew near, we scarcely breathed in our anticipation and desire to give all our thoughts and love to Him we had known as the Nameless One and for Whom we had worked for many years.

There was complete silence as 200,000 fairies and many discarnate humans waited for what proved to the most exciting, wonderful, awe-inspiring event of our lives.

The silence was broken for me by a single note from far away, which gradually came nearer, and on its journey produced an increasing number of varying tones all harmonizing with one another. The sound enfolded me. I lost my group; my senses were dimmed; I could not see, feel or register anything but this extraordinary, beguiling sound which was no longer separate because I became it. It was I who was forming the glorious music. My core vibrated in adoration and emitted a sequence of notes which blended together to herald the appearance of our beloved Lord. The sound gradually diminished and I changed back to myself again. Colour then enveloped me and I became all the hues of the many planes, separate and together, each one producing a different inner experience. The sound returned, but this time it was outside me; the colour withdrew from my being and lit up the sky as millions of stars moving in a joyous dance; at times they came closer and the power almost overwhelmed me.

By this time I was in a state of near ecstasy. Then in the centre of colour, sound and dance, He appeared first as Sai Baba in the long, orange robe He usually wears and His black halo of hair beaming multicoloured lights around His head. Then He changed to Maratumel, an enormous figure which dominated Earth and Sky with His Splendour. He was Light, brighter then the sun, softer than the moon, His glittering robe was studded with all the jewels I know and others I had never seen before. Then Sai Baba re-appeared and they stood side by side emitting a steady flow of pink Light surrounding all with Their Celestial Love. I felt myself compelled to move through this Light until I stood quite close to Them. A beam transfixed my heart and I knew that, in reality, I was part of Them. My love for Them almost dissolved me, but I held Myself together with my will. Then seemingly coming from both of them simultaneously, I heard, "You have unknowingly loved and worked for Me for many years and will continue to do so, increasing in knowledge and stature until you are worthy to share My Being. Take this rod; when you hold it in your left hand above your head, it will obey you – not yet, but as you continue to evolve and grow and Love and Wisdom rule you, so you will rule not only yourself but others who are also travelling along the path of Redemption." As I held out my hand the rod moved swiftly towards it and when I grasped it, I could feel its power in my whole being; and I knew that I had been given a treasure beyond my most exalted aspiration.

And so it proved itself to be. At first I was not very successful when I held the rod above my head, but then I conjured up the power I had felt when it first reached me. Gradually this force ceased to be a memory but a fact, and as I have grown in stature and Knowledge, so the rod has become obedient to my will as I had been promised. But I know that I must never feel that the power is mine, but that it has been sent to me according to my current needs, and that it must be used only for the vital cause of saving this Planet, for which innumerable fairies all over the World are each contributing their particle of power; but as countless grains of sand make a desert, and countless drops of water an ocean, so our tiny oblation plays its part in the Divine Plan.

– Festus

The New 'Physical Realm'
Fairy and Human Relations Congress

by Michael Pilarski

In 2000 I started a Fairy and Human Relations Congress in Washington State in honor of Daphne Charters and to carry on her work. The name is taken directly from Daphne's writings. This new congress is usually held in late June. Our 7th annual Congress will be held June 22-24, 2007. Human attendance at the first six congresses has ranged between 175 and 300 people. It is a family-oriented event and all ages attend, from babies to 92 year-olds. Four have been held at the Skalitude Retreat Center in the North Cascades of Washington state and two have been held at Riversong Forest Sanctuary on the Oregon side of the Columbia Gorge.

The Fairy and Human Relations Congress is a unique and special event. There are many spiritual gatherings in the world but nothing quite like the Congress with its specific mission to improve communications between the fairy and human realms. The Fairy & Human Relations Congress gives people interested in fairy communication a chance to share their experiences.

The humans are vastly outnumbered at the Congress by the fairies, devas and other Light beings who are in attendance. A warm thank you to all of them. It is a rare event for humans to experience so much fairy energy and such an outpouring of fairy/devic blessings.

In a sense we are creating an opening between our realms. A thinning of the veil. We create a middle ground where humans and fairies can come together and communicate.

Magical! Fun! Inspiring! Sweet! are some of the words used to describe the Fairy & Human Relations Congress. We enjoy ourselves immensely and almost everyone wants to come back next year and bring friends.

Congress highlights include:

- Friendships. The Congress is a great place to make new friendships and strengthen existing friendships. It is empowering and inspiring to be together with so many wonderful people
- Circles. We experience many joyful and uplifting circles with songs, dances, invocations, prayers, and attunements to the fairies.
- The joint human and fairy meditations are a powerful part of the Congress. The joint meditations are held daily, following which the humans have a quiet period to write down messages. The messages from past congresses can be found on www.fairycongress.com. These messages constitute one

way for the Congress to reach other humans with the fairies' messages. The meditations are sometimes followed by small discussion groups and a short plenary session in which people were able to share some of the extraordinary experiences they had during the meditation.

- The congress features 18 to 24 workshops each year which are high quality, interactive events. We have been fortunate to attract some of the best fairy communicators on the planet including: Dorothy Maclean and David Spangler of Findhorn; Peter Tompkins, author of The Secret Life of Plants; and notable fairy author, R. J. Stewart. Some presenters are less famous but all are talented. Our other congress presenters have included: Shoshanna Avree, Peter Berry, Paul Beyerl, Camilla Blossom, Morgan Brent, Sandy Fern Bunnell, Ginger Cloud, T. Thorn Coyle, Cynthia DeFay, Orion Foxwood, Mary J. Getten, John Michael Greer, Sarah Greer, Gary Hovda, Christan Hummel, Feather Jones, Eileen Kilgren, Neil Huckleberry Leonard, Little Feather, Charles Lightwalker, Jessica MacBeth, Robina McCurdy, Louisa Loonah McCuskey, Cindy McGonagle, Mark McNutt, MaryGold McNutt, Lisa Meserole, Catherine Morgan, Madi Nolan, Julie Charette Nunn, Lili Oma, Chuck Pettis, Diana Gay Pepper, Michael Pilarski, Anahata Pomeroy, Don Ollsin, Linda Quintana, Erin Raney, Raven, Ouapiti Robintree, Joseph Saine, Shemmaho J. Sioux, Paul Stamets, Steffan Vanel, Jennifer Vyhnak, and Shawn Black Wolf. Of course there are valuable contributions by all participants. We are all students and we are all teachers.

- The Fairy concert is held one evening each year. RJ Stewart has played guitar and sung for us every year, sometimes with his 77-string psaltry and always singing fairy ballads in his Scottish brogue. In 2005, the famous fairy band Woodland performed and in 2006 we were blessed by Lisa Thiel, accompanied by David MacVittie, David Wertzman and friends. MythMaker theatre troupe from Elfinstone Mountain, Sunshine Coast, British Columbia gave a riveting performance.

- The food is always delicious, participatory in preparation and filled with good vibrations. We camp out in beautiful mountain meadows.

- The Fairy Parade. The Fairy Parade is undoubtedly the high point of the Congress. Almost everyone costumes up to one degree or another and we have a costuming center to assist that. Almost every single person on site is there. And the numbers of fairies! Oh my gosh! And the Excitement! We are never quite sure what will happen during the parade. Sometimes we have a plan. It is always energetic, colorful and musical, full of dancing, circles and action. I think the reasons the fairies get so excited is that parading is a part of their experience for much of their evolution. The fairy literature abounds in accounts of fairies parading around in the moonlight and going about

323

in troupes. And according to Daphne Charters' accounts during large fairy parades the fairy participants get swept up into an exuberant wild abandon. At any rate, the excitement of the fairies affects the humans and vice versa. A grand time is had by all.

The Fairy & Human Relations Congress is one of the world's premier gatherings of fairy communicators and fairy seekers at this point in time. It is open to the public.

**Further details can be obtained online at
www.fairycongress.com**

APPENDICES

APPENDIX A

AN EXPLORATION OF THE QUESTION:
HOW MANY KINDS OF FAIRIES ARE THERE?
by Michael Pilarski

I often liken us humans describing the fairy realm to the parable of the group of blind men, all touching different parts of an elephant and having a wide range of descriptions of what an elephant looks like. The fairy realm is so vast that, although some humans can see into parts of it, they can have radically different descriptions of what it is like. For instance, there are many stages of growth, size and appearance of fairies as they reincarnate. The Deva Marusis describes these stages and they are listed farther on in this article. It is a vast universe and according to many of the authorities on the subject, it is teeming with life and the nature fairy/deva evolution is found working throughout much of the cosmos, giving power to, and tending, life forms and physical objects. Daphne Charters was all about improving communication and understanding between fairies and humans. These appendices helps carry this work forward into the current time.

Spelling

Consider these different spellings . . .
- fairy
- faery
- fairie
- faerie
- feri
- fari
- fae
- fay
- fey
- feé

These spellings can mean different things to different people. Daphne Charters uses the spelling "fairy" and that is the spelling you will find in *Volume I* except where it is spelled differently in a book title or in another writer's work mentioned in the appendices. If you asked a hundred people to define the word fairy you would get a wide range of definitions. The name or the spelling doesn't matter. What matters is that we know whom we are talking about (or talking with).

Many people in the world regard fairies (by whatever spelling) as total superstition, nonsense and fantasy. This condition is particularly rampant in Western industrial cultures. However, the percentage of humans in the world today who do believe in fairies is substantial and the percentage appears to be growing.

There are dozens of books on fairies, faerys, etc which use different names for different types of fairies and sometimes rather elaborate descriptions of the different types. This can be very confusing. In this article I attempt to clear up some of the confusion. Of course, this is not the final word on the subject.

Here is a very important point. Namely, that there are many kinds of beings from a number of evolutions that have been referred to as faery, fairy or the other ways of spelling. Depending on who you are talking to the word fairy (in all of its spellings) could mean: the nature fairy/deva evolution; the Sidhe/Elana; enchanters and enchantresses with supernatural power; and, for some people, various monsters and demons. *The Collected Fairy Manuscripts of Daphne Charters* are about the nature fairy/deva evolution.

There are some books on fairies (so-called) that are really libelous slander, which portray dark beings from lower planes as "fairies". While there are malevolent beings which are the basis for frightening stories, they are not from the nature fairy/deva evolution. The term "lower plane", as used here, is meant to refer to a lower vibration, rather than under the earth's surface. Some people mix fairies up with thought-forms, extra-terrestrials, ghosts, etc. In other words, don't swallow every faery or fairy book, hook-line-and-sinker. Use your intuition.

The Nature Fairy/Deva Evolution

These are the fairies you will find in Daphne Charter's manuscripts. As we are defining our subject matter here we mean the nature-spirits, fairies and devas, both small and large, who work with the plants, animals, streams, rivers, air, clouds, hills, valleys, mountains and other life forms and natural features of planet Earth. Our premise is that members of this evolution assist all life forms and natural processes on and within the Earth. The sizes and capabilities of the beings from this evolution range from tiny to titanic. They operate on a higher vibration than humans (the etheric plane) and hence are invisible to all but a few. Their ministrations are necessary for all life to exist on Earth, including humans.

The fairy/deva evolution is often said to be organized in a hierarchy. Each level advancing as they evolve and helping those below. It is said that the fairy/deva evolution is totally connected to and serving of the One Light/Creator

Source and do not have free will. The younger, smaller stages of fairies are said to be operating from a group mind (or hive) consciousness. On the other hand, Daphne's writings imply that at a certain stage of individualization fairies do acquire free will. Of course, like all life, the fairy/deva lifewave is not static, but is also changing and evolving. Obviously the fairies that Daphne works with are complex, intelligent individuals.

We can come to a better understanding of the inhabitants of the nature fairy/deva realms by comparing the accounts of a wide number of respected writers. You can do your own research. The following appendix contains the best books that I know of. There are differences between authors and there are similarities. Different authors may give a similar rundown on the different types of the fairies , but use different names. For example, "gnomes" are described in many texts, but some authors assign gnomes to levels from quite low to quite high in the fairy hierarchy. It is the reader's own inner knowingness that leads them to accept, reject or hold in abeyance that which is presented to them.

Stages in Fairy Evolution

Here is the nomenclature of the nature fairy/deva evolution given by the Deva Marusis to Daphne Charters as outlined in Manuscript Set #2 in *Volume I*.

How fairies first come into being: Elementals are capable of only one type of function within a single idea. Elementals come into being as the result of the Angelic Forces playing on matter in order to stimulate it into certain activities. To put it very simply, one might say that they are the "children" of Angels and matter and from them evolve the complexities, nature spirits and fairies.

Starting at the smallest:
- Rudimes
- Unitis
- Minutes
- Nomenes (gnomes)
- Elfines (elves and brownies)
- Fares (fairies)
- Farris
- Faralles, (farallis is singular)
- Aspirites
- Hiarus: The hiarus are those who are the governors.
- Ra-Arus: The Ra-Arus, in the Fairy evolution, are equal to the Archangels of Man.

- Marata/Maratumel. Also called the Nameless One by the fairies. Marata is the feminine aspect and is the Goddess of Nature. Maratumel is the male aspect.

Somewhere along this evolutionary line, fairies evolve into devas at the far-alles or aspirites level.

Flower A. Newhouse

Here is a list of the hierarchy of the nature intelligences dealing with the Earth, given by Flower A. Newhouse in her book *The Kingdom of the Shining Ones*, starting with the smallest:
- Frakins (FRAH kins)
- Gnomes
- Elves
- Oreads (Or ee adds)
- Tree Devas (DAY vahs)
- Allrays (ALL rays)
- Allsees (ALL sees)

The general thread of the description of the evolutions and their powers and functions are similar in both Charters' and Newhouse's accounts, even though the names differ.

The Sidhe – The Elana – The Faery Race

One of the reasons there are widely disparate accounts of the fairy realm may lie in the proposition that there are two different races of fairies (to use the term 'race' loosely). One is the fairy/deva evolutionary life-wave as just described. The other race of fairies is a flesh and blood evolution with souls. They have been referred to by many names. The Sidhe (pronounced shee), the Elana, and the faery race. I will use the terms Sidhi and Elana interchangeably in this article. I would also expect that most of the myths about the Tuatha De Danaan in Ireland could be sourced to interaction with the Sidhe. This race of beings used to live on the physical earth plane with humans, but were shoved out by human aggression. Some are hostile to humans. They are as large, or larger than, humans. They have many magical powers. It is unclear to me where this race of beings now resides. Where is "Tir na n'Og" where the Tuatha De Danaan retreated to? Some different vibrational realm of the earth? Off planet? Within the Earth? Here is what Eileen Kilgren says in her recent book *Memories*: "The Otherworld – the Realm of Faerie – is a remnant of the Land of Pan, which existed before Atlantis and

Mu, when the earth was much less solid. This fragment still exists in a dimension parallel to ours." Some of the Elana are still interfacing with humanity. Most Celtic folklore has to do with this faery race. Most modern-day, fairy sightings are probably of the fairy/deva evolution, rather than the Sidhe.

I have come across mention of this flesh and blood, soul race in some texts but many folk accounts also corroborate this premise, particularly Celtic accounts of hostile fairy forces. A recent, pertinent reference is the 2004 book by John Matthews, *The Sidhe: Wisdom from the Celtic Otherworld.* In the story, John is shown a recently discovered, ancient, undisturbed, underground chamber in Ireland. There he meets a tall figure dressed in archaic clothes. This representative of the Sidhe over the course of some time downloads information to John about the Sidhe. John Matthews' Sidhe is clearly the flesh and blood faery race of souls.

Another recent reference is Eileen Kilgren's books. Kilgren is being tutored by fire devas. A lot of her work is represented by colors and symbols, but she has also published several small books. Part of her teaching has to do with categorizing the different realms of beings. She clearly differentiates between the nature fairy/deva evolution and the flesh and blood fairy evolution which she terms "The Elana" – the fairies/devas being spirits and the Elana being souls – two separate, lines of evolution. Along with the Elana on the soul path are found the humans, angels and archangels [see Kilgren's accompanying diagram].

I don't know the details of when and where the difference happened between the spelling of 'fairy' and 'faery'; but I have a hunch that most people speaking of the Sidhe/Elana would use the spelling faery, rather then fairy. I am sure there are many instances where the different spellings are used for each race. The result being that at this point in time, you can never know for sure who/what people are talking about when they use the word fairy or faery or fairie or elves, and so forth. You have to listen to the author or speaker's description to ascertain which evolution they are talking about. You will not find the Sidhe in any of Daphne Charters' manuscripts. The word, nor the concept does not come up in any of Charters' manuscripts, insofar as I can ascertain.

Wikipedia Definition of Fairy

Here are several excerpts from *Wikipedia*:

> A fairy (sometimes seen as faery, faerie, or even fae; collectively wee folk, good folk, people of peace or many other euphemisms) is a spirit or supernatural being that is found in the legends, folklore, and mythology of many different cultures. There are many definitions of what constitutes a fairy, sometimes describing any magical creature,

like a goblin or gnome, and at other times to describe a specific type of creature, distinct from such creatures as hobgoblins.

They are generally portrayed as humanoid in their appearance and have supernatural abilities such as the ability to fly, cast spells and to influence or foresee the future. Although in modern culture they are often depicted as young, sometimes winged, females of small stature, they originally were of a much different image: tall, angelic beings and short, wizened trolls being some of the commonly mentioned fay. Diminutive fairies of one kind or another have been recorded for centuries, but occur alongside the human-sized beings; they can range from the size of human children to the tiny. Wings, however, are very rare in folklore; even very small fairies flew with magic, sometimes flying on ragwort stems.

– Wikipedia

Etymology [from Wikipedia]

The words fae and færie came to English from Old French which originated in the Latin word "Fata" which referred to the three mythological personifications of destiny . . . The Latin word gave modern Italian's fata, Catalan and Portuguese fada and Spanish hada, all of which mean fairy. The Old French fée, had the meaning "enchanter." Thus féerie meant a "state of fée" or "enchantment." Fairies are often depicted enchanting humans, casting illusions to alter emotions and perceptions so as to make themselves at times alluring, frightening, or invisible. Modern English inherited the two terms "fae" and "fairy," along with all the associations attached to them.

A similar word, "fey," has historically meant "doomed to die," mostly in Scotland, which tied in with the original meaning of fate. It has now gained the meaning "touched by otherworldly or magical quality; clairvoyant, supernatural." In modern English, the word seems to be conjoining into "fae" as variant spelling. If "fey" derives from "fata," then the word history of the two words is the same. [1]

Strictly, there should be distinctions between the usage of the two words "fae" and "faerie." "Fae" is a noun that refers to the specific group of otherworldly beings with mystical abilities (either the elves (or equivalent) in mythology or their insect-winged, floral descendants in English folklore), while "faerie" is an adjective meaning "of, like, or associated with fays, their otherworldly home, their activities, and their produced goods and effects." Thus, a leprechaun and a ring of mushrooms are both faerie things (a fairy leprechaun and a fairy ring), although in modern usage fairy has come to be used as a noun."

— *Wikipedia*

Closing Note: The fairies in *Daphne Charters' Collected Fairy Manuscripts* are from the nature fairy/deva evolution.

APPENDIX B

BOOKS ABOUT THE NATURE FAIRY/ DEVA EVOLUTION AND RELATED SUBJECTS
by Michael Pilarski

While Daphne Charters' collected manuscripts are a giant in the fairy literature, the following review of 60 "fairy-related" books points the way to further knowledge and understanding.

Here is my current best attempt at an overview of books about (or linked in some way with) the nature fairy/deva evolution. Arranged alphabetically by title rather then in any degree of importance. While I am familiar with many of these authors' works I cannot vouch for all of them. Different sources appeal to different readers at different times. Out of the 60 books reviewed, I have put an asterisks * by the ones I feel are especially good starting points.

There have been hundreds of books written on fairies and devas over the past century. Thirty years ago when I first started searching bookstores for serious books on fairies, they were few and far between with the main source being the Theosophical Society. The *Secret Life of Plants*, published in 1973, was a very influential book, promoting the idea of intelligence in nature. The Findhorn books made a big impact in the 1970s and the Perelandra books in the 1980s. More recently there has been a notable upsurge in fairy books being published, some of which are based on past literature and some of which are new material.

We also should remember that there are large repositories of fairy knowledge besides literature, such as: oral traditions, folklore, religions, spirituality, occultism, esotericism, and metaphysics. Much of this knowledge is invisible, kept within language groups, localities, families, or mystery schools. The knowledge is often kept secret because there is still repression in the world.

Then there is the phenomenon of increased communication with spirit realms happening worldwide. In the USA alone there are now millions of people communicating with various spiritual realms. A certain percentage of this is communication with the nature fairy/deva evolution. This body of current, experiential knowledge is immense and growing.

Use your intuition as to which books are right for you. Please send in reviews of books I have missed, corrections, and/or lengthier, more-in-depth reviews.

Angels & Devas. Torkom Saraydarian. 1996. Saraydarian Institute, PO Box 267, Sedona, AZ 86339. 47 pages. This is a compilation of writings from ten of Torkom's 50 books. The perspective of a spiritual master.

Behaving as if the God in all Life Mattered. Machaelle Small Wright. 1987. Perelandra, Jeffersonton, Virginia. 213 pages.

The Celtic Wisdom of Trees: Mysteries, Magic and Medicine. Jane Gifford. 2000. Godsfield Press. 160 pages. A compendium of knowledge about our relationship with trees. Presented according to the Celtic Tree Alphabet (each letter is associated with the name of a tree. A wealth of information on the mystical aspects of trees and their traditional healing properties. Recommended for the great photos.

Clairvoyant Investigations. Geoffrey Hodson. 1984. Quest Books, Theosophical Publishing, Wheaton, Illinois. 140 pages. A compilation of writings from Hodson's earlier years. Clairvoyant descriptions of large landscape devas. The color illustrations are among the best we have of devic form and color.

* *Complete Idiot's Guide to Elves & Fairies*. Sirona Knight. 2005. Alpha books, Penguin Group. New York. 328 pages. A great book for beginners as well as advanced readers. Something for everyone and in a readable, contemporary style. Here are a few quotes from R. J. Stewart's foreword: "a comprehensive book." "For the reader who wishes to know more about fairy tradition but is daunted by the wide range of books available (from heavily academic to speculative nonsense), this book will be a helpful guide." "Another excellent feature of this book is that it has many practical suggestions and insights for coming into genuine communion with fairy beings."

The Deva Handbook. Nathaniel Altman. 1995. Destiny Books, Rochester, NH. 164 pages. How to Work with Nature's Subtle Energies. A "how-to" book on communicating with devas and getting in touch with the power spots of nature.

Devas & Men: A Compilation of Theosophical Studies on the Angelic Kingdom. The Southern Centre of Theosophy, Robe, South Australia. 1977. 386 pages. This volume compiles the writings from 38 theosophical books as well as articles in *The Theosophist*. The bibliography is a guide to many of the major works on the subject until the 1970s. More angels than fairies and devas.

Devas, Fairies and Angels: A Modern Approach. William Bloom. 1988. Gothic Image Publications, Glastonbury, England. The author explains how the devas, fairies and angels can help us in our homes, our work and daily lives.

Earth Light. R. J. Stewart. 1992. Mercury Pub. Lake Toxaway, NC. 162 pages. Subtitled "The Ancient Path to Transformation - Rediscovering the Wisdom of Celtic and Faery Lore". Earth Light presents practical methods of working within the Faery Tradition through techniques of visualization and imagination. Also Power Within the Land R J Stewart, 1992, also The Well of Light (book and CD) R J Stewart, revised edition 2006. And other books from the same author: see www.rjstewart.net

The Elves of Lily Hill Farm: A Partnership with Nature. Penny Kelly. St. Paul, MN: Llewellyn, 1997. 265 pages. This book is the true tale of Penny Kelly's meeting with a group of resident elves. Kelly has also written *From the Soil to the Stomach: Notes on Healing from Lily Hill Farm.*

Emergence: The Birth of the Sacred. David Spangler. The Lorian Association, PO Box 1368, Issaquah, WA 98027. Spangler ranks among the top spiritual writers of the last half century, but none of his books focus specifically on the fairy/deva evolution. However, David is a good friend of the fairies. Spangler was director of the Findhorn Community for years and was instrumental in the successes of the Findhorn experiment.

Enchantment of the Faerie Realm: Communicate with Nature Spirits and Elementals. Ted Andrews. 1993. Llewellyn Publications. 240 pages.

Esoteric Music of the Deva Evolution. Cyril Scott. 2005. Kessinger Publishing Company. 72 pages.

Evolutionary Witchcraft. T. Thorn Coyle. 2004. Jeremy P. Tarcher/Penguin. New York. 302 pages. Coyle's book is designed to be read through once and then used as a ten-month training program with exercises involving movement, spells, right intention and occult ceremony. She is a Sorcerer in the Anderson Feri Tradition. Thorn teaches people how to bring more magic into one's life.

The Faeries Oracle. Jessica Macbeth, text. Artwork by Brian Froud. 2000. Simon and Schuster, New York. 205 pages. An oracle deck and accompanying book. Working with the faeries to find insight, wisdom and joy.

The Faery Faith: An Integration of Science with Spirit. Serena Roney-Dougal. 2003. Green Magic, BCM Inspire, London. 170 pages. A wide-ranging discussion of how faery lore can be of use today and how it relates to things such as magic, terrestrial magnetism, megaliths, apparitions, and UFO reports.

The Faery Teachings. Orion Foxwood. 2006, R J Stewart books, Arcata, CA. 203 pages. Orion is an Elder in Foxwood Temple, a wiccan tradition in Maryland. Foxwood combines his Wiccan background with his family lineage of American Southern folk magic into an introduction to faery teachings for contemporary use.

* Fairies at Work and Play. Geoffrey Hodson. 1982. Quest Books. 126 pages. Geoffrey Hodson is one of the greatest clairvoyants of the 20th century and author of over 40 books. This book is about the author's observations of the fairy realms. One of the best classics.

The Fairy Faith in Celtic Countries. W.Y. Evans-Wentz. First published in 1911. Citadel Press. 1994. 524 pages. A voluminous cataloging of oral Celtic folklore at the turn of the century. The information contains information on the fairy/deva evolution to some extent but is mainly about beings that would belong to the Elana/Faery race, and in some cases, darker beings from lower planes. Folklore, superstition and spiritual truths are often blended together in mysterious ways and the reader of books such as this one should not take the accounts literally. It can be like detective work. Looking at the clues to find the true spiritual truths. What are the allusions and metaphysical meanings? In a sense it is similar to ferreting out the spiritual truths in fairy tales and religions.

The Fairy Kingdom. Geoffrey Hodson. 1927. Re-published in 2003 by The Book Tribe, San Diego. 112 pages. A follow up to his book *Fairies at Work and Play*. He describes devas, sylphs, gnomes, fairies, brownies, manikins, Pan and examples of cooperation between devas and men.

Fire in the Head: Shamanism and the Celtic Spirit. Tom Cowan. 1993. HarperSanFrancisco. 240 pages. Cowan offers workshops on shamanism and Celtic spirituality around the country, including workshops on fairies.

* Findhorn Gardens. 1975. By The Findhorn Community. Harper & Row, Publishers. 180 pages. The Findhorn community in Scotland has become world famous as a place where people work with fairies to make beautiful gardens. There have been many books about Findhorn and many books by former Findhorn members. This particular book is authored by the phenomenal people who founded Findhorn and is the best book to get an understanding of what Findhorn was all about. Findhorn is now an international center for spirituality and the eco-village movement.

Garden Notes: From the Nature Devas. Cindy McGonagle. 1993. Botanic Reproductions, PO Box 40806, Portland, OR 97240. 94 pages. Helpful hints that enable you to communicate and learn on the devic level to heal the earth. She also has published *Sacred Places, Sacred Plants of the Columbia River Gorge.*

The Green Man: Spirit of Nature. John Matthews. 2002. Red Wheel Press. Boston. 64 pages. A small book on the historical figure of the green man in old Europe and ways to connect today.

Healing the Heart of the Earth. Marko Pogacnik. 1998. Findhorn Press. 270 pages. Pogacnik is internationally known for his land art and for applying communication with the nature realms to assist Earth Healing. Working with the devas for ecosystem restoration. Geomancers are now working with restorationists to remediate toxic sites. Pogacnik is one of the pioneers in this emerging field.

Hidden Side of Things. Charles W. Leadbeater. 1913. Theosophical Publishing House. 468 pages. One of the most famous occultists and clairvoyants of the 20th century. He has written many books. Several have included information on fairies and angels.

In Perfect Timing. Peter Caddy. 1997. 478 pages. Memoirs of a Man for the New Millennium. The autobiography of the co-founder of the Findhorn Community. This is not a book about fairies. It is a book about Caddy's remarkable life which helped create the germination plot for deva knowledge to broadcast to the whole planet.

* *The Kingdom of the Gods*. Geoffrey Hodson. 1952. Quest Books. 272 pages. An in-depth view of the angelic evolution which includes most of the information *in Fairies at Work and Play,* plus other information on the nature realms. It covers other aspects of the angelic evolutions besides those connected with Nature. The color illustrations of devas are among the best in print and very useful in visualizing devas.

***Kingdom of the Shining Ones*.** Flower A. Newhouse. 1955. The Christward Ministry, Escondido, California. 92 pages. Newhouse is a gifted Christian mystic and author of the last century. One of her life missions was increasing the world's knowledge and awareness of Angels from whom man receives assistance. This book is mainly about angels, but she also includes information on: nature intelligences dealing with the Earth, angels who influence animals, supervisors of fish and bird life, angels of the air kingdom, beings of the water world, and the Fire kingdom's shining presences. Here is one quote: "But he who has the wisdom and the thanksgiving of spirit to tread reverently into the strongholds and Devic temples of nature's servers shall find everlasting loyalty and devotion rendered him from constructive superphysical orders."

Letters on Occult Meditation. Alice Bailey. Lucis Trust, 120 Wall Street, 24th Floor, New York, NY 10005. 375 pages. The 24 books of Alice A. Bailey were written in cooperation with a Tibetan teacher between 1919-1949 and constitute a continuation of the Ageless Wisdom – a body of esoteric teaching handed down from ancient times. These books were channeled by Alice Bailey from The Master Djwal Kuhl, or as he is sometimes called, the Master D.K. It is probably the largest body of channeled material in the world library. None of the Alice Bailey books focuses on the fairy/deva evolution but there is relevant material scattered in her books. Many of the volumes are large and the type-font small, so the sheer volume of material is enormous. Few people have the mental stamina to read many of these books. They are somewhat akin to the occult writings of Rudolph Steiner. *Letters on Occult Meditation* is one of the shorter books and a good starting point for those inclined to try.

* The Living World of Faery. R. J. Stewart. 1995. Mercury Publishing, Lake Toxaway, NC. 217 pages. R. J. Stewart is Britain's leading expert on faery lore and magic. Stewart is one of the pre-eminent faery authors of our time with over 40 books to his credit. This book explores the living power of the Faery Tradition for the 21st Century. This particular book describes second sight, distance contact and powerful encounters with faery allies and co-walkers. There are practical techniques for enhancing communication, and a discussion on the relationship between faeries and angels in spiritual traditions. A good place to start if you haven't read any of Stewart's books.

Man as Symphony of the Creative Word. Rudolf Steiner. Steiner Books. 192 pages. Derived from a lecture given near the end of his life, Steiner here gives a unique and intimate description of the elemental nature spirits – the purely spiritual beings that complement plants and animals – and the cooperation that these beings offer to mankind.

Memories: The Past Recalled & Reclaimed. A History in Three Parts. Part One. How I Recovered from Amnesia. Eileen Kilgren. 2007. PO Box 70362, Seattle, WA 98107. 71 pages. $5.00 + $1.50 postage. This small book abounds in fascinating information and exciting encounters in other realms. Eileen's first two books introduced her first encounters and friendships with sprites, devas and faery beings. Mighty devas have been tutoring Eileen for years now and her latest book includes interactions with invaders from space, Ascended Masters, vampire slayers, The Hathors, and more.

Nature Spirits and Elemental Beings: Working with the Intelligences in Nature. Marko Pogacnik. 1995. Findhorn Press. 251 pages. Pogacnik is a Slovenian artist and geomancer who has written a number of books on fairy related topics. His writing are from his own personal experience.

Other Kingdoms. Hilarion. Channeled by Maurice B. Cooke. 1981. Marcus Books, 195 Randolph Road, Toronto, Ont. M4G 3S6, Canada. 238 pages. This is channeled material on the fairy realm with commentary by Cooke. The information is somewhat simplistic.

* Peralandra Garden Workbook: A Complete Guide to Gardening with Nature Intelligences. Machaelle Small Wright. 1987. Perelandra, Jeffersonton, Virginia. 240 pages. Based at Perelandra Garden in Virginia, Machaelle Wright has done more to advance the cause of working with nature spirits than any other person in North America in the twenty years since her books have been out. A very practical book about cooperation with the fairies to grow more food and beauty. Machaelle and other authors are moving humanity towards a practical cooperation with the nature fairy/deva evolution to clean up and heal the planet's damaged environments. It is perhaps in this field that our communication with the fairy/deva evolution is most urgent and needed. *The Garden Workbook* gives practical methods we can all use to communicate with our garden devas and fairies. A simple kinesiology technique with the fingers to get yes/no answers to questions.

Plants of Power. Alfred Savinelli. 1997 revised edition. Native Scents, Box 5639, Taos, NM 87571. 88 pages. Savinelli is a wildcafter and works with Native Peoples to gather plants in a sacred and ecological manner. Here he covers Native American ritual and medicinal uses for 20 plants.

Power Within the Land. R. J. Stewart. 1992. Mercury Publishing. Lake Toxaway, NC. 163 pages. The roots of Celtic and underworld traditions. Awakening the Sleepers and Regenerating the Earth. Visualizations and Exercises.

*** The Real World of Fairies.** Dora Van Gelder. Theosophical Publishing House, Wheaton, IL. 160 pages. Another first person account of what fairies are like. One of my favorites by a long-time theosophical clairvoyant. Dora has long been associated with Camp Indralaya on Orcas Island in the San Juan Archipelago of Washington State. The book includes an account of the angel of Mt. Constitution on Orcas Island. One of the best starter books.

Rediscovering the Angels. Flower A. Newhouse. 1950. Christward Ministry. 156 pages. This book includes the material from her book "Natives of Eternity".

The Rebirth of Nature: The Greening of Science and God. Rupert Sheldrake. 1992. Bantam. 260 pages. His theory of "morphic resonance" holds that self-organizing systems – molecules, crystals, cells, organisms, societies – respond to invisible regions of influence.

Regents of the Seven Spheres. H.K. Challoner. Theosophical Publishing House. 99 pages. 1920 or so was the date of first publishing. There are reprints available. A theosophist's writings on angels.

Sacred Ground to Sacred Space. Rowena Pattee Kryder. 1994. Bear & Co, Santa Fe. 319 pages. Visionary Ecology, Perennial Wisdom, Environmental Ritual and Art. An introduction to a wide range of earth-based spirituality practices including information from indigenous cultures. Consciousness in the landscape. Re-sacralizing the world. A how-to book with many experiential projects. A practical way to connect with the fairy/deva evolution without the European traditional trappings.

*** The Secret Life of Nature.** Peter Tompkins. 1997. HarperSanFrancisco. 228 pages. This book is subtitled: "Living in Harmony with the Hidden World of Nature Spirits from Fairies to Quarks". Peter Tompkins co-authored with Christopher Bird two previous books: *The Secret Life of Plants* and *Secrets of the Soil* which brought to public eyes many esoteric secrets about the nature realms. One of the things which makes Tompkins' book so original is his reporting on how occultists described the building blocks of the universe such as the elements, sub-atomic particles and quarks. Tompkins surveyed the literature of major fairy writers of the last century and synthesized and compared their findings – notably the publications of Findhorn, Dora Van Gelder, Geoffrey Hodson, Rudolph Steiner, Alice Bailey, Madame Blavatsky, Charles W. Leadbeater, and others. Tompkins was not aware of Daphne's work at the time. Tompkins has made a real contribution to the history of occult knowledge from ancient Hindus, Persians, Chaldeans,

Pythagoreans, Pharaonic Egyptians, neo-Platonists, Kabbalists and Rosicrucians down to the theosophists and anthroposophists of today. In a topic of this size and breadth, we can only get a glimpse of the vast amount of knowledge it hints at. Unfortunately the book has been out of print for years and copies now cost $200 or more. It deserves to be brought back into print.

The Secret Life of Plants. Peter Tompkins and Christopher Bird. 1973. HarperCollins Publishing. 402 pages. This influential book was a New York Times best seller for a long time

Robert Kirk, Walker Between Worlds: edited with commentary by R J Stewart (revised new edition 2007). This is the only edition of Robert Kirk's 1692 notebook, The Secret Commonwealth of Elves, Fauns and Fairies that includes notes and commentary from an esoteric perspective. Contains descriptions of second sight, of doublemen or co-walkers, and of fairy lives, customs and rituals.

Secrets of Sacred Space. Chuck Pettis. 1999. Llewellyn Publications, St Paul, MN. 277 pages. This book is focused on how people can use geomancy and dowsing to locate sacred sites and ley lines and how to build stone monuments a la stonehenge. It also includes a chapter on how to communicate with devas and spiritual beings.

Secrets of the Soil. Peter Tompkins and Christopher Bird. 1998. Earthpulse Press, Anchorage. 418 pages. Subtitled: New Solutions for Restoring Our Planet. The sequel to *The Secret Life of Plants.*

Seeds of Inspiration: Deva Flower Messages. Dorothy Maclean. 2004. The Lorian Association. 120 pages. It brings together for the first time most of her flower messages.

The Sidhe: Wisdom From the Celtic Otherworld. John Matthews. 2004. The Lorian Association, PO Box 1368, Issaquah, WA 98027. 115 pages. In the story, John is taken to an ancient, undisturbed, underground chamber in Ireland. There he meets a tall figure dressed in archaic clothes. This representative of the Sidhe (pronounced shee) over the course of some time downloads information to John about the Sidhe.

The Spirit Cord. R. J. Stewart. 2006. RJ Stewart Books, Arcata, CA. 188 pages. Practices from the mystical and ancestral traditions of the ancient world combined with contemporary methods for transforming consciousness.

Spiritual Beings in the Heavenly Bodies & in the Kingdoms of Nature. Rudolf Steiner. Anthroposophic Press. 1992 ed. 300 pages. Rudolf Steiner is one of the best-known personages in occult science. He is the founder of anthroposophy, bio-dynamic agriculture, Waldorf schools and eurythmy. Author of numerous books which take deep concentration to decipher and understand. In this lecture cycle he takes us deep into the angelic hierarchies operative in the Universe.

Summer with the Leprechauns: A True Story. Tanis Helliwell. 1997. Blue Dolphin Publishing. 191 pages. Helliwell is from Vancouver, British Columbia but spent a summer in Ireland during which a leprechaun becomes her friend.

Tales from the Spirit Realm: I and II. Eileen Kilgren. 1996. Published by the author, PO Box 70362, Seattle, WA 98107. 70 pages. $5 each. Stories of Eileen's adventures with water sprites, air spirits, and fire spirits. Eileen's relationship with the fairies is the closest to Daphne Charters' fairy relationship as I've found in my search of fairy books. Eileen has also put together a booklet of colored symbols, titled *Art of the Spirit Realm*, $20.

Talking with Nature. Michael J. Roads. 1985. H.J. Kramer, Inc., PO Box 1082, Tiburon, CA 94920. 151 pages. This is the story of a man who discovers he possesses the ability to commune intelligently with souls of plants, animals and even rock and rivers.

Talks with Trees: A Plant Psychic's Interviews with Vegetables, Flowers and Trees. Leslie Cabarga. 1997. Iconoclassics Publishing Co. Los Angeles. 173 pages.

* To Hear the Angels Sing. Dorothy Maclean. 1980. Lindisfarne Press. 217 pages. An Odyssey of Co-creation with the Devic Kingdom. An autobiography plus channeled messages from the devas. Dorothy was the Findhorn founder who communicates with the nature devas. It includes inspiring messages from the plants to humanity. Dorothy has been living in the Puget Sound area for the last decade. Maclean has done more to advance humanity's awareness of devas than any other person in the last century. Dorothy has been an honored presenter at the 2003, 2004, and 2005 Fairy & Human Relations Congress and will be a presenter at the 2007 congress.

To Honor the Earth. Dorothy Maclean. 1991. HarperSanFrancisco. 108 pages. Reflections on living in harmony with nature. A photographic coffee-table book with inspirational channelings from landscape devas.

Working with Angels and Nature Spirits. Lorna Todd. 1998. Kima Global Publishers, PO Box 374, Rondebosch, 7701, Cape Town, South Africa. 140 pages. Lorna Todd is a well-known British clairvoyant. Much of the book is messages from angels, devas, and the nature spirits of trees, flowers, animals and minerals.

We have not included in this literature review: fairy art books, classic children's fairy tales, modern children's fairy books, fantasy novels, folklore, witchcraft/pagan/wicca, indigenous, shamanism, and earth-based spirituality.

APPENDIX C

WHO'S WHO IN FAIRYLAND
HUMANS WHO HAVE ADVANCED THE FAIRY CAUSE.

Michael Pilarski has initiated a project to compile a list of people who have notably advanced the cause of human and fairy communication. This is an early draft based on current knowledge. This edition lists 78 people. I have listed web sites, where known. There are many deserving people who should be added to this list. Further editions will be posted on www.fairycongress.com

People are encouraged to send nominations for people to add to this list and/or additional comments on those presented herein. Send to michael@fairycongress. com

Listings are alphabetical rather than in any order of importance.

Category 1:
Notables who are no longer with us on the physical plane:

- Alice Bailey, channel for Djwal Kuhl. www.lucistrust.org
- Annie Besant, www.theosophical.org/
- Christopher Bird
- Peter Caddy, www.findhorn.org
- H.K. Challoner, www.adyar.com.au
- Daphne Charters, www.fairycongress.com
- W. Y. Evans-Wentz
- Manly P. Hall, www.frankperry.co.uk/MANLY%20PALMER%20HALL. htm
- Dora Van Gelder, www.questbooks.net/author.cfm?authornum=63
- Geoffrey Hodson, www.geoffreyhodson.iinet.net.au/index.htm
- Reverend Robert Kirk
- Charles W. Leadbeater, www.blavatskyarchives.com/leadbeaterbib.htm
- Flower A. Newhouse, www.questhaven.org
- Torkom Saraydarian, www.tsgfoundation.org/
- Cyril Scott, www.cyrilscott.net/index.html
- Rudolf Steiner, www.rsarchive.org

Category 2:
People currently active on the physical earth plane:

- Nathaniel Altman
- Ted Andrews, www.dragonhawkpublishing.com
- Paul Beyerl, www.thehermitsgrove.org
- Camilla Blossom, www.3flowershealing.com
- Morgan Brent, www.tribesofcreation.com
- Jim Butler, www.elfenproject.com
- William Bloom, www.williambloom.com
- Stephen Harrod Buhner
- Eileen Caddy, www.findhorn.org
- Joseph Cornell, www.dawnpub.com
- T. Thorn Coyle, www.thorncoyle.com
- Tom Cowan, www.riverdrum.com/
- Avatar DeDannan
- Dr. Geo, www.geocities.com/mkaastrup/
- Adrienne Dumas, www.myspace.com/AdrienneDumas
- John C. Fox, http://hilarion.com/jonchan.html
- Orion Foxwood, www.foxwood-temple.net
- Brian Froud, www.worldoffroud.com
- Mary J. Getten, www.MaryGetten.com
- Jane Gifford
- John Michael Greer
- Gurudas
- Ronni Hall, http://thefairyfieldguide.blogspot.com
- Tanis Helliwell, www.iitransform.com/
- Ellen Evert Hopman, www.geocities.com/gaias_song/willow.html
- Christan Hummel, www.earthtransitions.com
- Sandra Ingerman, www.sandraingerman.com
- Eileen Kilgren
- Sharon Knight, www.SharonKnight.net
- Sirona Knight, www.sironaknight.com
- Rowena Pattee Kryder, www.creative-harmonics.org
- Amy Leigh, www.ContinuumPress.com
- David Lertzman
- Jessica MacBeth
- Dorothy Maclean, www.lorian.org
- Marcia Zina Mager, www.marcia-zina-mager.com
- John and Caitlin Matthews, www.hallowquest.org.uk

- Cindy McGonagle, www.cindymcgonagle.com
- Mark and MaryGold McNutt, www.aerious.org
- Catherine Morgan, www.tasaris.com
- Robert Moss, www.mossdreams.com
- Hugh Mynne
- Don Ollsin, www.herbalhealingpathway.com
- Christopher Penczak, www.christopherpenczak.com
- Diana Gay Pepper, www.treefrogfarm.com
- Michael Perlman
- Chuck Pettis, www.geo.org
- Marko Pogacnik, www.pogacnikmarko.org
- Raven, www.ravenmedium.com
- Michael J. Roads, www.michaelroads.com
- Ouapiti Robintrcc, www.hummingbirdremedies.com
- Serena Roney-Dougal, www.psi-researchcentre.co.uk/
- Sathaya Sai Baba. www.sathyasai.org
- Molly Sheehan, www.greenhopeessences.com
- Rupert Sheldrake, www.sheldrake.org
- David Spangler, www.lorian.org
- Ariel Spilsbury, www.holographicgoddess.com/
- R. J. Stewart, www.rjstewart.net
- Lisa Thiel, www.sacreddream.com
- Lorna Todd, www.ascension-workshop.co.za
- Peter Tompkins
- Doreen Virtue, www.angelintuitive.com.au
- Jennifer Vyhnak
- Machaelle Small Wright, www.perelandra-ltd.com/

This list reflects my current information base. There are many, many more I do not know about or who are locally known. To add people to this list contact Michael@fairycongress.com

APPENDIX D

TABLE OF CONTENTS FOR
VOLUMES II AND III OF *THE COLLECTED*
FAIRY MANUSCRIPTS OF DAPHNE CHARTERS

VOLUME II:
FORTY YEARS WITH THE FAIRIES, PART 2

Table of Contents
Introduction

Manuscript Set #9
  The House Fairies (The lives of house fairies are much more exciting than you might suppose.)
  - Serrus and Fello *by themselves*
  - Serrus and Fello *by Bill*
  - Sheena *by herself*
  - Pino *by himself*
  - Sheena and Pino *by Cecil*
  - Herus *by Himself*
  - Herus *by Betty*
  - Maire *by herself*
  - Mairus *by himself*
  - Maire, Mairus, Herus *by Jack*
  - Healing Powers *by Maire*
  - Thought-Formations *by Daphne*
  - Thought-Formations *by Maire*
  - Thought Formations *by Perima*

Manuscript Set #10
  Stories about visiting the realms of other evolutions (Meet members of the evolutions of color, sound, scent, movement, and mind.)
  - A Fairy in the Land of Colour *by Normus*
  - We Visit the Land of the Thormes *by Jack*

- The Land of the Gravines *by Peter*
- Daphne, Normus and the Other Fairies in the Harnele Sector *by Normus*
- A Visit to the Land of the Harneles *by Maire*
- Harneles *by George*
- The Temple on the Astral *by Herus*
- Maire & Mairus visit the Ra-Arus *by Maire*
- Another Journey *by Maire*
- Maire, Mairus, Herus and Jack Meet the Marano *by Jack*
- Two Young Ceres Meet the Ramano *by Rimago*
- A Group Lesson from a Ceris *by Rimago*
- The Fairies in Cooperation with the Ceres *by Maire*
- Ceres *by Father John*
- Flowers Too Tall in Colchester Garden *by Normus*
  Third Plane, Reception given by Father John *by Rimago*
  Footnote *by Daphne in 1989*

Manuscript Set #11

Blending and Becoming (Stories about fairies, humans and members of other evolutions blending their energies to create new beings incorporating elements of all involved.)

- Blending and Becoming *by Father John*
- Soperon *by Rimago*
- Ponterinus *by Maire*
- Co-operation between the Aspects *by Maire*
- In Conclusion *by Father John*
- Father John talks to Daphne
- Jack and Daphne *by Jack*

Manuscript Set #12

The Underworld (Fairies and humans descend into lower vibration realms to rescue lost humans and fairies.)

- Fairies in the Underworld *by Father John*
- The Underworld *by Rimago*
- Deva in the Underworld (thought formations) *by Maire*
- A Musician's Work with the Lost Ones *by Rudolph*
- Beasts of the Underworld *by Daphne*
- Rays for the Lost Ones *by Ronald*
- Work with a Lost One of the Fairy Evolution *by Movus*
- Denizens of the Deep *by Father John*
- Underworld *by Rimago*

Manuscript Set #13
Tales from Beyond the Sunrise (Stories by humans living on the astral plane about the realm they live in and their work with Daphne and the fairies.)

- Simon & Joe, Part I *by Simon*
- Simon & Joe, Part II *by Simon*
- Dawn *by Daphne*
- The Man Who Loved Motorbikes *by Ronald*
- The Experience of Love *by Peter*
- A Pilgrimage into the Past *by Ludwig*
- Peter *by himself*
- Fairy Animals *by Andrew*
- A Lesson for John, Betty, Andrew and the Fairies *by John*
- Fairies – Experience with Betty and Andrew *by John*
- Fairy Instruments *by Father John*
- Fairy Instruments *by Jack*
- The Silence *unsigned*
- Purpose in Music Composition *by Rudolph*

Appendices: Revised and updated from Volume I.

VOLUME III
PERIMA: THE ADVENTURES OF A HOUSE FAIRY

In "Perima: The Story of a House Fairy", the fairies Perima and Tepi with their human friend, Augustine, travel into the realms of hell to rescue a soul fragment of Tepi. This was written long before soul retrieval became such a well-known topic in today's neo-shamanistic circles. This book is unlike Daphne's other writings in that it is an action-packed adventure and much of it takes place in the lower realms.

Table of Contents

Part I: My Youthful Years
- My Childhood Home
- The Centre of Culture
- A New Family
- The Seminary
- The Student Teacher
- The Wilderness
- Another door Opens

Part II: Tepi and I

Part III: Sulic and I

Appendices

Volumes II and III will be published by RJ Stewart Books in 2007 or 2008. Announcements will be posted at www.fairycongress.com and www.rjstewart.net

APPENDIX E

WHAT'S NEXT?
Developments and Proposals relating to
The Collected Fairy Manuscripts
of Daphne Charters

Exciting news! New manuscripts found

In preparation for publishing *Volume I*, I have come across several translations of Daphne's works which I had previously overlooked. I just found a complete Spanish translation of *A True Fairy Tale* which was published in Buenos Aires, Argentina in 1969 and a smaller publication on fairies by Daphne translated into French in 1951. Does anyone know anything about the history of these two publications?

Un Veridico Cuento De Hadas
(A True Fairy Tale)

Buenos Aires. 1969. Lily Helen Kelly. 275 pages.
I am assuming that Kelly is the translator as well as the publisher. The copy I have is autographed by Lily Kelly to Daphne Charters and reads:

> Dear Mrs. Charters,
>   This is your book dressed up in Argentine clothes. Now you have
>   a chance to learn Spanish browsing through these pages. Hope it
>   arrives safely.
> With best wishes,
> Lily Kelly
> Bs. Aires, August 25, 1969.

Les Origines, La Vie et L'Evolution des Fees
(The Origins, Life and Evolution of the Fairies)

Traduit es adapté de l'anglais par Henri E. Boitel
Membre de l'Union Spirite Française
Membre du Comité de Photographic Transcendale.

La Diffusion Spirituale, Éditeur. 1951. Paris. 37 pages. Autographed by Henri Boitel, the French translator. This is a French translation of Daphne Charter's 1951 manuscript entitled *The Origin, Life and Evolution of the Fairies*. In Volume 1 of the Collected Fairy Manuscripts of Daphne Charters, this corresponds to Manuscript Set #2, The Deva Marusis Speaks.

Anyone interested in republishing the Spanish or French translations, or translating into other languages, should contact Michael Pilarski.

Illustrations Solicited for the Collected Fairy Manuscripts of Daphne Charters

We are looking for artists to illustrate Daphne's manuscripts. This can include;
1) A cover illustration for a particular story.
2) Illustrations for a whole story for publication as a children's fairy tale book. Daphne's works would lend themselves to a long series of children's books.

Fairy Movies

One of our goals is to see movies produced which are based on Daphne Charters' manuscripts. Movies can be animated or 3-D combining animation and real people. Volume III, Perima, is especially suited for this. Would anyone like to be on the movie team or have contacts in the movie industry?

Volume II and Volume III will be published by RJ Stewart Books in 2007 or 2008.

Proposals for collaboration should be sent to:

Michael Pilarski
PO Box 253
Twisp, WA 98856
(360) 927-1274
michael@fairycongress.com

CPSIA information can be obtained
at www.ICGtesting.com
Printed in the USA
BVHW061003250221
600596BV00001B/1